CASSELL STUDIES IN PASTORAL CARE AND PERSONAL AND SOCIAL EDUCATION

PASTORAL CARE AND PERSONAL-SOCIAL EDUCATION

Books in this series

P. Lang, R. Best and A. Lichtenberg (editors): *Caring for Children: International Perspectives on Pastoral Care and PSE*

O. Leaman: *Death and Loss: An Educational Response*

J. McGuiness: *Teachers, Pupils and Behaviour: A Managerial Approach*

P. Whitaker: *Active and Experiential Learning*

CASSELL STUDIES IN PASTORAL CARE AND PERSONAL AND SOCIAL EDUCATION

PASTORAL CARE AND PERSONAL-SOCIAL EDUCATION

Entitlement and Provision

Edited by

Ron Best, Peter Lang, Caroline Lodge and Chris Watkins

in Association with the National Association for Pastoral Care in Education

CASSELL

Cassell
Wellington House
125 Strand
London WC2R 0BB

387 Park Avenue South
New York
NY 10016–8810

First published 1995

British Library Cataloguing-in-Publication Data
A catalogue record for this book is available from the British Library.

ISBN 0-304-32781-6 (hardback)
0-304-32780-8 (paperback)

Typeset by Create Typesetting
Printed and bound in Great Britain by Biddles Limited, Guildford and King's Lynn

Contents

Series Editors' Foreword

The antecedents of this book are spelled out at some length in the editors' introductory chapter, as are its scope and purpose. Suffice to say that in its attempt to cover the broad range of concerns and activities associated with the concepts of pastoral care and personal-social education, it is in the tradition of Marland's *Pastoral Care* (London, Heinemann, 1974), Hamblin's *The Teacher and Pastoral Care* (Oxford, Blackwell, 1978), Best *et al.*'s *Perspectives on Pastoral Care* (London, Heinemann, 1980) and Lang and Marland's *New Directions in Pastoral Care* (Oxford, Blackwell, 1986). Each of those books sought to combine theory and practice in ways which would advance both the quality of support provided by schools and colleges and the quality of analysis and reflection that ought to accompany it. Each book was, in its way, a milestone in the development of affective education in the UK.

A comparison of the present book with any of those from the 1970s and 1980s would be instructive from an historical point of view, for the changes in focus and emphasis thus identified would be very considerable. They are indicative of the depth and range of the changes which have taken place in education in recent years, not least through the requirements of the 1988 Education Reform Act and all that follows from it.

Change is a recurring theme throughout the book. If change is to continue at anything like the present rate, it is difficult to see how any book about the current state of education can avoid becoming dated all too quickly. Yet it is because things are changing so rapidly that teachers and others with a professional concern for education need regular and up-to-date statements of sound principle and good practice. In reflecting the current concerns of pastoral care and PSE, and in offering some important pointers for the future, this book provides a much-needed statement of entitlement and provision for the 1990s and ahead.

The entitlement of children to be valued, supported and developed as whole persons is at the heart of the work of the National Association for Pastoral Care in Education (NAPCE), and it is NAPCE that we have to thank for the present volume. The original idea for the book came from a meeting of the Publications Committee of the Association in October 1992, and was immediately supported by the National Committee. The editors were drawn from the National Committee, the vast majority of contributors are NAPCE members, and the editorial work was funded by the Association. All the editors' royalties will go to the Association.

We are delighted to include this volume in the series.

Peter Lang
Ron Best

Notes on Contributors

Steve Adams is advisory teacher for child protection for Derbyshire LEA, and has been providing training for school and other education staff in pastoral care, personal-social education, counselling and child protection since 1986. He taught for sixteen years, eight as head of house in a Derbyshire comprehensive school. He is author of *A Guide to Creative Tutoring* (London: Kogan Page, 1989) and many papers and articles on pastoral care and child protection.

Phil Bayliss is a lecturer in special educational needs at the University of Exeter School of Education. As a practitioner he has worked in special and mainstream schools and further education, setting up integrated provision for students with special needs. His research interests centre on the integration of children and adults with severe learning difficulties.

Ron Best is assistant dean and professor in the Faculty of Education at Roehampton Institute, London, and a former chairperson of NAPCE. He has researched and published on numerous aspects of education including school libraries, initial teacher education and provision for children with special needs. He is executive editor of NAPCE's journal *Pastoral Care in Education*.

Bernard Clarke has been headteacher at Peers School for five years. His original training was in social work and he has also worked at schools in India, Bristol and Loughborough. He is married with four children, all of whom have attended the schools in which he has worked.

Martin Desforges is a senior psychologist with Sheffield MDC, with responsibility for continuing professional development, and tutor to the M.Sc. in Educational Psychology at the University of Sheffield. He is interested in the emotional development of children and ways that caregivers – parents, teachers and other professionals – can support emotional development.

Phil Griffiths is now working independently as a counsellor, supervisor and trainer. He was formerly Senior Counsellor in the Educational Psychology and Counselling service of Dudley LEA, and before that was a member of the Schools Council Project: Health Education 13–18. He is the co-author with Keith Sherman of *The Form Tutor: New Approaches to Tutoring in the 1990s* (Oxford: Blackwell, 1991), and of other articles on tutoring and counselling. He has a particular interest in the management of tutors and in the pastoral care of staff.

Brenda Hopper lectures in counselling and related studies at Edge Hill College of Higher Education, Lancashire. She taught in secondary schools in Nottinghamshire before moving into higher education to work with teachers and other professionals on in-service programmes. She is a member of the North-West NAPCE committee and an elected member of the National Executive.

Mary James is a lecturer in education at the University of Cambridge Institute of Education. Her special interests are in curriculum, evaluation and applied research methods. She edits *The Curriculum Journal*. Formerly she taught in secondary schools, where she was a head of year and head of a social studies department.

Peter Lang is a senior lecturer in education at the University of Warwick. He is papers editor of the journal *Pastoral Care in Education*. He has taught, written about and researched the areas of pastoral care and personal-social education. Currently he is working on comparative research within a European context.

Caroline Lodge is the headteacher of George Orwell School in Islington, and is vice chair of NAPCE. She is co-editor of *Gender and Pastoral Care* (Oxford: Blackwell, 1991).

John McGuiness is director of counselling courses at the School of Education, Durham University, and the author of several books on the foundational importance of socio-emotional factors in the learning process. He is a trainer in commercial/industrial contexts as well as in education and is constantly surprised to find hard-headed accountants valuing exactly what is currently being removed from the educational experience of children.

Colleen McLaughlin is tutor in personal and social education at the University of Cambridge Institute of Education. She is very interested in the development of counselling work in the school setting and she runs courses for teachers in this and allied fields.

Michael Marland is headteacher at North Westminster Community School, and honorary professor of education at the University of Warwick. He is a founder-member and first chairperson on NAPCE, and has a worldwide reputation as a writer and speaker on all aspects of education. His books include *Pastoral Care* (London: Heinemann), *The Craft of the Classroom* (London: Heinemann) and *The Tutor and the Tutor Group* (Harlow: Longman).

Stephen Munby is currently Senior Adviser in the Quality Development Service, Oldham Education Authority. He has been inspecting schools for several years and has worked widely as a consultant and trainer, both in the UK and abroad.

Fergus O'Sullivan is senior lecturer in the Centre for Education Management, Leeds Metropolitan University. He has worked as an education officer, senior inspector and INSET coordinator in LEAs and as a teacher and deputy head in secondary schools. His current interests are management development, teaching and research, particularly in the field of the 'learning organization' and collaborative organizational evaluation.

John Thacker is a senior lecturer in education and course tutor to the M.Ed. in Educational Psychology at the University of Exeter School of Education. He has a long-standing interest in pastoral care and PSE in both primary and secondary schools and is currently looking at the part played by organizational culture in personal and social education.

Sally Tomlinson is dean of education and professor of education policy at Goldsmiths' College, University of London. She has written and researched for many years in the areas of home–school relations, effective schooling, special education and multi-cultural education.

Patsy Wagner is the deputy principal educational psychologist for Kensington and Chelsea, having previously been a head of department for compensatory education in a London comprehensive. She is a qualified family therapist, an active NAPCE member, and currently secretary of the NAPCE London committee.

Chris Watkins is a course tutor in pastoral care and PSE at the Institute of Education, University of London, and also works in areas of school behaviour and mentoring. At the time of writing he is officer in the chair of NAPCE.

Introduction

DEVELOPMENTS IN PASTORAL CARE AND PERSONAL-SOCIAL EDUCATION

There are aspects of pastoral care that originated before the 1944 Education Act, and in some cases in the last century. The same applies to personal-social education, though generally its origins seem to have been more recent. However, people have been writing about pastoral care for a much more limited period. It was not until the 1970s that the first books on how to 'do' pastoral care appeared. Michael Marland's *Pastoral Care* (1974), Keith Blackburn's *The Tutor* (1975) and Douglas Hamblin's *The Teacher and Pastoral Care* (1978) made important contributions to people's ideas and practice of pastoral care. It was also in the 1970s that the first critiques of pastoral care were published. Both Best, Jarvis and Ribbins (1977) and Lang (1977) drew attention to a number of problems about pastoral care – lack of clarity regarding its meaning, its use as a means of control and an over-emphasis on structure at the expense of practice. Later Lang (1983) suggested these two strands might be characterized as a literature of technique and a literature of critique. He went on to argue for the need for the two strands to be combined in the same writings.

The 1980s were in many ways a decade of progress in so far as pastoral care was concerned. In 1982 the National Association for Pastoral Care in Education (NAPCE) was founded and developed into a significant professional organization. Papers in its journal *Pastoral Care in Education* both reflected the growing amount of good and innovative practice and encouraged innovation and development within schools. Training at both initial and in-service levels increased. The idea that the practice of pastoral care needed not only intuition and good nature but skill and a developed pedagogy was reinforced by the promotion of 'active tutorial work'. The publication of Michael Marland's paper 'The pastoral curriculum' (1980) was a key first step in what was in some ways the most critical development of the 1980s. This was the move from a fragmented and bolt-on approach to pastoral care to a more integrated whole curriculum and whole-school approach.

It was also during the 1980s that two influential books appeared. Best, Jarvis and Ribbins's *Perspectives on Pastoral Care* (1980) and Lang and Marland's *New Directions in Pastoral Care* (1986). Both were edited collections of papers and both had a wide appeal to practising teachers, teacher educators and those involved in research.

An important reason for this wide appeal was the fact that both books contained a critique and technical discussion. They pointed the way towards action but at the same time encouraged thought. Another of their strengths was their breadth of coverage. They provided a wide-ranging view of pastoral care and its concerns.

The editors believe that one important aspect of the current volume is its continuation and updating of a tradition established by these books in the 1980s. This book again takes a broad view of pastoral care; critically, it seeks to encourage both action and reflection, and to underline the vital link between the two activities.

THE CURRENT CONTEXT FOR PASTORAL CARE AND PERSONAL-SOCIAL EDUCATION

The current context for pastoral care and personal-social education also reinforces the importance of continuing to present good practice and research alongside critiques. Some of the unresolved issues and tensions of the 1980s remain and have been obscured or further complicated by the need to respond to and adapt to more recent educational changes.

Some of the government-imposed reforms have exacerbated already existing problems. The introduction of the so-called National Curriculum very often reinforced the fragmentation of a child's learning experience in the secondary school, and created a fragmentation in the primary school where the curriculum had tended to be more integrated up to then. Local management funding formulae and the creation of grant-maintained status have given schools more power over how to distribute diminishing resources, and at worst this has been at the cost of some pastoral posts. At best, it has produced some creative and imaginative new roles into which pastoral team leaders have been able to extend their work and further assist the effective learning of the students. Some decisions have been thoughtful and strategic, but at worst the changes have been reactive and unplanned and have weakened pastoral care and the effectiveness of personal-social education. There are schools which offer the National Curriculum five cross-curricular themes as a course, and schools which have abandoned pastoral programmes, cut the available time for tutors to work with their groups and dispensed with heads of year. No overall pattern has yet emerged, but it is clear that the current context for pastoral care, no less than the rest of schools' work, remains confused and in flux.

Education policy at national level has always marginalized or ignored pastoral care and personal-social education. This has been especially true since the Education Reform Act (1988) with its emphasis on the National Curriculum and its assessment. This legislation resulted in a large increase in the volume of work for teachers, related to the subjects included in the National Curriculum. Those interested in promoting the value of pastoral care and personal-social education have had to defend and promote their position in this difficult context. There have been more positive reactions, encouraged and facilitated by NAPCE and by other factors, such as the Technical and Vocational Education Initiative (TVEI). As a result of the legislation, each school has had to make decisions which affect pastoral care provision. As a consequence practitioners have continued to develop their expertise, theorists have been testing their hypotheses, research has been carried out and reported in journals such as NAPCE's *Pastoral Care in Education*. Ideas and practice have been refined, redefined and tested. Further, pastoral care and personal-social education have gained much from complementing and enhancing the work done through TVEI and its extension, drugs education, health and sex education, including HIV education, the Business and Technician Education Council and records of achievement. However, changes have tended to be parochial, and no overall picture is yet emerging.

WHY BOTHER WITH THIS BOOK?

So long as it has something to contribute to improving educational practice, a book on pastoral care and personal-social education should be of value at any time. This book is intended to go further and to restate principles which lie behind good practice.

At present a great deal of talk, change and action in schools is being generated as a response to what is published as an outcome of the Education Reform Act (1988) or subsequent legislation, and originates with central government or its quangos: statutory orders, arrangements for testing, discussion documents, consultation papers, curriculum booklets and so on. The editors intend to reclaim some of the agenda with this book, to remind schools and educationalists generally that there are still large areas of autonomy and that the National Curriculum need be only one part of the whole curriculum of any school. We intend to restate the crucial importance of pastoral care and personal-social education, while offering substance for this claim through contributions from respected practitioners and researchers.

There is a demand for practical resources for teachers in this area. The evidence for this demand is in the numbers who attend courses, who subscribe to journals and who purchase training packs and other materials. For example, the publication activity of NAPCE has expanded considerably since 1990.

Training work in pastoral care and personal-social education has always been *ad hoc*, and has had to compete with other aspects of school life and other school priorities for time, financial resourcing and LEA or teacher interest. The training scene at initial training or post-initial qualification is changing rapidly, with much more focus on school-based and school-focused training and development opportunities. A book which reports the state of the art in pastoral care and personal-social education will be useful to those who have little access to other forms of staff development, and will complement the experience of those fortunate to have such opportunities.

THE CONTENTS AND STRUCTURE OF THIS BOOK

Pastoral care and personal-social education are, to some people, difficult areas to structure and arrange. They are areas which contain a large number of topics, and the vocabulary for describing them is not always shared. To us, as editors, the task of creating an initial map of the proposed contents was not simple, but was helped by the overall structure of parts which you now see on the contents page.

First, there is a need to examine definitions and concepts in these areas. Different people may mean different things when they use the terms; definitions of pastoral care and personal-social education vary in what they include and in the aspects which they omit. Ron Best's chapter traces and analyses a range of definitions.

Second, the particular and sometimes peculiar context of the school has a major influence on what pastoral care and personal-social education may be. Thus it is important to address aspects of the school as an organization: its structures, management, teams and their development. Caroline Lodge and Fergus O'Sullivan examine some of these aspects in an important whole-school way. This part is completed by addressing a theme which has bedevilled the history of pastoral care, especially when it has not been treated as a whole-school matter: the issue of care and control is critically considered by John McGuiness, reminding us that control is never an end in itself but an outcome of learning.

The face-to-face work of teachers with pupils is examined in three parts which address individual work, planned work with groups and responsive work.

'Working with individuals' is a part comprising three chapters. Colleen McLaughlin examines the notion of counselling in schools, its recent history, models and prospects. Phil Griffiths examines the process of tutoring and guidance, its recent development as a whole-school task, some models and the implications for staff support. Brenda Hopper provides useful ideas for understanding individuals in the context in which we often find them in schools – that of the group. This chapter makes a bridge to the next part, which addresses planned learning with groups.

'The curriculum' is a much used but poorly understood phrase. Michael Marland traces some of the history of curriculum pronouncements in Britain, reminds us of the key powers to be exercised by the school and examines approaches to planning the whole curriculum. Chris Watkins takes the whole curriculum as a starting point for examining personal-social education, reviews recent developments and proposes models for further work. Steve Munby makes the argument that assessment issues must be addressed in a book such as this, and identifies seven important assumptions for effective practice in a whole-child, person-centred approach. Phil Bayliss and John Thacker give an extra focus to special educational needs as interactive and complex, and consider how to access a whole-school curriculum for personal-social education.

No matter how much schools and teachers plan their pastoral work and personal-social curriculum, there are some experiences which will influence the lives and learnings of pupils and teachers and which arrive in an unpredicted way. In a part entitled 'Trauma', three chapters address a selection of themes in this area. Steve Adams examines child protection and the role of the school, before proposing a pastoral contribution. Martin Desforges examines separation and divorce, children's reactions and the various contributions which the school can make. Patsy Wagner explores ideas about death and loss and examines practical action by the school.

Personal-social learning is not confined within the walls of the school. Influences on self come from a wide range of sources. Recognizing this means that the school needs to nurture links with home and community. Bernard Clarke outlines the numerous communities of the school from the local world of work to the global community, and points to some important considerations in building a working community. Sally Tomlinson analyses links between school and home, the problems inherent in creating partnerships, and policies for development.

The final part brings together two chapters under the heading of 'Developments'. Mary James looks at processes in using action-research and evaluation in the area of pastoral care and personal-social education: specifically the issues of deciding criteria and evidence. Peter Lang looks at developments in a range of countries and proposes that we have something to learn from each of them. In the concluding chapter, the editors survey the potential of pastoral care and re-state the key principles upon which it must be based if this potential is to be realized.

REFERENCES

Best, R., Jarvis, C. and Ribbins, P. (1977) Pastoral care: concept and process. *British Journal of Educational Studies*, **25**(2), 124–35.

Best, R., Jarvis, C. and Ribbins, P. (eds) (1980) *Perspectives on Pastoral Care*. London: Heinemann.

Blackburn, K. (1975) *The Tutor*. London: Heinemann.

Hamblin, D. (1978) *The Teacher and Pastoral Care*. Oxford: Blackwell.

Lang, P. (1977) It is easier to punish us in small groups. *Times Educational Supplement*, 6 May.

Lang, P. (1983) Review of *Perspectives on Pastoral Care* [eds R. Best, C. Jarvis and P. Ribbins], *Pastoral Care in Education*, **1**(1), 61–3.

Lang, P. and Marland, M. (eds) (1986) *New Directions in Pastoral Care*. Oxford: Blackwell/NAPCE/ESRC.

Marland, M. (1974) *Pastoral Care*. London: Heinemann.

Marland, M. (1980) The pastoral curriculum. In Best, R., Jarvis, C. and Ribbins, P. (eds) *Perspectives on Pastoral Care*. London: Heinemann.

Part 1

Definitions and Concepts

CHAPTER 1

Concepts in pastoral care and PSE

Ron Best

INTRODUCTION

I suspect that many of those who underwent initial or award-bearing in-service training as teachers in the 1960s and early 1970s found the then-fashionable conceptual analytic approach to the philosophy of education rather tiresome. Certainly, the study of how Peters, Hirst and Dearden employed words like 'teaching', 'training' and 'instruction' seemed rather remote from my preoccupations as a geography teacher at that time in the East End of London. Yet to explore the concepts we use in both our descriptions and our prescriptions for schooling is more than academic self-indulgence. It has the potential to clarify action as well as thought, and to contribute insights which guide and inform educational reform.

There are a number of concepts used in the discussion of schools' concern for meeting the needs of children as more than empty buckets to be filled with knowledge (Haigh, 1975). Like 'education', 'training', 'instruction' and so forth, these concepts share a 'family resemblance', yet their coexistence suggests their distinctiveness. These concepts include: *pastoral care*, *affective education*, *guidance*, *counselling* and *personal and social education* (PSE).

It is the purpose of this chapter to explore some of these concepts. However, the analysis will not follow strictly the model of the philosophers of education of the 1960s but will range more widely both historically and empirically. A model, originating a decade ago (Best *et al.*, 1983) and much refined since (see, for example, Best and Ribbins, 1983; Lang and Ribbins, 1985; Best, 1989), will be employed to propose some logically determined dimensions of pastoral work, and some prevailing tensions will be identified.

PASTORAL CARE

'Pastoral care' is a distinctively British concept. Its use in other cultures typically results in puzzlement. Where it has been used meaningfully in other cultures it has been as an inheritance, for example, in Australia

(Committee of Enquiry ..., 1980) or has been imported as a conscious policy, for example, in Singapore (SEAS, 1988).

Etymologically, pastoral care has its roots in the teachings and organization of the Christian Church. From the Latin root *pascere* (to feed) and articulated by the powerful metaphor of the Good Shepherd, pastoral care describes the spiritually and morally sustaining concern of the pastor for his or her flock (Dooley, 1980).

In the days when most institutionalized education was provided through Church schools, non-conforming academies and the exclusively Anglican foundations at Oxford and Cambridge, the application of the concept – though curiously not the words themselves – to education might have been a natural enough extension of its clerical context. What was less natural was its application in the system of secular State schools which grew up after 1870 and, in a much later wave of State provision, again after the Second World War. Paradoxically, it seems to be in State comprehensive schools from 1965 onwards that the term came into greatest use (Ribbins and Best, 1985).

Defining pastoral care in the educational context has proved extremely difficult. From Michael Marland's seminal volume of that title in 1974, twenty years of discussion, writing and theorizing have failed to achieve much more than a working consensus.

Whether 'pastoral care' was ever an entirely appropriate word to use in regard to education is debatable. Two early objections were those of Dooley (1980) and Hughes (1980). Dooley argued that the term brought with it from its New Testament roots a concept of dependence which leaves little room for exercise of freedom of choice between alternative courses of action, essential to moral action, and thus does not square well with the goal of education as rational and moral autonomy (Dooley, 1980, pp. 21–3).

Hughes located the term within 'the public school tradition written about at length in the latter part of the nineteenth century and the early nineteen hundreds', and, like Dooley, noted the assumed dependence of the cared-for upon those who are superior, whether socially or in wisdom, which rested uneasily with the aims of education (Hughes, 1980, pp. 26–7). Such attitudes were, he argued, 'strikingly out of step with those most basic changes in attitude towards the welfare of children which have characterized the development of the education system in Britain' (Hughes, 1980, p. 29).

In the years since those critiques were published, theoretical and empirical research has done much to differentiate between the various aspects of pastoral care. Its identification with the guidance and counselling of individual pupils has been complemented by its application to aspects of both official and 'hidden' curriculums, and to the way in which teachers carry out the more conventional roles of delivering the academic curriculum and maintaining order. In the process, an already diffuse concept has become more so.

One recent and authoritative definition comes from the report of an inspection of aspects of pastoral care in twenty-seven comprehensive schools, carried out by Her Majesty's Inspectorate in 1987–8:

pastoral care is concerned with promoting pupils' personal and social development and fostering positive attitudes: through the quality of teaching and learning; through the nature of relationships amongst pupils, teachers and adults other than teachers; through arrangements for monitoring pupils' overall progress, academic, personal and social; through specific pastoral structures and support systems; and through extra-curricular activities and the school ethos. Pastoral care, accordingly should help a school to achieve success. In such a context it offers support for the learning, behaviour and welfare of all pupils, and addresses the particular difficulties some individual pupils may be experiencing. It seems to help ensure that all pupils, and particularly girls and members of ethnic minorities, are enabled to benefit from the full range of educational opportunities which a school has available.

(DES, 1989, p. 3)

This definition demonstrates the breadth of the concept and the diversity and pervasiveness of the term's referents throughout the school. Pastoral care is seen to be achieved through structures, systems, relationships, teaching quality, monitoring arrangements, extra-curricular activities and ethos. In its diffuseness,this definition compares closely with teachers' use of the concept of 'pastoral care' which I have encountered through years of research and in-service training.

I have found that for many teachers, pastoral care is most easily identified with the structures of roles which schools have devised to parallel the academic structures of subject responsibilities, heads of department/faculty and so on. In a research context, teachers frequently respond to questions about what pastoral care means within their school with statements like: 'Oh, we have a house system (or a year system)', as though the structure *was* pastoral care rather than a means by which the responsibilities for *doing* pastoral care are allocated.

Since 'to care' is a verb, it is clear that pastoral care is something we do, and not merely an institutional form. Indeed, it is arguable that caring sometimes goes on despite the systems or structures which it is claimed have been created to facilitate it (Best *et al.*, 1983). So for other teachers, pastoral care is the multifarious activities – guiding, counselling, interviewing, recording, meeting parents, attending case conferences, disciplining, negotiating and so on – in which they engage, albeit in roles which are institutionalized and designated 'pastoral'.

Another response is to argue that pastoral care is not so much the activities or practices which teachers engage in, as the way in which those activities are performed. While there are logical arguments to the effect that one could not be said to be engaged in (say) counselling if one was behaving in an uncaring way, it is clear that there are enormous variations amongst teachers in the way they approach the activities associated with pastoral care. Some interviews with children (or parents) are carried out in more caring ways than others. Even punishing someone can be done in a more or less caring way.

Pastoral care may be seen in the caring quality of relationships between people, whether between teachers and pupils, pupils and pupils, teachers and teachers, teachers and parents or, for that matter, any of the groups who are stakeholders in the school. I recall one headteacher's response to a researcher's request for a definition of 'pastoral care': 'It all comes down to relationships; if you get those right, all else follows. If you don't then you won't achieve very much of anything.'

What seem to underlie the quality of teachers' pastoral role performance, and of the relationships which exist generally within the school, are the *attitudes* which the actors adopt towards one another. These, in turn, reflect the values which they hold. Social interaction between (say) a teacher and a child may be described as 'pastoral' not because the interaction takes place in distinctively 'pastoral' or 'caring' roles – for example counsellor–client, tutor–tutee – but because of the attitudes which the actors adopt: polite, respectful, concerned, thoughtful. These attitudes are in turn manifestations of particular *values* which the actors hold: such values as respect for persons, regard for truth, fairness and so on.

It is because we use pastoral care as a concept which embraces the less tangible (but more profound) realms of relationships, values and attitudes, as well as the more tangible and structured role-positions and their associated duties and practices, that it is possible to apply it corporately to the climate or ethos of a school. As a researcher, if I ask of a teacher: 'Is this a caring school?', the response is most often to describe the quality of relationships between teachers and children – and the attitudes, values etc. which these encapsulate – rather than to describe the structure of the school. Very often, the fact that teachers *like* their pupils is cited as evidence for the caring ethos of the school.

PASTORAL CARE, GUIDANCE AND COUNSELLING

We have seen that, despite the connotations of dependency and subordination which derive from its origins in the theology and practice of the Christian Church, pastoral care is a popular and enduring concept which has wide and diffuse application in education. To summarise, it is variously used to refer to:

- a bureaucratic structure of status positions and role definitions;
- activities or practices performed by the role incumbents;
- the way in which those practices are carried out;
- the quality of relationships between members of the school;
- the attitudes members adopt towards one another, and the values to which these give expression;
- the ethos or climate of the school as a whole.

In its comprehensiveness – and to some extent the lack of a *systematic* differentiation between its various applications – one might conclude that little has changed since Hughes's (1971, p. 156) rendering of pastoral care as 'multifarious kinds of personalised service'. It is therefore surprising to find some recent commentators making rather simpler and altogether more restrictive formulations for it.

In *The Tutor and the Tutor Group*, a book produced to accompany Longman's recent addition to the stock of tutorial materials for use in form periods, Michael Marland asserts that '[t]he best definition of pastoral care, that peculiar British educational phrase, is "personal, educational, and vocational guidance"' (Marland, 1989, p. 15). He goes on to argue that in helping youngsters to learn what it is to be a pupil or student, and to begin to think about their future careers from an early point in their lives, educational and vocational guidance complement personal guidance in 'enabling the young person to face that question "Who am I?"'. Pastoral care, then, has as its focus personal development (Marland, 1989, p. 15).

In equating pastoral care with guidance, Marland may be responding to the widespread use of the term as something of a synonym for pastoral care in other cultures, some close to home. As early as 1968, the Scottish Education Department's document *Guidance in Scottish Secondary Schools* employed a broad concept of guidance which had many of the features of 'pastoral care' in England. It also seems to have suffered from some of the same ambiguities. One commentator (Bennett) is reported to have concluded that 'the guidance systems which were subsequently established in Scotland were often characterized by serious disagreements about the organization, function and purpose of pastoral care within the schools' (Best *et al.*, 1980, p. 7).

An equivalence between pastoral care and guidance is also made where guidance is defined very broadly. Consider, for example, Milner's (1980) definitions:

> guidance is about helping young people to begin to find themselves, to develop their sense of identity, to begin to know who they really are, what they have and what they do not have; what they can do easily, what they can do with difficulty and what they probably cannot do at all, in terms of education, occupations, relationships, values and society ... A very simple definition of guidance describes it as a process of helping individuals, through their own efforts, to discover and develop their potentialities for personal happiness and social usefulness.
>
> (Milner, 1980, pp. 123–4)

Such a definition does indeed resonate with the broad concept of person-centred service which pastoral care seems to encompass. Yet the equation of pastoral care with guidance seems inappropriate for several reasons.

First, in common use 'guidance' is too narrow a concept to serve the altogether broader field of reference of pastoral care. If I seek guidance, I seek advice. If I am travelling and seek a guide, it is because, although I have some notion of where it is I want to go, I recognize that I lack knowledge of the transport routes, the passable terrain and so on. Guidance within education – whether advice about academic destinations (what subjects to choose, what examinations to sit etc.), about career possibilities or personal relationships – does not necessarily require the full range of attitudes, values, relationships, personal knowledge, empathy and so on which we have seen pastoral care to connote. There is more to pastoral care than guidance.

Second, in common use, 'guidance' does not necessarily entail the eventual moral and intellectual autonomy of the individual. I may employ a guide to get me from one place to another without ever intending to make the trip again, let alone intending to acquire the detailed knowledge necessary to be able to make the trip next time unaided. However, within education, the premium placed upon the eventual independence of the pupil leads to a slightly different interpretation of the role of a guide within such a metaphor. Citing a policy statement produced by the NFER in 1953, and elaborated by Morris in 1955, Watts and Fawcett (1980) comment:

> In this view, the teacher's role can be compared with the guide on a long mountaineering expedition, in which the 'actual objectives, the routes, the stages, the pace and the equipment must all be chosen to suit the climber', and in which one of the aims is 'that the pupils should gradually become independent of the guide and able to climb unaided'.
>
> (Watts and Fawcett, 1980, p. 107)

Within such guidance, the novice would be receiving instruction, coupled with experiential learning, in order to acquire the knowledge and skills necessary to achieve independence in this context. And it is true that, in education, giving guidance often entails transmitting certain concepts and facts without which the pupil cannot be guided to a satisfactory destination, such that, in the fullness of time, the pupil will be capable of charting her or his own course without our assistance. But to guide is active, to be guided passive; so the concept is being stretched to the limit in building in the ultimate independence clause. That is why the limits of the concept are commonly acknowledged. For instance, those involved in careers *education* are frequently at pains to distinguish it from careers *guidance*, precisely because their project is deemed to promote knowledge and understanding which have worth far beyond their immediate application to career choice (Watts and Fawcett, 1980, pp. 109–10).

Elsewhere, the application of the term to aspects of what Marland termed the 'pastoral curriculum' (Marland, 1980), have further complicated matters. Thus, in Queensland (Australia) 'guidance tutoring' is a near synonym for a tutorial programme, and in other States for programmes of personal and social education. In terms of the analysis of common-sense applications of the role of a 'guide', this again seems inappropriate, for, if the earlier argument is correct, guides are not usually called upon to teach their clients anything. Indeed, it may be against their own interests so to do, since their livelihood may depend upon the continued dependency of their clients.

There is no doubt that the activities encompassed by 'guidance' are activities which teachers engage in when they are 'doing' pastoral care. Since in order to give guidance we need to know something of the child's aspirations, 'pastoral' activities like interviewing and recording information about decisions may play a part in guidance. But there are other aspects of pastoral care – including the quality of relationships, the giving of moral and emotional support in times of stress or anxiety – which seem to lie outside it.

The distinction between 'guidance' and 'counselling' merits comment at this point. There is a strong 'family resemblance' between these two concepts and this is recognizable in the way that they are often run together in speech and publication. (The existence of the influential *British Journal of Guidance and Counselling* epitomizes this confluence). They have in common their service to a client. Both are to do with providing assistance of some kind, in a helping relationship, yet their coexistence is evidence enough of their difference.

Traditionally, guidance in schools entailed three main activities: the giving of information, the diagnosis or analysis of the individual's need or problem, and the provision of advice. It is against this that the distinguishing characteristics of counselling may be identified. Writing of careers counselling, Watts and Fawcett observe that

> the object of the counsellor is not to diagnose the pupil's attributes and then recommend appropriate occupations, but rather to help him [*sic*] work through his problem, articulating his perceptions both of himself and of the options open to him, and subjecting them to scrutiny, until he is able to reach his own decision. The skills required of the counsellor, in short, are primarily not diagnostic but facilitative, and are concerned less with the outcomes of decision-making than with its process ... they are focused not on helping pupils to *make wise decisions* (with the assumption that he knows what these should be), but on helping them to *make decisions wisely*.
>
> (Watts and Fawcett, 1980, pp. 110–11)

While it is true that different theories of counselling may place more or less importance on the counsellor remaining neutral, the client-centred paradigm (most often associated with Rogers) provides a very clear basis for the distinction I am talking about here. The crux is the degree to which the help that is given is based upon expert knowledge, whether that knowledge is knowledge of processes or outcomes, and where, in the giving and receiving of this help, the independence of the client figures. The broader the definition of 'guidance' (see Milner's definitions quoted on page 7), the easier it is to see counselling as one set of practices which are employed in guidance. The more constrained the concept of guidance, the more clearly it differs from counselling in the emphases given to client autonomy and the need for direction.

At this point we may wonder whether it really matters what things are called. Surely (it may be argued) it is less important what label we attach to something than what we actually *do* under that label? If so, perhaps all the foregoing has been a waste of time? I think not. As I have already indicated, the clarification of issues (including discrepancies between ideals and practice) is an important outcome of the process of conceptual analysis, and a number of such issues have emerged already: rational and moral autonomy as an important goal for pastoral care, the proper place of direction within guidance and counselling and so on. None the less, I think there is some force to this argument.

Whether I consider myself to be engaged in 'counselling', 'guidance', 'pastoral care' or any other name I happen to adopt, what is most important is that my actions are likely to be successful in achieving those goals I set myself in the first place, that the goals themselves are worth achieving and that the methods used to achieve them are the most appropriate given the set of values which I hold in regard to this and other aspects of my work. One thing which gives these concepts their 'family resemblance' is their common commitment to the welfare or well-being of the individual child in the context of her or his total social and personal development. How this commitment is achieved is a matter of identifying the welfare and developmental needs of the individual. These needs are too often taken for granted in what is said and written about pastoral care and PSE. That is true, for example, of the HMI definition noted earlier (see pp. 4–5), which describes what pastoral care is concerned with, through what it is made manifest, and so on, but does not articulate the precise needs of the children whom it is supposed to serve.

The next section will address the nature of needs directly, in the context of a model which aims to clarify further the goals, processes and practices of pastoral care.

PASTORAL CARE AND NEEDS

One helpful distinction is that between reactive, proactive and developmental pastoral care (see Chapter 18 by Peter Lang below). *Reactive* pastoral care refers to the response which teachers make, in the form of counselling, guidance and so on, when children need support with a problem, usually of a personal, social or emotional kind. For some teachers this remains the heartland of pastoral care: form tutors are expected to get to know their tutees primarily in order to be able to recognize when they have a problem with which they require help.

It is now recognized that to be merely *re*active is not enough: it reduces pastoral work to what Hamblin long ago termed 'emotional first-aid' (Hamblin, 1978). The force of the metaphor is, of course, to direct attention to the need to prevent crises by anticipating needs. Prevention is better than cure. *Proactive* pastoral care refers to schools' attempts to anticipate 'critical incidents' in children's school careers and to provide children in advance with the coping skills necessary to handle them before they achieve crisis proportions (Hamblin, 1978).

Developmental pastoral care goes beyond coping strategies, by engaging children in activities which are designed to contribute to their personal and social development, and thus enhance the potential quality of their lives inside, outside and after school. This is often linked with PSE.

These distinctions are useful, but stop short of differentiating the kinds of need which might be met by each.

I suggest that there are four identifiable types of need which schools attempt to meet in setting up the structures, undertaking the activities, establishing the relationships, adopting the values and attitudes, and in creating the climate or ethos which we identify as 'pastoral care'. Each type of need is associated with a particular status the child enjoys; each may be associated with particular roles teachers play; and each may be identified with an organizational dimension of the school as an institution. Let us call schools' attempts to meet these four kinds of need 'pastoral tasks'.

There are four pastoral tasks. Three of them – 'casework', 'curriculum' and 'management' – were originally distinguished by Watkins (1985), and served to correct the idea that pastoral care was limited to the counselling and support associated with reactive services. The fourth – which I shall call 'control/community' – is a necessary addition in order to accommodate both those disciplinary problems which seem always to have placed heavy demands on the time and energies of teachers in positions of 'pastoral' responsibility, and the pastoral work which may be achieved through the 'hidden curriculum', ethos or climate of the school.

Although these four tasks may be distinguished for purposes of analysis, it is important to note that they are frequently combined in complex patterns of behaviour on the part of teachers and pupils in schools. Let us look briefly at each.

Casework

In the early years of state secondary schooling after the Second World War, and especially with comprehensive reorganization following DES Circular 10/65, pastoral care was virtually synonymous with casework. It is here that teachers *in loco parentis* attempt to meet the needs of the child in the status *child*. The teacher is the responsible adult upon whose maturity the child may reasonably depend.

When teachers do casework, they are not in quite the same position as the doctor, lawyer, social worker or counsellor – because, unlike the clients who fill their casebooks, the child's needs are not merely 'medical', 'legal', 'social' or 'personal'. Pastoral casework may concern any or all of these: what is distinctive about it is the fact that as teachers we respond to the pupil as one who, by virtue of her or his tender years, has needs which we, as adults, are in some measure able to meet.

These needs include the need for security, the need for guidance and the need for moral or emotional support. They may include on occasions physical needs – a change of clothing, for example, or a hot meal. And they certainly include the need for understanding and patience in the face of irrationality and childishness, and for forgiveness, warmth and acceptance when rules are broken or behaviour is otherwise unacceptable. In a word, they need love. The activities traditionally associated with pastoral care as reactive – guidance, counselling, listening, defending, representing and so on – are schools' attempts to meet these needs.

It is sometimes thought that the justification for casework is in the removal of impediments to successful learning, that casework performs some kind of underlabourer role for the curriculum. Certainly this is one of its functions, for no child will learn much if it is hungry, distressed or desperately unhappy. These needs demand resolution first. However, casework is justified on more than these instrumental grounds. The commitment of responsible adults to the well-being of children is intrinsically worthwhile and requires no further justification.

Curriculum

The pastoral curriculum includes the school's attempts to be both proactive and developmental through the intentional provision of learning experiences which relate to the child's welfare and contribute to her or his personal and social development. One important consideration in organizing the curriculum is, of course, the age of the child. We would not offer the same set of learning experiences to a 5-year-old as we would to an 18-year-old. But it is not the status 'child' which is central here: rather, it is in its status as a learner or *pupil* that the child has curricular needs.

What are the needs of the individual as a pupil? Marland (1980) notes in his definitive chapter about the pastoral curriculum that it is not in principle different from any of the other sets of learning experiences (subjects) which schools provide. Like the curriculum in English or geography, the pastoral curriculum comprises concepts, facts, attitudes and skills. Therefore, the needs of the pupil may be seen to be opportunities to acquire concepts, learn facts, practise skills and develop attitudes. However, since the pastoral curriculum is distinctively to do with the pupil's personal and social development, I think we need to add to these: opportunities to *examine beliefs* and *explore feelings*.

Here, too, there is a distinction to be made between instrumental and intrinsic justifications. The pastoral curriculum may anticipate 'critical incidents' (Hamblin, 1978) in a career path through the academic curriculum and forestall those crises which are both personally injurious and detrimental to further learning. The inclusion of study skills in tutorial programmes is an example.

But the pastoral curriculum goes further than this. It may include content which is important (if not essential) to the personal and social development of the individual – and to which the child is therefore entitled – and which is not available elsewhere in the curriculum. Thus, PSE, health education, careers education and so on, together with much of the tutorial programme, are justified by virtue of their direct contribution to the individual's personal and social growth.

It is necessary at this point to say something about PSE, not least because there is a deal of confusion about the relationship between tutorial programmes, PSE courses and subjects with a 'pastoral flavour' (for example, health education), and how all these relate to the concept of the pastoral curriculum.

Much of the confusion arises because different authorities have chosen to use different words to describe similar developments. I think this is in part due to the different backgrounds and traditions from which those who are active and interested in this whole area have come. As primarily a teacher (and headteacher), it is natural enough for Marland to use the concept of the *curriculum* to describe this pastoral task. For Richard Pring, a *philosophical* analysis of what it is to be a 'person' provides the rationale for his map of personal and social education in the curriculum. (Pring, 1984; cited in Lang, 1988, pp. 43–4). Coming from a background in *social and developmental psychology*, Watkins chooses to focus upon the concept of the 'self' in describing personal and social education (and, later, guidance) as a school's attempt to promote directly the development of bodily, sexual, social, vocational and moral/political selves, together with the self as a learner and the self in the organization that is the school (Watkins, 1992). Others expand the PSE label to include health (PSHE) or moral education (PSME) because they have come to this enlarged curriculum concept from specialisms in one of these areas.

Of these labels, that of *personal and social education* has acquired considerable currency in recent years, because of its endorsement within the National Curriculum as the umbrella for a range of cross-curricular themes, dimensions and skills (NCC, 1990, pp. 2–7). However, as we saw in the earlier discussion of guidance and counselling, differences in labels may be less significant than the common aims and ideals of those who employ them. I suspect Pring speaks for them all when he identifies the following characteristics of the person as providing the necessary orientation for all work of this kind:

the capacity to think, to reflect, to engage critically with the received values, beliefs, and assumptions that one is confronted with ... [in short] the powers of the mind ...

the capacity to recognize others as persons – as centres of consciousness and reason like oneself...

that one acts intentionally, deliberately, and thus can be held responsible for what one does...

consciousness not only of others as persons but of oneself – a sense of one's own unity as a person, one's own value and dignity, one's own capacity to think through a problem, to persevere when things get tough, to establish a platform of values and beliefs whereby one can exercise some control over one's own destiny.

(Pring, 1988, pp. 43–4)

I find it easiest to take Marland's (1980) distinction between the pastoral curriculum and the tutorial programme as my starting-point. This leads to the following equation:

Pastoral Curriculum
=
the tutorial programme
+
subjects with a distinctive pastoral 'flavour'
e.g. health education, PSE, life skills, skills for adolescents
careers education, social education, education for citizenship, etc.
+
pastoral content/process in 'academic' or conventional subjects
i.e. 'PSE across the curriculum'

Control/Community

When I began researching pastoral care in 1976, it was apparent that pastoral 'middle managers' spent a good deal of their time responding to class-teachers' problems of control. To me it seemed that they spent a lot more time disciplining than (say) counselling, and that it was the problems of teachers rather than of children which were being addressed. Research in progress indicates that it remains true that many of the problems which teachers attempt to solve – much of their casework – are linked with, or manifested initially in, what teachers construe as unacceptable behaviour.

For this reason, much of our talk about order in schools is couched in terms of *dis*order. Our attention is devoted more to the misbehaviour of the deviant minority than to the conforming behaviour of the majority. As a result, the status which the child is accorded is that of 'deviant' or 'rule-breaker', the equivalent of the 'criminal' in society at large. While it is true that deviants have needs – help in correcting their behaviour, developing self-control and so on – this is a strikingly negative stance to adopt.

Concepts like 'deviant' and 'criminal' are social categories. One can only have such a status within a social group in which there is a shared code of behaviour. In established societies, the pattern of acceptable conduct is enshrined in formal rules or laws. However, in seeking to promote moral order in schools, matters cannot be left at the level of informal group norms, or in the form of institutionalized and reified 'laws of society'. Indeed, the laws of a repressive society may exclude the freedom to exercise one's moral autonomy. We need the moral force of the concept of the *community* to enlighten our attitudes to non-conformity.

It follows that the appropriate status to afford the child is that of *citizen* in the community that is the school. This is so whether or not the child is perceived to conform. Even the criminal is first and foremost a citizen: how else could s/he acquire criminal status?

The question we need to ask, therefore, is: what are the needs of the citizen in the community of the school? I suggest that they are the needs of the citizen in *any* community: the right to live one's life in a peaceful environment; a set of sensible rules and a system of sanctions to ensure that the one's freedom is not infringed by the excessive behaviour of others; opportunities to participate in corporate activities (including decision-making) and to develop a positive self-image; and opportunities to feel that one belongs and thus to share in mutual concern for the well-being of one's fellow citizens. Pastoral *control* cannot be divorced from the creation of a *caring community*.

Management

The fourth pastoral task is different in kind from the other three. Although it has the same ultimate aim – to meet the needs of the individual child's well-being and personal/social development – pastoral management does not do this directly. Rather, it is facilitative of the other three tasks, providing the infrastructure without which teachers' work would tend to be unsystematic, uncoordinated and ineffective. In short, pastoral management should be shaped as much by the needs of the *teachers* as by the needs of the pupil.

What do teachers need if they are effectively to perform the tasks of casework, curriculum and control/community? I suggest that at the very least teachers need:

- leadership, co-ordination, motivation and inspiration;
- resources and facilities including time and rooms for counselling and interviewing;
- clear job descriptions, sensitive appraisal, feedback and staff development opportunities;
- meetings which are regular, purposeful, carefully planned and competently managed;
- opportunities to participate in corporate activities and to feel valued as members of the team;
- to be appreciated and to develop a positive self-image;
- a framework of shared norms, procedures and (when necessary) sanctions;
- counselling, guidance and moral support in the face of the demands and stresses of their pastoral work.

HOLISTIC EDUCATION

We have seen that 'pastoral care' is a very comprehensive concept, expressing a commitment to the welfare, well-being and fullest development of the individual. In its etymology, and with the associated connotations of dependency and paternalism, it is probably inappropriate, but it endures. No alternative known to me can encompass the range and diversity of structures, practices, attitudes, values, relationships and so on which 'pastoral care' denotes.

Concepts of tutoring, guidance, counselling and the like are certainly not alternatives; rather, they seem to describe specific sets of activities in which teachers engage in order to carry out the various tasks which make up pastoral work. Guidance and counselling may figure prominently in casework and control; tutoring and personal and social education in the pastoral curriculum. They are constitutive of the reactive, proactive and developmental goals of pastoral care and not synonymous with it.

The comprehensiveness of the concept is a weakness as well as a strength. Necessarily, it lacks precision. In offering a model which permits the analysis of the four pastoral tasks – casework, curriculum, control/community and management – I have attempted to provide a basis for spelling out more precisely the nature of pastoral work aimed at meeting the needs of the child in its various statuses. I believe this is necessary to give direction to our planning, to provide a framework for monitoring and evaluation, and to identify staff-development targets (Best, 1990).

But there are dangers. The distinguishing of different pastoral tasks through conceptual analysis may create the illusion that these tasks are always distinguishable in real life. They are not. On the contrary, teachers' work is often a seamless robe, in which casework blurs into curriculum, curriculum into control and the creation of community, and so on. One activity may at one and the same time be contributing to the performance of all the tasks. Leading a tutor group exercise to explore the idea of respect for others, sparked by an instance of playground bullying, would be an example. An inference to the effect that there must be a division of labour amongst teachers according to these tasks is clearly invalid. Indeed, it is comparable to the inference that the pastoral and the academic are necessarily separate, and should be institutionalized separately in the school's bureaucracy: the well-known and much denigrated 'pastoral/academic split' (Best and Ribbins, 1983).

What schools should be looking for is *unity*. Unity *in diversity* maybe, but unity none the less. The plethora of labels and the diversity of roles and systems must not blind us to what they ought to share, and often do share: the ultimate common goal of the total well-being and fullest development of the whole person. Pring's characteristics of the person (see p. 13) seem to underpin all pastoral work, recognizing personhood as rational and moral autonomy within conditions of social interdependence. Yet surely this is no less than to state the goal not just of pastoral care and PSE but of *education* itself.

It is something of a cliché that education must be concerned with the development of the whole child. It is true none the less. That is why Pring can argue that to be involved in education is necessarily to be involved in *personal* and *social* education (Pring, 1988). That is why Watkins calls for schools to 'seek a whole curriculum approach which is genuinely whole-pupil, that relates to their needs and covers time-honoured rather than politically fashionable themes which presently come under a range of titles' (Watkins, 1992, p 5). The point is to recognize that a full understanding of education as concerned with the affective, aesthetic, moral, spiritual and so on as well as the cognitive or intellectual, entails a whole-school approach to human and social development. The power of the concept of pastoral care lies in its capacity to remind us that this is so, and thus to make schools more caring communities. And that requires commitment and planning. As Tomlinson warns:

> the caring school does not emerge simply as a by-product of good intentions. It presents a goal that has to be deliberately planned and worked towards. For that reason, in determining its policies, the school should identify objectives which will enable it to translate caring intentions into action.
>
> (Tomlinson, 1988, p. 8)

The definition of such objectives requires a clarity of thought which is often hindered by the confusions of current terminology. I hope this chapter has made some contribution to clarity of thought and purpose in this important aspect of education.

REFERENCES

Best, R. (1989) Pastoral care: some reflections and a restatement. *Pastoral Care in Education*, **7**(4), 7–14.

Best, R. (1990) Pastoral care in schools: some implications for teacher training. *Australian Journal of Teacher Education*, **15**(1), 14–23.

Best, R., Jarvis, C. and Ribbins, P. (1980) Pastoral care: concept and process. In Best, R., Jarvis, C. and Ribbins, P. (eds) *Perspectives on Pastoral Care*. London: Heinemann.

Best, R. and Ribbins, P. (1983) Rethinking the pastoral–academic split. *Pastoral Care in Education*, **1**(1), 11–18.

Best, R., Ribbins, P., Jarvis, C. and Oddy, D. (1983) *Education and Care*. London: Heinemann.

Committee of Inquiry into Pupil Behaviour and Discipline in Schools (1980) *Self-Discipline and Pastoral Care*. Sydney.

Department of Education and Science (1989) *Report of Her Majesty's Inspectors on Pastoral Care in Secondary Schools: An Inspection of Some Aspects of Pastoral Care in 1987–8*. Stanmore: DES.

Dooley, S. (1980) The relationship between the concepts of 'pastoral care' and 'authority'. In Best, R., Jarvis, C. and Ribbins, P (eds) *Perspectives on Pastoral Care*. London: Heinemann.

Haigh, G. (1975) *Pastoral Care*. London: Pitman Publishing.

Hamblin, D. H. (1978) *The Teacher and Pastoral Care*. Oxford, Blackwell.

Hughes, P. M. (1971) *Guidance and Counselling in Schools*. Oxford: Pergamon.

Hughes, P. M. (1980) Pastoral care: the historical context. In Best, R., Jarvis, C. and Ribbins, P. (eds) *Perspectives on Pastoral Care*. London: Heinemann.

Lang, P. (ed.) (1988) *Thinking about . . . Personal and Social Education in the Primary School*. Oxford, Blackwell.

Lang, P. and Ribbins, P. (1985) Pastoral care in education. In *International Encyclopedia of Education*. Oxford: Pergamon.

Marland, M. (1974) *Pastoral Care*. London: Heinemann.

Marland, M. (1980) The pastoral curriculum. In Best, R., Jarvis, C. and Ribbins, P. (eds) *Perspectives on Pastoral Care*. London: Heinemann.

Marland, M. (1989) *The Tutor and the Tutor Group*. Harlow: Longman.

Milner, P. (1980) Guidance and counselling: changing patterns of care in schools. In Best, R., Jarvis, C. and Ribbins, P. (eds) *Perspectives on Pastoral Care*. London: Heinemann.

National Curriculum Council (1990) *The Whole Curriculum*, Curriculum Guidance 3. York.

Pring, R. (1984) *Personal and Social Education in the Curriculum*. Sevenoaks: Hodder & Stoughton.

Pring, R. (1988) Personal and social education in the primary school. In Lang, P. (ed.) *Thinking about . . . Personal and Social Education in the Primary School*. Oxford: Blackwell.

Ribbins, P. and Best, R. (1985) Pastoral care: theory, practice and the growth of research. In Lang, P. and Marland, M. (eds) *New Directions in Pastoral Care*. Oxford. Blackwell/NAPCE.

Scottish Education Department (1968) *Guidance in Scottish Secondary Schools*. Edinburgh: HMSO.

Singapore Educational Administration Society (1988) *The Pupil's Growth – Our Major Concern*. Singapore: SEAS.

Tomlinson, J. (1988) What is pastoral care and how does it relate to the other dimensions of schooling? In Singapore Educational Administration Society *The Pupil's Growth – Our Major Concern*. Singapore: SEAS.

Watkins, C. (1985) Does pastoral care = personal and social education? *Pastoral Care in Education*, **3**(3), 179–83.

Watkins, C. (1992) *Guidance in UK Schools*. Coventry: NAPCE.

Watts, A. G. and Fawcett, B. (1980) Pastoral care and careers education. In Best, R., Jarvis, C. and Ribbins, P. (eds) *Perspectives on Pastoral Care*. London: Heinemann.

Part 2

The School and the Teachers

CHAPTER 2

School Management for Pastoral Care and PSE

Caroline Lodge

INTRODUCTION

This chapter starts by making the case that the need to provide effective pastoral care is as great as ever, despite reports that some secondary schools have cut down on tutorial times, PSE lessons and pastoral posts following the Education Reform Act (1988). After reviewing the pastoral goals of schools, a case is made for the importance of managing pastoral care in a school in a way which provides a force for coherence. It is suggested that traditional models or systems for providing pastoral care may need to be adapted to take account of new influences.

PASTORAL GOALS OF THE SCHOOL

The following list is a summary of the goals of a pastoral system which was defined as long ago as 1986 by the National Association for Pastoral Care in Education (NAPCE) in a publication on in-service training for pastoral care (NAPCE, 1986). The case for each of the goals, as part of a whole-school approach, is examined.

- to provide a point of personal contact with every pupil;
- to provide a point of personal contact with parents;
- to monitor pupil progress across the curriculum;
- to provide support and guidance for pupil achievement;
- to encourage a caring and orderly environment;
- to promote a school which meets pupils' needs;
- to provide colleagues with information to adapt teaching;
- to engage wider networks as appropriate.

To provide a point of personal contact with every pupil

The average size of a secondary school is now only 750 pupils, and perhaps a hundred staff (teaching and support), yet there is still a need for each pupil to know one teacher, and to have their progress monitored and guided by that one person. There are many changes and permutations for each pupil to negotiate each day in secondary schools (different lessons, teachers, rooms, homeworks), each year (critical incidents) and the major passage into choices at 16 plus. The child has her or his own personal change and development to negotiate, and to try to control or direct. There is a need for parents, other teachers and the pupils themselves to have a point of reference. The person who usually takes this role is the tutor. Tutors use their personal contact to hear the pupils' perspectives on themselves and their future. Marland (1989, p. 14) has described the tutor as:

> the heart of the school, the specialist whose specialism is bringing everything together, whose subject is the student herself, who struggles for the tutee's entitlement, and who enables the pupil to make the best use of the school and develop her person.

A child in a primary school has fewer changes to negotiate each day, and the point of contact is usually provided by the class teacher. Teachers in primary schools still need to be explicit about their pastoral role, however.

To provide a point of personal contact with parents

Schools cannot ignore the contribution of parents to the education of young people and they have a greater impact on educational choices than do teachers (see also Chapter 16 by Sally Tomlinson, below). However, schools frequently do ignore parents, although their support for and understanding of school processes is essential, and they need access to information and to the key people in their child's school. Secondary schools can present a difficult and off-putting face but parents will persevere when they have a name and a familiar face to find. Schools need a channel for communications home if the school is to make anything of its home–school links or partnerships. Schools need to identify the most appropriate person to hear the parents' perceptions, aspirations and fears for their child and to gather and reflect on information about the pupil and to discuss this with the parent and child. The person with the closest contact with the child is likely to be the tutor, who is therefore best suited to be the contact for parents.

To monitor pupil progress across the curriculum

To achieve this goal schools need efficient procedures to assess, record and monitor pupils' progress. There must also be appropriate access and co-ordination of the information in order that action can come out of the information and that the pupil can be helped.

This goal does not refer only to individual pupils but also to the need for curriculum areas to reflect on their curriculum offer and delivery, and for those charged with overseeing the whole curriculum picture to reflect on the curriculum experience across all subjects. Plans for teaching specific skills, competencies and information need to be mapped across the curriculum if pupil outcomes are to be matched with intentions.

To provide support and guidance for pupil achievement

With the personal contacts described above, some pastoral systems did not develop beyond the rationale of 'getting to know the pupils'. The purpose of knowing pupils and parents better is to use this knowledge to help pupils get more from themselves and their school.

Recent changes in curriculum and assessment arrangements have highlighted the importance of a structure to monitor, guide and record achievement, and to support pupils. There is still the need to give constructive and planned help at the critical transition moments (for example transfer at 11, choices at 16 plus). Learning about the individual's development in the class, in society and as a person still needs careful planning.

During 1990 HM Inspectorate made a survey of guidance in schools and sixth form colleges, and the report (HMI, 1992) concluded that guidance is most effective where it is clear, part of a planned policy and integrated with other aspects of the school. The report was critical of the failure to coordinate record systems and guidance. These comments remind us that effective support and guidance for pupils' learning requires coordination and planning. It cannot exist as a stand-alone feature of a school. Planning for guidance means ensuring that the PSE programme is carefully thought out, whether delivered by tutors or specialists, as an integral part of the rest of the learning offer, or by some combination or other arrangement. It means that subject teachers must be aware of the wider aspects of their subjects (for example the vocational relevance and opportunities of their subject, or the personal-social perspective of the subject). It means ensuring that opportunities for individual counselling are available for every pupil.

To encourage a caring and orderly environment

Pastoral care has always had a great deal to contribute to fostering an orderly environment. Clearly this is an aspect of school life which is the responsibility of all staff (and pupils) and one which cannot be effectively entrusted to a few discipline specialists. The Elton Report (1988) made clear that schools manage pupil behaviour best where there is a whole-school approach. In some schools, however, 'pastoral care' has been distorted so that discipline has become the main function of pastoral staff. It can be difficult in these schools to move out of this trap. 'Someone has to do the discipline.' In general the answer is that everyone has to (see Watkins and Wagner, 1987).

Without a caring and orderly atmosphere learning will suffer. The personal-social aspects of the curriculum explore the pupil's role in the school and the groups to which they belong and the part they can play in making these effective learning groups. The tutor has a part to play in understanding individual difficulties with learning, or other difficulties which are preventing effective learning – a casework role. Both the curriculum and the casework need careful planning.

To promote a school which meets pupils' needs

This goal reflects the need for schools to be responsive institutions, listening to pupils, to parents and to their own staff, and acting upon the information gained. This implies structures which can identify needs, can be channels for information, for making contact with parents. These structures may take the form of school and year councils, parental information sessions and surgeries, for example. It implies that the school will develop an ethos which conveys the importance and value placed on listening and good communications. The contribution of those in contact with pupils, teachers, tutors, support staff of all kinds, can greatly support this ethos.

This goal implies that the school staff will be alert to identifying pupil needs. These will range from curriculum adaptations and alterations to teaching styles through to providing specialist support for individual pupils. It will also include other individual needs (for example, sympathetic treatment of traumatized children, catering for the social and physical needs of children with disabilities). It will include needs of groups of children (for example, the needs of children arriving in school with little or no English – see Lodge (1992), or dealing with bullying within a group). It will include identifying the needs of all the pupils (for example, the sudden death of a member of the school community, or celebrations in which all are involved).

Above all, this goal implies effective communications between all members of the school community. Any aspect which makes communication less effective is therefore a concern, and the pastoral care of staff is therefore also on the agenda.

To provide colleagues with information to adapt teaching

This goal is closely related to the previous two. Schools must respond to pupil needs and to information collected about progress. A common trap here is to blame the child for failure to respond to the school's offer, without looking for any institutional obstructions to learning. Information about *groups* of pupils and their responses is also needed. The implications for management of these three goals are for good communications and for efficient co-ordination.

To engage wider networks as appropriate

It is necessary from time to time to seek assistance and guidance from outside agencies or individuals to work with individual or groups of children who are experiencing difficulties. This can be achieved also through links with parents and community networks, world of work networks and so on.

It is clear that each of these goals still has a central place in secondary schools. The current context may be leading schools to emphasize the importance of the monitoring of pupil progress and curriculum provision more than previously. The remainder of this chapter will consider the management of these goals.

THE CHANGING CONTEXT FOR THESE GOALS

The context in which schools are operating is changing very fast. Of the most recent changes, those involving more central control of the curriculum and pupil assessment most impinge upon the goals as originally conceived and upon the ways schools work towards achieving them.

There are other changes, including local management of schools (LMS), parental 'choice', increased power of governors, choosing grant-maintained status (GMS) and the diminishing powers of the local education authorities (LEAs). These are all triggers for changes to the organization and structures of schools. Sometimes these have been the driving force behind changing staffing structures, including some reduction in posts of specific responsibility for leading pastoral teams.

Invited to consider what factors are contributing to fragmentation, and which to coherence, participants in recent courses on the changing role of the head of year produced some interesting lists. The following influences have been listed, among others, under the heading of 'factors producing fragmentation':

- phased and piecemeal introduction of the National Curriculum;
- lack of time;
- lack of money and other resources;
- too many new initiatives;
- LMS;
- staff insecurity and redundancies;
- management style;
- Standard Assessment Tasks (SATs) and other assessment demands;
- decline of the LEAs;
- appraisal.

Such a list invites the comment, 'it all depends on the way each of these factors is responded to'; and subsequent discussion would involve considering some of the same factors being placed on the following list.

The following influences have appeared under the heading of 'factors increasing coherence':

- management;
- tutorial work;
- co-ordinator roles;
- TVEI (if managed well);
- National Curriculum subjects if part of whole curriculum;
- appraisal (if supported and well resourced);
- institutional development plans (IDPs) if collegiate;
- whole-school policies;
- planning and wide consultation.

Some of the factors are outside the control of the school. Some can be mediated in their effects through good management and adequate resourcing. However, good management will not provide an antidote to all the worst effects of these changes, but the framework of whole-school policies and planning is an essential feature of counterbalancing fragmentation in our schools.

The influence of the package of changes, mainly introduced through the Education Reform Act (ERA) of 1988, has sharpened some of the perceptions about practice and forced some decisions, usually for financial and not educational reasons. Some schools have taken the opportunity for some radical thinking about structures, roles and the management of pastoral care.

The changing context in which schools work has already begun to influence traditional pastoral roles, especially those of heads of year and heads of house. There is evidence for this in changes to role titles, so that recently teachers have been appointed to such posts as year co-ordinator, year leader, even year manager, and pastoral community leader, key stage 3 co-ordinator, cross-curricular co-ordinator and other such titles. Some of these new titles are just that: new titles, with no possibility of being effective in the role change signalled by the title change. Making co-ordinating roles effective will be examined later in this chapter (pp. 28–32). In other instances it is clear that schools are making effective experiments and progress in developing a role which will help achieve the pastoral goals of the school. The emphasis on co-ordination is an important and interesting one.

Not everything is changing, of course. Some of the issues remain. In Britain the 11 to 18 curriculum has traditionally been developed in a vertical manner, that is subject by subject. The difficulties of gaining an understanding of the whole curriculum experience of the pupil have always been immense. Teachers have, on the whole, regarded their subject teaching role as more important than their role as tutor. HMI (1989) inspected some aspects of pastoral care in secondary schools in 1987–8, and concluded that pastoral and academic approaches should support each other, and some schools, they found, had begun to explore ways of integrating their approaches.

> Schools need to consider how teaching and learning procedures can most appropriately benefit from promoting the care and overall development of pupils. Approaches will doubtless need to vary from school to school. Nevertheless the more schools are able to promote pastoral care through the curriculum, the more efficient and effective they are likely to be. Of course, if this is so, there will be no place for teachers who claim they are only interested in subjects, not young people, or vice versa.
>
> (HMI, 1989, p. 47)

The same report commented on incoherence in structures and lack of clear job descriptions, and reported on the need for individual tutors to be given sufficient support for their role; accessibility of records; and a whole range of other recommendations for the management of pastoral care. The pace of change, and with it the need for good management, has increased since HMI published their report.

MANAGEMENT OF PASTORAL CARE

This section examines more closely the management issues raised by implementing the pastoral goals as described and discussed above and suggests some practical approaches to these issues.

It is evident that any management of these goals must involve a whole-school approach. A coherent whole-school approach will be achieved through co-ordination, good communications, teamwork, clear procedures, integration of approaches and a shared understanding of the goals and how they will be implemented.

The building-blocks for this whole-school approach include:

- a pastoral policy;
- structures for effective co-ordination and good communications;
- working in teams;
- training for teachers.

I will look at each of these building blocks in turn, while keeping in mind that they are interrelated.

A pastoral policy

The value of a pastoral policy to a school comes in two ways. First, the process of developing a policy through full consultation and discussion is one which will help all members of the school community to explore together the pastoral goals of the school and the ways in which they can best be implemented.

Second, a policy document is a useful reference document against which to work, to measure and to monitor the progress of the implementation of the policy. It is one of the few policies required by the statutory regulations for headteachers in Teachers' Conditions of Service and Pay (see DES 1994): 'Professional Duty 11: determining and ensuring the implementation of a policy for the pastoral care of pupils'.

A policy which contains the following is more like to lead to effective practice:

- the background and need for this policy;
- pastoral goals of the school;
- the policy in practice: structure, roles, tasks, curriculum, casework procedures, etc.;
- resources to support the policy, including money, staff and time;
- action to be taken, by whom and when;
- communicating the policy;
- arrangements for monitoring and reviewing the policy.

Some other aspects of an effective policy need to be mentioned. First, policies need to be flexible and to be reviewed at planned intervals. The review procedures need to be spelled out in the policy itself, but the policy should not be so inflexible that adjustments cannot be made as practice develops through implementation of the policy plans. A pastoral policy will reflect the needs of the particular school, and will require adjustment to the school's own population and changing circumstances.

Second, policies which relate to the school institutional development plan (IDP), with the developmental aspects of the policy clearly indicated in the plan and indications of target dates, expected outcomes and responsibilities allocated to named people, are more likely to be effectively implemented. The IDP should also include identified training needs, with some idea about how they will be met.

Third, a sound pastoral policy then will, ideally, be part of a pattern or web of whole-school planning. It will relate to other policies, such as those on equal opportunities, staff development and so on. It will provide an opportunity for professional development for the staff of the school in drawing up the policy. It will act as a point of reference for planning and be flexible enough to change year by year.

Structures for effective co-ordination and good communication

Traditionally subject departments in secondary schools have operated like a series of mini-schools, each department having a considerable autonomy over curriculum, assessment, resource allocation, staff development, discipline and so on. From the late 1960s, pastoral systems began to operate in many secondary schools, and as they developed they had to find a way to work around these previously existing power bases. Occasionally secondary schools developed with pastoral, rather than subject, 'barons'; but with the attention given to the adaptation of each school's curriculum to the National Curriculum requirements, attention has often been narrowly focused on subject teaching.

In the current context, in order to achieve the pastoral goals set out above, it is clear that there must be a high level of co-ordination in the school. There are three stages to co-ordination:

1 *monitoring* (which includes gathering information and examining it to find patterns);
2 *evaluating* (which means comparing actual with intended outcomes);
3 *decision-making* (which means planning for changes in the light of (1) and (2)).

Effective co-ordination also requires two further decisions: *how* are these three stages going to be carried out, and *who* will do this work?

The need for clear structures is closely linked, then, to the need for effective co-ordination. Structures are the means whereby responsibilities are allocated within a school; they describe the differences in responsibilities and show the links between these people. A staffing structure must therefore describe two elements: the role descriptions of staff (who is responsible for what), and the communications routes between these post-holders. Roles can only be effective within a structure which enables and facilitates role-holders to carry out their responsibilities. There has been a recent increase in the number of job titles which include the word 'co-ordinator', but school staffing structures have remained constant, and because they are based on vertical structures (subject departments) do not easily allow effective co-ordination. Some of the difficulties for post-holders who are 'cross-curricular themes co-ordinators' or 'PSE co-ordinators' may have arisen because only one element, the job description, in the structure was attended to, while the structure within which they had to operate remained unchanged.

Concern about 'the pastoral/academic split' has led schools to experiment with their structures and mechanisms for co-ordination for some time. Traditional school structures can be represented in the following ways. Figure 2.1 indicates that it is disconnected at all levels of the hierarchy. A modified version of the same model is linked at senior management level but disconnected at middle management (Figure 2.2). Some schools have modified the model further and try to build in links at

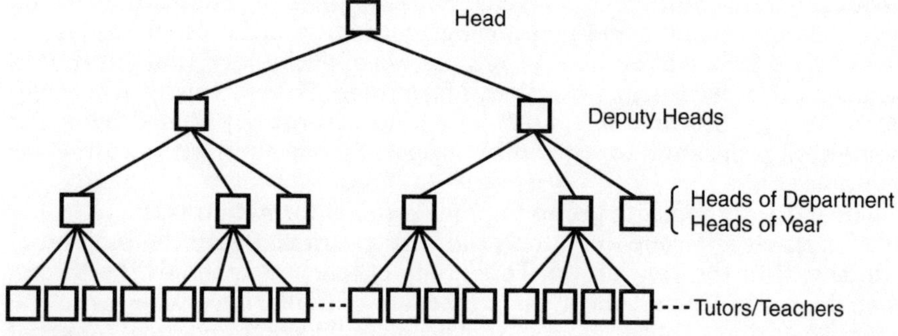

Figure 2.1

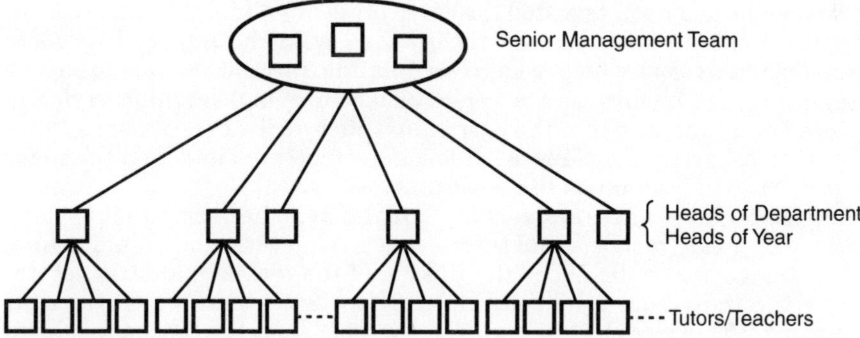

Figure 2.2

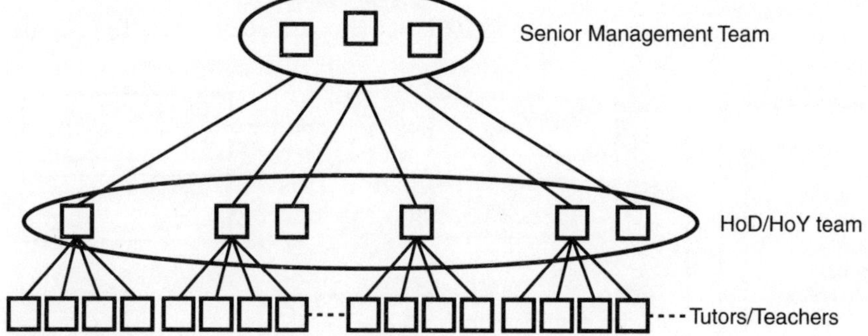

Figure 2.3

middle management level (HoD/HoY meetings and the like) (Figure 2.3). What each of these models has in common is that any co-ordination is expected to happen by co-ordinating post-holders, usually in meetings. While this kind of co-ordination is important, it is rarely effective, because it is trying to glue together two systems.

A different approach starts by determining what needs to be co-ordinated, and then asks what are the best means of co-ordination. In order to achieve their pastoral goals, schools need to co-ordinate information about the curriculum for each year: content, aims, teaching and learning methods, assessment and monitoring procedures. It is also necessary to co-ordinate information about the progress of each individual pupil. It is not enough, of course, just to collect information. The responsive school will examine the information, and take action accordingly – modifying the homework programme or providing support for one pupil with reading, for example.

The most appropriate group to provide this information is the teaching staff most closely concerned with the year group and with the individual pupils within the year group. This group of teachers includes the tutors, their team leader and the subject teachers of the forms or classes in the year. The number of teachers in this group will vary from school to school and depend upon a number of factors: the number of forms in the year cohort; the number of teachers who are both tutors and subject teachers of their own form; how integrated the curriculum offer is; and so on. We have identified the group most directly involved with the pupils. It is *their knowledge and work* which needs co-ordinating, to avoid overlap, to ensure progression, to ensure that a range of teaching and learning styles is utilized and to ensure that the curriculum offer, delivery, assessment and review is coherent. This approach leads to structures in which the team (and not the individual) is the basic unit.

Figure 2.4, shows a team structure, built up from the basic building block of the year team (teachers and tutors) and linking with curriculum teams. (This diagram only describes the linking of the teams, and does not describe the individual roles within it.) There are a number of practical reactions to this model. How big are the teams? Does the RE teacher have to belong to every year team? How will it work in a small school? What happens to the pastoral role of the year teams? Do the power bases in the school alter?

There is no attempt to promote this as the correct model, the single

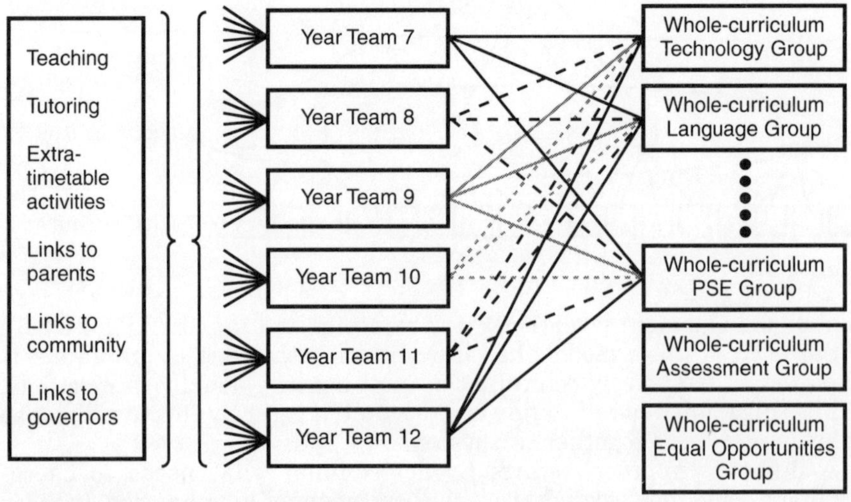

Figure 2.4 (from Whalley and Watkins, 1991, p. 20)

simple answer to problems of co-ordination and the old pastoral/academic split. But it may offer some practical pointers for those reviewing structures in their own institutions. It is different from the traditional models described previously which reinforce separation. Adaptation of current structures, to meet some of the purposes of this different model, may be possible despite this model being built up from a different base. For example, any year seven team of teachers would find it useful to meet and discuss a common approach to the first half term in the new secondary school, or to review that first half term.

The collection of information is also not a new field for most schools. Some methods are routine in many schools, some may take organization and imagination to achieve. Methods for getting appropriate information include:

- pupil pursuit;
- curriculum mapping;
- class diaries filled in by each teacher and tutor;
- pupil interviews;
- monitoring of records of achievement;
- monitoring of homework diaries;
- collecting information on teaching of specific skills, e.g. numeracy skills;
- monitoring pupil progress, e.g. by snapshots of progress in each subject;
- inter-curricular maps, e.g. information technology skills, human rights information.

The right person for this information gathering will differ from institution to institution. A year team or curriculum co-ordinator may already have this responsibility described on their job description. Many job descriptions of heads of year contain such phrases as:

> Maintaining an overview of the curriculum in the school as it is experienced by pupils as individuals, monitoring the impact of the variety of teaching and approaches and learning experiences, promoting a coherence and wholeness in the curriculum of the Year and advising Heads of Faculty/Department and Senior Staff of potential cross-curricular links.[1]

What is more difficult for people with this responsibility to establish is how all this can be effectively carried out, and what mechanisms exist to effect change as a result of their work.

The collection of this information is of any value only if it is then examined by asking the appropriate questions of the appropriate people, and if there is an expectation that action of some kind will follow. Managing co-ordination therefore also means bringing the right people together. Very often this will be the year team of the tutors and their team leader and the subject teachers.

It may be that a more appropriate group, in some organizations, would be heads of faculties and the pastoral team leaders. However, members of

[1] This responsibility was twenty-first out of twenty-two listed responsibilities for senior year tutor.

these groups are notoriously bad at seeing a whole-school perspective, and, if asked to consider the range of subjects to be offered at key stage 4, for example, they may not be able to contribute to the decision beyond a narrow subject interest (for example, to keep a 'marginal' subject in the option list).

Monitoring the setting of homework is an example which can reveal how information is gathered, examined and evaluated, and finally how decisions are made in a school. At one training session course members were asked to find out what form tutors in their school would do if they discovered that their form was not being set homework by one teacher, in contradiction of the school's policy. The task provided participants with a great deal of information about their organization, and how it handled information. Would the tutor find out this information? If so, what would the result be of the tutor having that information? Who else would be told? Would anything happen to rectify the situation? The answers ranged from 'the tutors wouldn't know' to a description of a structure for regular monitoring of homework, as well as to providing information to parents about homework being set, and detailing clear steps to rectify the situation if homework was not set.

In order for communication channels to be clear, it is important for all post-holders to have a clear job description, one that sets out the main purpose of the post, the main tasks and responsibilities, the resources available to support the post, the skills required to carry it out and how the post relates to the others in the structure. An example is given, for a year co-ordinator, at the end of this chapter. Such clarity helps to avoid misunderstandings about role, which have especially dogged pastoral team leaders. More clarity in job descriptions will emerge as a result of appraisal. It will also help identify training needs (see next page).

It is clear that, in order to achieve some of the pastoral goals, structures must operate in school to promote co-ordination and the flow of information. Only by ensuring that information is collected and passed on to the right teams and individuals will schools become responsive. Only if the right teams and individual leaders have information will they be able to adapt teaching, promote assessment of pupil progress and provide the feedback we need to ensure that schools are providing the best for the pupils.

Working in teams

The pastoral work of the school can be effective only if done in teams, in partnership. Identifying the needs of pupils, generating the information which will allow teaching to respond, support and guidance for pupils, fostering a caring and orderly environment: these are all the tasks of many members of staff. In order for these different people to work together effectively for the pupils' benefit they need to be organized into teams.

These teams need clear goals, tasks and responsibilities and resources. It would be possible to draw up a team job description in the same way as for an individual post-holder. An attempt to do this is included at the end of this chapter. The teams also need leadership, and someone to take responsibility for keeping the team on track, monitoring the work done and being accountable to others for that work. Team leadership is becoming more recognized as an important skill for schools.

Training for teachers

Training in the pastoral aspects of a teacher's job has always been neglected. Neither initial training nor in-service training has given more than cursory attention to pastoral work (Maher and Best, 1985). The new arrangements for initial training courses, being based more in schools, may have the merit of enabling initial training to include more treatment of pastoral aspects, especially the role of the tutor.

In secondary schools teachers need skills which relate to their pastoral role and need to develop these alongside their other expertise. Identifying skills needed for, say, tutoring is a useful team-building exercise in itself. One attempt, which still has a great deal of merit, was published as long ago as 1986 by NAPCE. *Preparing for Pastoral Care: In-service Training for the Pastoral Aspect of the Teacher's Role* (NAPCE, 1986) identified goals, tasks, skills and resources needed for a number of pastoral roles: the form tutor, the pastoral leader, and senior staff. This position statement was intended to help schools to identify training needs at a time when the funding of In-service Education and Training (INSET) was about to change fundamentally, and was about to become more responsive to the identification of needs by schools and LEAs. Funding arrangements for training have changed fundamentally several times since then, but the importance of identifying needs and providing appropriate training has remained.

CONCLUSIONS

This chapter has focused on the changing emphasis within established pastoral goals; an emphasis which is moving away from a preoccupation with casework and towards curriculum and pupil monitoring and co-ordination. This changing emphasis is already affecting job descriptions and structures in some schools. In others, only job titles or descriptions are changing, without the structures being in place for post-holders to achieve the tasks they are set. I have been careful not to prescribe which post-holders are most suited to the many tasks involved with monitoring and co-ordination: this is because different institutions will respond to change in different ways, and have different structures already in place with different degrees of rigidity.

Current circumstances are highlighting this monitoring role. This is not a new departure, but rather an enhancement of the pastoral aspect of the secondary school. There is a great deal of excellent practice in pastoral care in secondary schools: individual tutors and team leaders, teachers who offer guidance and counselling, structures created to support individuals and groups of pupils. In this chapter I have argued for extending the existing support network for pupils' personal and social development to a structure which will enable the school to become much more responsive to pupils' needs. HMI in 1989 in *Personal and Social Education from 5 to 16* (HMI, 1989) stressed that all the teaching staff have a role to play in pastoral care and PSE: 'the role of all teachers is vital because personal and social development and responsibility are intrinsic to the nature of education. It is something from which no teacher can opt out' (para. 2, p. 1). I have gone further and suggested that the school structures must support the monitoring and co-ordination of pupil progress and the planned curriculum in order to support pupils' learning.

EXAMPLES

Year co-ordinator

Goals:

to co-ordinate the support and guidance to students through the tutors' personal contact with students, parents and involvement of outside agencies and other teachers as necessary;

to promote a caring and secure learning environment in which all students can achieve;

to ensure cohesion of and to evaluate the curriculum for Year ... including delivery of cross-curricular themes, skills and dimensions in line with whole-school policies.

Responsibilities:

1 to lead a team of tutors and students;
2 to identify professional development needs of tutor teams and ensure they are met;
3 to organize parents' meetings (e.g. Home School Association, reports)
4 to co-ordinate the team's liaison with outside agencies;
5 to work with students and teachers to develop routines and skills which promote a caring and secure learning environment;
6 to co-ordinate the monitoring and evaluation of the curriculum for Year...;
7 to co-ordinate the monitoring and evaluation of student progress for Year...;
8 to facilitate the year council meetings and the communications with tutor groups and school council.

Skills:

1 leadership and team-building skills;
2 identifying and delivering appropriate staff development programme
3 organizing parents' meetings;
4 co-ordinating team's liaison with outside agencies;
5 skills of listening, counselling, guidance;
6 knowledge of whole-school policies, cross-curricular dimensions, skills and themes;
7 knowledge of curriculum monitoring strategies, and monitoring of students and their achievements;
8 ability to work co-operatively with other team leaders.

Structure:

1 The year co-ordinator is a member of a team of year co-ordinators who are led by the senior teacher – pastoral (a member of the senior management team);

2 The year co-ordinator leads a team of tutors and subject teachers of Year . . .;
3 S/he is supported by a member of the senior management team;
4 Year teams meet for fifty minutes every three weeks. Year co-ordinators meet every six weeks.

Resources:

1 Time – the teaching load of a year co-ordinator is about fifteen out of twenty-five periods per week.
2 Space – each year co-ordinator has a private office with an outside telephone line and has charge of students' records for the year;
3 Support staff – the year co-ordinator can call upon the office general assistant for approximately thirty minutes of filing every two weeks, and has access to the school's typist as necessary;
4 Financial resources are allocated on the formula, and the year co-ordinator is responsible for a budget equivalent to one unit per student in the year group.

Year team

Goals:

to co-ordinate the support and guidance to students through the tutors' personal contact with students, parents and involvement of outside agencies and other teachers as necessary;

to promote a caring and secure learning environment in which all students can achieve;

to assist the year co-ordinator in evaluating the curriculum for Year . . . including delivery of cross-curricular themes, skills and dimensions in line with whole-school policies.

Responsibilities:

1 to plan and review the work of the team in support and guidance of students and in promoting the effective learning environment;
2 to identify professional development needs of the team and individuals in the team;
3 to review information gathered on student progress;
4 to review information gathered on the curriculum for Year . . .;
5 to take note of matters discussed at year council meetings.

Skills:

1 teamwork skills

Structure:

1 The year team is lead by the year co-ordinator who is a member of a team of year co-ordinators, led by the senior teacher – pastoral (a member of the senior management team);
2 Year teams include the year co-ordinator, year tutors and subject teachers of Year . . ., supported by a member of the senior management team;

3 Year Teams meet for fifty minutes every three weeks. Year co-ordinators meet every six weeks.

Resources:

1 Time – fifty minutes' meeting time every three weeks;
2 Space – access to the year co-ordinator's private office with an outside telephone line and students' records;
3 Financial resources are allocated on the formula, and the year co-ordinator is responsible for a budget equivalent to one unit per student in the year group.

REFERENCES

Department of Education and Science (1994) *School Teachers' Pay and Conditions Document*. London: HMSO.

Elton Report (1988). London: HMSO.

HMI (1989) *Pastoral Care in Secondary School. An Inspection of Some Aspects of Pastoral Care in 1987–88*, Ref. NS76/87. London: HMSO.

HMI (1989), *Personal and Social Education from 5 to 16*, Curriculum Matters 14. London: HMSO/DES.

HMI (1992) *Survey of Guidance 13–19 in Schools and Sixth Form Colleges, Spring–Autumn 1990*, Ref. 21/92/NS. London: HMSO.

Lodge, C. (1992) Integrating pupils who speak no English. *Pastoral Care in Education* **10**(2), 32–5.

Maher, P. and Best, R. (1985) Preparation and support for pastoral care: a survey of current provision. In Lang, P. and Marland, M. (eds) *New Directions in Pastoral Care*. Oxford: Blackwell/NAPCE.

Marland, M. (1989) *The Tutor and the Tutor Group*. Harlow: Longman.

National Association for Pastoral Care in Education (1986) *Preparing for Pastoral Care: In-Service Training for the Pastoral Aspect of the Teacher's Role*. Coventry: NAPCE.

Watkins, C. and Wagner, P. (1987) *School Discipline: A Whole-school Approach*. Oxford: Blackwell.

Whalley, C. and Watkins, C. (1991) Managing the whole curriculum in the secondary school – a structure. *Management in Education* **5**(3) 19–22.

CHAPTER 3

Training and support for pastoral care

Fergus O'Sullivan

INTRODUCTION

People are the single most valuable asset any organization has. In schools, as far as the pupils are concerned, this is recognized in good practice through such aspects as the pastoral care system, the use of records of achievement, active learning strategies involving pupil interaction and an emphasis on individual and group responsibility. These all support the individual in the learning context and ensure the maximum benefit from the educational opportunities provided through the formal curriculum.

Underpinning such an approach is the belief that education is fundamentally a social activity and that individuals' predispositions for learning are improved if they are in a receptive frame of mind and sensitive to the needs of others. The presence of a pastoral curriculum and arrangements for its delivery is objective evidence of the importance attached to this viewpoint by a school.

If we apply such an approach to teachers themselves, the arrangements made for staff development and appraisal can be seen as 'pastoral care for teachers'. The cycle of activity given in the National Steering Group's (NSG) report (DES, 1989) can be seen as the first steps of the process to be outlined in this chapter (see Figure 3.1 overleaf).

Those of us working in staff development have long been aware of the need to support adult learning by moving from a transmission model of In-service Education and Training (INSET) to a collaborative learning model. However, the focus of specific county- and school-based INSET events still tends to be a substantive area (such as, in recent times, a National Curriculum subject, assessment or local management of schools). In response to this, LEA trainers, college departments of education and private INSET providers now tend to use a variety of learning strategies which recognize the need to build into their courses the rich veins of experience and expertise adult learners bring with them. However, there is a need to consolidate such approaches into a 'training curriculum' where the key prerogative is a sensitivity to the needs of the individual, the group, the work context, the employer, the community and ultimately, through these, to the pupils themselves.

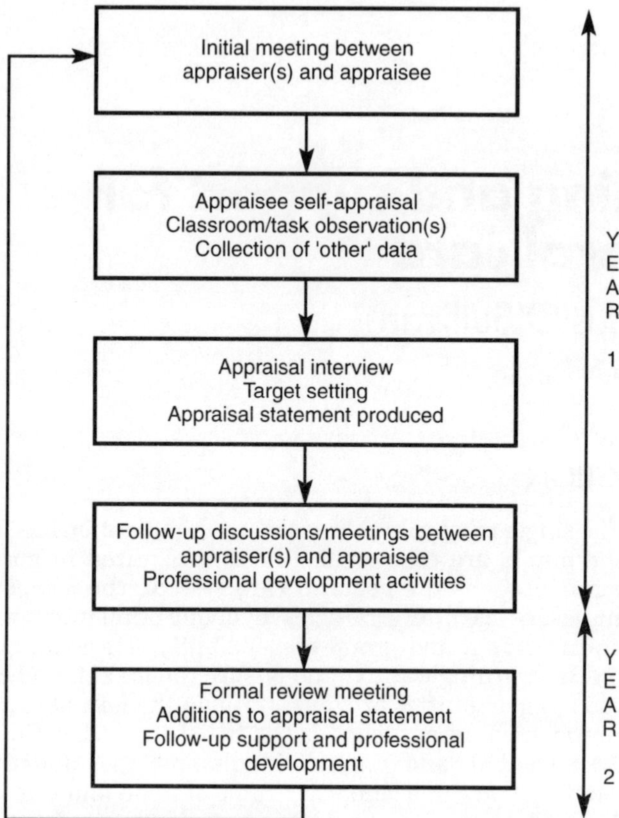

Figure 3.1 Components in the appraisal process: a biennial cycle (from DES, 1989)

Such a training curriculum would need to consider the whole individual and his or her role as a team player in the organization. It would need to adopt an approach which used a cycle of activities and techniques drawn from a counselling perspective (Figure 3.2). The aim needs to be one of empowerment of the individual and the work group through the use of a reflective approach to support on-going learning. In embryo we have such an approach in current group practice in INSET and the stages of the NSG Framework for Appraisal. It is the objective of this chapter to map out this framework as it relates specifically to supporting pastoral care through a cohesive approach to staff development.

THE STAFF DEVELOPMENT PROCESS

The two key processes which underpin an understanding of the development of staff are those of, first, dialogue with individuals using a counselling perspective and, second, the framework of the organizational development cycle. Thus organizational development requires the consideration of both the needs of the individual and those of the workplace team. To create support for the development of skills for pastoral care, it is

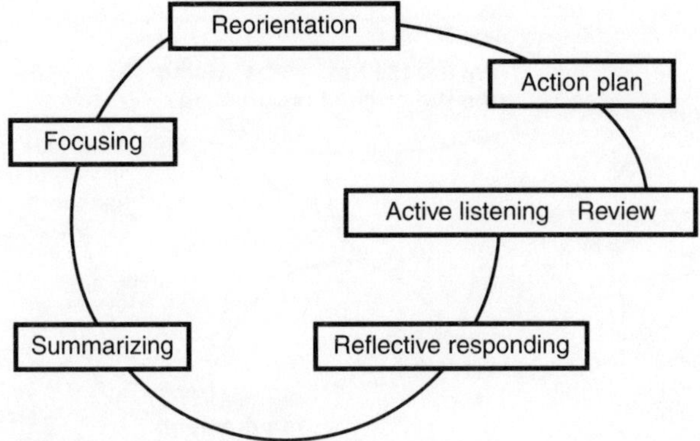

Figure 3.2 Stages in the counselling cycle

particularly important to pay attention to both these aspects in designing the staff development programme.

Figure 3.3 (overleaf) conveys, I believe, in graphical form some of the dynamics of the process. The version printed here differs from the original (O'Sullivan *et al.*, 1988, p. 59), in that we have now realized that, whereas the original had 'monitoring' as a discrete stage in the process, the 'eddies' which spring from the main cycle represent, in fact, the process of monitoring itself. Thus they form 'iterative loops' which give a feedback (and feedforward) aspect to the process. For this reason we do not now see monitoring as a separate activity but as one which ensures a review of current practice and generates data which can later be used in evaluation.

Like the pastoral care provision in a school, the process for staff development has to respond to the individual's entitlement to further development as well as providing a supportive structure and cycle of activity designed to cater for the needs of the section/team. Therefore, this section, in examining the stages of the development cycle, will cover the needs of the organization. The next section will address the needs of the individual in a discussion of the strategies that could be used in implementing the cycle.

The value of conceptualizing the process in this way is that it can represent the stages both for an individual staff development activity and for the institutional development cycle. Indeed, close parallels can be drawn between this cycle and that for counselling individual pupils or appraising teachers. I would also maintain that it follows the requirements of Kolb's (Kolb and Fry, 1975) Experiential Learning Cycle (Experimentation–Experience–Reflection–Learning) as well as those identified by Brandes and Ginnis (1986) for active student-centred learning:

- The learner has full responsibility for his or her own learning.
- The subject matter has relevance and meaning for the learner.
- Involvement and participation are necessary for learning.
- The teacher becomes a facilitator and resource person.
- There is a positive relationship between learners.

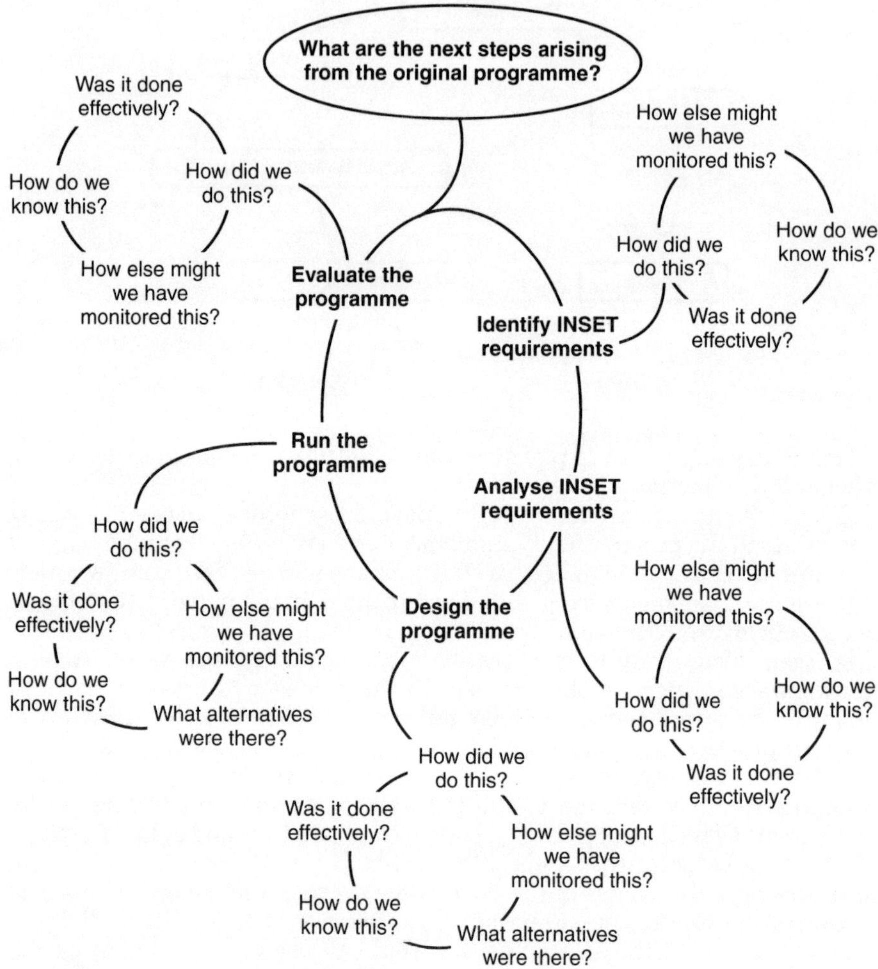

Figure 3.3 The staff development cycle

- The learner sees himself or herself differently as a result of the learning experience.
- The learner experiences 'confluence' in his or her education.

The term 'confluence' is used by Brandes and Ginnis to mean a 'flowing together' of what Bloom (1956; 1964) refers to as the cognitive (thinking) and affective (feeling) domains. Although there is debate currently about a more formal approach to the teaching of children, such models of the learning process remain important in informing the organization of activities for adult learners in the staff development process. The validity of this statement can be seen in the use of a student-driven competency-based framework for the General and National Vocational Qualifications (G/NVQ) which relates staff development and training to the needs of the learner on and close to the job.

Over the past five years I have collected numerous versions of 'development cycles' and it is interesting to note how these have become more and more complicated and multi-dimensional in an attempt to represent real life more accurately. For the purposes of planning and delivering staff development, however, the simple inner cycle of Figure 3.3, Needs–Analysis–Plan–Deliver–Evaluate, is perfectly adequate to act as a framework. Representing the process as a single cycle is also a convenient shorthand, though in practice many different INSET activities and the individuals participating in them will be at different points on the cycle at any particular time.

This emerging understanding is important when considering the development of staff for pastoral care, as it has implications both for the way staff appraisal is approached and, through a direct experience of a supportive process, for the ability and skills of all staff to support *pupils* in their own learning. Activities such as the process of dialogue between pupil and tutor in the recording of achievement and the use of individual action plans are examples of the development cycle in action. This is particularly significant in that recent work in organizational development and management has moved away from mechanistic models such as line and branch hierarchies, personnel management through job descriptions or formal appraisal systems and production management through a high degree of specialization of labour to more organic, flexible, team-based, customer-oriented and problem-solving approaches (Handy, 1985; Peters and Waterman, 1982; Brown and Lauder, 1992). The adoption of the development cycle given here is supportive to both initiating and sustaining this latter approach.

I should like to conclude this section with a word of warning and one of re-assurance. The emphasis in planning a staff development cycle has been on a systematic process which goes through easily recognizable stages and where the relationship between the trainers, participants and learning experience is one which focuses on improvement and development. In practice, however, the process operates at many levels and easily becomes hidden from view – people being people, their own agenda and interaction will colour their perception of the effectiveness of the process. The warning, therefore, is that much of the time the nice logical structure of the cycle is messy and feels out of control. In the hurly-burly of everyday life in a large learning organization this is quite normal! The important thing to remember is that if the *stages* of the cycle are followed as a framework for organizing staff development, it is more likely that the organization itself will develop and, most of the time, that most of the individuals will also develop.

IMPLEMENTING THE DEVELOPMENT CYCLE

Following the general principles that staff development activities need to relate directly to the needs of both the individual and the organization and be carried out in such a way as to enhance flexibility and responsiveness, the suggestions given below can be regarded only as exemplars. In response to the tendency for the pressure of day-to-day action to frustrate the process, many schools have designated a staff development co-ordinator

(SDC). It is important for the pastoral care team (or any section team) to identify one person who can be responsible for liaising with the school SDC and possibly serving on the staff development committee (see pages 46–7). This person needs also to ensure that training providers engaged to deliver training events for pastoral care are aware of the needs to use and build on the skills and expertise of the experienced adults participating.

Identifying needs

The process of identifying needs has to be done at the individual, team and organizational levels. Aggregated individual lists of needs through a process of review and audit may or may not give a good picture of the needs of the organization, so steps must be taken to generate needs at a variety of levels. As an illustration, however, I shall focus on the individual and whole-organizational levels. Pages 45 to 46 give an example of an evaluation activity which could be adapted for needs identification at the team level.

At the individual level there are two main approaches – questionnaire and interview (though these can be combined). I feel that, whichever is chosen, it is important for individuals to have the opportunity to discuss their needs with a senior colleague, as staff development is an intensely social, as well as personal, process. This colleague can be the year head or pastoral deputy for the pastoral team, though there may be advantage in this group being a panel from which tutors can choose their preferred 'mentor'. In any case the outcomes of the process should be fed through to the SDC. An example which could be used as either a structured interview schedule or a questionnaire is given below. In carrying out this process the skills required by the co-ordinator are, for example, data analysis in the case of a questionnaire and interviewing or counselling skills if the task is carried out as a dialogue.

Question schedule for identifying staff training needs

1 At which particular aspects of your job do you regard yourself as being particularly successful?
(pastoral care, knowledge, skills, tutor group administration, management, etc.)

2 How do you think you could share these with colleagues?
(model pastoral activities, workshops, lecture, notes / summary, study packs, etc.)

3 In which aspects of your job do you think you will need training over the next year or two?
(pastoral care skill acquisition, updating knowledge, management, other)

4 What pattern of training do you prefer for these targets?
(distance learning, evening, day, residential, part-time / full-time / sandwich, other)

5 How would you see outcomes from future training being applied at tutor group level?

6 How would you see yourself achieving further professional development in pastoral care?
(short course, long course, diploma, degree, post-graduate)

7 Any other points you would like to raise?

At the end of the personal discussion which ought to accompany this process, in keeping with counselling practice, an action plan should be agreed which identifies what the individual and interviewer each needs to do before the next meeting.

At the organizational level, there are many published inventories and procedures which can help to identify needs as well as the normal cycle of meetings at different levels which most organizations run regularly. One of the most common is the Guidelines for Review and Internal Development in Schools (GRIDS) process (McMahon *et al.*, 1984). The published pack gives detailed instructions and reproducible copies of the questionnaires and analysis sheets. The review is especially valuable for identifying and focusing on a particular concern and will help to identify a task group of staff to investigate the issue and produce an action plan. The process can be specifically targeted on pastoral care but is often rather lengthy, the questionnaires taking a week or so to complete, the analysis somewhat longer and the whole cycle leading to implementation of the action plan, up to a year.

A shorter, but less detailed, inventory is available from Pavic Productions: Diagnosis of Individual and Organisational Needs (DION – Elliott-Kemp and Williams, 1980). This has a 66-question list but, as the answers are tick-boxes, the process can be carried out more speedily, is quick to analyse and can form part of a meeting if the questions are prepared as overhead projection transparencies. In my experience this inventory not only groups the responses into major categories (such as leadership, teamwork, problem solving, management, relationships with the community, etc.) but also identifies the single item which the whole staff think needs attention. Although this may not be significant in the eyes of the senior management, if something is done quickly the vast majority of the staff will see action resulting from the process – one of the problems with other techniques is that often action takes some time to be visible!

Such approaches can be categorized under the generic term 'school-based review' (SBR), the purpose of which is to identify areas for development through a systematic review of current practice. Although SBR goes beyond merely identifying needs to the preparation of a plan for the implementation of change, as it is a process internal to the organization, it tends itself to give opportunities for staff development during which staff will also be developing a set of specific skills. Staff will therefore become more 'empowered' and open to innovation, thus generating a positive climate for the whole process (Hopkins 1987).

The outcomes from these 'needs identification' procedures can then be used to inform the preparation of an overall plan for a year's programme of activity. Specifications for specific training activities can then be developed addressing the following issues:

Drawing up the training event specification

1 *Area / topic of training.* Has the provider appropriate qualifications, expertise, experience, credibility in pastoral care?
2 *Skill to be enhanced.* This is linked to the delivery method. Even if a course is not specifically targeted on a skill (for instance counselling, appraisal, interviewing) it is useful to map out skills such as these which could be practised during the event.

3 *Delivery method*. Is the provider familiar with the style of delivery proposed (e.g. activity/groupwork), what resources will be required (e.g. overhead projectors, video), what learning materials (handouts, booklists) will be prepared, and who will produce them?

4 *Tutors/providers*. For groups larger than ten, normally at least two tutors will be needed plus group leaders (possibly from the participants); provide them with a detailed brief and hold a facilitators' meeting if necessary.

5 *Trainees/participants*. Numbers, status, expertise and previous training of participants should be logged, plus any other guests (e.g. HMI, advisers, officers, evaluators, etc.).

6 *Venue/domestic arrangements*. It should be agreed whether the provider or the course organizer is covering this and to whom the bill should be sent.

7 *Monitoring and evaluating outcomes*. Normally the provider should be asked to present an evaluation of the training event itself; it is important to agree how this is to be done.

8 *Costs*. These should be identified and agreed; if development work is necessary a fee needs to be agreed. Beware of 'plus expenses' – large unexpected bills can be run up! Try to negotiate an all-inclusive fee or agree rates and estimates for travel, accommodation, subsistence, preparation/duplication of materials, etc.

9 *Follow-up*. Ensure the provider fulfils the terms of the contract, pay promptly and courteously if satisfied, negotiate for future events as soon as possible if required – good providers are always in demand! Determine whether the course can be provided 'in house' – possibly by one of the group leaders or other participants.

Delivering the programme

Staff development should be seen as an organization-wide process. Not all the needs identified at the individual or organizational level require formal training events; often opportunities can be found to satisfy at least part of an individual's need by opportunities such as involvement in a wider work group, job shadowing, job rotation or internal consultancy. Therefore, in drawing up the overall programme and planning each training event, a range of methods, techniques and skills should be considered and an appropriate selection made. The list opposite shows examples particularly relevant to pastoral care, though most of these would also feature in any programme of staff development.

Descriptions of the use of these techniques and skills are available in established texts and training manuals such as *School-based Staff Development Activities* (Oldroyd, Smith and Lee, 1984); *Staff Development for Pastoral Care* (Hamblin, 1989); *Teacher Appraisal and Self-evaluation* (Hancock and Settle, 1990); and *Staff Development for School Improvement* (Wideen and Andrews, 1987).

Once the staff development programme has been agreed and published (though many activities will be identified only by title at this stage and others will emerge during the implementation phase of the cycle), individual training events need to be planned and training providers identified

Methods/techniques	Skills
brainstorming	interviewing
pair/share	counselling
triads	negotiation
buzz groups	contracting
witness sessions	consultancy
presentations	empowerment
simulation/role play	leadership
work shadowing	'followership'
job exchange/rotation	team building
problem solving	group participation
giving/receiving feedback	action planning
evaluation	costing
	evaluating

and engaged. Through the emphasis on objective criteria and cost effectiveness in initiatives such as Technical and Vocational Education Initiative and its Extension (TVEI/E), TVEI-Related In-service Training (TRIST); Local Education Authorities Training Grant Scheme (LEATGS), Grants for Education Support and Training (GEST) and Local Management of Schools and Colleges (LMS/LMC), most schools and colleges are now familiar with this process.

Process of contracting for a training service

1 *Specification / bid*. The nine issues outlined on pp. 43–44 can be advertised for providers to submit tenders or form a specification for a chosen provider.

2 *Contract*. Once costs have been applied to the specification and delivery agreed with a training provider, a formal contract can be drawn up confirming the arrangements. This can be varied through negotiation between the parties if necessary.

3 *Claim / payment*. This should relate to the specification and the agreed contract and is normally submitted in arrears by the provider. However, payment of all or some of the fee can be made in advance. (This can be useful at the end of financial years!)

This might appear over-formal for a simple training activity but, even if the provider is an in-house teacher, following a shorter version of this process (possibly without costs but requiring an evaluation report) is good practice. As a technique for managing the implementation of training for pastoral care it is valuable, as it resembles the process of establishing a learning contract in student-led courses such as the Business and Technician Education Council (BTEC), City and Guilds (CGLI) and other G/NVQ-validated courses, as well as mirroring the counselling and negotiation processes used in relationships between student and tutor and between student and pastoral section head.

Evaluating the programme

Perhaps the most problematic aspect of staff development is that of identifying outcomes and evaluating the success of individual training events and the programme as a whole. As pastoral care frequently requires rapid response to immediate issues, the discipline of making time for review can get squeezed out. It is vitally important (as in counselling) that time is taken at appropriate points to review action plans and progress made. If the strategy given above to contract training events is followed, the training provider can be asked to complete a simple form as part of their claim. Such a form would test the programme title, the evaluation strategy, data type and analysis method. Of course this should be part of the negotiation of the contract itself – it is totally unfair (and may well be impossible) to ask for a detailed evaluation after the event has happened and the opportunity for data gathering past!

The participants themselves can also benefit from actively evaluating the INSET event or their staff development programme, and this can be arranged as an activity in the event or a specific event in itself. In any case, as a contrast to the almost inevitable 'happy hour' evaluation sheets (which of course are valuable activities in their own right!) a 'buzz-group' format could be employed; for example:

Pastoral team evaluation activity

Target audience:	Year tutors
Group sizes:	Four to six
Time:	20–30 minutes (plus 15 minutes plenary if required)
Instructions:	Tackle each question in turn. Rotate the Chair so each team member looks after one question. Record the team's views on flipcharts. Do not get bogged down in contentious issues – record them for further debate!
Questions:	Has the activity/event/programme met the objectives set? Which aspects were perceived as particularly useful? Which aspects could be improved and how? Were the domestic arrangements satisfactory? What were the specific and general outcomes of the training? How might these be implemented? What further needs have been identified?

ORGANIZATIONAL ISSUES

There are two main aspects to the organization of staff development for pastoral care: first, the internal structure set up to support the process outlined above and, second, the relationship between the organization and the external environment. Both are important in a consideration of the entitlement of teachers to staff development and in the management of INSET provision.

Internal structures for the management of staff development

It is important that the process outlined in this chapter should be delivered in the organization through a management structure recognized by all staff; thus, there needs to be a systematic relationship between the various interested groups. One possible such structure for pastoral care is given in Figure 3.4.

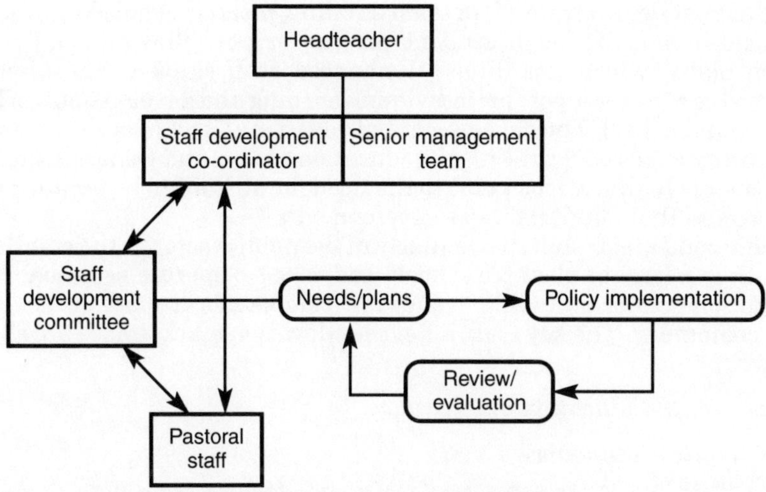

Figure 3.4 Management structure for pastoral staff development

The staff development committee can be a representative body, a task group or an *ad hoc* group, but in any event it is useful to have a 'rolling' membership, as serving on such a committee is a valuable staff development activity in itself.

Any structure such as this needs to be understood as an *aide memoire* under which the process can operate. It should not be so rigid that it is closed to change and modification. There is often a tendency for structures (particularly administrative ones) to take over as masters rather than servants of the process which they are designed to support! In the case of training and support for pastoral care, this is especially important as the aim is a learning environment within which both staff and students feel their social and psychological needs are being catered for. In this respect, the pastoral team should, through their staff development co-ordinator, ensure their interests are represented on the staff development committee to achieve a suitable balance between pastoral and academic training events in the programme.

Staff development and the external context

In this concluding section I want to look at the wider context of developments in education, schooling and the political and legislative framework and their relationship with staff development for pastoral care. The three strands which can be identified are: closer and more collaborative links between schools and the world of work; the creation of a public service marketplace; and a focus in organizational development on 'people' and 'quality'. All of these have implications for staff and pupils in schools and the way in which the school works as an organization.

One of the outcomes from Prime Minister James Callaghan's Ruskin College speech (1976) which initiated the 'Great Debate' in education was the call for a greater relationship with the world of work. It has been argued that the original objective of the TVEI was subsumed by a focus on broad general and transferable skills (DES/HMI 1991). Out of this has come a great deal of training in team building, interpersonal skills, recording achievement through student profiles or portfolios and individual action plans, which has directly enhanced staff skills in the arena of pastoral care as a support for individual learning and development (of both pupil and teacher). The development of a National Record of Achievement (now being explored for the higher education sector) and General/National Vocational Qualifications point to the need for all staff to be familiar with the process that supports these developments.

The second major shift, particularly in the public sector, is the creation of a 'market orientation' where schools and colleges operate as autonomous institutions under a funding agency and compete for a share of the available 'customers'. The key features of the education marketplace are shown below:

Features of the education marketplace

School / college autonomy
in a context of:

- control
- competition
- isolation

The funding authority
as an 'enabler' through:

- strategic planning
- funding formula
- audit and evaluation

Agency provision of services
such as:

- finance
- personnel
- property
- legal
- curriculum
- INSET
- inspection
- management support

In this context, the acquisition of interpersonal and managerial skills plays a vital part in preparing the organization for, and supporting it in, this new relationship. These features are underlain by a market ideology which maintains that a centrally planned economy is bureaucratic, producer-led, wasteful and inefficient. The repercussions of this can be clearly seen in the health service and other local authority services (Flynn, 1990) which have been subject to compulsory competitive tendering (refuse disposal, cleaning, grounds maintenance, etc.). The implications for staff development here are that, first, the internal context of the school has changed as it becomes more locally managed and, second, the external world of work requires individuals who are able to work in a context of smaller agencies or business/service units and with a 'customer orientation'.

By contrast, as has been mentioned on pp. 38–41, movements in organizational development (Peters and Waterman, 1982; Handy, 1985) and their counterparts in education (Reid *et al.*, 1987) trace a clear line away from rigid hierarchical structures and economies of scale towards flatter structures, smaller work groups, flexibility and total quality management (Garratt, 1990; Handy, 1984). On the basis of these changes in organizational structures, I believe that, whether the current trend to privatization of the public sector continues or not, individual organizations will move in these directions. A powerful stimulus to this is that many middle and senior management staff are attending training courses and bringing in marketing consultants in the context of competition under local management/incorporation of schools and colleges and will therefore be exposed to these ideas.

This is relevant to a consideration of the role of staff training and support for pastoral care for both intrinsic and extrinsic reasons. Research in organizational development has demonstrated that a focus on staff, and fostering their growth both as individuals and as members of teams, benefits both the individuals themselves and the organization in terms of increased job satisfaction, the release of latent creativity and greater involvement and commitment. The school can then become a 'learning organization' (Garratt, 1990) and adopt a positive approach to quality through people. Therefore, the training of staff, all of whom under this model have a pastoral role, to be more familiar and comfortable with a range of interpersonal and team skills will encourage a 'synergy' in the school in terms of support for each other and a positive orientation to the development of pupils.

As well as such internal benefits for individuals and the school, there are, however, external reasons also for an orientation more towards 'people'. A positive ethos in the organization is fundamental to creating a favourable image for marketing the school or college and in demonstrating this to visitors. Organizations and their leaders tend to approach the creation of such an ethos and image through 'mission statements' but, for these to permeate throughout the organization, a staff development policy and process which values people and pays attention to their needs is vital to enable all persons to 'live the mission' and thus establish a 'quality culture'. Those responsible for pastoral care in any organization can therefore be of vital importance in assisting colleagues to acquire such skills and to establish and maintain such a culture. Recent initiatives such as the Department of Trade and Industry's Quality Standard (BS 5750) and the Department of Employment's *Investors in People* standard are concrete examples of whole-organization approaches to this and are being taken up by an increasing number of schools and colleges.

In conclusion, staff development is the engine of creativity which enables the organization to learn and renew itself in response to the needs of the staff and the external environment. It needs to be funded as such, although some activities can be accommodated with minor alterations to working practices rather than a 'course'. For such development to take place and to become part of the organization's culture, pastoral care skills need to be identified and enhanced so that all staff become more familiar and expert in their use. It is for these reasons that the development of such skills is an entitlement in the 'training curriculum' for all staff. This chapter has given some pointers as to how such a provision may be organized.

REFERENCES

Bloom, B. (ed.) (1956) *Taxonomy of Educational Objectives. Handbook I: Cognitive Domain*. London: Longman.

Bloom, B. (ed.) (1964) *Taxonomy of Educational Objectives. Handbook II: Affective Domain*. London: Longman.

Brandes, D. and Ginnis, P. (1986) *A Guide to Student Centred Learning*. Oxford: Blackwell.

Brown, P. and Lauder, H. (1992) *Education for Economic Survival: From Fordism to post-Fordism?* London: Routledge.

Department of Education and Science (1989) *School Teacher Appraisal: A National Framework*, Report of the School Teacher Appraisal Pilot Study. London: HMSO.

Department of Education and Science/HMI (1991) *Technical and Vocational Education Initiative (TVEI): England and Wales 1983–90*. London: HMSO.

Elliott-Kemp, J. and Williams, G. (1980) *The DION Handbook* (Diagnosis of Individual and Organisational Needs). Sheffield: Pavic Productions. Department of Educational Services, Sheffield City Polytechnic.

Flynn, N. (1990) *Public Sector Management*. London: Harvester Wheatsheaf.

Garratt, B. (1990) *Creating a Learning Organisation: A Guide to Leadership, Learning and Development*. Cambridge: Director Books.

Hamblin, D. (1989) *Staff Development for Pastoral Care*. Oxford: Blackwell.

Hancock, R. and Settle, D. (1990) *Teacher Appraisal and Self-Evaluation: A Practical Guide*. Oxford: Blackwell.

Handy, C. (1984) *Taken for Granted? Understanding Schools as Organisations*. York: Longman.

Handy, C. (1985) *Understanding Organisations*. London: Penguin.

Hopkins, D. (1987) School based review and staff development. In Wideen, M. and Andrews, I. (eds) (1987) *Staff Development for School Improvement: A Focus on the Teacher*. London: Falmer.

Kolb, D. and Fry, R. (1975) Towards an applied theory of experiential learning. In Cooper, L. (ed.) *Theories of Group Processes*. Chichester: Wiley.

McMahon, A., Bolam, R., Abbott, R. and Holly, P. (1984) *Guidelines for Review and Internal Development in Schools* (GRIDS). York: Longman.

Oldroyd, D., Smith K. and Lee, J. (1984) *School-based Staff Development Activities: A Handbook for Secondary Schools*. York: Longman.

O'Sullivan, F., Jones, K. and Reid, K. (1988) *Staff Development in Secondary Schools*. Sevenoaks: Hodder & Stoughton.

Peters, T. and Waterman, R. (1982) *In Search of Excellence: Lessons from America's Best Run Companies*. London: Harper & Row.

Reid, K., Hopkins, D. and Holly, P. (1987) *Towards the Effective School*. Oxford: Blackwell.

Wideen, M. and Andrews, I. (eds) (1987) *Staff Development for School Improvement: A Focus on the Teacher*. London: Falmer.

CHAPTER 4

Personal and social education: pupil behaviour

John McGuiness

HOW TEACHERS MIGHT CREATE PUPIL MISBEHAVIOUR

Some time ago, I attended a lecture by a senior police officer in which he described how crime figures can be massaged up or down. You want to suggest that we are in the midst of a crime wave of unprecedented severity, perhaps to persuade a police authority that their officers really do need that new computer system, or ten new squad cars? Then all vandalism is categorized as criminal damage to get it on to the crime statistics. If on the other hand you want to signal real success in the fight against crime, the reverse process takes place, in which serious crime is designated a misdemeanour, and thus removed from the statistics, which are assembled on the serious crimes reported. Wadsworth (1979) assembled chastening evidence to indicate that our trust in Home Office statistics about crime figures should take us beyond mathematics into definition. He found that when suspects are approached, white, conforming individuals are less likely to be arrested; if arrested, less likely to be charged; if charged less likely to be found guilty; if found guilty less likely to be given a custodial sentence than a non-conformist member of an ethnic minority.

Perhaps the connection with pupil behaviour in school is not immediately obvious. The general point that I think it is worth our while bearing in mind is Erikson's (1966) observation that it is the 'social audience' that confers the quality 'criminal' on certain actions. Banks *et al.* (1975) found that there exists an implicit scale of 'social offensiveness' that bears no relationship to the law, but which governs police interest in and response to delinquent behaviour. Is it possible that similar constructions of reality impinge on our response to pupil behaviour in school? Are certain pupils, or classes of pupils, subconsciously deemed more likely to be offenders, and have we, as individuals or as school staff, some implicit scales of social offensiveness that exist independently of school regulations? Our perception of pupil behaviour is not objective, it is socially influenced, and so is pupil perception of our behaviour. Equally, both pupil and teacher behaviour is strongly influenced by the social ambience within which it occurs – that is, the school.

I emphasize the importance of the social influences on pupil behaviour to provide a contrast with a more traditional approach which looks at responses to disruptive pupils. Of course it is important to analyse with great care the range of methods we can use to cope with the defiant, the aggressive, the insolent and the inconsiderate pupil – McGuiness (1993a), Watkins and Wagner (1987) and Wheldell (1992) offer detail on that. This chapter takes a more proactive line – how can a school use personal and social education to pre-empt misbehaviour, to create a school ethos in which antisocial behaviour is a rarity, and positive co-operative behaviour as much a school objective as any other outcome required by the National Curriculum? Extensive research (assembled and analysed by Smith, 1989) suggests that the focus for strategies for pupil behaviour should not be the rare major incidents but the normal challenge of fundamentally co-operative young people coping with the challenge of growing up. Elton (1989) is in no doubt that the lurid events the press delights in 'are rare' and seeks to 'stress the importance of personal and social education as a means of promoting the values of mutual respect, self-discipline, and social responsibility which underlie good behaviour' (p. 13).

WHOLE-SCHOOL PERSONAL AND SOCIAL EDUCATION

The idea of appointing a person who lacks personal competence in languages as a modern linguist to develop pupils' competence in language is an evident lunacy, yet we are strangely willing to presume the existence of personal and social competence in ourselves as we set out to meet the requirements of the National Curriculum in this area. It seems less exposed to scrutiny, less open to assessment than the core and foundation elements of the curriculum. The National Curriculum Council's exhortation (1990) that whole-school PSE 'cannot be left to chance' and that it needs to be an 'explicit part of the school's curriculum policy' suggests that a more hard-headed analysis is expected. I feel able to make these statements not from some perceived vantage point of personal, social excellence but from an awareness of the myriad ways in which my behaviour in the classroom affects the pupils' personal and social development. HMI (1987) unequivocally land me with that burden, asserting that 'through good models of adult behaviour, there is constant encouragement to develop self-esteem, self-discipline and autonomous adherence to high standards' (p. 29). Elsewhere (1989) the Inspectorate urge that 'the role of all teachers is vital . . . no teacher can opt out' (p. 1).

THE PSE TEACHER: QUALIFICATIONS?

As a schoolteacher I worked as a modern linguist, but interest and circumstance gradually moved me into the field of psychology, with special reference to counselling. I was particularly intrigued by Egan's (1986) exhortation that a key requirement of the trainee counsellor was 'to come to terms with the problematic in himself'. I was encouraged in training to pursue vigorously the question, 'what bits of me, what personal traits reduce my interpersonal effectiveness?' That feels now like a pretty relevant, and very professional question for me to ask myself as a teacher. Are there issues about me, parts of my intra- and interpersonal style that reduce my claim to be socially and personally developed? And if there are such elements, what impact do they have on me as a PSE teacher and on the pupils who, as HMI claim, use my behaviour as a model for their PSE learning? And – what can I do about it?

On training courses with professionals from a range of 'human client' areas (education, medicine, nursing, management, social work), I have explored the concept of the destructive and the facilitative practitioner using the following exercise. Each member of the group is asked to draw to mind some member of their own profession who they believed was destructive, ineffective or damaging to clients in some way. Thus teachers were invited to imagine that their partner in the exercise was such a remembered 'destructive' teacher. They were then asked to offer to that destructive teacher completions of such sentences as, 'you damaged me when you used to . . .' or, 'you diminished me by . . .'. or 'I was hurt when you . . .'. Doctors, nurses, social workers, industrial and commercial managers on other occasions undertook a similar task. Within and across groups, though they had very different specific professional foci, there was remarkable consistency in the lists they produced when they were asked to complete the exercise by identifying the key characteristics of 'destructive' teachers (or doctors, social workers, etc.). What follows is a combination of a teachers' and a doctors' list, but all lists followed basically the same pattern. Destructive professionals are:

condescending/all-powerful	scornful/sarcastic
angry/bad-tempered	rough/violent/aggressive
two-faced/(no match)	teasing/(no match)
prejudiced/do not believe you	sexist/sexist
humiliating/insulting	(no match)/cold hands

The most noticeable phenomenon with all groups was how rarely specific elements of professional tasks were cited. The vast majority of people doing the exercise identify psycho-social characteristics as crucial. In discussion afterwards, no group viewed such skills as subject expertise for teachers, pharmacological skills in GPs or chemical engineering skill in an industrial manager as unimportant, but there was unanimity on the centrality of psychological and social factors in work with human subjects, as the medium within which effective task performance had to occur. We also found ourselves happily 'projecting' on to other people traits that on reflection we thought ourselves capable of!

A similar, obverse patterning occurs when groups are asked to identify 'facilitative' professionals – effective teachers, doctors, nurses and so on. Then lists emerge containing such characteristics as:

approachable	encouraging
patient	gentle
positive	understanding
humorous	believes in me
makes me believe in myself	enthusiastic
gives time	listens
organized	

Very occasionally specific skills in professional tasks are identified in the positive list, but the overwhelming majority consists of psycho-social elements. Groups are frequently surprised to see the tendency, and as a result become more open to the wide range of psychological research predicting that such experiential data is to be expected – research into self-esteem (Snygg and Combs, 1959), risk-taking (Rogers, 1983), mental health (Heisler, 1961) and 'life success' (Heath, 1977), would lead us to expect that, before humans can address the challenge of a new task, they need to feel *safe*. McGuiness (1993b) puts the same idea differently:

> how many of our reluctant learners are not presenting cognitive or intellectual difficulties ... [but rather] ... saying to us, 'I'm sorry, but I cannot address the material you are offering me at the moment. I have a much more pressing need to establish myself as a being of intrinsic value.' Perhaps our pupils are more astute at establishing the priorities of the classroom than we are. (p. 109)

The priority, then, is a classroom that is infused with the values, skills and interactions of personal and social education.

To respond to the interrogation mark at the beginning of this section, to be as qualified as possible for my PSE responsibilities, I (and I must leave each person to do their own self-audit on this) need to minimize my tendency to 'destructive' professional behaviours, and enhance my abilities on the positive list; in a phrase, to learn how to communicate respect to pupils (DES, 1987). And – no teacher can opt out. I am left with a vivid recollection of the GP who, in discussing the socio-emotional side-effects (as he called them) of say French or chemistry, likened them to the side-effects of medically prescribed drugs – 'and anyone who ignores those influential side effects', he commented, 'is being grossly unprofessional'. It is the same message as the HMI (1989) citation earlier – 'all teachers ... no opting out', but phrased in a slightly more challenging way.

PERSONAL AND SOCIAL EDUCATION: CONTENT AND PROCESS

So far I have tried to argue that we need to develop an awareness of the difficulties in crystallizing a clear concept of pupil 'delinquency' and the role that school ethos can play in increasing or diminishing the perceived amounts of such behaviour; I have pushed hard for the position that no teacher can opt out of PSE (and its implications for pupil behaviour) and remain fully professional; and I have explored, at least as much for my own teaching as for the reader's, what I need to pay attention to if I am to contribute professionally to the personal and social development of my pupils. Before moving on to both the content and process of PSE, with particular reference to the National Curriculum, and its potential impact on pupil behaviour, it seems appropriate at least to mention the larger context within which all this occurs.

Since 1979 (DES) we have seen a move at governmental level from words like 'personal' and 'social' to a new vocabulary crystallized in the 1988 Act, which tends to 'moral' and 'spiritual'. I hope that my unease with the new thrust is not an indication of my own lack of spirituality or morality, but I am sure the language change is not accidental – where the 1970s mode had a feel of process, movement, awareness of the dignity of the individual and the importance of the community, the new language gives me a sense of the static, eternal verities and content of 'moral behaviour'. The problem is whose verities ought to fill the PSE curriculum. If, as suggested earlier, the modelling effect of behaviour by teachers is seen as highly significant, we can expect a similar influence to be exercised by society in general and government in particular. Pupils will be vaguely aware of 'being economical with the truth' becoming an instrument of government policy in the 1980s, and the more able have certainly heard of Westland, British Aerospace, secret arms sales to a government which systematically gassed a people, and covert party political donations. We all contextualize our activities, consciously or unconsciously, and I am sure that any absence of congruence between the rhetoric of PSE documents and the practice of governments, schools and ourselves as individual teachers affects pupil response to it. Coincidentally, while writing this piece I saw Lord Tebbitt being interviewed by Kenneth Baker, the architect of the Education Reform Act, about the resignation of Margaret Thatcher – 'I will go and lie for you, Margaret, for the last time', Lord Tebbitt recalled saying to his premier. There was no apology, no hint that the lie was undesirable, immoral (BBC 2, 7.35, 25 September 1993). What are teachers of PSE (and their pupils) to make of it? One is bound to wonder, too, that if there is no such thing as society, as Margaret Thatcher proclaimed, what meaning can 'social' have?

PSE AND PUPIL BEHAVIOUR: CONTENT AND PROCESS

Elton is unequivocal. 'We stress the importance of personal and social education as a means of promoting the values of mutual respect, self-discipline, and social responsibility which underlie good behaviour' (p. 13). The report strongly supports the strategy that emphasizes positive, pre-emptive action rather than reaction to trouble after it has occurred. How, then, is a school to adopt such a strategy, given that PSE no longer merits a curriculum guidelines document of its own? Beyond the general exhortation of the need for a 'whole curriculum response', we have to use the guidelines on the themes of health education, citizenship, careers education, economic and industrial understanding and environmental education to pursue the cross-curricular dimension of PSE (and its attendant, more specifically stated skills). The apparently arbitrary conceptual jumble in documents on PSE is excellently clarified and focused by Buck and Inman (1992), and they offer, too, some clear management models for this area of school activity.

For the purposes of PSE and its relationship with pupil behaviour, it may be useful to summarize the 'delivery modes' and key content elements (Table 4.1). Any element of PSE is presented to pupils in at least three modes – the ethos of the school, in subject teaching and in specialist presentations of cross-curricular themes, dimensions or skills. Thus, gender sensitivity is developed via the school's ambience, within core and foundation subject teaching, and on, for example, a PSE course.

Placing 'attitudes and values' in the first column is a recognition that they have the most powerful influence on behaviour. Pupils can 'know' a lot about rights and responsibilities (as indeed can ministers), can possess

Table 4.1 Using PSE to enhance positive pupil behaviour

	Attitudes and values	*Skills and competencies*	*Concepts and knowledge*
Ethos/whole school	self-esteem confidence assertiveness respect for self/others for truth for property	interpersonal questioning teamwork critical thinking planning reflective	social political economic moral historical cultural markets
↓			
Core/foundation			
↓			
Cross-curricular themes Specialist input			

real skills in articulation, problem analysis and decision-making, but at the same time have such an amoral view of, say, truth, that the lack of honesty as a dominant value leads to knowledgeable, skilled but amoral behaviour. The knowledge base of PSE can be established in a way that has minimal impact on positive behaviour: if PSE wants seriously to influence pupil *behaviour*, it must concentrate on pupil attitudes, values and feelings, the psycho-social elements identified earlier. If the knowledge base draws on the documentation on *content*, the attitudinal and value bases need to infuse and flow from the process and ethos within which the teaching occurs.

It is possible, as Buck and Inman (1992) have done, to derive a list of aims from the plethora of literature available to us. They would meet little dissent from their assertion that we are concerned to produce adults who are:

- confident and assertive
- knowledgeable about themselves
- able to maintain effective interpersonal relationships
- understanding of and sensitive to the beliefs, values and ways of life of others
- informed about the world
- able to question assumptions and beliefs
- able to think critically
- concerned about promoting justice and equality on an interpersonal, societal and global level
- skilled in how to work collaboratively
- able to reflect on their learning and plan for future developments (p. 7)

Obviously the key challenge is how to operationalize these aims. What can teachers do to help ensure that such adults do emerge from our schools? My own analysis of the list would place 'information about the world' in the concept/knowledge box, and would involve a careful, balanced presentation of what pupils ought to know – problematic in itself. Requests for 'hard knowledge' fail to take into account how little of that there is!

We have, then, a number of skills – interpersonal skills (with a crucial foundational attitude of respect for self and others), skills in questioning assumptions (values about truth and openness), critical thinking (thoroughness and precision), collaborative skills (again respect for self and others), the ability to reflect and plan (awareness of the consequential elements of decisions and actions) – all things for us to learn to do, which rely on our ways of perceiving, valuing, construing and feeling about experiences.

At the heart of the aims is the concept of the self-valuing individual – from that flow the skills, the approaches to knowledge, the confident, assertive, respecting and open behaviour, which emerge in good behaviour. Good behaviour is the manifestation of good feelings about ourselves, and if there is one measure of effective PSE in school it lies in the answer to this question: 'Does my school/classroom help/permit pupils to establish, maintain and enhance their self-esteem?' To the extent that the answer to the question is an unequivocal yes, the contribution of PSE to positive pupil behaviour is assured – every diminution of the sense of self-worth will produce an equal, opposite, often disruptive pupil defence of that esteem, described by Snygg and Combs (1959) as 'the single most important motivator of all human behaviour'.

REFERENCES

Banks, C., Maloney, E. and Willcock, H. D. (1975), Public attitudes to the penal system. *British Journal of Criminology*, **15**, 228.

Buck, M. and Inman, S. (1992) *Whole School Provision for Personal and Social Development: The Role of Cross-curricular Elements*. Goldsmiths' College, University of London.

DES/HMI (1987), *Good Behaviour and Discipline in Schools, Education Observed*, 5. London: HMSO.

DES/HMI, (1989), *Personal and Social Education, 11–16, Curriculum Matters*, 14. London: HMSO.

Egan, G. (1986), *The Skilled Helper: A Systematic Approach to Effective Helping*. Monterey, Cal.: Brookes-Cole Publishing.

Elton Report (1989), *Discipline in Schools: Report of the Commission of Enquiry Chaired by Lord Elton*. London: DES/HMSO.

Erikson, K. (1966), *Wayward Puritans: A Study in the Sociology of Deviance*. New York: Wiley.

Heath, D. H. (1977), *Maturity and Competence*. New York: Gardener.

Heisler, V. (1961), Towards a process model of psychological health. *Journal of Counselling Psychology*, **11**(1), 59–62.

HMI, *see* DES.

McGuiness, J. (1993a), *Teachers, Pupils and Behaviour: A Managerial Approach*. London: Cassell.

McGuiness, J. (1993b), The National Curriculum: the manufacture of pig's ears from best silk. *British Journal of Guidance and Counselling*, **21**(1), January.

National Curriculum Council, 1990, *Curriculum Guidance No. 3, The Whole Curriculum*. London: NCC.

Rogers, C. (1983), *Freedom to Learn for the Eighties*. Columbus, Ohio: Merrill.

Smith, G. (1989), Recent research on disruption in schools, unpublished paper, prepared for HMI Course A319.

Snygg, A. W. and Combs, D. (1959), *Individual Behaviour*. New York: Harper & Row.

Wadsworth, M. (1979), *The Roots of Delinquency*. London: Martin Robertson.

Watkins, C. and Wagner, P. (1987), *School Discipline: A Whole School Approach*. Oxford: Blackwell.

Wheldall, K. (1992), *Discipline in Schools: Psychological Perspectives on the Elton Report*. London: Routledge.

Part 3
Working with Individuals

CHAPTER 5

Counselling in schools: its place and purpose

Colleen McLaughlin

INTRODUCTION

In this chapter I intend to look at the background to counselling in schools, the place and purposes of counselling and the current issues, some of which are near to being resolved and many of which are unresolved. I will explore the different range of counselling work in schools: from more intensive counselling to the wider use of counselling skills. Counselling, guidance and pastoral care are fairly new areas in terms of educational history. However, they are growing up and it is time to move beyond the 'conventional wisdom' (Best *et al.*, 1983) and take a more searching look at the problems and issues of the work in schools.

A HISTORICAL OVERVIEW OF COUNSELLING IN SCHOOLS

To explore the approaches to counselling in schools is also to mirror wider developments in counselling in Britain. To attempt an overview which marks out phases and stages is also to risk objectifying a process which is often less clear and more messy than might be suggested. It is not a process of development where teachers and their practice move neatly from one phase into another: it is more like a rolling stone: new aspects are collected and added so that the final picture is more confused. Practice and attitudes in schools today will bear the hallmarks of many different philosophies and approaches. However, it is helpful to know what these different elements are.

Up to the early 1960s counselling had received little attention in British schools. In society at large psychotherapy was already well known. It was based largely on a psychoanalytic model. It was viewed as 'somewhat marginal and mystical' (Proctor, 1993). The view of helping at this time could be caricatured as being based on a medical model: the patient went to the expert who interpreted his or her experience and administered a cure. These attitudes have not disappeared and can be seen today. For instance, when I was an advisory teacher I worked with a pupil who had been causing great concern in a school. I had my first session and a week later returned to the school. When I asked how things were the teacher said in a very disgruntled tone, 'She's worse since she saw you!' Often in referring or discussing the suitability of counselling for a pupil there is still the expectation of a magical cure. This expectation may also be explained by looking at the development of the counselling movement in British schools, which Hamblin (1982) shows was rooted in the mental health movement and in vocational guidance. The traditional views of 'normality' and 'deviance' which could be seen in the mental health movement at that time could lead to expectations of cure. These views could also lead to the danger of amplifying 'deviance', and this was one of the reasons why Richardson (1979) pointed out the dangers of personal counselling in schools.

The behavioural and humanistic approaches to counselling could be seen as reactions to the predominance of the psychoanalytic. They were adapted and used in schools. The behaviourist view places great importance on the environment and attempts to modify behaviour by altering the responses to a behaviour. Many of the behavioural techniques were adopted in schools. Token economy systems and the like were used to work with individual pupils in schools and some educational psychologists advocated many of these approaches. Many such approaches are still used, particularly with so-called 'disruptive' pupils. The complexity of the classroom environment meant that for many teachers this approach seemed over-simplistic, although it helped in many instances to refocus teachers' attitudes to 'negative' behaviours.

In the mid-1960s there was the advent of the first university training courses for school counsellors. The humanistic approach to counselling was predominant in many of these courses, although many were more eclectic in their philosophy. Carl Rogers's work had a great impact, particularly his view of counselling as 'good communication within and between men'. 'Daws (1974) suggests that the Fullbright scholars brought in to assist the trainers of courses produced counsellors who were fascinated by the Rogerian non-directive and client-centred approach' (Hamblin, 1982). The view of counselling as rooted firmly in a particular quality of relationship and the view of the client as 'a pilot not a robot' were predominant. Counselling was often described as a 'non-directive' process with the client in charge. About one in ten LEAs appointed counsellors in schools (see Fuller, 1980). This coincided with an acknowledgement that pupils were experiencing the effects of rapid social change and that schools had a clear role in meeting the welfare needs of these young people.

In the early 1970s there were many changes which affected counselling. First, cuts in education began and many LEAs and schools saw counsellors as a luxury, so they were the first to be cut. Counsellors in schools are now very rare birds. Second, some were beginning to question the appropriateness of this arrangement. For example, Elizabeth Richardson (1973) in her study of Nailsea School showed that there were tensions between the counsellor and the teachers and that many issues of boundaries, roles and purposes had not been resolved. Law (1977 and 1978) made a major contribution to this debate by researching the system-versus-person orientation. The importing into education of the one-to-one model of counselling, where the 'expert' is in a specialist role, was being questioned. The purist Rogerian approach was in decline and in its place was a greater emphasis on the *skills* of counselling. The work of Gerard Egan (Egan, 1986) and others was becoming more dominant in some circles.

During the 1980s counselling came to be seen as a valid activity for *all* teachers, and *counselling skills* were seen as necessary for teaching. Concepts of guidance had become much clearer, and vocational, educational and personal guidance were viewed as a necessary part of the work of pastoral care in schools. There was also a move to integrate and use many of the ideas which had come from counselling in the curriculum for pupils. Tutorial activities and personal and social education courses included listening skills and work on self-esteem, for example. Many of the counselling theorists had written on education and worked to adapt their ideas to the work of teaching and learning: Carl Rogers's (1983) book *Freedom to Learn for the Eighties* is an example. There was also an acknowledgement that counselling in applied settings was a different task from counselling in settings where it was the prime task of the organization.

Initiatives such as records of achievement and teacher appraisal, which were concerned with processes of self-assessment and reviewing, relied heavily on skills which were drawn from counselling. In many cases this led to greater confusion about what counselling was. Generally, though, it lead to a greater acceptance and wider use of counselling skills.

As stated earlier, these phases and stages can be detected by looking at the literature and aspects of practice, but this is not a description of the state of counselling in all British schools and there are still many problems related to working in schools. The attitudes of teachers still reflect the spectrum: there are teachers who do not feel that counselling has any part to play in schools, there are those who wish to have the specialist one-to-one model and there are those who are aiming to explore in a realistic fashion the complexities of counselling in schools. The history of counselling in schools has affected present practice and developments for there are tensions between these different models. These need exploring if we are to develop current practice.

WHAT IS COUNSELLING?

Before exploring counselling in a school setting, I want to clarify what we mean by counselling and counselling skills. I will explore counselling under five main headings: the process and task of counselling; the structure of the counselling process; ethics; the relationship between counsellor and participant; and the types of intervention or skills.

The process and task of counselling

Counselling is a conscious process and it is aimed at helping someone to develop self-understanding and self-acceptance. The British Association of Counselling (BAC) defines it thus: 'Counselling is the skilled and principled use of relationship to facilitate self-knowledge, emotional acceptance and growth, and the optimal development of personal resources. The overall aim is to provide an opportunity to work towards living more satisfyingly and resourcefully' (1991, p. 1). This definition is useful for it highlights many important elements of counselling. First, the focus is on the participant and the learning about him- or herself. There is no *other* content to be learned. The aim of this learning is to facilitate understanding and acceptance: it is to build on more of the good that exists. It is not a process of remediation. This process should also aim to develop control from within rather than control from without, which is why counsellors do not usually give advice, although they will give information, and do not take control away from the participants. The technical term for this sense of inner direction is internal locus of control and it is important in school settings. For example, research has shown that an internal locus of control is related to achievement in learning. Licht and Dweck (1983) showed that many girls suffered from a sense of helplessness in mathematics and that teacher feedback can enhance or reduce this sense of learned helplessness or external locus of control.

The tentative language in the BAC definition also alerts us to another issue. Counselling is not magical and it not about *solving* problems. It is about developing coping strategies and living effectively, but this is rooted in reality. This has implications for the types of intervention which occur and it implies that the process will be characterized by challenge as well as by support. The process will be characterized also by a focus on feeling, thinking and acting. This is an eclectic approach and takes elements from all the different elements of the humanistic tradition.

The structure of the counselling process

There is also much agreement that the process has different stages (see Egan, 1986: Hamblin, 1993). These stages can be described as an exploratory phase; a problem-solving or understanding phase; and a stage which focuses on action. The exploratory phase is concerned with creating the conditions to explore the issues for the student and the exploration by both the participant and the student of these issues. However, since, as stated in the previous section, the process is aimed at self-understanding, the aim here is to help the participant reach the understanding or clarification as well as the counsellor.

The next stage of understanding is a more focused process, where the particular concern or concerns of the student are explored with a view to developing new understandings or new perspectives. This may involve acceptance of limits and restrictions of power as well as focusing on arenas for potential action. The final stage is concerned with making decisions and taking action, if that is appropriate. These stages make different demands on both the counsellor and the student and require different interventions and skills.

Ethics

Since counselling has specific aims, certain structures and ethical procedures have grown up around the activity. The aim is that counselling should be a non-exploitative activity, as well as one which protects the safety and promotes the development of the participant. The first issue is that of choice and the boundaries of the process. The British Association of Counselling describes counselling as a 'conscious process'. This requires the participants to know that they are undertaking counselling. It means that students should be aware that they are in a counselling interaction and that counselling should be invitational, that is there should be an invitation to talk. It is *not* to suggest that all students should be self-referred. I am suggesting that there is a significant difference between inviting a student to discuss or share something and sending a message that it is expected. Phrases such as 'Would you like to talk about this?' are invitational.

The BAC definition also implies that students should be aware of the nature of the contract, which then raises the issue of confidentiality. Traditionally confidentiality is seen as a right in counselling. 'Confidentiality is a means of providing the client with safety and privacy. For this reason any limitation on the degree of confidentiality offered is likely to diminish the usefulness of counselling' (BAC, 1991, p. 2). This may be true of settings where counselling is the prime task of the organization or where the relationship between counsellor and participant is that *only* of counsellor and client. This is not the case in schools and colleges. Teachers have certain statutory obligations to disclose information, for example, in the case of child abuse, and the law regarding the teacher's role in certain areas has been debated and is still confused to many, for example, in the area of giving advice on contraception (NAPCE, 1988). What is clear is that students need to know the status and limits of confidentiality. This suggests that teachers need to be clear about and communicate to pupils the limits of confidentiality. The Brook Advisory Centres' (1990) document on confidentiality in secondary schools argues that it is essential that schools discuss the advisability of:

- having an ethical code of practice for professional staff (i.e. teachers, counsellors, school doctors and nurses);
- developing self-awareness by publishing guidelines on confidentiality so that all staff and *pupils* are aware of them;
- developing a policy for storing information and protecting confidentiality.

Other ethical requirements according to the BAC Code of Ethics are to do with client safety, client autonomy and competence. 'Reasonable steps' (BAC, 1991) need to be taken to ensure the safety of the participant. This automatically means that steps have to be taken to monitor the competence of those counselling, including an examination of the provision for training and supervision. There is also the requirement that those who undertake counselling engage with the responsibility to explore their own practice and development, particularly looking at how their own emotional issues may affect their practice. Client autonomy has already been touched on but if there is an ethical requirement to promote the control and autonomy of the participant, then many issues need to be explored. For example: do we act on behalf of the participant? How do we maintain and identify boundaries between the counselling relationship and other relationships? Teachers need opportunities to clarify how to maintain these boundaries and deal with any conflicts which may arise. There is a danger of treating counselling as a 'sacred' activity and thus not engaging with these issues in schools where teachers play many roles. I will now look at the relationship between the counsellor and the participant, which is central to this work.

The counselling relationship

The counselling relationship is the basis for counselling work. It is the safe base. The counsellor is aiming to create a place in which it is possible for the student to air the most vulnerable and tender parts of herself: aspects of her or his self which may seem shameful or impossible to talk about for fear of ridicule or rejection. In order for change to occur the student needs to feel sure of acceptance and needs to establish a sure foundation from which to take risks. Carl Rogers's (1951) description of the characteristics of this relationship captures its complexity and subtlety.

Rogers believed that there were core conditions which needed to be present in a counselling relationship and that these conditions were necessary for a facilitative environment. The core conditions were much researched (Rogers, 1959). They were congruence, acceptance and empathy and they needed not only to be present in the relationship but also *felt* by the client, that is they needed to be communicated clearly to the client. *Congruence* was in Rogers's eyes the most fundamental of the core conditions. It is the condition of genuineness. The counsellor attempts to be a real person, not to hide behind a façade or professional role. It demands self-awareness of the counsellor so that s/he can distinguish between feelings which belong to herself or himself and those which belong to the participant.

The second core condition is acceptance or *unconditional positive regard*. Rogers argued that in order to develop a healthy sense of self each of us needs 'unconditional positive regard'. The counselling relationship should contain this since many have never experienced it and it is a necessary foundation for healthy development. Rogers saw the need for positive regard as a universal human need. He believed that our self-regard or our need to feel good about ourselves is related to how we function in the world. Those who have received only very selective affirmation from those around them whom they care about will find it hard to feel good about themselves and function effectively in the world. Unconditional positive regard in the counselling relationship is not about agreeing or colluding with someone but concerns unconditionally accepting and communicating respect. It implies a caring where the counsellor attempts to be aware of the judgements and evaluations which could contaminate the other.

The third core condition is *empathy*.

> It involves being sensitive, moment to moment, to the changing felt meanings which flow in this other person, to the fear or rage or tenderness or confusion or whatever, that s/he is experiencing. It means temporarily living in his/her life, moving about in it delicately without making judgements, sensing meaning of which s/he is scarcely aware, but not trying to uncover feelings of which the person is totally unaware, since this would be too threatening. It includes communicating your sensings of his/her world as you look with fresh and unfrightened eyes at elements of which the individual is fearful. It means frequently checking with him/her as to the accuracy of your sensings and being guided by the responses you receive. You are a confident companion to the person in his/her inner world.
>
> (Rogers, 1980, p. 215)

There is much agreement that these are the necessary conditions for counselling. Some research has also suggested these qualities are significant in teachers and in relationships between teachers and pupils (Heron, 1975; Ingram, 1988).

Types of intervention and skills

Skills alone are not enough. Not only do counsellors need to possess the ability to use certain skills but they also need to know the appropriate purpose and use of the skill. John Heron (1975) has devised a useful framework for the use of skills. He describes two categories of intervention in a helping situation: authoritative and facilitative interventions. Authoritative interventions are those where the intervener takes more initiative and has more authority in the intervention. Facilitative interventions are more open-ended.

Authoritative

Prescriptive	Aims to direct behaviour by instructing, advising or evaluating.
Informative	Aims to impart new knowledge.
Confronting	Aims to challenge or give direct feedback.

Facilitative

Cathartic	Aims to release feelings.
Catalytic	Aims to help the other to rethink or re-examine.
Supportive	Aims to support and affirm worth.

Those undertaking counselling or those using counselling skills need to know when it is appropriate to use which intervention, as well as having the skills to use these interventions. Heron suggests that professionals in a helping situation tend to use the authoritative interventions rather than the facilitative ones. This would apply to teachers too. He suggests that the intervention most frequently avoided is the cathartic one. Teachers need to explore whether they are able to use the full range of interventions and whether the one they choose is the most appropriate in the situation. Many teachers use many authoritative interventions as part of teaching and they may feel that, as Heron suggests, it is the facilitative interventions which they need to develop.

In order to use these interventions appropriately and skilfully counsellors need to master the following skills:

- the skills of attending and listening actively: this includes the ability to paraphrase, summarize and reflect back;
- the skills of appropriate questioning;
- the ability to communicate empathic understanding, non-critical acceptance and genuineness;
- the ability to challenge;
- the ability to share feelings and experiences in an appropriate way;
- the ability to help the participant set goals;
- and finally the ability to help someone solve problems and work on action.

This list is a very crude one, and fuller descriptions of these skills can be found in Egan (1986) and Hamblin (1993). The previously discussed requirement on teachers and others to monitor and be responsible for their competence in this field is relevant here. Heron's work may provide a useful framework for training and development.

Having sketched a very general and broad picture of counselling, I will now explore the issues raised about counselling in the setting of a school or college. The theory and practices described so far arose largely out of practice in settings where counselling was the prime task. This is not the case in schools and the transition is not an easy one, nor do I think it is complete.

COUNSELLING IN SCHOOLS – ITS PLACE AND PURPOSE

Schools are complex institutions and therefore complex settings for counselling. The model of counselling which has been tried is largely the one imported from settings where counselling is the prime work. So the one-to-one model is often seen as the aim for those wanting to develop counselling in schools. Other countries, such as the USA, have adopted this model. This does not seem to be the route which has developed or will develop in Britain, partly because of the resource implications and partly because of the current developments in counselling in schools. This search to establish counsellors in schools has created some tension and I think hindered the development of counselling in schools. We need to acknowledge fully that teachers are teachers primarily and that they will and should use counselling in schools, but that we need to face the issues which this dual role involves. This would be to redirect the debate from one about resources, that is how to acquire the time and space to import untouched the one-to-one model, to how can we develop counselling in a school setting, acknowledging the complexity of the task and facing the issues this raises. Before discussing what I think some of these issues are, I would like to explore the place and purpose of counselling in schools in a more general sense.

In thinking about counselling and its place in schools it may be helpful to distinguish between *proactive or educative* work, which is to do with the improvement of communication and the use of counselling theory and skills, and more *responsive* work, where the teacher is responding to a specific pupil need and where the prime focus of the interaction is a counselling one. It seems to me that there is some confusion about this distinction at the moment, so that the use of skills in appraisal interviews or records of achievement reviews is described wrongly as counselling because they draw on counselling skills and the body of knowledge which has arisen in this area. The prime focus of these activities is not a counselling one, as I have defined counselling in this chapter, and the danger is that the ethical dimensions and the voluntariness of counselling do not apply to these settings.

The first arena of work I described was the proactive or educative application of counselling theory and psychology. There is much we can do in this area where we take from counselling theory and apply it to the education of pupils and the running of the school. Part of this work is involved with 'giving psychology away' or to aiming to contribute to the good mental health of our pupils. This involves looking at the whole person in the school and, if we use Best's (1989) framework, we examine what counselling theory and psychology have to contribute in the areas of the curriculum, the control dimension, the welfare dimension and the management of staff. In the area of the curriculum, counselling theory contributes an element to the personal and social education of pupils. Counselling theory and psychology have already contributed much here. Instead of adopting a remediation approach, where the experts, that is the teachers, keep the skills and the knowledge and use it, they give the skills and knowledge away, teaching pupils how to listen to each other, state their needs and talk through their feelings. Generally, it is the development of an education for the emotional development of pupils, using what we know contributes to good mental health. It is connected to affective education too.

The curriculum area is also to do with the development of effective learning and learners. The task of learning and the social or emotional dimensions are closely connected. Learning involves risk and the ability to tolerate ambiguity or incompetence for a while so that what is already known can be accommodated. The creation by teachers and pupils of a safe or risk-taking climate is important. John Holt (1983) showed the power of fear of failure on learning in schools. Counselling theory has much to contribute here, and Rogers (1983) in particular, has written much on this. This places a requirement on teachers to have what have been described as first-level counselling skills (Hamblin, 1993), that is an ability to listen and respond to feelings, to make reasonable demands on pupils, to adapt appropriately to individuals and groups, to reinforce and support. Much development has taken place in this area and there are schemes of work such as *Skills for Adolescence* (Tacade, 1986) which address issues of creating a safe climate in the classroom where all can be respected and listened to. The pastoral team may locate some of this work in tutorial time, and these skills are essential for tutors to have to perform their work in an effective manner but they are also part of the skills of good classroom teaching.

In the curriculum there is also the more direct application of counselling skills and the process of reviewing and setting action plans in records of achievement and careers education is an example. The skills of reviewing and the process of facilitating self-assessment to move towards setting targets and action plans is very similar to the counselling process and many of the skills are the same. However, this is a very different use of the skills. The boundaries, the focus of the work and choice of the pupil to be there are not the same as a counselling interview and for the protection of pupils the distinction needs to be clear and maintained. The issue of confidentiality is also an important one here. Training in the use and application of skills drawn from counselling is useful but the differences must be maintained.

The impact of the school and its practices is another aspect of curriculum, that which has been called the 'hidden' curriculum. Here we need to review many aspects of the school's practice and its impact on pupils. For example, what impact do some classroom and organizational practices have on the self-image and motivation of pupils? In 1974 Hamblin first wrote about counselling and counsellors in school, 'If the counsellor is concerned with the understanding and prevention of alienation and the production of attitudes which allow pupils to avail themselves of the resources of the school, then s/he cannot afford to separate him/herself from the daily life of the school' (Hamblin, 2nd edn, 1993, p. 282).

The control dimension of the school's work is one where there has been much done in the name of counselling. Hamblin (1993) argues that one of the abuses of counselling in schools has been to use it as a mechanism of social control and personality change. There is a danger that we can locate the problem in the pupil when it is more appropriately located in the school or the context. Counselling can be abused in this way and can be used as a mechanism for changing pupils or as a vehicle for labelling pupils different and in need of help. These labellings may be inappropriate, for they may be based on prejudice and moralizing. Recently there has been much development of a more proactive nature where, for example, the theory of rational emotive therapy has been adapted and used in creating effective discipline in classrooms (Rogers, 1989; Glasser, 1986). The emphasis is not on punishment or remediation of individuals but rather on creating positive behaviour and on diagnosing situations in order to work constructively on problems. Initiatives in bullying and child abuse are also examples where teachers and other professionals are taking children's feelings far more seriously and where issues of the use of power are being rethought. So for example, schools are taking seriously what pupils feel and working with them to alter the climate which allows bullying to be acceptable (cf. Besag, 1992). Pastoral leaders need to take on the management and development of this area of work.

I shall consider the welfare dimensions after looking at the management of staff. Recently, there has been much debate about the pastoral care of staff, and aspects of counselling have been drawn on, for example, the application of techniques of stress management. There is a danger that such approaches can replace looking at the contributing factors. For example, initiatives can focus on individual stress management techniques for teachers, thus locating the problem in the individual teacher's reaction or management of the role, when the problems of teacher stress may reside in other areas and need to be addressed in a different way. For example, recent studies have suggested that the management of and pace of change is a major factor in teacher stress and that initiatives which look at supporting teachers in their professional role can be helpful (Lodge *et al.*, 1992). However, with the proviso that such approaches are not being used to focus in the wrong area, some aspects of counselling theory and psychology can be useful. The use of counselling skills to facilitate better communication and the adoption of humanistic or other approaches can contribute much in this area. Counselling skills have been drawn upon in areas such as appraisal interviewing and in developing interpersonal skills etc.

I will now turn to what I described as the *responsive* use of counselling, which overlaps greatly with the welfare dimension of the school's role. By using the term 'responsive' I do not wish to imply that the role is a passive one, whereby the teacher waits for the knock on the staffroom door and there is a child saying 'Please, Miss, I wish to be counselled.' Nor do I intend to imply that the counselling is restricted to individuals for I would wish to include activities such as group counselling and peer counselling in this bracket. Part of the responsive role of the pastoral team should include the setting-up of groups to focus on specific issues identified as a need, for example social skills or behavioural issues. Peer counselling, where a peer helps a student, is vastly unaddressed and has much to recommend it. Mead's and Timmins's work (1993) is an example of the use of peer support groups and their value. By using the term 'responsive' I mean that the use of counselling is much more focused on reacting to pupil need and the prime focus is a much more 'traditional' counselling one. Some of these needs may be predictable. So, for example, we may anticipate that pupils will need individual guidance and counselling at times of transition or choice; times such as making a vocational or transition choice at 16 plus, or when moving to a new course or from a new school. Opportunities will be given for pupils to avail themselves of counselling support if necessary.

Some of the occasions when pupils will need counselling will not be totally predictable: times of personal or educational difficulty, for example. Hamblin's (1993) concept of levels of work is very useful in this area. He identifies three levels of work within a school – the immediate, the intermediate and the intensive. The different levels require different levels of training and they should not be seen as hierarchical. The *immediate* is a level which can be required of *all* teachers in their capacity as tutors. This will involve working with issues which arise in the personal and subject domains. As has been mentioned already, work in this arena requires teachers also to be aware of signs of stress and tension in pupils, as well as to have the ability to respond appropriately to situations where the pupil may be dealing with emotions or problems. It demands the use of basic counselling skills and knowledge of the theoretical and ethical base of the skills. The second, or *intermediate*, level is concerned with the maintenance of care and concern. It may involve coordinating resources both within and outside the school in order to meet the welfare needs of the pupil. It will also involve the establishment of systems for the detection of such needs and the co-ordination of information gathering and sharing within the school. I would want to argue that this level is also concerned with the establishment of some policy issues and the provision of an arena for debate about some of the difficult practical and ethical issues for teachers working with counselling. There is a need to draw up and communicate policy in this area. HMI in their survey of guidance in secondary schools and colleges found that:

> Generally speaking the greatest *strength* of the guidance seen lay in its pervasiveness ... There were, however, *weaknesses* in the provision of guidance. It was seldom co-ordinated and there were rarely policies relevant to guidance ... finally, more attention needed to be given to analysing the outcomes of guidance, and relating findings to planning of provision. If schools and colleges are to offer guidance of good quality they need to develop approaches which, in the light of their circumstances, achieve and maintain a proper balance between meeting the needs of the individual and of society; and between reacting to problems and taking the initiative.
>
> (DES, 1990, pp. 79–81)

The third, *intensive*, level is the level of in-depth work with a pupil. This will involve more specialist counselling by those with relevant training. Time and the use of such skills are clearly an issue for schools to debate here. There are teachers who have the skills to work at this level and their work needs to be acknowledged and developed by those responsible for policy development. The HMI (DES, 1990) report identified many issues here: the lack of use of such expertise; the lack of adequate facilities for counselling; the lack of consistency in various practices adopted by different teachers; and resources to do the work, including time and money.

ISSUES WHICH ARISE FROM COUNSELLING WORK IN SCHOOLS

In summary, then, this chapter has raised many issues about counselling in schools and has tried to suggest some avenues to proceed down in order to clarify matters. There is a need to have the sort of debate and clarification which normally occurs around the formation of policy. Included in that debate need to be the uses of counselling in the school; the choice pupils are offered and the implications of this; the school's policy on confidentiality and information exchange; the support and training necessary and available to teachers in this area of their work; a code of ethics *for teachers*, including the issue of power and its use by teachers; and the establishment of systems of referral and contact with other agencies.

Douglas Hamblin (1993) warns of the potential abuses of counselling in school: they are that counselling could become subtle control or manipulation, that it is sometimes seen as being concerned with changing personality rather than developing growth, that it is often offered only to those who are seen as deviant or disadvantaged and that it could also be seen as a process of probing interviews. In many schools this has changed (cf. DES, 1990) and many current practices are based on the appropriate use of counselling skills; counselling psychology is more widely accepted and used. The HMI survey found that the best responses were characterized by:

- clarity and precision;
- evidence of a coherent underlying policy;
- an integrated approach (bringing together personal and social education, pastoral work, the role of subject teaching, relationships with parents and outside agencies, ethos, teaching and learning styles);
- a recognition that the quality of guidance was influenced by the school–student–home partnership;
- a relating of the guidance provision to students' needs and perceptions; and
- evidence of a link between intentions and practice.

However, the survey also indicated that there is still much work to be done, and pastoral staff have much to do in developing a policy and practice which is pervasive and effective. We are at a point, though, where the agenda for action is clearer.

REFERENCES

Besag, V. (1992) *We Don't Have Bullies Here!* Valerie Besag, 57 Manor House Road, Jesmond, Newcastle upon Tyne NE2 2LY, England.

Best, R. (1989) Pastoral care – some reflections and a restatement. *Pastoral Care in Education*, **7**(4), 7–14.

Best, R., Ribbins, P., Jarvis, C. and Oddy, D. (1983) *Education and Care*. London: Heinemann.

British Association for Counselling (1991) *Code of Ethics and Practice for Counsellors*. Rugby: BAC.

Brook Advisory Centres (1990) *Confidentiality in Secondary Schools: England and Wales*. Brook Advisory Centres Publications Unit, 24 Albert Street, Birmingham B7 7UD.

Daws, P. (1974) *Early Days*. Cambridge: CRAC.

Department of Education and Science (1990) *HMI Survey of Guidance 13–19 in Schools and Sixth Form Colleges*. London: DES.

Egan, G. (1986) *The Skilled Helper*. Monterey: Brooks Cole.

Fuller, A. (1980) Counselling in schools in 1980. *The New Era*, **61**(5), 165–8.

Glasser, W. (1986) *Control Theory in the Classroom*. New York: Harper & Row.

Hamblin, D. H. (1982) Counselling and pastoral care. In Cohen, L., Thomas, J. and Manion, L. *Educational Research and Development in Great Britain 1970–1981* Slough: NFER–Nelson.

Hamblin, D. H. (1993) *The Teacher and Counselling*, 2nd edn. Oxford: Simon & Schuster.

Heron, J. (1975) *Six Category Intervention Analysis*. Guildford: University of Surrey.

Holt, J. (1983) *How Children Fail*. Rev. edn. London: Penguin.

Ingram, M. (1988) *It Pays to be Human in the Classroom*. Unpublished diploma dissertation, Cambridge University Institute of Education.

Law, W. (1977) Systems orientation: a dilemma for the role conceptualisation of counsellors in schools. *British Journal of Guidance and Counselling*, **5**(2), 129–48.

Law, W. (1978) The concomitants of system orientation in secondary school counsellors. *British Journal of Guidance and Counselling*, **6**(2), 161–74.

Licht, B. and Dweck, C. (1983) Sex differences in achievement orientations: consequences for academic choices and attainments. In Marland M. *Sex Differentiation and Schooling*. London: Heinemann.

Lodge, C., McLaughlin, C. and Best, R. (1992) Organizing pastoral support for teachers: some comments and a model. *Pastoral Care in Education*, **10**(2), 7–12.

Mead, C. and Timmins, P. (1993) Peer support groups and whole school development. In Bovair, K. and McLaughlin, C. *Counselling in Schools*. London: David Fulton.

NAPCE (1988) *Sex Education in Schools*, NAPCE discussion document. Warwick: NAPCE.

Proctor, B. (1993) Overview of counselling in Britain today. In Bovair, K. and McLaughlin, C. *Counselling in Schools*. London: David Fulton.

Richardson, E. (1973) *The Teacher, the School and the Task of Management*. London: Heinemann.

Richardson, J. (1979) Objections to personal counselling in schools. *British Journal of Guidance and Counselling*, **7**(2), 129–43.

Rogers, C. (1951) *Client Centred Therapy*. Boston: Houghton Mifflin.

Rogers, C. (1959) A theory of therapy, personality and interpersonal relationships as developed in the client-centred framework. In Koch, S. (ed.) *Psychology: A Study of Science. Vol. 3, Formulations of the Person and Social Context*. New York: McGraw-Hill.

Rogers, C. (1980) *A Way of Being*. Boston: Houghton Mifflin.

Rogers, C. (1983) *Freedom to Learn for the Eighties*. Ohio: Charles Merrill.

Rogers, W. (1989) *Decisive Discipline*. Geelong, Australia: Institute of Educational Administration.

Tacade (1986) *Skills of Adolescence*. Manchester: Tacade.

CHAPTER 6

Guidance and tutoring

Phil Griffiths

Pause for a moment and look through the corridor window. Two people can be seen, seated around the corner of a table, in an otherwise empty classroom. It is clear that they are a teacher and a pupil, and even if we ignore the differences in age and dress it is possible to make assumptions from the postures about which is which. The teacher is leaning forward, elbow on the table, the pupil sitting back, a little away from the table and rather upright on his chair. The teacher is asking questions, using the movements of her hand to throw the questions across to the pupil, the pupil is responding with words and nods. As the session goes on the questions become shorter, the pupil's answers become longer. Slowly the postures change; the teacher leans back a little in her chair and this movement is echoed by the pupil who also relaxes a little. A pause. and the pupil this time leans forward, picks up a piece of paper from the table and asks a question. The teacher replies and the pupil follows up his question with another. The postures for the moment have been reversed, with the pupil leaning forward, the teacher leaning back. A little later both are leaning forward to share the paper, then both are leaning back and the session has moved from question and answer to discussion.

I have described a moving picture, a silent film since no voices can be heard through the corridor window, of a guidance session by a teacher – a tutor, a year head or a subject teacher – in which the physical actions and postures of the two people involved reflect a movement of initiative and responsibility from one person to the other. We have no idea of what was being said, of the content of the session or of its purpose. I want to suggest, however, merely from watching the picture, that, whatever action resulted from the meeting, the teacher was *successful* in managing the process of the session.

I use the word 'successful' because what the teacher did, in the short space of the guidance session, was to translate into action what I suggest is the basic principle and purpose of all tutorial and guidance work; *to help the students or pupils to take increased and increasing responsibility for themselves – for their academic work, for their behaviour and for their actions*. Whether the guidance is with individuals or with whole classes, whether by subject teachers or by form tutors and whatever the content and purpose – academic review, behaviour management or personal difficulties and problems – the aim and principle remain the same.

It is worth examining that basic principle to see how it fits with wider educational aims, how its use has developed over the past few years and what impact the new climate in education and new demands such as the National Curriculum and Standard Attainment Targets (SATs) will have on it. I shall look also at the process of a guidance session to examine the skills, attitudes and values needed, at how that principle can be translated into action in one model of working, and at the support structures and procedures I believe the school must create to help staff offer effective guidance.

BACKGROUND

For many teachers, encounters like that described above are most readily seen as the work of the form tutor; and indeed the skills needed for the process of one-to-one guidance are basic requirements for those in that role. However, neither the skills nor the process are restricted to teachers in that role alone.

Two key developments in the last few years have pushed tutoring and guidance towards the centre of schools' activities. The first of these was TVEI with its insistence on discussion, negotiation and 'counselling' or 'review and guidance'. The student was expected to take part in the planning and review of his or her own work and money, time and space were made available. Money was a key factor; more than one school used TVEI money to create a 'counselling suite', of small offices and a waiting room, to further this work. The important point to note is that they used the Technical and Vocation Education (TVE) money to take them in the direction they wanted to go.

GCSE followed, with an emphasis on coursework which made similar demands for individual supervision, discussion and negotiation. While this was focused largely on years ten and eleven many schools extended downwards the 'review and guidance' sessions to include all pupils. These two activities grew out of and were reinforced by other developments; profiling, records of achievement, pupil-centred learning and flexible learning for example. Each of these demanded from staff skills which were rarely touched on in initial training: the basic skills of tutoring and guidance, of reviewing, negotiating and planning for individuals and of that whole area known as 'listening skills'. And each development had as a key element what I described above as the basic principle of guidance – helping the individual students to take increasing responsibility for planning their own work, setting their own targets, creating their own aims and recording their own achievements.

The necessary skills for this had been acquired and developed by some teachers, mainly pastoral staff, but now had to be taken on board by staff responsible for TVEI and GCSE – a range of subject teachers and form tutors – by those involved in records of achievement and by those developing flexible learning. Tutoring and guidance, in one form or another, inside the classroom and out, have become the responsibility of the majority of staff and not just of those in pastoral positions. Much of the guidance is focused on the academic work of individuals, but this is frequently carried out by form tutors in a general review in which academic work, effort, behaviour and personal difficulties are considered. What were regarded as 'pastoral' skills are being applied directly to further academic work and achievement, with a consequent merging of the pastoral and academic 'sides' of schools and a spread of those skills among all staff. Tutoring and guidance have become not an 'academic' or a 'pastoral' task but a 'teacher's' task.

There are two further, and significant, points to be made here. The first is that in helping students and pupils to take responsibility for themselves the tutorial process is making a major contribution to what HMI described as the central purpose of education – 'the personal and social development of the pupil; (*Aspects of Secondary Education* (HMI, 1979), chapter 9. 1.2 p. 206). This is used in the widest sense so that personal development would include academic work and achievement and is obviously a 'whole-school' task in which almost everything in the school plays a part; what is taught and how it is taught, structures and management, attitudes and values. But equally obviously, accepting increased responsibility for self plays a large part in the movement towards adulthood and hence in 'personal development'.

The second point is that when the tutorial and guidance process becomes a responsibility of all teachers in the school, becomes central to a school's activities and is used equally for academic review and the management of behaviour, then the pastoral/academic divide disappears. As part of 'academic' work a subject teacher may sit down with an individual pupil or work with a group or whole class to review work and achievement. On the 'pastoral' side a form tutor may talk with a member of his or her form about behaviour or work on PSE with the whole class. The content of those sessions may be very different but the underlying aims, the strategies used to achieve those aims and the process within the sessions will be the same.

This consistency of aims, strategies and process is made easier by the frequently forgotten fact that subject teachers, heads of department and form tutors are the same people. We tend to think and talk about them as if they were different people and confuse the role with the person, but about two-thirds of the teachers in a school act as form tutors at any given time, including many heads of subjects or departments, and almost all teachers either have been or will be form tutors at some time. For about 90 per cent of their time, when they are not being form tutors, they are teaching their subject. It would be absurd to assume that they then become different people with different attitudes, values, experiences, skills, ways of speaking to pupils, understanding them or relating to them.

Tutoring therefore – or guidance and tutoring – is not something only done by tutors. It is an interaction between a member of staff and one or more students which is shaped and determined by specific principles, which demands certain skills on the part of the member of staff and which is aimed at helping the students to take responsibility for themselves.

A GUIDANCE MODEL

If those are the aims and principles, then whatever happens in the guidance session itself must be consistent with them. The session should be a model for the whole process, a time and place in which the student learns, and is encouraged to take some responsibility for what is said and some responsibility for the actions that are agreed.

We need to remember that just as staff develop the skills of guidance and of tutoring, so too do the students need to develop the skills of being guided and tutored, particularly when they are expected to take an active part. They most certainly need help in taking responsibility. I have very carefully used the words 'some' or 'a degree' of responsibility when talking about this, a reflection of the fact that responsibility is not handed over but shared. Where the balance lies will obviously depend on the age of the student and the teacher's professional skill and expertise in assessing the student's competence, confidence and level of ability. Accepting responsibility is a process of growth, and a skill that has to develop so it is probably wise to 'start small', but the only real way of knowing what responsibility the student can bear is to take the risk – and stand by to pick up the pieces. Let me expand a little on the picture used at the beginning.

Mrs Jones, the Head of English Department, is sitting down with David Peterson, a member of her year ten tutor group, to review his work. He has collected marks and comments from his subject teachers, and she has had a number of conversations over the past term with many of those teachers. She has a picture in her mind, from the marks, comments and conversations, of the way David is working and of his possible levels of achievement. David has his own pictures, both of himself and, having seen the marks and comments, of how his teachers see him. The various pictures are not identical. In addition David may well have ideas of what he wants to achieve and of the likelihood of success, and he will have positive or negative feelings about the comments his teachers have made. It is February, so David has had six months of GCSE work, and Mrs Jones has known him well for nearly two years, having been his form tutor since the beginning of year nine.

On the basis of David's marks and the comments from and conversations with his teachers Mrs Jones probably has some idea of the points she wants to make. This will be one aspect of her 'agenda' for the meeting. David will have an 'agenda' of his own which, if the marks and comments are not particularly good, may well be resentful and defensive; he may, however, be delighted with what has been said, satisfied with his work and marks and be expecting little but praise. His agenda may not match that of Mrs Jones at any point.

Mrs Jones will know nothing of David's feelings, although she may well guess some of them, but, in addition to making her points:

- She will want David to hear and understand any comments she has to make and recognize them as legitimate concerns.
- She will want to explore David's reactions to the comments and to leave David feeling that he has been heard.

- She will want David to come out of the session feeling positive about himself and his chances of success.
- She will want David to take some responsibility for any changes and actions needed following the review.

A MODEL RELATIONSHIP

How Mrs Jones starts, what she says and what she does in the session will depend largely on her relationship with David, but also on her sensitivity, perceptiveness and skills. There are some key words in that sentence which demand some clarification, beginning with that overused word 'relationship'.

The problem with 'relationship', as it is often used in the educational literature, is the words used in association with it; 'warm', 'positive' 'accepting', 'trusting', 'friendly'. Of course these qualities are necessary but, as Keith Sherman and I have pointed out elsewhere:

> Less often are the words 'powerful', 'responsible', 'adult', 'authoritative' and 'controlling' used ... [Yet teachers] are adults who cannot abdicate from that position, who have power and authority over those in their care and who are responsible for exercising control.
>
> (Griffiths and Sherman, 1991)

Power, control and authority are not necessarily in conflict with the previous set of words, and in a proper and productive relationship the authority and adult status is used to provide a 'framework from within which the friendliness, warmth and acceptance can be offered'. In terms of the guidance session Mrs Jones must use her authority to take the lead, to establish what the meeting is about, to set the atmosphere, to some degree set the agenda and to establish the boundaries. She will also be responsible for keeping the session focused on the task, and for the time limits. She will remain firmly in charge, but her very authority and confidence will enable her to put over to David more convincingly her genuine concern for a positive outcome.

The concept of boundaries is important. Within limits David is free to say what he likes in the session, but, for example, scurrilous abuse of another member of staff – or of herself – is outside those limits. Respect, mutual respect, is necessary. This needs to come first from Mrs Jones, and indeed it will be the respectful way in which she deals with David which will to a large extent establish the atmosphere and boundaries. The process of establishing these will go on throughout the session – it certainly cannot be achieved by telling David at the beginning what the boundaries are. In effect Mrs Jones must offer to David, through her own behaviour, a model of how to relate properly and productively to another person.

As the purpose, agenda and boundaries are established David must be given time, space and freedom within those boundaries to put forward his own thoughts, reactions, ideas and solutions; must in fact be encouraged to take some responsibility for what is happening and what is decided.

The model for a working relationship being suggested here is based on that of Coopersmith (1967) in *The Antecedents of Self-esteem*. He proposed four basic conditions which together might create a framework for positive development:

- respectful, accepting and concerned treatment by 'significant others';
- appropriate boundaries;
- freedom within those boundaries for individual actions and decisions;
- a history of success.

The fourth condition is difficult to achieve within the guidance session, although it is obvious that Mrs Jones can emphasize any successes in David's list of marks and comments, and if David leaves the session feeling that he has been heard and was contributing to any decisions this too could be seen as a success.

I must emphasize that this is only one suggested model for a productive relationship between a teacher and student. It is, however, a model which addresses some fundamental human needs of both adults and children – and indeed might be applied to the whole area of teacher appraisal. Teachers too are in need of 'respectful, accepting and concerned treatment by significant others', and at no time more than today.

A MODEL FRAMEWORK

Having suggested a model for the relationship within the guidance session, I want to turn to a model for the session itself.

Egan (1975) in *The Skilled Helper* put forward a basic three-stage model for 'the helping interview' in which the first stage was concerned with listening and exploring, the second with clarifying and expanding the understanding of both parties, and the third with taking mutually agreed action and decisions. I believe this model is an appropriate one which can be applied, with a degree of flexibility, to all tutorial or guidance sessions.

Mrs Jones and David begin the session with some shared knowledge and information – the marks and comments from his teachers. Mrs Jones's first task will be to explore with David his understanding of that information and his reactions to it – exploration, in other words, both of factual knowledge and of its emotional content. She will start there in accordance with the well-tried counselling rule of starting where the client is. In fact there is little point in starting anywhere else since if David has not grasped what the comments mean – or is angry and resentful because of them – his level of understanding and his feelings could interfere with any progress the session might make. This will be the first stage of listening and exploring.

The second stage, of clarifying and expanding the understanding of both parties, is likely to be the appropriate time for Mrs Jones to make her own input. This then becomes information that she and David can share and explore before going on to the third stage. There are no rigid boundaries, however, between the stages and she may well have contributed some of her own assessments in the first part. The descriptions of the work to be done at each stage are descriptions of the focus and balance of that stage rather than prohibitions.

The third stage will come when Mrs Jones and David, having arrived at a mutual understanding of what the situation is, and perhaps what the problems are, discuss what actions need to be taken. It is very important that the session is seen to have an outcome in terms of what each person does, in other words that it results in mutually agreed actions. These may be very simple, an agreement to meet next week to continue for example; or they may be more complex and involve talking with other people or a trial period followed by a further meeting. The important thing is that they are seen to be actions resulting from the session, and that they are followed up.

If David is to take some responsibility, it is equally important that as far as possible the actions are mutually agreed. I put it that way because Mrs Jones is likely to have a clearer understanding than David of what needs to be done and a better understanding of the consequences of any course of action – or inaction. She is likely to be able to produce a wider range of possible strategies and may have to persuade David to adopt what looks like the most effective. This is part of her adult and authoritative role, but the long-term result is likely to be better if her efforts go to persuasion rather than coercion. How easy or successful this will be will again depends on the relationship she has fostered.

NECESSARY SKILLS

Let us assume, then, that Mrs Jones has a reasonable working relationship with David, that a degree of trust exists between them and that she has planned the session in terms of the three-stage model. She needs in addition a range of skills which will enable her to manage and monitor the process and progress of the session.

We began with a description of positions, postures and movements, and one of the basic skills is an awareness of their significance. I described two people 'sitting around the corner of a table'. This position is an easy and convenient one. It allows the table to be used to spread materials while the corner, intruding slightly between the teacher and the student, gives each a degree of protection and personal space without acting as too much of a barrier. Few of us have the luxury of a private office with easy chairs, and the table corner can be found in any classroom or science lab.

Our understanding of the significance of positions, postures and movements must include not only an awareness of how the student is sitting or moving – does it show confidence or nervousness, openness or defensiveness, eagerness or apathy? – but an awareness of the possible effect of our own postures and actions. There are few absolute rights and wrongs in this area, and subtle differences can have widely different effects on different people. Sitting well back in a chair can be seen as relaxing and helping the student to relax; but it can also be interpreted as 'dominant' behaviour since this may not be something we do if we are talking to someone of greater status. We can all laugh, for example, at the thought of wagging a finger hard in the face of the student, but given the right context and the right relationship it may not be inappropriate or be perceived as threatening.

What we do need is a conscious awareness and self-awareness, an ability to monitor and change our own postures and gestures to make them appropriate or to create a desired change.

This is not as difficult or as complicated as it sounds, although I do not want to suggest we have nothing to learn. But as normally functioning social beings we do note people's stances and postures, we do interpret them and change our own in response. We do not have to learn a new language, merely become more aware and bring into consciousness the knowledge we unconsciously possess.

That basic level of sensitivity to postures, gestures, tones of voice, etc. – the whole area of 'non-verbal' messages – is a part of what are frequently described as 'listening skills'. Active listening demands much more than sitting silent; it demands sensitivity to the non-verbal messages, a posture that makes the other person aware of attentiveness, appropriate and timely acknowledgements – nods, verbal encouragement and responses.

Closely connected with active listening is the ability to *reflect back* to the other person what you understand to have been said. We are all, as human beings, capable of hearing what we want and expect to hear, of fitting what was said into our own framework and 'sets'. Accurate reflection does two things; it reassures the speaker that they are being heard and understood and it allows the listener to check our their own understanding of what is being said. It is also a means of exploring, clarifying and expanding. 'What I hear you saying is . . .' 'You mean . . .' An extension of this skill is the ability to pick up and reflect back not only the factual content of what is being said but the feelings that come over with it. 'When you said that you seemed really pleased', 'Whenever you talk about . . . your voice changes, as if you're angry.' It is important to recognize that in using reflection the listener takes responsibility for what she has heard and understood. If she has misheard she has to accept her own error. She is, however, giving the speaker a chance to correct any misapprehensions.

At appropriate points throughout the session it is a useful and necessary skill to be able to stop the dialogue and *summarize* what has been said so far. In fact those words can be used. 'Can we stop there for a moment and look at what has been said so far?' Certainly summarizing can be used, perhaps should be used, when the teacher feels that the end of one of the stages has been reached. Such interventions as *reflecting* and *summarizing* enable the teacher to punctuate and pace the session, to move on to another aspect or to draw something to a conclusion. Developing such skills gives the teacher a greater degree of control of the session and allows her to 'fine-tune' and manage the process.

Finally what Mrs Jones will need, as I suggested earlier, is to be able to come up with a range of strategies for action in the third stage – strategies for the student to use in dealing with other members of staff, strategies for self-monitoring of work, for time allocation at home and at school, for prioritizing conflicting interests and activities. Even in a 'review and guidance' session of academic work she will be dealing with matters outside as well as inside school and with the 'whole life' of a whole person, and the strategies need to recognize this.

Although the example I have used to illustrate the models is one of an academic review, they have a much wider application. Careers guidance, for example, is based on a respect for the individual student. It requires an exploration of knowledge, understanding and feeling, a clarification and expansion of existing knowledge and finally plans for action – the basic three-stage framework. It demands an awareness of non-verbal signals and the 'active listening' skills of reflection and summarizing. And its aim is to help the student to arrive at, and feel responsible for, her or his own conclusions and decisions.

In tutorial work on personal and social difficulties or on behaviour management, the same fundamental aims and principles still hold. For example McNamara's (1992) article 'Motivational interviewing: the Gateway to pupil self-management' discusses the process of behaviour management; the key concept is the fact that unless the pupil accepts the need for change then change will not take place. Helping students to take responsibility for themselves, their work and their behaviour is not just an abstract ideal but a pragmatic necessity if change, growth and development are to be encouraged.

Again, although the example used is of a one-to-one interview, the relationships model, the three-stage model of exploring issues and the principle of helping students to take responsibility for themselves, can all be applied directly and easily to tutorial and guidance work with groups and whole classes. They are also relevant to subject teaching. The basic questions of the three-stage model – where are you now? where do you want to be? how can you get there? and what help do you need? – are teaching and learning questions as well as helping ones.

In offering the two models I have aimed not just to suggest how things ought to be but to illustrate the sort of work I have observed being developed in a number of schools. Mrs Jones, though a fictional character, has the skills, values, understanding and expertise being used and developed by many teachers I have worked with, and by many others throughout the country. The precise models may differ from school to school and from teacher to teacher, but the basic aims and principles and the values implicit in them – the emphasis on the 'personal and social growth' of the individual student for example – have gained universal recognition.

STAFF SUPPORT

Implicit in the process of tutorial and guidance work is the understanding that discussion, exploration of feelings and ideas, sharing of difficulties, talking something through with another person, are productive procedures which give support and also offer the chance of change, growth and development. It is an understanding that has been grasped by many teachers and shapes their behaviour towards the students. What is surprising is that this understanding is not applied in any consistent and coherent fashion to the needs of staff.

Schools seem to have been reluctant to take on board the idea that staff too are in need of support – and never before quite so much as now – and that staff too have personal and professional dilemmas and developmental needs. To meet those needs it is not enough to depend on the informal network of contacts within departments and in the staffroom – which can be a place where much stress is experienced, and where frequently a façade of competence and confidence, of being a good teacher, has to be maintained.

I suggest it is the responsibility of teachers themselves, but even more of management in schools, to create the means by which support and supervision can be offered and personal and professional dilemmas explored. By 'personal' I do not necessarily mean, for example, difficulties coming from home about relationships with partners or children. In the middle of a tutorial session teachers are using their own 'selves', their own sensitivities, experiences, feelings and perceptions to understand and help the students in front of them. They cannot help but be engaged and involved on a personal as well as a professional level and they have a right to proper support of the 'whole person'.

We suffer, I think, in schools from an isolation in our work and from what has been described elsewhere as the 'mythology of self-sufficiency' (Griffiths and Sherman, 1991). In that mythology asking for help is seen as a weakness and an admission of failure, and support is seen as necessary only for those who cannot cope, as a crutch for the inadequate. We need to move away from that limited, damaging and stress-creating concept towards the concept of a more co-operative and supportive culture.

Professional support, in the sense in which it is used in social work, counselling, probationary work and increasingly in medicine, personnel work and management in industry, is not about weakness, failure or inadequacy. Its purpose is to monitor, enhance and make more effective the work of the individual. We need to adopt in schools the strategies being developed elsewhere and to learn to share, in groups or one-to-one sessions with our peers and our managers, the aims and objectives, difficulties and dilemmas, successes and failures in what we do. This 'interactive professionalism' as Fullan and Hargreaves (1992) have termed it, is an important factor in creating and sustaining mutually supportive working environments.

The Elton Report suggested that we should develop 'peer support groups' to combat isolation, to increase effectiveness and to reduce stress. (*Discipline in Schools*, 1989). If time constraints prove too tight to develop these, we can at least look to increasing the effectiveness of the meetings we do hold, that is to running departmental meetings in ways which further the task, maintain the group and offer mutual support, a sharing of difficulties and a chance of professional and personal growth. To do this, however, we must become more aware of staff needs. Proper support or supervision sessions with immediate managers could produce the same benefits.

Let me suggest therefore, as one further model, that each teacher concerned with tutoring and guidance has an entitlement to regular management supervision sessions which have a similar framework to the guidance sessions with the students. As I remarked earlier, teachers too need 'respectful, accepting and concerned treatment'. They need appropriate boundaries, if only to feel that they are not responsible for everything. They need freedom of action within those boundaries, areas of responsibility where they take the decisions. They too need to focus on successes, and on failures if only in order to learn from them. Like their students, teachers need a framework for personal and professional growth and development.

Such a supervision session would have the same three-stage framework I suggested for guidance: 'where are you now? where do you want to get to? what do you need to do to get there?' And it would use the same skills of listening, reflecting and summarizing. It would provide, in other words, an experiential and learning/teaching model for the tutor in her or his work with students.

It would do more than that. My suggestion is based on the firm belief that proper care for the students depends upon proper care for the staff – by management and by each other; that unless schools care for their staff the cost for individual teachers in caring for the students will ultimately prove too high; that we need to develop a consistent set of values, an ethos of care which emphasizes support, growth and development and which applies to staff and students alike. As Fullan and Hargreaves (1992) point out, as one of their guidelines to greater effectiveness teachers should 'monitor and strengthen the connection between [their] development and the students' development'. Such a consistent model would affirm and support the values implicit in guidance work of personal growth and development for all members of the organization.

SUSTAINING THE ETHOS

A question for all teachers at this moment is whether such values and aims, for themselves and their students, can be sustained in the face of the determined onslaught on teacher's skills, competence, values and attitudes which we experience almost daily and have endured for the past ten years, and in the face of the massive increase in work and pressures the new demands have created.

There is little in the imposition of a National Curriculum, or SATs, or in the movement towards grant-maintained status that of itself directly threatens the tutoring process, although the restrictions on GCSE coursework and an increasing rigidity of prescription limit the real choices students can make and hence reduce the need for them to take responsible decisions. However, at the time of writing, work on records of achievement is still being encouraged and that demands the same skills and values and the same philosophy. Some schools who have taken the grant-maintained leap claim that they have been able to take on more staff and focus more easily on individual needs. The philosophy of diversity and independence implicit in the grant-maintained movement suggests that they would wish to encourage and develop the skills of taking responsibility for themselves among their students. Whether the levels of funding will permit this when there are 3,000 – or 23,000 – grant-maintained schools rather than 300 is anyone's guess.

The impact in the area of values and philosophy is difficult to assess. I would suggest that this is because there is a degree of dissonance between the verbal messages coming from our masters in the DFE and their actions. The words are about independence, choice, diversity, taking responsibility for oneself, standing on one's own feet, etc. The actions are about what *The Times* called the 'nationalization' of education: rigid central control with more powers going to the centre with every passing Education Bill, increasing (and contradictory) absolute prescription and a limitation of choice. We have an expressed political philosophy which preaches individual responsibility and self-determination but policies which take away local self-determination, insist on central control, and take from teachers the means by which they can encourage the very qualities this government would praise. In this climate judgements and forecasts are impossible.

I do believe, however, that the work, effort, values and principles of tutoring and guidance are under threat, and the threat comes not directly but through two separate but connected factors of school life. The first is time.

Recent research – the ATL (AMMA) research from Warwick University for example (ATL/Warwick University, 1991a, 1991b) – has highlighted the astounding number of hours worked by primary and secondary teachers both inside and outside school. One reason so much work is taken home (at least fifteen hours a week) is that the school day has become far more congested and the demands on teachers for and during contact time far greater. The impact of SATs on secondary schools will make this much worse. To add further confusion, budgetary limits in 1993/4 are likely to lead to a general reduction in staffing levels. The problem for tutoring and guidance is that it is extremely time-consuming. It may well be that one-to-one work with students, and tutorial time in general, will fall victim to the increased pressures on staff time whatever the wishes and priorities of individual staff and schools.

The second factor – or set of factors – which threatens proper tutorial and guidance work is the lowering of staff morale and possible changes in what can be described as the 'professional culture'. The major reason for the excessive workloads of staff in both the primary and secondary surveys (ATL (AMMA)/Warwick University 1991a, 1991b) was what the reports describe as the 'conscientiousness factor': teachers' commitment and sense of obligation to their students, which appears at the moment to be unrelated to salary level or incentive allowance held. This could well change. The secondary report comments that 'Teaching is not yet a contract-led profession', in spite of 1265 hours and all that, but also notes:

> It remains to be seen how far the new climate under LMS, performance indicators, teacher appraisal and performance-related pay will be able to induce a change in such a culture ... Such a change could be in the direction of reduced commitment and time on work ... The process may be encouraged by repeated changes in nationally-imposed requirements, so their [the teachers'] preparation time is wasted as schemes become obsolete.
>
> (ATL (AMMA)/Warwick University, 1991b, p. 44)

Lack of time, lowered morale and a reduction in the 'conscientiousness factor' are the real threats to tutorial work. Time has never been adequate and at the moment much of the individual guidance and tutorial work is squeezed into odd moments of preparation time and depends very much on teacher goodwill. Other things are brushed aside – to be taken home perhaps. If we do become more contract-minded, if the commitment falls, then the will to find the time will disappear. We have not yet reached that stage; as one young teacher said to me the other day, 'At least in the classroom, working with the kids, you can forget all this.' 'Working with the kids' remains the thing most teachers get most reward from, although it now accounts for much less than half the workload (AMMA/Warwick University, 1991b). Long may it remain a refuge from the plethora of paperwork and politics.

Nevertheless, although I do not want to exaggerate it, we do face a problem in schools of lowered morale, over-work, uncertainty, high levels of stress and the danger of a consequent reduction in effectiveness. There seems little chance in the next few years of schools and teachers receiving help with these difficulties from anyone other than themselves.

In fact if the staff were students, the pastoral and tutorial systems would be operating at full stretch to offer support. This makes the creation of structures and strategies of support for staff even more urgent: not only for the sake of the staff and the school, but as the 'basic and necessary foundation for the school's task of caring for its pupils' (Griffiths and Sherman, 1991).

REFERENCES

ATL (AMMA)/Warwick University (1991a) *Workload Achievement and Stress*. Coventry: Department of Education, University of Warwick.

ATL (AMMA)/Warwick University (1991b) *The Workloads of Secondary School Teachers*. Coventry: Department of Education, University of Warwick.

Coopersmith, S. (1967) *The Antecedents of Self-Esteem*. San Francisco: Freeman.

Egan, G. (1975) *The Skilled Helper*. Monterey, Cal.: Brookes Cole.

Elton Report (1989) *Discipline in Schools*. London: HMSO.

Fullan, M. and Hargreaves, A. (1992) *What's Worth Fighting for in Your School*. Buckingham: Open University Press/Ontario Public School Teachers Federation.

Griffiths, P. and Sherman, K. (1991) *The Form Tutor*. Oxford: Blackwell/Simon & Schuster.

HMI (1979) *Aspects of Secondary Education in England*. London: HMSO.

McNamara, E. (1992) Motivational interviewing: the gateway to pupil self-management. *Pastoral Care in Education*, **10**(3), 22–8.

CHAPTER 7

Using groups to develop pupils' learning skills

Brenda Hopper

INTRODUCTION

This chapter is written for teachers in classrooms who wish to develop ways of using groups to help pupils to develop learning skills. It is based on the premise that all groups have the potential for power and influence, both in relation to their members and in relation to other groups and individuals, and that the research (see, for example, Rowan, 1976; Thibaut and Kelley. 1986) that has been done into group processes over recent years has important implications for the teacher. Some understanding of the principles of group development and group dynamics will be of value to the teacher who wishes to promote the personal and social development of the pupils within the groups that she or he teaches. As a member of an effective working group, an individual can experience the caring, support and trust that enables her to face the challenge of new learning, of having existing beliefs, values and understandings questioned and acquire new knowledge, skills and ways of perceiving the world. Interpersonal communication can be enhanced, leadership skills can be developed and effective problem-solving strategies can be acquired.

Groups provide a valuable context within which a range of learning opportunities can be accessed. Experiential learning, which pays attention to the 'how' as well as the 'what' of learning, involves a process of activity, reviewing the activity, learning and application (Figure 7.1). This cycle highlights the importance of learners reviewing what they have done, usually within a small group. The effective as well as the cognitive domains are highlighted, and learning becomes a process which engages the pupil at an emotional as well as an intellectual level. Reflection on experience is essential, if that experience is to contribute to greater awareness and understanding. A group provides a potentially safe environment within which this reflection, and subsequent learning, can occur.

Throughout their school life young people spend much of their time as members of different groups – class groups, tutor groups, gender groups, small working groups, friendship groups, and many others. From the moment they arrive in school on the first day, they join a group of peers with whom they will spend much of their school life. Some of these will

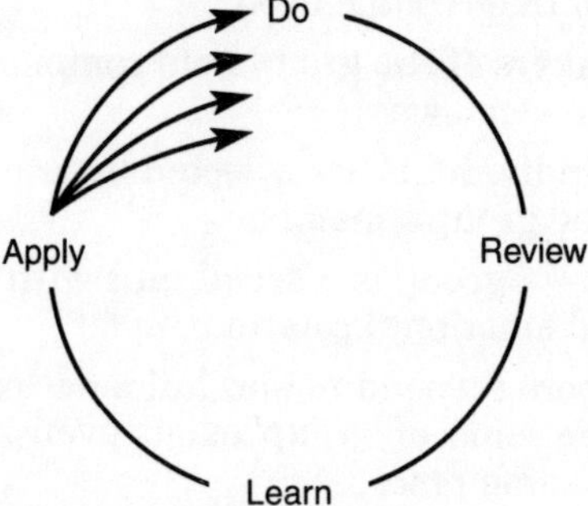

Figure 7.1 (from Kirk, 1987)

become friends – others they will hardly know, despite spending many hours in close proximity in the same room. However close and significant these relationships with others may become at an individual level, there is no doubt that young people's social identity is intimately bound up with membership of the groups to which they belong. In this chapter I will consider:

- the nature of groups;
- some theories of group development;
- communication in groups;
- power and authority and the role of the teacher;
- the individual within the group;
- some practical ideas for the classroom.

THE NATURE OF GROUPS

A learning group within a school context may be defined as a whole class group, or as a small group of pupils who are engaged in a particular task or activity. A group of between twenty and thirty will have very different characteristics to a group of three to four: a group of less than six offers greater intimacy and opportunity for face-to-face interaction, and is more likely to have a fluid leadership with little structure. With more than twenty-five or so, there is little opportunity for face-to-face interaction between everyone, and positive leadership is necessary for the group to work effectively. In schools, pupils will belong to small, often task-focused groups, working together on assignments and other activities, and also to larger class or tutor groups which meet on a frequent and regular basis. While there are some significant differences between these two types of groups, many of the processes and stages through which the groups pass will be the same.

Most writers define a group as a number of individuals, generally more than two, who are interrelated in some way. Some of the features which determine a group are:

- *collective perception* – the members are conscious of their existence as a group;

- *needs* – the group satisfies some need;
- *shared aims* – members of the group hold common aims or ideals which unify them in some way;
- *interdependence* – individuals are affected by and respond to events that affect any of the group's members;
- *social organization* – a group is a social unit with norms, roles, statuses, power and emotional relationships;
- *interaction* – members respond to and influence each other in communicating. The sense of 'group' exists even when members are not together in the same place;
- *cohesiveness* – members want to remain part of the group, to join in its activities and contribute to the group;
- *membership* – two or more people interacting for longer than a few minutes constitute a group.

(after Jaques, 1984, p. 1)

From this list it can be seen that, to a greater or lesser extent, the pupils within a particular class or tutor group constitute a group, and within this there will be a number of smaller sub-groups, some of which are self-selected and others which are determined by the organization within the classroom. Not all the features listed above will be present in classroom groups, and some will be more evident in smaller, task-focused groups. By attending to those features which promote coherence and interdependence, the teacher can develop the whole class as a group which offers support, security and challenge to individuals in their learning, and can also help small groups to operate more productively and effectively in the tasks they are engaged in, and in the social-emotional dimensions of group work.

SOME THEORIES OF GROUP DEVELOPMENT

Research into the ways in which groups work has been a relatively recent development, with much of the literature emerging over the past two decades (see, for example, Napier and Gershenfeld, 1983; Brown, 1988). One of the better-known models of group development, and one which is fairly easily committed to memory, is based on the work of Tuckman (1965), who described the stages through which a group passes as:

Forming	The orientation stage when the group is initially coming together, and individuals are exploring issues such as 'What is going to happen here?', 'Who are the other people in this group?', 'How will I relate to these people?'	This initial 'coming together' stage will occur in the life of every new group. Each time the teacher reorganizes groupings in the classroom, she will need to recognize and acknowledge the hesitation and uncertainty which will be generated within individuals in this new group. This may appear to be an unproductive stage in the life of

		the group, but will be helping individuals to orientate themselves.
Storming	The stage at which disagreements and tensions arise, and in which conflict begins to emerge.	Learning to work co-operatively means testing out existing 'rules' and ways of working. Sometimes this means challenging others in the group, and vying for leadership.
Norming	The stage at which ways of working are established, 'rules' are developed, understood and accepted, and individuals in the group learn to work together.	Having tested out different roles and ways of working, patterns can be established for *this* group, individuals come to know and understand how they and others work, and the group can move into being fully productive.
Performing	The stage of productivity in which the group is able to work effectively, to resolve tensions and disagreements in a way which is acceptable to everyone in the group, and to move forward on the task in hand.	If a group manages to reach this stage – and many do not – it can become self-directing and self-managing. Tasks will be achieved and the group will be able to look after its members.

(after Tuckman, 1965)

In this, as in other similar models of group development, the stages are sequential and successive, as at each stage the ways in which the group addresses and resolves issues is dependent upon the resolutions made in previous stages. A group which does not pass through a 'storming' stage at least once, is unlikely to become fully productive. Many teachers try group-work in their classrooms, only to discover that there are disagreements and difficulties within some of the groups. Helping a group to deal with its difficulties, by offering support, by intervening in helpful ways, and by offering structured opportunities for difficulties to be expressed, may be more useful in the long run than abandoning this way of working.

The stages of this development model are also cyclical – a group will revisit many issues in different contexts each time it meets a new situation. The fact that a group has established its norms and ways of working does not necessarily mean that these will hold good on other occasions. A new experience of working together may require a new set of norms to be developed.

A brief look at another model (Glassman and Kates, 1990), which considers the various psychological themes which may be particularly relevant, may help the reader to gain an insight into the types of issues which may be addressed by a group at any particular stage in its development. These social-emotional issues are important features of a group's existence, and will be present at some level throughout the life of a group. I have considered these in the context of the whole-class group:

Stage 1: Pre-affiliation
'We're not in charge'
Recognizable to the teacher who meets a new class or tutor group at the beginning of the school year. Pupils will generally be quite cautious, waiting to see what is going to happen. They do not know the 'rules', and are waiting for some structure and direction to tell them what is acceptable behaviour. They may be trying to gain approval, from one another and possibly from the teacher.

Stage 2: Power and control
'We are in charge'
'We're taking you on'
The testing which occurs after the initial 'honeymoon' period is over. At this stage rules will be challenged, authority is asserted and boundaries are tested. It is at this stage that power relationships are confronted, and shifts of power may occur. Even if the group has set its own ground rules, these will be tested out. The teacher who is trying to work democratically in the classroom may find that she is being pushed towards re-taking control. It is as if the group is saying 'we do not want this responsibility', or 'we do not trust that you are really willing to give us responsibility'. While it may not make the situation any more comfortable at the time, it may be helpful to know that this process happens in all groups that meet together to work over a period of time. It is an important stage in the life of the group and, while it can be worked through, it cannot be avoided if the group is to become productive.

Stage 3: Intimacy
Sanctuary
The point at which the group feels good to belong to, and at which things seem to be going really well. Having worked successfully through the issues of the previous stages, group members are now able to work effectively together, to make decisions and take responsibility for themselves. For the teacher who manages to reach this point with her group, the rewards can be immense. She is able to take her place within the group – still with overall responsibility but able to participate as a member of the group whose needs and wishes are taken account of, along with everyone else's.

Stage 4: Differentiation
'This isn't good any more'
followed by 'We're okay and able'
When the expectation of things going well which has arisen from the previous stage is seriously threatened. The group seems to take a backward step. Conflicts and tensions re-emerge, and the group just does not seem able to work well together. It is almost as if the group is back in stage 2, needing to re-establish ways of working before it can once again become effective.

Stage 5: Separation
'Just a little longer'
As the group moves towards the end of its time together, there is a feeling of loss and regret. So much more could have been achieved if there was just a little more time. Emotional attachments may be strong, and the members of a group that has successfully worked through the earlier stages of its development may have strong feelings of needing the group, and of not wanting to leave. For most pupils in school, this will not happen until they leave at the end of year eleven or thirteen, but even the prospect of leaving a particular situation, perhaps with a tutor or teacher whom they have come to like and respect, can elicit feelings of loss and separation.

(after Glassman and Kates, 1990)

One implication of this model is that groups will have different needs at different stages of their development, and that these needs can be addressed by careful planning and structuring of learning opportunities. Within a pastoral structure, the group tutor will have an overview of the group, and can plan a developmental programme which responds to the identified needs of the both small groups and the tutor group as a whole, as they emerge. At the opposite end of this continuum is the teacher who may meet many groups in a single day, have very little contact with any of them during any given week, and may then be faced with the task of building an effective group with minimal contact. In this case the process will be slower and relationships will take longer to develop. As most teachers will know from experience, the relationships which can be built with a group with which there is frequent and regular contact are very different in quality from those which can be built when opportunities for working together are few and far between.

At the beginning of a new school year, time spent on clarifying expectations and generating a set of ground rules based on 'what are our rights in this classroom?' (including, of course, those of the teacher) and 'what responsibilities are associated with the protection of those rights?' can quickly establish ways of working which give pupils some responsibility within a very clear framework. Many tutors already do this with their tutor groups – but a variety of different subject groupings generates a need for this process to occur in each new group (though perhaps not always in the same way – spending the first week of a new year setting ground rules in every lesson is probably not highly motivating either to teachers or to pupils). Group-building games and activities (see, for example, Brandes, 1982, Brandes and Phillips, 1978), which enable pupils to work together and get to know one another, can be built into tutorial programmes and PSE programmes, and many of these can be adapted for use within specific subject lessons. Planning a topic, theme or module within a specific curriculum area can include planning for the developmental processes within the whole group, and within individual small groups. Activities which help groups to move through the different stages in the model, and address the themes which are particularly relevant at those times, can be built into schemes of work and become part of the day-to-day lesson-planning process. The daily contact which a tutor has with her group can provide an opportunity for planned activity, even if the tutor period is no more than ten minutes long – even small amounts of time can be used productively!

Working with other people, being a member of a group and sharing in collaborative activity are essential skills, not just in employment terms but in other aspects of everyday living. Understanding the processes through which groups grow and develop helps to demystify what can be a frustrating and difficult experience – and it is reassuring to know that tensions, conflicts and feelings of frustration and alienation are normal responses to what is happening in a group. I am indebted to a colleague who once suggested to me that I 'trust the process'. It is tempting to try to rush in and rescue a situation which is feeling difficult, or to impose a structure or intervene in a way which avoids facing issues and addressing tensions.

While in the short term this may be an expedient strategy, the cost in the longer term is that the group is denied an opportunity to work through its difficulties and arrive at a productive stage.

GROUP SKILLS

Communication

Interpersonal communication is essentially the sending and receiving of messages, and 'effective communication exists between two persons when the receiver interprets the sender's message in the same way the sender intended it' (Johnson and Johnson, 1991, p. 107). In a group situation, the opportunities for misunderstanding are increased as the size of the group increases. It is interesting to check out understandings within a group – even though everyone has effectively received the same message, there will be a wide range of different interpretations. Individuals may claim to have listened and heard, and yet what they hear is influenced by their perceptions in a way which often filters and distorts the message. The skills of sending clear messages, of listening carefully and checking out understanding are essential to good communication in any situation, and particularly within groups.

The process of sending and receiving messages is a complex one, and yet interpersonal communication skills are generally not explicitly learned – we assume that we can communicate effectively, and only occasionally discover that we thought we were being very clear and yet our messages are misunderstood or misinterpreted. The ability to offer support to someone who is experiencing difficulty in expressing themselves, to challenge in a way that enhances rather than diminishes the self-worth of the individual being challenged, to check perceptions and recognize differences in perception, are just as important in a group context as they are in one-to-one interaction. These skills are readily identifiable and can be taught to pupils of all ages, either through exercises and activities specifically designed for that purpose (see, for example, Bond, 1986; Settle and Wise, 1986; Timmerman and Ballard, 1975, 1978) or through using the day-to-day interactions which occur in the classroom as learning opportunities.

Decision-making

There are a number of different strategies for making decisions in groups, each of which will have a different outcome in terms of its effect on the group. While no one strategy is necessarily better than the others, different strategies will be appropriate for different occasions. A fully functioning group will be able to use a wide range of strategies, and will be able to choose which is the most appropriate in any given circumstances.

- *Decision by authority*. Often the teacher in the classroom. This is an effective strategy in terms of speed of outcome, but involves little or no interaction or participation, and consequently there is little commitment by the members of the group to the decision made. Resentment and frustration may result, and individuals may then try to sabotage the decision, either overtly or by more subtle means.

- *Decision by majority*. Probably the most common 'democratic' way of making decisions. While there is greater commitment on the part of those who voted in favour, there will often be a substantial minority of dissatisfied members, who may feel alienated and lacking in commitment.
- *Decision by minority*. While not a unilateral decision, this has similar drawbacks to a majority decision, except that the process utilizes the resources of even fewer group members, and there is likely to be even less commitment to the decision.
- *Decision by consensus*. 'a collective opinion arrived at by a group of individuals working together under conditions that permit communications to be sufficiently open – and the group climate to be sufficiently supportive – for everyone in the group to feel that he or she has had a fair chance to influence the decision' (Johnson and Johnson, 1991, p. 220). Although time-consuming, this often produces a creative, high-quality decision which receives the support and commitment of all group members, even those who might have preferred a different outcome. This strategy is appropriate in situations where the decision to be made is particularly complex or important.

Arriving at a consensus in a group requires a range of skills – listening carefully to everyone's point of view, listening to and understanding people's feelings, considering issues from a different perspective, working out compromises, communicating openly and honestly. The teacher can help these skills to be learned by:

- explaining what is meant by a consensus, and frequently checking out that decisions made in a group have the support of all its members;
- modelling consensus-seeking, and continuing to work at arriving at a consensus even if one or two vocal members of the group have already indicated their agreement. In consensus-seeking, silence does not indicate consent – *all* points of view are elicited and checked out;
- inviting pupils who are not in agreement to say why, and explain their opinions, making sure that these are heard, acknowledged and valued;
- constantly seeking ways of offering opportunities for decisions to be made by consensus, and challenging occasions when majority rule has prevailed.

There are a number of decision-making exercises which can be used to help pupils to examine the ways in which they make decisions in groups (see, for example, Gene Stanford's book *Developing Effective Classroom Groups*, 1977). While they are of some use, the investment that individuals have in the outcome may be limited. It is important to ensure that there are also opportunities to make *real* decisions, the outcome of which are significant to the members of the group, and to which they will feel some real commitment.

Managing conflict

Whenever groups of individuals work together on a task, there will

Figure 7.2

inevitably be some conflict. For many teachers, indeed for many people, conflict is something which must be avoided at all costs. Expression of emotions such as irritation, anger, frustration are not considered to be acceptable in the classroom, and yet these emotions are a normal part of everyday life, and an important element of our spectrum of feelings. Avoiding conflict is not usually helpful in the longer term – it leads to a build-up of feelings and unexpressed emotions which, if bottled up, will inevitably either leak out or erupt somewhere, often inappropriately. Conflict in itself is not damaging to relationships, either one-to-one or group relationships. What is important is whether or not the conflict is addressed and resolved, and the way in which it is resolved. Learning to work through conflict and to deal constructively with it is an important part of the personal and social education process.

In school pupils can learn assertiveness skills which will help them to deal with conflicts in a more productive way. One model of possible ways of behaving in conflict situations is illustrated in the 'OK Corral' diagram (Figure 7.2). Each quadrant represents a particular standpoint, or way of perceiving a relationship. The 'I'm OK, You're OK' standpoint presents a way of managing difficult situations which is based on a problem-solving model; where everyone's views are heard, everyone's feelings are listened to and understood and a resolution is arrived at which may not meet everyone's needs but recognizes and acknowledges them and preserves their feelings of self-worth. The other three quadrants all illustrate ways of behaving which do not fully acknowledge and value the experiences and feelings of all concerned. Pupils are as skilled as any adult at recognizing put-downs, and the natural reaction to an aggressive comment is to retaliate in an aggressive way, thereby starting a cycle of aggression. The teacher can intervene in a helpful way, not by attempting to solve the problem or resolve the conflict but by encouraging pupils to express their views and their feelings in a direct way, without blaming or criticizing others. Using 'I' statements is a helpful way of doing this, so that pupils are 'owning' their thoughts and feelings and not blaming others (for example, 'I am mad at you', rather than 'You make me mad'). Asking pupils to explain *what* they are doing, and what they see as the consequences of that behaviour is often more helpful than asking *why* they are doing something – 'why' questions invite rationalizations and can lead to a defensive response. Gordon (1974) identifies a list of 'communication roadblocks' (such as criticizing, blaming, moralizing, threatening, analysing, sympathizing) which teachers may use with pupils, and which are likely to be unhelpful, communicate unacceptance and may elicit feelings of anger and resentment. These same messages can be unhelpful when used by pupils with one another, and may increase tension rather than resolve the conflict. Focusing on what is happening, rather than trying to analyse the reasons behind a particular point of view, may help to avoid a build-up of tension, and enable group members to express their feelings without fear of judgement or criticism. The teacher can provide a powerful model of these behaviours, and can help pupils to work through, rather than avoid, issues and difficulties.

POWER AND AUTHORITY AND THE ROLE OF THE TEACHER

No discussion about groups and group processes would be complete without considering issues associated with power and authority. I have already identified power and control as a central theme in any group. The power and authority of the teacher is an additional factor in the classroom, as the way in which she uses it can so easily undermine the work that she is trying to do in encouraging pupils to take responsibility for themselves and for their commitment to others.

Many teachers will have experienced the frustration that comes from trying to encourage pupils to take responsibility for making decisions for themselves, and for taking action, only to find that they are highly dependent on being told what to do. Working within a group provides some safety, when a decision has been arrived at by a group of people, and they can share the responsibility that accompanies that decision. Moving from a way of working based on dependency on the teacher to one based on personal responsibility is a lengthy and often difficult process, and cannot be achieved simply by changing expectations. Through working in groups, and developing appropriate skills for working together, pupils learn that it is acceptable to say what they think and feel, that mistakes are allowed, even welcomed, and that when the teacher says that they can make choices for themselves, she really means it and will not overrule them later.

Pupils may be reluctant to take responsibility for themselves because:

- Making decisions and taking responsibility is risky. What happens if it all goes wrong? Taking responsibility for making a decision implies being held responsible for its outcome.

- They have learned to be 'teacher-pleasers', in other words to say and do what they think the teacher will want to hear and see. This condition can easily be reinforced by the teacher who gives generalized praise, rather than specific feedback.
- The classroom is not a safe and supportive place, where risks are encouraged and mistakes are valued as learning opportunities, rather than condemned or derided. There is a lack of acceptance, by the teacher, by other pupils, or both.

Giving groups real decisions to make, and supporting them in that process of decision-making, enables pupils to learn to take responsibility and to experience the shift of control from a totally teacher-determined situation to one where power and control are shared.

I have already suggested that the teacher's role in managing and supporting groups in the classroom is a very active one, though it may be quite different from the traditional model of a teacher's role. The teacher is very much a participant in the learning process, supporting, encouraging, structuring activities and managing the classroom environment, talking and listening to pupils and intervening whenever a learning opportunity presents itself. The locus of control may have shifted, from being located totally within the teacher to being shared with the pupils, but the teacher maintains an involvement in and shared responsibility for the way the classroom is managed and ordered. Ground rules may be devised, and codes of conduct established, but these are negotiated between teacher and pupils. The teacher, as a member of the group, has a particular set of needs. She will ultimately be held responsible for what happens in the classroom, and will need to establish some boundaries, and be clear in the way these are communicated.

THE INDIVIDUAL WITHIN THE GROUP

The discussion so far has largely focused on the group, and the ways in which groups develop and work together. Within this framework, it is important not to lose sight of the fact that a group is a collection of individuals, and that as individuals they have their own needs, desires, aspirations and anxieties. By helping groups, both small and whole-class groups, to examine the way they work together, to ensure that all their members are listened to and heard, and by encouraging the development of active listening skills, individual needs can be expressed and addressed, and every individual can learn from and contribute towards the work of the group.

The teacher in the classroom will operate in a way which reflects her or his beliefs and underlying assumptions about the nature of people and the way in which they behave. One set of assumptions, which has its roots in humanistic group-work practice, may offer a useful framework:

- people have inherent worth and capacities regardless of race, class, status, age and gender, as well as physical and psychological condition
- people are responsible for and to one another because social life is a natural and necessary human characteristic
- people have a right to belong and to be included

- people, having emotional and intellectual voices that are essential to their existence, have a right to take part and be heard
- people have the right to freedom of speech, and freedom of expression
- differences among members are enriching to one another
- people have a right to freedom of choice, to determine their own destinies
- people have the right to question and challenge those professionals who have sanction to guide and direct their lives

(Glassman and Kates, 1990, pp. 23–4)

Recent developments in teaching and learning emphasize the role of the individual within the group. Teachers who work in this way ensure that their classroom is a place where pupils are active participants in the decision-making processes, where they feel a sense of involvement and ownership of the curriculum, where relationships between pupils and between teacher and pupils are based on honesty, integrity and mutual respect and where the range of learning experiences on offer ensures that the individual needs of everyone in the group are catered for. Strategies and structures by themselves do not make for a supportive, positive learning environment; the underlying ethos of the classroom is a far more powerful communicator of values than anything which may be said by the teacher.

While the focus so far in this chapter has been on groups of pupils and teachers in classrooms, it will no doubt be clear to the reader that everything that has been said in relation to pupil learners is equally valid for groups of teachers within the wider context of the school. The ethos of the school needs to support the work of individual teachers in classrooms by offering opportunities for involvement in decision-making and by ensuring that individuals are listened to and feel that they have been heard. An institutional commitment to valuing individual members of the school community needs to go further than a statement in the school aims – it needs to be experienced by pupils, teaching staff, non-teacher staff, visitors and all who have contact with the school.

SOME PRACTICAL IDEAS FOR THE CLASSROOM

There are a number of strategies for starting the move towards ways of working which pay attention to the learning potential of groups. Just as pupils need to feel secure in order to take risks, so teachers need to ensure that they take small, measured steps in trying anything new. Pupils will have a set of expectations based on their previous experiences in the classroom. They may take time to adapt to change, to adjust to new ways of working.

Some practical ways in which the teacher can work towards developing effective groupwork include:

- trying different ways of structuring groups:

  ask pupils to choose a partner, and then assign them randomly to groups of four as a way of mixing up friendship groups in a not-too-threatening way;

  use activities to sort pupils into completely random groups (for example, find matching colours from small pieces of card, find other pieces of a simple jigsaw), or partly pre-determined groups (asking the class to arrange themselves in a line in order of height and then count off will often result in a gender-mix).

- introducing pupils to group-work gently, perhaps by asking them to work in pairs to begin with. Pairs can then come together to make groups of four, bringing with them something they have already discussed.
- setting carefully structured tasks with clear boundaries, and checking that everyone understands the task before they begin to work on it.
- ensuring that you have a set of 'ground rules' or guidelines for working together, and drawing the groups' attention to these.
- building in opportunities for small groups to review how they are working together. Simple questions such as 'What went well? What didn't go so well? What could we have done to help us to work together better?' invite reflection and do not take long to consider.
- acknowledging what is happening in the classroom, and how people are feeling about what is happening. Try not to make judgements, but focus on observations. Encourage individuals to evaluate their own and each others' behaviour, while giving feedback based on what you have seen.
- modelling helpful behaviours. Let pupils know that you will not tolerate put-downs and ridicule in the classroom by dealing firmly with any incidents. Make clear, direct statements which do not criticize the offender but indicate that their behaviour is unacceptable.
- looking for opportunities to engage pupils in real decision-making. Help them to develop the skills to make decisions in a way which acknowledges everyone's opinions and feelings.
- spending time developing the 'classroom community', working with the whole group or class. Consider different seating arrangements, and look for ways of encouraging everyone to contribute.
- helping groups to identify specific skills which will help them to work together effectively, and then ask them to use those skills and assess themselves and each other at the end of a lesson or activity.
- encouraging pupils to express their feelings, especially when there are disagreements or tensions. Make sure these are listened to and acknowledged, and offer an example by letting pupils know how you are feeling.
- avoiding stepping in to solve problems or resolve difficulties for groups – instead, help them to work through issues for themselves. Encourage active listening and understanding of other people's points of view, and help groups to consider a range of alternative strategies and explore different solutions.
- giving groups as much freedom as possible to make decisions about how they will work. Be available as a resource person, but allow the group to manage its own activity. Try to observe what is happening in

the groups, so that you can offer your observations when the group is considering how it worked.

- being clear about your own boundaries. A democratic classroom is still a place of order and discipline – the difference lies in the nature of the order and the responsibility for the discipline. Involve pupils in discussion problem behaviours. Focus on positives rather than negatives – rewards rather than punishments. Explain clearly your limits and any sanctions you intend to use, and be firm and consistent in your use of these.

CONCLUDING THOUGHTS

Just as a knowledge and understanding of group processes is important for the teacher, so too is this understanding valuable learning for the pupils. By reflecting upon their own experiences and listening to those of others, and by examining the ways in which interactions occur, young people can begin to understand what is happening and can more readily take control of their own actions and responses in a group situation. Feedback from others provides valuable material for learning; checking out assumptions, listening to others' points of view, learning to work through conflict in a constructive way, rather than avoid it, are all important aspects of social development and contribute to the enhancement of social skills. Interaction with others is an important context within which young people develop their sense of identity. Through interaction they can develop their awareness and understanding of themselves as social beings, able to communicate effectively, to co-operate with others and to recognize the uniqueness of their own experience while also appreciating that they are not alone in their doubts, concerns and anxieties. As members of a group, young people can experience for themselves the potential to make decisions and to effect change within an organization. They can examine the effect that their behaviour has on other members of the group, and also the impact that the behaviour of a group may have on other groups. They can experiment with different styles of leadership, and develop skills and approaches to leadership which help a group to work effectively. They can learn to value the contribution that other members of the group may make, and recognize that the contribution of each individual will be unique. They will face the challenge of someone who is disrupting or sabotaging the work of the group, and can explore ways of managing this. They can learn that acceptance of their own and others' thoughts and feelings is an essential mediator in helping individuals to feel secure enough to take risks and to learn. By building group-work into the classroom, by planning experiences and activities which focus on aspects of working together, and by intervening in ways which draw attention to group processes, the teacher can enhance the personal and social development of individuals through their experience of group life.

REFERENCES AND FURTHER READING

Brown, R. (1988) *Group Processes: Dynamics Within and Between Groups*. Oxford: Blackwell.

Corey, M. S. and Corey, G. (1987) *Groups: Process and Practice*, 3rd edn Monterey, Cal.: Brooks/Cole.

Glassman, U. and Kates, L. (1990) *Group Work: A Humanistic Approach*. London: Sage.

Gordon, T. (1974) *Teacher Effectiveness Training*. New York: David McKay.

Harrison, A. A. (1976) *Individuals and Groups*. Monterey, Cal.: Brooks/Cole.

Jaques, D. (1984) *Learning in Groups*. Beckenham: Croom Helm.

Jenkin, F. (1989) *Making Small Groups Work*. Exeter: Pergamon.

Johnson, D. W. and Johnson, F. P. (1991) *Joining Together: Group Theory and Group Skills*, 4th edn. Englewood Cliffs, NJ: Prentice-Hall.

Napier, R. W. and Gershenfeld, M. K. (1983) *Making Groups Work: A Guide for Group Leaders*. Boston: Houghton Mifflin.

Napier, R. W. and Gershenfeld, M. K. (1987) *Groups: Theory and Experience*, 4th edn. Boston: Houghton Mifflin.

Rowan, J. (1976) *The Power of the Group*. London: Davis-Poynter.

Schmuck, R. A. and Schmuck, P. A. (1974) *A Humanistic Psychology of Education: Making the School Everybody's House*. Palo Alto, Cal.: National Press Books.

Thibaut, J. W. and Kelley, H. H. (1986) *The Social Psychology of Groups*. London: Hutchinson.

Tuckman, B. (1965) Developmental sequence in small groups. *Psychological Bulletin*, **63**(6), 384–99.

IDEAS AND ACTIVITIES FOR USE IN CLASSROOMS

Bond, T. (1986) *Games for Social and Life Skills*. London: Hutchinson.

Brandes, D. (1982) *Gamesters' Handbook Two*. London: Hutchinson.

Brandes, D. and Ginnis, P. (1986) *A Guide to Student-centred Learning*. Oxford: Blackwell.

Brandes, D. and Phillips, H. (1978) *Gamesters' Handbook*. London: Hutchinson.

Kirk, R. (1987) *Learning in Action*. Oxford: Blackwell.

Kreidler, W. J. (1984) *Creative Conflict Resolution*. Glenview, Ill.: Scott, Foresman.

Settle, D. and Wise, C. (1986) *Choices: Materials and Methods for Personal and Social Education*. Oxford: Blackwell.

Stanford, G. (1977) *Developing Effective Classroom Groups*. New York: A & W Publishers.

Timmerman, T. and Ballard, J. (1975) *Strategies in Humanistic Education: Vol. One*. Amherst, Mass.: Mandala.

Timmerman, T. and Ballard, J. (1978) *Strategies in Humanistic Education: Vol. Three*. Amherst, Mass.: Mandala.

Part 4

The Curriculum

CHAPTER 8

The whole curriculum

Michael Marland

INTRODUCTION

The entitlement to pastoral care and personal-social education requires comprehensive, school-wide curriculum planning, not merely a bolt-on of pastoral care, however good. To achieve this it is necessary to understand where our curriculum planning has come from and its true legal position now. In the heavily-loaded busy-ness of schools it is difficult to look back and even more difficult to take a firm grasp on the underlying legal structure – for interpretations abound which are inaccurate and confusing, often even from those in official positions. In particular, it is too easy to lose sight, since 1988, of the *school's* responsibility for curriculum planning and the importance of whole-school planning, not limited to discrete 'National Curriculum' courses.

THE IN-SCHOOL PLANNING PROCESS

Although it is not always possible to discipline planning into its logical sequences, the process has four discrete steps: first, the aims of the school should be established (in accordance with section 18 of the 1986 legislation); second, a range of whole-school policies should be established, for instance on aspects such as equity (cf. Runnymede, 1993), cultural diversity and breadth; then, and only then, should the overall curriculum be divided into 'planning divisions' and their content established in detail; and, finally, the contents of those planning divisions should be distributed into 'delivery modes'. The art is to endeavour not to move to the end too quickly, and above all not to confuse 'the timetable' with 'the curriculum'. We should timetable a curriculum, staff a timetable, and educate a staff, rather than working upwards from the current knowledge and skills of the staff. It is profession-centric to start with what we are able to do now. It is certainly worth spending time defining the aims and having drafts discussed carefully by students, families, staff, local groups and the governors. Everything else derives logically from those aims, and the depth and precision of that wording is most important.

These policies are not very dissimilar from those which the National

Curriculum Council started by calling 'dimensions'. They should, of course, derive from the aims and section 1 of the Education Reform Act, 1988. These policies should be informed by the concept of 'a global culture', but one which is still respectful of the roots of people, and should share a cultural universality with the technicalities of the modern world, especially information technology, as 'the defining technology of our age'. By including the personal, social, linguistic, cultural, occupational and social aspects of today, there is a sound basis for a curriculum that enables effective pastoral care.

The planning divisions should not be regarded solely as what has been traditionally known as 'subjects'. The true division of 'curriculum content' includes attitudes, concept or understanding, fact and skills. It is not adequate to make the planning divisions merely those of traditional subjects, for there have to be some which are larger than those. For instance, South Australia has in its state curriculum 'information skills' as a basic skill before the subjects are listed.

As the contents of the various planning divisions will be re-arranged later, the actual divisions do not matter and the definition of the divisions is largely a matter of convenience and the availability of planning knowledge. For instance, for planning purposes 'sexuality' can be regarded as a part of 'health education' or as part of 'personal and social education'. Similarly, 'citizenship' can be planned as a single entity for later distribution, or again put under 'personal and social education'. 'English' exists as a statutory planning division as the 'core' subject, but does not have to be planned in that way within a school. At North Westminster Community School, for instance, 'English' in National Curriculum terms is divided up into a number of 'curriculum planning divisions', as follows (Table 8.1).

From a pastoral point of view, it is particularly important that these planning divisions are comprehensive, with, for instance, this example making separate planning divisions of 1, 12, 13, 14, 15, 16, 17, and 18. There are, of course, other ways of dividing up, and certainly from a pastoral point of view the planners would need to ensure that what have been called 'the seven selves' are included: bodily, sexual, social, vocational, moral/political, as learner and in the organization (Watkins, 1989).

Only at this point, logically, does the school consider what I prefer to call 'delivery modes'. It is most important that there should be a planned disjunction between the 'planning divisions' and the 'delivery modes'. Whilst there may sometimes be a strong measure of synchrony between the two, for example in 'mathematics', which is likely to be both a planning division and a 'course', there will be many planning divisions, the contents of which are delivered through a number of delivery modes. Few courses can be 'self-contained'. In this planning, there is of course a tension between what I call the 'specialised' and the 'disseminated', or the 'specific' and the 'contextual', that is whether the best mode of delivery is a linear sequence focusing on the aspect of content or whether that aspect should be met in a variety of contexts. This is particularly true, for instance, of information technology, knowledge about language, knowledge about self and aspects of communication. This tension has an especial pastoral aspect.

Table 8.1

Curriculum planning divisions	*Statutory sources including NC 'subjects'*
1 Information-handling skills	English
2 Information technology	Technology
3 Language	
Knowledge about language	English and Modern languages
Languages other than English	Modern languages
Reading	English and history
Oracy	English and modern languages
Writing	English + others
4 Mathematics	Mathematics
5 Science	Science
6 History	History (+ English and Arts)
7 Arts	
Culture	English, PE, Art, Music
Art	Art
Dance	Physical education
Literature	English
Drama	English
Music	Music
Media	English and art
8 Craft, design and technology	Technology and art
9 Environment	
Geography	Geography
The natural environment	Geography and science
The built environment	Technology and art
10 Economic awareness	
11 Physical development & games	Physical education
12 Health	Physical education and Science
13 Religion	(Section 8 of 1988 & SACRE)
14 Sexuality	(Section 44 of 1986 Act)
15 Occupations	
16 Organizations	
17 Citizenship	
18 Decision-making	

(North Westminster Community School)

People have thought of 'subjects' as the main, indeed in some schools the only, mode of delivery. I prefer a fourfold division: the environment, the communal life of the school, the tutorial programme and the courses. For instance, the displays and the planned exhibitions in a school, as well as the experiences which its aesthetic and practical environment offers, actually teach. How can interpersonal relationships be properly taught without the environment to encourage them, and how much better they can be taught if there are exhibitions of works of art to illuminate some aspects. The aesthetic environment relates to the interpersonal understanding.

The communal life of the school includes assemblies, specially arranged events, interrelationship with the local community and such activities as collecting for charities. The tutorial programme must have its own content, as well as supporting the courses. Finally, the courses themselves must have their content so planned that they are not myopic. For instance, from a pastoral point of view the course on science should include what scientists are, the course on languages what linguists do, and the course on English include interpersonal communication. An aspect like sexuality is likely to be included in arts courses, literature courses, science courses and the tutorial programme. 'Facts about' are necessary to underpin guidance and counselling. For instance, the relationship of health education to pastoral care is illustrated by the fact that over five times as many girls as boys are referred to professionals after reporting instances of sexual abuse. However, confidential interviews with adults found that three times as many men had been abused when boys as had reported it at the time. Why are all those boys keeping it to themselves?

Of course, the effects of the location of content in the four modes are very important, and many aspects of content require an 'integrative centre' (Marland, 1989) to assist a pupil's bringing together. This is true of aspects of health education, information-handling skills and understanding of self.

The crucial tension of curriculum planning is to balance breadth and variety on the one hand with depth and specialism on the other. It is important to plan a coherent school curriculum derived from its aims, incorporating the National Curriculum requirements, through a series of whole-school policies, expressed in specific planning division content lists. Some content will be specifically delivered and some contextualized. The pastoral impact demands a subtle complementary balance. Time spent on those aspects is richly rewarded when it comes to distribution into delivery modes.

THE STATUTORY BASIS OF CURRICULUM PLANNING

Since the legislation of 1986, 1988, and 1993 it is now clear where power and control lies: the headteacher is responsible to the governors 'for the determination and organisation of the secular curriculum' (Education (no. 2) Act, 1986, 18 (5)), against the governors' acceptance or modification of the Local Education Authority curriculum policy and against the broad criteria of section 1 of the Education Reform Act, 1988, and the detailed 'building regulations' of section 2 – the National Curriculum requirements.

Governors are now the node of power in curriculum planning, with their duties laid down in the Education (no 2) Act, 1986. The LEA is obliged to formulate a 'curriculum policy' under section 17 of that Act. The governors then have to 'consider' that, but they have power to 'modify' and the very important curriculum duty to establish the school's aims:

> The articles of government for every county, controlled and maintained special school shall provide for it to be the duty of the governing body to consider –
>
> (a) the policy of the local education authority as to the secular curriculum for the authority's schools, as expressed in the statement made by the authority under section 17 of this Act;

(b) what, in their opinion, should be the aims of the secular curriculum for the school; and

(c) how (if at all) the authority's policy with regard to matters other than sex education should in their opinion be modified in relation to the school; and to make, and keep up to date, a written statement of their conclusions.

(Education (no. 2) Act, 1986), section 18 (1))

The governors must 'have regard to any representations which are made to them ... by any persons connected with the community served by the school and ... by the chief officer of police' (*ibid.*, (3)).

Despite the weight and detail of the National Curriculum requirements arising from section 2 of the Education Reform Act, 1988, they are only the national regulations against which the *school* curriculum has to be planned. They limit freedom but do not take away the Head's responsibility for the school to devise its own curriculum:

The articles of government for every such school shall provide for the determination and organisation of the secular curriculum for the school to be the responsibility of the head teacher and for it to be his duty to secure that that curriculum is followed within the school.

(Education (no. 2) Act 1986, section 18 (5))

There are, however, two components, both of which have especial importance to personal-social education and pastoral care, which have a different legislative basis.

'Religious education' has been required since 1944 but the Education Reform Act 're-enacts and reinforces this requirement' (DES Circular 3/89, para. 19). The school's content has to meet the requirements of the local SACRE (Standing Advisory Committee on Religious Education) syllabus, but, again, the timing and mode of delivery can be the school's shaping. Although the SACRE control of the religious education aspect is considerable, it is meant to have a local flavour and focus, and is amenable to the school's influence, especially that of the parents.

'Sex education' is the other exception. The main legislative requirement is that every school must include sex education, but that parents have a right to withdraw their child (Education Act, 1993). Further, sex education should be 'given in such a manner as to encourage those pupils to have due regard to moral considerations and the value of family life' (Education (no. 2) Act, 1986, section 46). Of course, Section 1(b) of the 1988 legislation also remains an overriding requirement (cf. p. 106) and it strengthens the pastoral aspects of sex education.

The components of both religious education and sex education, it will be seen, can be shaped to support the *school's* aims, to blend into its curriculum, and support its pastoral care.

As if to pre-empt the common misunderstanding that the Education Reform Act, 1988, the DES, or the Secretary of State are controlling the totality, shape, style, or delivery pattern of a school's curriculum, there is, in the Act itself, a firm denial of the Secretary of State's right to control anything other than the definition of the National Curriculum components:

(3) An order made under subsection (2) above may not require –

(a) that any particular period or periods of time should be allocated during any key stage to the teaching of any programme of study or any matter, skill or process forming part of it; or

(b) that provision of any particular kind should be made in school timetables for the periods to be allocated to such teaching during any such stage.

(1988, section 4, para. (3))

Each School is thus required from its aims to develop its own curriculum, and has to incorporate the National Curriculum content. However, the scope for variety and a school's own content and shaping is very great indeed.

BRITISH POSTWAR CURRICULUM HISTORY

The weakest aspect of British secondary schools has long been their overall curriculum planning, and that has undermined equality of opportunity and pastoral care. This is not a comfortable claim, and many, with memories of their hard work in syllabus planning and class preparation, resent it. However, any study shows that we have run schools by curriculum presumption: it appeared obvious what pupils should learn and the debate focused on method rather than content. The listing of accepted 'subjects' was all that was required to define 'the curriculum' of a school. Then heads of departments were appointed and they and their 'subject teachers' decided what should be taught under those agreed labels and also its pedagogy.

In the United Kingdom, there was a major realignment of the dispersal of power and decision-making in the schooling systems at the start of the 1990s, and much misunderstanding and mistrust resulted from the changes, rapidly devised and even more rapidly implemented.

The underlying weakness of immediate postwar British legislation, the Education Act, 1944, was that it confused the location of power. The classic textbook phrase was that Britain has had 'a national education system locally administered'. However, this disguised more than it revealed. The attempts in 1944 to set up a postwar education system that would produce a measure of equality omitted who was going to control which aspects. At a time when many teachers are complaining that there is too much central control that has resulted from the legislation of 1988, it is worth remembering that during the war years central government were determined to increase the degree of central control, with the secretary of the central government's Board of Education declaring that before the war the Board of Education was 'too inclined to follow and insufficient to lead'. The Education Act, 1944 gave the 'direction' of education to the Minister for Education – where the prewar phrase had only been 'the superintendence'. In the 1940s far greater central control was planned for the postwar reconstruction. This was not to be so.

The resulting legislation in 1944 had a number of aspects which were admirable, including especially free secondary education for all, but in it were the germs of later problems, including those of today. First, the separation of secondary schools into grammar, secondary modern and technical – a division of children which parents were never fully going to accept, and above all a division of the curriculum between those children that was to continue to cause trouble and still does today. Second, the location in section 23 of the Act of the 'Control of secular curriculum' in the newly-created local education authorities. In fact that control was barely exercised, and even the most energetic and dogmatic education authorities endeavoured to work only by exhortation and influence, and hardly by anything that can be called 'control'. What was singularly missing was an attempt to clarify the content of the curriculum or to establish a clear relationship between the wishes of parents and the control of education.

From the 1950s to the 1980s the underlying question in education was 'Who decides what?' Whenever anyone endeavoured to ask questions or influence schools, the person to whom they addressed the question always said that she or he did not have the power of making that decision – power always lay elsewhere. This was frustrating to all – especially parents: headteachers, when challenged about any aspect of the work of their schools, could always blame 'them' outside the school.

Much of the talk in England and Wales in the early 1990s was of 'the National Curriculum'. In fact, whilst the requirements of the curriculum content described under that title are massive, this is an inaccurate way of looking at British curriculum planning now. To understand the new established dispersal of powers we have to look back.

By the end of the 1950s there were serious doubts about the existing curriculum in all schools. The comprehensive school had come about partly as a result of pressure against the differentiated curriculum of the secondary modern school: no foreign language, very little science. The present concept of the 'core curriculum' came about partly from the pressure of parents of children in the early comprehensive schools against the similarly differentiated 'streams': 'academic', 'general', 'practical' were, for instance, used as labels for the groups of pupils in some comprehensive schools.

In 1962, the DES established study groups for the curriculum in the hope of influencing schools, but the Association of Education Committees argued against what it feared as the growth in ministerial control. The following summer, the teachers' unions and LEAs met, with the Minister of Education in the chair. The key DES officer, Derek Morrell, and Lord Alexander, the chair of the AEC, between them devised what became the Schools Council. The Schools Council funded a number of excellent projects, and had some influence, but it did not lead to full curriculum planning in LEAs or most schools. Further, its strict and narrow interpretation of 'curriculum' rigorously kept out any consideration of pastoral care.

It became clear by the early 1980s that LEA curriculum direction had failed. A select committee of the House of Commons, chaired by the Labour MP Christopher Price, reported about responsibility for the curriculum:

In our experience the extent of passing powers and the responsibilities down the line in education frequently makes it very difficult for the ordinary citizen to know just who is held responsible for many parts of the system, and this is perhaps especially true of the curriculum. There is, too, a disturbing tendency in a devolved system for necessary action to be shrugged off and passed backwards and forwards because none will readily own up to being responsible for action.

(DES, 1981)

The Select Committee argued that a national consensus should lead to a right 'for all children in all schools and not some children in some schools'. HMI were also arguing for 'an entitlement curriculum'.

Out of widespread confusion about who was responsible, and much dissatisfaction with the offer of many schools, came the requirements of the 1988 Act that the school curriculum should be one that is:

a balanced and broadly based curriculum which –

(a) promotes the spiritual, moral, cultural, mental and physical development of pupils at the school and of society; and

(b) prepares such pupils for the opportunities, responsibilities and experiences of adult life.

(1988, para. 2)

This over-arching pair of requirements, which are legally prior to the National Curriculum requirements, could have been drafted by a pastoral care enthusiast. Indeed (*b*) is virtually a succinct statement of the central aims of pastoral care.

This is made stronger and more *pastorally* orientated than the 1944 definition by adding 'cultural' and by the whole of (*b*) (cf. Education Act, 1944, section 7). The DES's own commentary to Members of Parliament at the time of the debates spells out this subsection (2)(*b*) and uses phrases directly leading to PSE and pastoral care: '"Adult life" embraces all aspects of adult experiences – home life, employment, citizenship and social responsibility, etc.' (DES, 1987, p. 2). Paragraph 2 is the springboard for the 1988 Act and the planning of a school's curriculum and cannot be conscientiously attempted without pastoral care and PSE.

The curriculum content for pastoral care was further spelt out by HMI in an overview:

Personal and social education is concerned with qualities and attitudes, knowledge and understanding, and abilities and skills in relation to oneself and others, social responsibilities and morality. It helps pupils to be considerate and enterprising in the present, while it prepares them for an informed and active involvement in family, social, economic and civil life. It plays an important part in bringing relevance, breadth and balance to the curriculum.

(HMI, 1989, p. 1)

Then, and only then, in section 2 is the demand that the minimum content of the 'National Curriculum' should be incorporated. The school curriculum must incorporate the contents of the National Curriculum 'core and foundation subjects' as defined by Statutory Order.

After the general preamble of section 1, which sets out the criteria against which each school has to judge its overall curriculum, the Act requires religious education and a set of compulsory 'subjects'. The 'core' subjects are mathematics, English and science. The other 'foundation' subjects are history, geography, technology and physical education at all stages; up to the end of key stage 3, music, art; and for pupils in key stages 3 and 4, a modern foreign language.

Most importantly, the DES specifies that more than this is required, and that there is a form of statutory obligation for 'cross-curriculum' issues and other 'subjects'. The DES's own statement is the clearest way to see this:

Cross-Curricular Issues and Other Subjects
3.8 The foundation subjects are certainly not a complete curriculum; they are necessary but not sufficient to ensure a curriculum which meets the purposes and covers the elements identified by HMI and others. In particular, they will cover fully the acquisition of certain key cross-curricular competences: literacy, numeracy and information technology skills. More will, however, be needed to secure the kind of curriculum required by section 1 of the ERA (see paragraphs 2.1–2.2). The whole curriculum for all pupils will certainly need to include in appropriate (and in some cases all) stages:

- careers education and guidance;
- health education;
- other aspects of personal and social education; and
- coverage across the curriculum of gender and multi-cultural issues.

These areas of the curriculum are not separately identified as part of the statutory National Curriculum because all the requirements associated with foundation subjects could not appropriately be applied to them in all respects. But they are clearly requirements in the curriculum which all pupils are entitled to by virtue of section 1 of the Act. A great deal of learning related to these themes can and should be covered for all pupils in the context of the foundation subjects, and some elements will certainly be contained in the attainment targets and programmes of study.

(DES, 1989b, para. 3.8)

Some of those aspects of education, such as multi-cultural education and personal and social education, which are slowly being established in schools but which many feared the Act would prevent, are therefore, made virtually obligatory.

In today's dispensation the curriculum system is school-based, incorporating national elements, planned against national criteria, and judged externally by the Office for Standards in Education (Ofsted). Compare the work of an architect. If we were architects commissioned to design a building, there would be minimum space specifications, minimum safety specifications and various facilities required by national 'building regulations' – but style, the interrelationship, the layout, the ambience and the way of meeting the needs of the users would be devised by the architects themselves in conjunction with their clients.

It is interesting that some of the more vulnerable aspects of the curriculum could be given more emphasis since 1988 than before, especially personal and social education and the arts. Whilst art and music are not compulsory for 15- and 16-year-olds, there is a greater emphasis than before, and even dance has a stronger position than before until the end of key stage 3. As in the 1980s only 8 per cent of 12-year-old boys had access to dance, this will be a step forward. The proper place of these affective subjects has important pastoral implications.

Especially important from the pastoral point of view is the DES's interpretation of 'cultural' and of preparation for the 'opportunities, responsibilities and experiences of adult life' in its Circular, insisting on 'diversity':

> This restates and extends the list of central purposes for the curriculum in section 7 of the 1944 Act, in particular, it emphasises the need for breadth and balance in what pupils study, and that cultural development and the development of society should be promoted. It is intended that the curriculum should reflect the culturally diverse society to which pupils belong and of which they will become adult members. It should benefit them as they grow in maturity and help to prepare them for adult life and experience – home life and parenthood; responsibilities as a citizen towards the community and society nationally and internationally; enterprise, employment and other work.
>
> (DES, 1989b, p. 7)

Thus, theoretically at least, the curriculum will not be legal unless the school can demonstrate that societal and cultural diversity is properly prepared for. Certainly many of the National Curriculum descriptions of content are admirably diverse – such as technology, requiring the study of design forms of other cultures; English, including the reading of literature from other cultures; and the arts, having a cultural diversity built into them.

CURRICULUM CONTENT AND PASTORAL CARE

In the years that pastoral care stood aside from the curriculum, the content of the latter appeared almost irrelevant to the achievements of the former. In fact the core of pastoral care requires growth in skills, concepts and knowledge. In the sixteenth century an early description of the core of the pastoral content of the curriculum was set out by the French philosopher Michel de Montaigne:

> Teach the [child] ... what principles govern our emotions and the physiology of so many and diverse stirrings within us. For it seems to me that the first lessons with which we should irrigate his mind should be those which teach him to know himself.
>
> (Montaigne, 1991, p. 178)

A school's curriculum should have this as its heart. Indeed modern research could be seen as expanding on Montaigne.

A range of specialist studies from the fields of health education, child psychology and psychiatry, cultural and racial interaction, information-handling and gender has shown the possibilities and importance of helping young people develop their sense of themselves and their skills as 'life managers' (the Grubb Institute's phrase). What these studies have shown us is the relationship between behaviours and self-esteem, decision-making skills and self-understanding. In particular they have demonstrated the inadequacy of 'facts about' a topic to influence behaviour. So powerful is the peer group for the adolescent that it penetrates, or distantly controls, even the intimate and private activities of sex. We must mobilize the group, and free the individual from the dominance of the group.

Dr Linda Del Greco of Bridgewater State College in Massachusetts has documented the numerous studies showing that 'susceptibility to peer pressure and conformity were highly correlated with the initiation and continuation of cigarette smoking' (Del Greco, 1980, p. 80). (There are similar pressures with sexual behaviour.) She concludes:

> Adolescents, therefore, need to be equipped with skills that will permit them to express their own desires and beliefs. Since the peer group is essential to the adolescent's lifestyle, it is imperative that adolescents learn how to express themselves, follow their own convictions ... and yet not alienate themselves from their peer group.
>
> (Del Greco, 1980)

Most research workers have shown that 'shock-horror tactics are unlikely to work'. The studies of American and Canadian drug and substance-abuse programmes and of smoking-prevention programmes reveal that to be effective such programmes must teach an adolescent freedom of thought, expression and action without alienation from the peer group. Del Greco goes on to argue that the teaching of assertiveness satisfies both criteria and is the best way to fight smoking. Similarly, the American researcher Botvin shows that while US knowledge-based programmes succeed in changing students' knowledge and attitudes about cigarette smoking, they have little impact on actual smoking behaviour: 'Apparently knowledge and attitudes of the dangers of cigarette smoking in itself is not a deterrent for most students' (Botvin *et al.*, 1980, p. 140). His New York study of fourth and sixth formers concluded that 'any increases in smoking knowledge played only a minor role in reducing the incidence of new smoking'.

What then does work? The most likely means of enabling young people to make their own decisions includes not only knowledge or fear. We need to remind ourselves that the task of being able to use that information for making personal decisions is not necessarily inherent in being taught and learning the facts. A programme that works will help young people to think, to talk, to communicate, to feel proud, to trust and to have faith in themselves. The most difficult part is to enable students to have their own freedom of thought and decision-making without alienation from the peer-group (Eiser *et al.*, 1988).

This example can be generalized to other aspects of personal, social, educational and vocational guidance. HIV-related behaviour is a well-researched recent example. Thus the planning of a *school's* curriculum from aims, through policies and planning divisions, to delivery modes should have pastoral components built in as an integral aspect from the first.

CONCLUSION

The burden and the stresses of external demands on schools need not be allowed to mask the essential truths of curriculum planning from the pastoral point of view: the school is the centre of power for curriculum planning against national criteria; the curriculum distribution is entirely the school's decisions; and the curriculum as a whole must be shown to be meeting section 1, para. 2: meeting the needs of 'the opportunities, experience, and responsibilities of adult life'. *There* is the pastoral burden of the central curriculum criteria. There is the statutory justification of building pastoral care into the curriculum.

REFERENCES AND FURTHER READING

Botvin, G., Eng, A. and Williams, C. (1980) Preventing the onset of cigarette smoking through life skills training. *Preventive Medicine*, **9**, 135–43.

Del Greco, L. (1980), Assertiveness training for adolescents: a potentially useful tool in the prevention of cigarette smoking. *Health Education Journal*, **39**(5a part 3), 80–3.

Department of Education and Science (1981) *Select Committee on Education Report*. London: HMSO.

Department of Education and Science (1987) *Education Reform Bill, Notes on Clauses (Commons)*. London: DES.

Department of Education and Science (1989a) *Education Reform Act 1988: Religious Education and Collective Worship* (Circular 3/89). London: DES.

Department of Education and Science (1989b) *Education Reform Act 1988: The School Curriculum and Assessment* (Circular 5/89). London: HMSO.

Department of Education and Science (1989c) *From Policy to Practice*. London: DES.

Education Act 1944. London: HMSO.

Education (no 2) Act, 1986. London: HMSO.

Education Reform Act, 1988. London: HMSO.

Education Act, 1993. London: HMSO.

Eiser, J. R., Morgan, M. and Gammage, P. (1988) Social education is good for health. *Education Research*, **30**(1), 20–5.

HMI (1989) *Personal and Social Education from 5 to 16. Curriculum Matters 14*. London: HMSO.

Macbeth, A. (1989) *Involving Parents*. London: Heinemann.

Marland, M. (1974) *Pastoral Care*. London: Heinemann.

Marland, M. (1980) The pastoral curriculum. In Best. R., Jarvis, C. and Ribbins, P. (eds) *Perspectives on Pastoral Care*. London: Heinemann.

Marland, M. (1989) *The Tutor and the Tutor Group*. Harlow: Longman.

Montaigne, M. de (1991) *The Complete Essays*, trans. Screech, M. A. London: Allen Lane.

National Curriculum Council (1989) *Interim Report on Cross-Curricular Issues*. York: NCC.

Runnymede Trust (1993) *Equality Assurance*. Stoke on Trent: Trentham Books for Runnymede Trust.

Watkins, C. (1989) *Whole-School Policies for Personal-Social Education: The Ingredients and the Processes*. Warwick: NAPCE.

CHAPTER 9

Personal-social education and the whole curriculum

Chris Watkins

INTRODUCTION

In this chapter I offer a brief review of some of the changes which have affected personal-social education in the late 1980s and early 1990s in English (and to a lesser extent Welsh) secondary schools. I then propose some concepts and practices which may support further development in the next period. In particular I shall be taking a 'whole-curriculum' view of personal-social education – a term which I aim to clarify.

WHOLE CURRICULUM STARTING POINTS

I take PSE to mean the intentional promotion of the personal and social development of pupils through the whole curriculum and the whole school experience. It is immediately clear that this definition is not simply referring to timetabled courses labelled personal and social education (or any of the other various titles which have been used).

The late 1980s proved an important time for PSE in many schools in that the notion that a timetabled course was sufficient provision for this aspect of learning came increasingly under question and increasingly lacked credibility. The 'ghettoization' of PSE courses was a common concern (Brown, 1990), as was the mismatch which could be found between the content and aims of such courses and the pupils' experience in the rest of school. Sometimes proactive PSE courses came up against reactive schools, on other occasions schools which were trying to be empowering came up against PSE courses which seemed controlling and negative in style.

Moves beyond PSE as solely a timetabled course have been tackled in a variety of ways, the best of which placed the contribution of specialist courses in the context of broader planning. This is one aspect of a whole curriculum view, and is in contrast with the minimalist view that whole curriculum means 'through the subjects'. Evidence is now more available of the benefits of a PSE course in the total provision (see Appendix 2 on the value of pastoral care and PSE).

There has also developed, in some schools but not all, a more effective view of the role of the tutorial, again within a whole-school picture. Earlier use of terms such as 'pastoral curriculum' had been criticized as divisive. Even when the term was used in a wide sense (Bulman and Jenkins, 1989), it was suggested that the term *necessarily* implied a divided system of pastoral care in schools. The phrase 'pastoral aspects of the curriculum' was sometimes more useful. However, ways of describing or analysing the interrelation between pastoral care and PSE were not available: one view (Watkins, 1985), seemed (judging by the number of references made to it) to identify this gap, and perhaps to go some way to filling it.

THE TERM PSE: CHANGING USE

In some ways the 1980s have seen the meaning of the term 'personal and social education' change. Donovan (1989) suggested that there were still a few schools operating the underlying notion that PSE was for lower ability pupils who would be following a non-exam timetable in their fourth and fifth years of school. There are still schools which seem capable only of viewing PSE as a timetabled course where a notional 'team' of colleagues is burdened with all the anxiety-provoking, personally demanding and controversial issues. More often the English secondary school seems to have accepted the place of both timetabled and broader personal-social considerations for all pupils.

PSE has not always had a good name: a new tutor in an inner London school once said to me, 'I know what PSE stands for – perfectly sordid experience'. In a context where small periods of a pupil's timetable were characterized by 'Death by 1,000 worksheets' (and of the personally intrusive variety), I could see the point she was making.

Perhaps it was these sorts of distortions, and the wish to distance from them, which led to attempts in some quarters to use a different term – PSD, personal-social development. This happened in some projects funded by the Technical and Vocational Education Initiative (TVEI). Teachers forged a number of important achievements under this banner in the 1980s, not least an increasingly open discussion of teaching approaches, more negotiated learning, and the development of records of achievement. However, at worst the term PSD put at risk the notion of pupils' entitlement, as it could be read to imply that an educational programme was not necessary to promote such development.

Terms have also been used which give an extra highlight to *one aspect* of PSE: examples include PSHE (personal, social and health education), PSME (personal, social and moral education) and SPACE (social, personal and careers education). This may reflect the specialist background of the innovative staff in PSE. But it is common to find health educators who do not see their connections with careers educators, and vice versa. I prefer a unifying term rather than a partisan one. I have also chosen to use the phrase personal-social education (with the hyphen) in order to show the redundancy of the 'and' which is commonly used: it seems to me that you cannot have personal education without it being social, nor social education without it being personal.

Statements regarding personal-social education have rarely been found in central government views of the curriculum, but the way government addresses the curriculum has a major effect on PSE at the local level. The

1944 Education Act lacked any detailed statement about the school curriculum: this attracted central government interest in the 1970s and took a changing course culminating in the Education Act of 1988. It is to that which we now turn.

PSE AND THE DEVELOPMENT OF THE NATIONAL CURRICULUM: A BRIEF REVIEW

A major issue which has been affecting PSE in the late 1980s has been the development of the National Curriculum. It is worth recording some of the events which are not generally known or are too often forgotten.

In 1985 the government White Paper *Better Schools* said: 'The Secretaries of State's policies for the range and pattern of the 5 to 16 curriculum will not lead to national syllabuses. Diversity at local education authority and school level is healthy, accords well with the English and Welsh tradition of school education, and makes for liveliness and innovation' (p. 4). In the summer vacation of 1987 the same government published a 'consultation document' (DES, 1987c) which took the opposite approach and outlined a national curriculum composed of a string of traditional school subjects and percentages of time allocated to them. It is reported that seventeen van-loads of responses arrived at the DES, most of which questioned the lack of reference to personal-social education. A minor DES publication (DES, 1987a) followed up with a minor reference to personal-social education, but this portrayed it as 'another topic' alongside the core and foundation subjects.

In the detailed specification of core and foundation subjects, each working group was given guidance that it should specify how the subject contributed to 'the development of personal-social qualities ... for example self-reliance, self-discipline, a spirit of enterprise, a sense of social responsibility, the ability to work harmoniously with others' (DES, 1987b, p. 4). However, it was clear that this would not be a major priority, nor would there be a co-ordinated approach across subject working groups. Simple attempts to assess 'personal qualities', as were contained in the first report of the mathematics working party, showed the age-old difficulties of measurement in this area, were not credible or face valid, and were removed.

Attention then became focused on the NCC 'Interim Whole Curriculum Committee' which was asked to 'give early consideration to the nature and place of cross-curricular issues, in particular personal and social education'. It made an interim report to the Secretary of State in April 1989 which was not published. Important points from that report included:

- Personal and social education (PSE) is arguably the most important of the cross-curricular dimensions to which schools need to give attention. PSE can be seen as the promotion of the personal and social development of pupils through the school curriculum. It is concerned with fundamental educational aims and permeates the whole curriculum. It should be the responsibility of the teachers and a priority for school management.

- Personal and social education, in its broad sense, is part of every pupil's entitlement to a curriculum which promotes the purposes of education laid down by the Act. No component of the school curriculum is without its potential influence on personal and social development.
- Schools will need to develop an explicit whole school policy for PSE ... It should make clear that all teachers are responsible for promoting the personal and social development of pupils in their care.
- In key stages 3 and 4 it must be part of a school's policy to supplement curriculum-wide PSE provision with allocations of time for PSE objectives not adequately met elsewhere.
- In key stages 3 and 4 a guidance and support structure for pupils should be a central feature of school policy. Each pupil should relate personally to one tutor who is responsible for overseeing his or her individual welfare and progress. The role of guidance should be to help pupils to discuss, agree and review programmes of work, and to plan pathways towards future careers. Guidance is an integral part of each pupil's experience in school, not just provision for when things go wrong.

(National Curriculum Council, 1989a, paras 4.1, 4.3, 4.5, 4.7)

These were important statements, and readers looked for them to be followed up. But the report remained unpublished. The Chairman and Chief Executive of the National Curriculum Council describes the pressure from the Department of Education and Science against working on matters of the whole curriculum, in the form of a letter from the Minister telling NCC to abandon such work (Graham, 1993, p. 20). Recognizing that many schools wanted to hear an answer to the question 'Where's PSE?', NCC published extracts of the Whole Curriculum Committee report themselves (*NCC News*, June 1989).

October 1989 saw the publication of NCC Circular 6 (National Curriculum Council, 1989b), *The National Curriculum and Whole Curriculum Planning*, which included the following:

To achieve these whole curriculum aims, schools need to ensure that the planned contribution of different subjects is not made in isolation but in the light of their contribution to pupils' learning as a whole.

(para. 7)

Personal and social development through the curriculum cannot be left to chance but needs to be coordinated as an explicit part of a school's whole curriculum policy, both inside and outside the formal timetable. Personal and social development involves aspects of teaching and learning which should permeate all of the curriculum. Whilst secondary schools may offer courses of personal and social education, it is the responsibility of all teachers and is equally important in all phases of education.

All teachers recognize their responsibility for promoting the personal and social development of their pupils. This can be assisted by giving priority to making links between what they teach and what their pupils learn at other times and in other parts of the curriculum. They should have a clear view of how their teaching contributes to the whole curriculum experience of their pupils.

The introduction of the National Curriculum provides a new opportunity to promote these links. Attainment targets and programmes of study are the bricks with which the new curriculum must be built. Cross-curricular strategies bond these bricks into a cohesive structure.

(paras 10, 18, 19)

The above-quoted publications demonstrated the view adopted by the Council at that time, that PSE courses were not to disappear, nor was everything going to be incorporated into core and foundation subjects, but that a more whole-school approach would be needed. However the detail was not clearly spelled out, and a confusion was born between the phrases 'whole curriculum' and 'cross-curriculum'.

Further guidance on the whole curriculum was promised, and in 1990 a very slim, uninspiring document was published (National Curriculum Council, 1990c). This lacked any overall model of the curriculum, and became another of the weak English publications in this area (Lord, 1986; Schools Council, 1975). The disappointment was further compounded by the fact that the first guidance document on 'cross-curricular themes' was published at the same time: *Economic and Industrial Understanding* (which had been moved up the list of themes and hurried in its production to be published at the same time) was fatter, glossier, and contained colour photos (as well as a narrow conception of economic and industrial understanding). The message was that a particular set of cross-curricular themes was to be given prominence, thereby increasing the possibility of fragmenting whole curriculum matters such as PSE.

Originally the Whole Curriculum Committee had made some effective distinctions between cross-curricular dimensions, themes and skills. Cross-curricular *dimensions* were stated as:

- personal and social education;
- equal opportunities;
- multicultural education.

(National Curriculum Council, 1989a, para. 1.3)

These were described as 'interwoven in the curriculum, both formal and informal' (National Curriculum Council, 1989a, para. 1.3), whereas *examples* of cross-curricular *themes* had been listed as:

- health education;
- environmental education;
- economic and industrial understanding.

Their defining feature was 'a strong component of knowledge and understanding, in addition to skills'. They were said to be 'less pervasive than the cross-curricular dimensions' (National Curriculum Council, 1989a, para. 1.3).

By 1990 there were five themes:

- economic and industrial understanding;
- careers education and guidance;
- health education;
- education for citizenship;

- environmental education.

(National Curriculum Council, 1990c, pp. 4–6).

The rationale for the choice of the above five 'themes', and for their separation, was not made clear: it was merely claimed that 'although by no means a conclusive list, [they] seem to most people to be pre-eminent' (National Curriculum Council, 1990c, p. 4). They soon passed from 'examples' to what many schools took as a complete set. This is particularly interesting in the light of an earlier unpublished draft of the guidance on whole curriculum which included the following list of cross-curricular themes:

- economic and industrial understanding;
- careers education and guidance;
- health;
- citizenship;
- environmental education;
- information technology;
- media education;
- family studies;
- leisure;

followed by the comment 'This list is not exhaustive but gives an indication of the variety of themes in which schools have been interested'.

The status of these themes is still misunderstood. Some have regarded cross-curricular themes as a basic entitlement. This is not the NCC view: consultants drafting the guidance on themes have told me that on several occasions they were told not to use the word 'entitlement' – the last use of this important term was in the 1989 report on the place of PSE.

It is distressing that teachers do not critically examine the 'provenance' of the guidance in these NCC publications. One consultant is reported to have been instructed to take all the adjectives out of a draft. The guidance on 'citizenship' is reported to have been written by three members of the NCC after the final draft from the working group had been thrown out.

The creation of the English five themes has not met with acceptance elsewhere. In Wales a cross-curricular theme of community understanding has been substituted (Curriculum Council for Wales, 1992). In Northern Ireland the cross-curricular themes start with education for mutual understanding, and cultural heritage (Northern Ireland Curriculum Council, 1989). The focus on the five themes meant that further detailed attention to the development of dimensions was not forthcoming.

THE NATIONAL CURRICULUM IMPACT ON PSE

It is possible to view the above account with a range of feelings, from disappointment that PSE has not achieved the status of national prescription, to elation that it avoided the clutches of an alien and illiberal form of control. Whatever the feelings about National Curriculum developments from 1988 to 1993, the impact on PSE can be evaluated under four headings:

- the effects of subject-based testing;
- the weakness of whole-curriculum guidance;
- the status of 'cross-curricular' elements;
- the status of aspects outside the National Curriculum framework.

The effects of subject-based testing

The main statutes in the Education Act of 1988 which specify the National Curriculum are not about curriculum, nor even about subjects: they are about testing. The assessment tail wags the curriculum dog.

The use of school subjects as the building blocks for the National Curriculum can be traced back to earlier years, when good teaching became equated with good subject teaching (Goodson, 1990). It is no coincidence that subject categorizations were chosen as the building blocks of a back-to-basics centralizing legislation. Despite their vague and arbitrary nature, school subjects are used for national paper and pencil tests. In this sense 'subjects' are controllable and controlling, in contrast to more person-centred goals for education.

A subject-based curriculum:

- treats subjects as though they were ends in themselves;
- becomes content-based to the exclusion of concepts and skills;
- does not cope with the enormous growth of knowledge and the demands for more economical ways of organizing it for the purposes of learning;
- draws arbitrary boundaries around subjects;
- may terminate worthwhile study that is not confined within subject areas;
- fails to make a link between subject matters, and hence one subject is not supported by another;
- leads to learning difficulties occurring when learners are switched from one subject area to another.

Such a curriculum with extensive national testing is in tension with the stated goals of the 1988 Education Act, to 'prepare pupils for the opportunities, responsibilities and experiences of adult life' (section 1(2)(a)). It is also in tension with views of employers who have suggested that subject-based study does not suit school leavers well (CBI, 1989, para. 57).

The general impact of subject testing on secondary schools in the period 1988 to 1993 has been:

- an understandable wish to get the statutory aspects of subject testing 'under their belts', a wish which was regularly frustrated by government changes of policy over the forms of assessment;
- a hardening of subject teaching boundaries in some schools, fuelled by accountability fears, despite the clear DES statement, 'The use of subjects to define the National Curriculum does not mean that teaching has to be organised and delivered within prescribed subject boundaries' (DES, 1989, para. 4.3);

- a concomitant reduction in cross-subject working (Hall (1992) refers to an NCC survey which showed evidence of this);
- at worst, infighting over the amount of timetabled time allocated to the subjects.

This despite the statement:

> The Secretary of State:
> – may not prescribe how much *time* should be spent on any programme of study
> – may not require particular ways of providing a subject in the school timetable
> – will not specify teaching methods or materials
> (National Curriculum Council, 1990a, sheet A6 referring to section 4, sub-sections 2 and 3 of the 1988 Act and DES Circular 5/89)

The particular impact of subject-based testing on PSE has been:

- that it is clear that PSE is not a government priority, and consequently
- that PSE development (as has been the case in the past) works from local starting points and develops a local character.

The weakness of whole-curriculum guidance

Given a National Curriculum composed of subjects, the government, DES and NCC were not also going to specify whole curriculum matters which might be seen to divert attention away from the subjects.

Ways of describing the whole curriculum have not advanced since the work developing from the HMI 'areas of experience' (HMI, 1983). Some LEAs have continued to use this approach in their advice to schools, and Scottish developments have taken a similar direction (Scottish Consultative Committee on the Curriculum, 1989). The body in Wales charged with implementing the National Curriculum made an important contribution. In its document *The Whole Curriculum 5–16* eight areas of experience are proposed as planning centres for the curriculum (Curriculum Council for Wales, 1991). By not giving primacy to subjects they appear to follow the Northern Ireland example (Northern Ireland Curriculum Council, 1989), which agreed six cross-curricular themes before specifying objectives in the context of subject teaching.

The overall impact of weak guidance in England has been to allow the fragmentation of subject treatment in the secondary school, and, in a time of coping with imposed change, most schools have not made innovations in their whole curriculum management.

The status of 'cross-curricular' elements

The phrase 'cross-curricular' is unclear in its meaning. The credibility of discussions using it is often compromised. Does it mean across the subjects of the National Curriculum? across the basic curriculum? across the whole curriculum? everywhere? dimensions or themes? and how does anyone decide what is 'across' and what is within? *What could a curriculum be such that some of it is across itself?*

The confusion could have been avoided if the original distinctions made by the NCC Whole Curriculum Committee (cited above) had been maintained, but in slightly different language, as follows.

For aspects of learning to which every occasion in school has a contribution to make (albeit sometimes unplanned), the term 'dimension' is meaningful. But (by definition) we are here talking about the whole curriculum. The examples of PSE, equal opportunities and multi-cultural education are good ones. Developing these dimensions requires active whole-school approaches and policies.

For areas of more specific knowledge, to which some subjects (particularly defined) make a partial contribution, 'themes' may be an appropriate term. Their development may be advanced by discussion and agreement between subject teaching teams.

Thus we have:

All locations	*whole-curriculum dimensions*	whole-school policy
Some locations	*inter-subject themes*	departmental agreements

In schools the impact of the NCC's 'cross-curricular guidance' varies. The influence of pieces of paper which are centrally published as guidance on the curriculum is as weak as it has ever been. It is frequently difficult to find these guidance publications in a particular school.

Schools adopted various strategies to the 'cross-curricular guidance'. Some failed to recognize that NCC guidance on cross-curricular themes is non-statutory (and therefore may be put to one side and replaced by something better) – sometimes because of the uninformed behaviour of inspectors and others who collude with or support the cry 'we have to do this now'. Some evidence suggests (Whitty *et al.*, 1993) that only 11 per cent of schools have adopted these five themes. Other schools examine the NCC publications alongside other such guidance, from LEAs and elsewhere.

At worst, schools have responded in a fragmented way, appointing for example a co-ordinator for each new theme, and attempting to plan in a haphazard way. One example I came across operated like this: identify all the possible learning objectives in all the NCC guidance booklets (I think it was 127); group these into a number of headings (around thirty); circulate these headings to subject departments asking if they 'do' any of them; departments which say they do become the 'lead departments' for that heading – end of problem. This fragmented response is perhaps not as alarming as the trivialized approach which allocates thirty-five minutes per week to a slot called 'cross-curricular work'!

Recent research (Whitty and Rowe, 1993; Whitty *et al.*, 1993) suggests that the different NCC themes are handled in different ways by schools. Those with a history and tradition (careers and health education) are often found in a timetabled PSE course. Environmental education is shared out between geography and science (a good example of the 'inter-subject theme' defined above). Education for industrial understanding is the most 'permeated' through a number of subjects, and citizenship is hard to find (in English secondary schools, that is – it does not apply in Wales, where 'community studies' is chosen).

Evidence is also starting to emerge that even the well-supported themes such as careers education are being squeezed from the timetable (NACGT and ICG, 1993).

The status of aspects outside the National Curriculum framework

In some cases it seemed to be forgotten that the National Curriculum is not everything. Notwithstanding the various NCC and DES statements, such as:

> The whole curriculum is broader than the basic curriculum. It includes:
>
> - provision beyond the basic curriculum (other subjects and extra-curricular activities)
> - cross-curricular elements
>
> (National Curriculum Council, 1990a)

some schools forgot that the National Curriculum indicated that it would take up about 70 per cent of pupil time (DES, 1987c, p. 7). Some LEAs have continued to remind schools of this, as has the Curriculum Council for Wales, proposing 15 per cent of pupil time for enrichment beyond the National Curriculum. But schools were led to believe the National Curriculum is everything by this very talk of percentages: what originated as some informal advice to subject working groups was exaggerated by the efforts of others including subject teaching associations, to the point that some people argued that the core and foundation would take 120 per cent of the time available. Such nonsense emanates from viewing the National Curriculum as specifying all of a subject and its time, contrary to the 1988 Act. NCC appeared to collude in this, and sailed very close to the wind in terms of the legal prohibition against specifying timetables when referring to percentages in Circular 10 (National Curriculum Council, 1990b), but described these as illustrations of what schools do, rather than NCC recommendations.

In the light of the four elements above, the overall picture shows important features of how schools vary:

- Some or many seem frightened and destabilized, acting to 'get things right' and forgetting their own professional judgement.
- Some have a non-reactive perspective, thinking about the various aspects of change, holding on to their existing confidence including that in PSE.
- Some have been stimulated to address PSE anew (to my knowledge this has included high-status independent schools).
- Most have recognized that they will not find central government support for PSE and will have to clarify their own purposes and practices in the area.

NATIONAL CURRICULUM – ANOTHER REVIEW

The review of the National Curriculum undertaken by Sir Ron Dearing (Dearing, 1993) has discussed some of the factors referred to above. The proposals, which were immediately accepted by government, are for a period of greater stability, for the excessive prescription of the National Curriculum to be removed, and a revised approach to assessment. The excessive content is related to the subject base: 'The Orders have, however, been devised individually and at different times by subject specialists who were naturally keen to see that their subject was well covered' (para. 3.14). Surely there is a parallel message here for all schools: devising a curriculum by starting with subject interests leads to distortion.

The clear message that the National Curriculum is not the whole curriculum is supported by the proposal to occupy 75–80 per cent of teaching time on statutory National Curriculum and religious education in the early years of secondary school, and a more flexible curriculum in the later years. As the report states, 'The time released by slimming down the statutorily prescribed content of curriculum would be used to [amongst others] cover issues such as health education and careers education' (para. 3.29).

I take the view that the Dearing proposals offer a breathing space for schools, in which they may take a more rational and less pressured look at their curriculum offer. The possibilities for improved whole-curriculum thinking are there, and they include giving attention to the personal-social dimension of the whole curriculum. The statement 'we can't run a PSE course because of the National Curriculum', which in my experience was more often anticipated than heard, and which was always a misattribution, is now more clearly erroneous.

Notwithstanding this window of opportunity, it would be unwise to ignore the changes on areas other than curriculum which government introduced in the period 1988–93. Whatever the developments in curriculum prescription and testing, the quality of school life is affected by other developments. It is in the climate of schools that we see change occurring. School climate may be difficult to assess, but it is fundamentally important in a discussion of personal-social education. In the 1990s I see examples of schools becoming more competitive, both within themselves and in their stance towards others, more parochial in their goals and their view of their role, and less accepting, as shown through the increasing number of exclusions, for example. If this were the whole picture it would be extremely worrying. Perhaps it has always been the case that in poorly managed schools the needs of the institution take precedence over the needs of the pupils. Now the possible increase in some aspects of school autonomy raises the possibility of more schools taking on the characteristics of closed systems.

In the next period schools' approaches to PSE will doubtless continue to differ, and perhaps such differences will increase. But there will be a new opening for whole-curriculum considerations and for schools to clarify their provision in this area.

PUPILS' ENTITLEMENT IN PSE

Although many schools have accepted that they make a planned contribution in the area of personal-social education, it does not follow that they make an explicit statement of pupils' curriculum entitlement in this area.

In training events I ask teachers to examine such statements of entitlement as the following:

Pupils' personal-social entitlement

Pupils are entitled to respect, dignity and promotion of self-reliance; and knowledge, skills and understanding which help them to:

1 *maximize their academic achievement at school:*

- communication skills;
- skills of learning in classrooms;
- co-operative work;
- skills of managing study;
- reflection and review.

2 *maximize the use of their academic achievements after school:*

- skills of understanding themselves, their opportunities and their choices;
- personal-social skills, including skills of self-presentation;
- interpersonal skills for their future work and non-work contexts.

3 *maximize their contribution to and satisfactions from adult life:*

- maintain bodily health, psychological health and a healthy lifestyle;
- develop interpersonal relationships including intimate and sexual ones;
- understand social relations in family, work and community;
- promote positive relationships, identify and avoid negative relationships;
- skills of making moral judgements and developing appropriate action;
- understand democratic and political processes;
- skills in communicating ideas and opinions to influence social change;
- understand and respect the beliefs, faiths and cultures by which people interpret life and on which they base their behaviours;
- cope with change;
- combat prejudice.

An important feature of such statements is that they incorporate both *general* aspects, to which all teachers can imagine making a contribution, and *specific* aspects to which the teacher with some specialist training can make an extra contribution. This can be very important in moving past the view of PSE as all the difficult personal and controversial issues to do with sexuality, drugs, AIDS and so on (a portrayal which led many teaching colleagues to feel inadequate if support was not available), to a more balanced position where those highlighted issues take their place in the context of the broader themes of development and achievement.

The issue of the relation of PSE to 'academic achievement' is also made clear in such statements. This again can help to take us beyond the point where PSE is portrayed as something separate from (or even an antidote to) the school's proper concerns with achievement. Underlying these polarizations there sometimes lurks a very narrow view of how pupils achieve, that is by being 'taught at'. In general terms this sort of polarization has waned as schools become more effective at talking about effective teaching and learning. However, outside pressures such as those towards 'traditional methods' and 'learning the facts' sometimes cause it to resurface. This is despite the available evidence that co-operative learning enhances and does not reduce academic achievement. The most comprehensive research review of the effects of co-operative teaching approaches (Slavin, 1986) identified forty-five studies done between 1972 and 1986 investigating the effects of student team learning on achievement. Thirty-seven out of forty-five studies showed that student team learning classes significantly outperform control group classes in academic achievement. Eight studies found no differences. None showed negative effects for co-operative learning.

PUPILS', PARENTS' AND OTHERS' VIEWS OF NEEDS IN PSE

Pupils' views of their own needs in personal-social learning are gathered all too rarely it seems. This is a missed opportunity, as PSE can then degenerate into teachers suggesting the content and then cajoling pupils into it. Simple survey devices (such as the example in Watkins, 1991) can prove engaging and illuminating for younger pupils. A different style of eliciting concerns would be appropriate for more mature pupils, and equally important.

Some of the evidence of pupils' and parents' views gathered through cross-school research surveys is included in this volume – see Appendix 2, 'The value of pastoral care and PSE'.

Parents are not generally asked their view about PSE. However, even on those aspects which some wish to make the most 'controversial', parents are supportive. An important survey on sex education (Allen, 1987) demonstrated that 96 per cent of parents wanted sex education to take place in school. And on a more local level, I have been told about many occasions when teachers ran a parents' evening on PSE, using the methods and materials they normally would with pupils, and found enthusiastic support from parents, sometimes contrary to the teachers' own expectations.

The Confederation of British Industry (CBI, 1989) argued for a greater prominence for cross-curricular elements, careers education and guidance amounting to at least one period of teaching a week in years 9 to 11, and a higher prominence to core skills rather than subject knowledge:

- values and integrity;
- applications of numeracy;
- understanding of work and the world;
- problem-solving;
- effective communication;
- applications of technology;
- personal and interpersonal skills;
- positive attitudes to change.

It is interesting that these views were not obviously incorporated into national curriculum reforms of the late 1980s: it is important for each school to engage such views at a local level when reviewing and developing its curriculum.

DESCRIBING A CURRICULUM

I take the curriculum to mean the planned learning offer of the school. Describing a curriculum is then about key questions such as what learning should be offered, when, in what order, through which approaches, and so on. At a national level it may be difficult or impossible to achieve a consensus over such matters, so the categories of school subjects are used.

However, at the local school level there is real scope for describing the curriculum (see Marland, p. 107 above). It becomes possible with appropriate whole-school management to build a consensus on just these matters.

Developing the personal-social curriculum in a whole-school sense requires a statement to be agreed on the following aspects of the learning offer:

- goals in PSE
- the content of PSE: a cohering model
- locations for learning: a whole-school approach
- personal-social aspects of all classrooms
- teaching skills and methods

Each of these will now be discussed in turn.

Goals in PSE

Goals may be framed in a variety of ways with different results. It is important to discuss the goals in PSE in order to clarify what is really possible for the school to contribute in this area (Watkins, 1991), and to put aside the distortions which can arise. It is crucial to discuss how goals relate to the goals of the school, as the relation is often considerable. Schools have given increasing attention to their statements of goals: it is one element in increasing purposefulness and direction which can enhance PSE.

Goal statements in PSE link back to a view of entitlement. It can be valuable to consider statements such as:

- to develop rational thinking skills and critical faculties in order to make informed decisions;
- to promote responsible attitudes towards the maintenance of good health through an understanding of the factors leading to healthy lifestyles;
- to provide opportunities for the development of effective interpersonal relationships;
- to develop the ability to assimilate knowledge, to study independently and to have a positive attitude towards continued learning;
- to provide opportunities for students to develop skills in communicating ideas and opinions to influence social change;
- to provide an opportunity for students to understand and respect the beliefs, faiths and cultures by which people interpret life and on which they base their behaviours;
- to make sense of their present personal and social experience.

As a device for planning, goals statements are insufficient. Teachers plan their classrooms on the basis of content and activity. These need to be covered in some appropriate way.

The content of PSE: A cohering model

The days when PSE was described by its proponents as more importantly process than content are behind us. Teachers, pupils and parents want to know what it's about. Here the difficulty of phrasing arises which may

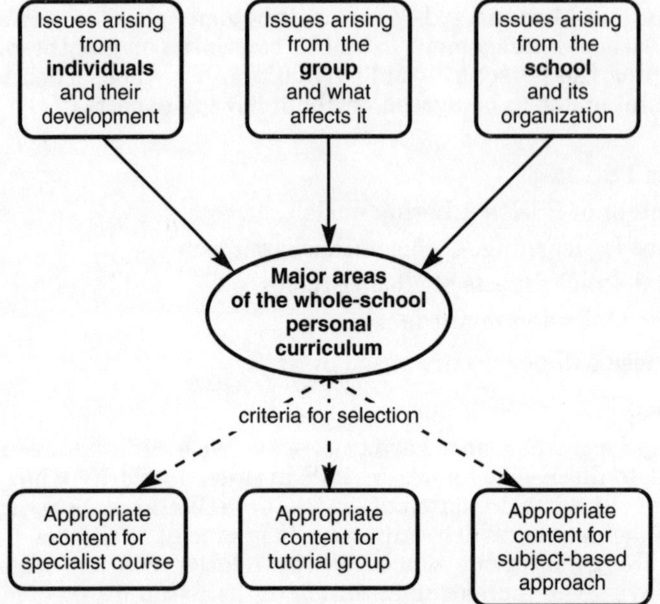

Figure 9.1 The sources and locations of the whole-school personal curriculum

explain those past references to process. The content of personal-social education is clearly not a set of testable facts or depersonalized knowledge. It does contain knowledge, of a more personal and open-ended sort than that which typically composes subjects. It also contains procedural knowledge, about how the social world works. The open-endedness may raise anxiety levels for some teachers, until they see what role the teacher plays in providing structures which help pupils extend this sort of knowledge, rather than being the source of it all themselves.

Content of PSE is distorted by reacting to the latest 'moral panic' especially when associated with a demand, 'what's the school doing about this?' Sex, drugs, gambling, juvenile crime ... – all these may be real issues which adolescents wish to address, but not in a way which is stimulated through adults' anxieties.

Schools need to develop an approach to PSE content which is open-ended yet stable.

If one asks the question, 'where does the content of PSE come from?', the model in Figure 9.1 (Watkins, 1992a; Watkins and Thacker, 1993) highlights three main sources and the need to clarify criteria for the distribution of the learning offer.

The following set of headings may bring coherence and completeness to a whole-school personal curriculum.

- *Bodily self*. Understanding changes and their variety; reflecting on the impact of these; addressing the use and misuse of the body, including through substance abuse.
- *Sexual self*. Understanding sexual development; the role of sexuality in relationships.

- *Social self*. Understanding others' perspectives and their role in relationships; making sense of others and their judgements; coping with conflicts; presenting oneself in a range of situations; working with others.
- *Vocational self*. Developing awareness of adult roles, lifestyles and preferences; taking a wider look at what sort of contributing adult to become; valuing a range of contributions; transition to adult roles.
- *Moral/political self*. The making of judgements; resolving moral dilemmas; taking action on issues.
- *Self as a learner*. Understanding strengths and competences; reflecting on approaches to learning.
- *Self in the organization*. Becoming an active member of a school; making sense of the organization and getting the most from it.

For a further expansion see Watkins (1992b). These extend from the work of Wall (1947, 1977), in order to pick up some time-honoured themes in adolescent development. The repeated use of the notion of self reminds us that students' views of themselves are developing fast in adolescence, and that student-centred teaching approaches are required. Also these seven approaches give a reasonably 'whole-person' result, and are framed at a sufficiently general level to engage the concerns of the vast majority of teachers.

These headings have proved attractive to schools (Saywell, 1992), including those featured by the BBC (BBC Education, 1992), to LEAs (Surrey County Council, 1991; Hertfordshire County Council, 1993; Norfolk County Council Education Committee, 1992), and have even received passing mention by NCC (National Curriculum Council, 1990c, p. 7).

In practice they prove useful for:

- helping teachers talk about pupils developmental needs in various years;
- planning aspects of an overall programme;
- discussing the contribution to pupils' personal-social development made by subject classrooms;
- thinking through the messages in the school's climate and organization;
- constructing a whole-school picture and policy;
- communicating with parents;
- promoting communication between adolescents and parents.

(Watkins, 1982)

Locations for learning: a whole-school approach

A whole-school approach to PSE means:

- an approach in which all teachers recognize they have a contribution to make;
- an approach which engages the perspectives of the whole school –

teachers, pupils, other staff, and so on. It is likely that this will be supported and achieved through an active whole-school policy, which spells out the whole-school cycles of review and action.

- an approach in which different teams complete different tasks, and the contribution of *all* 'locations for learning' are examined:

  tutorial programmes
  specialist guidance lessons with a specialist team
  subject lessons (some specific ones/all)
  the para-curriculum of classrooms
  extra-timetable activities
  residential experience, work experience
  school organization and climate
  links to community.

Adopting such an approach will not be constructive for planning until questions such as 'how do you distribute the content?' are raised. Criteria for distributing are needed, and have often been in short supply, resulting in either competition (say between tutorials and specialists in PSE, and between both of those and subjects) or dumping (especially on the tutorial occasion which might be characterized as addressing sex and drugs and litter).

Watkins and Thacker (1993) make the following suggestion. Personal tutors might initiate considerations which link to:

- previous knowledge of the pupil and his/her development, social relations;
- knowledge of the parents and their views, hopes, etc.;
- knowledge of the pupil's performance across subjects;
- broader school-related themes.

Subject tutors might initiate considerations which link to:

- particular aspects of the subject and its study;
- specific issues in the classroom they manage;
- particular learning needs of pupils in a subject.

Personal-social aspects of all classrooms

It is surprisingly rare for teachers to talk about their teaching and classrooms, especially across subject boundaries. The National Curriculum stress on subjects has made it more likely that talk across classrooms may be couched in terms of subject overlap and the like. There is an urgent need to develop the language which overarches subject considerations, with which we can start to talk about the contribution a subject-teaching classroom makes to some superordinate goals. The four major categories below can provide a start.

- *The goals of the subject.* How the subject contributes to a young person's competence in the world; what's the point of it, etc. Statements on this may be found in what the subject says it's for, and why teachers are enthusiastic about it, and justify it.

- *The content of the subject*. Particular topics and themes which are included in the subject.
- *The skills developed in the classroom*. Communication, problem-solving, reflection, action-planning, assertion.
- *The learning methods used in the classroom*. The sorts of teaching and learning activities which are employed.

Such categories can start to generate important discussions and exchange across subject-teaching classrooms, both in terms of the overall picture of the curriculum which is created and also in terms of the contributions each makes to pupils' personal-social development. Further developments of these headings are given in Watkins and Thacker (1993).

In such discussions the overall picture created from subject classrooms will no doubt show that pupils' specialist entitlement in PSE, in such areas as health and careers, is not met through the core and foundation subjects but that the experience of these subjects is important to discuss in personal-social terms.

Evidence is available to show that action-learning programmes in PSE have greater impact than those focusing on fact-learning programmes in subjects (see Appendix 2). An emphasis on all classrooms must not be at the expense of a well-targeted programme.

Teaching skills and methods

Teaching methods remain a central issue in PSE. In the face of some attempts to challenge the validity of action learning, and a general trend to see teaching as 'delivery', teachers will continue to need occasions to review and reaffirm the rationales for group-work. Groups offer:

- more efficient arrangements for the teacher;
- increased communication and engagement about a learning task;
- a range of ideas and perspectives.

Groups demand:

- the use of communication skills;
- collaboration on some occasions or some tasks;
- group processes when faced with problems to solve;
- skills of identifying and making decisions.

Groups may:

- recognize and enhance the social processes which support learning;
- become supportive places, including for learning;
- be used to simulate social processes which occur elsewhere;
- provide a platform for preparing for other group experiences, outside the group, in the future, etc.;

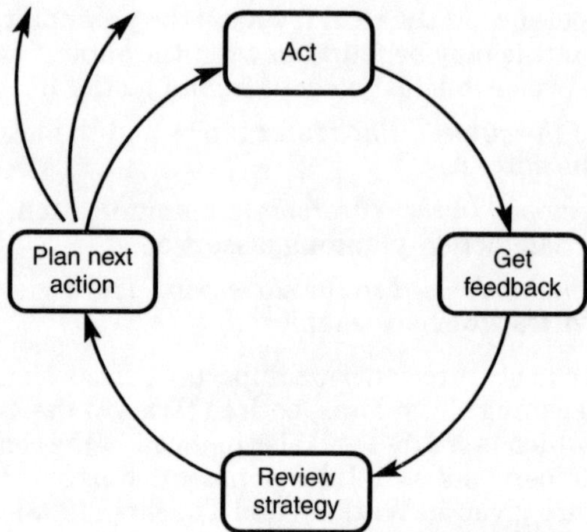

Figure 9.2 The process of personal-social learning in adolescence

- provide a context for reflecting on our own performance;
- provide opportunities for people to give and receive personal feedback;
- become safe contexts for supporting growth and experiment.

It is useful to recognize that some rationales for group-work are distinct from rationales for reflection and action-learning. These latter also need review and re-affirmation.

If personal-social education is to support and enhance personal-social development, then it needs to be built on an understanding of how such learning occurs.

Much adolescent learning in such areas may be described by the process characterized in Figure 9.2. Through a process such as this adolescents learn strategies, skills, perceptions and the associated understandings.

It is most useful for personal-social education (wherever it takes place) to operate in support of this process, through a cycle which is sometimes called action-learning, and which is characterized in Figure 9.3.

The 'Do' phase might be an activity in the classroom – a case study, a simulation, a learning activity – or it might be some experience outside the classroom. The 'Review' phase is a structured way of looking at the important points. The 'Learn' phase is where pupils learn from different approaches and identify what more they wish to learn. The 'Apply' phase asks them to transfer their learning to situations they know, to plan some action and to set goals.

The role of the teacher is to provide the necessary structures for pupils to progress through this process. Action-learning at its best is a highly structured (but still open-ended) process, not a sloppy interminable discussion.

CONTEMPORARY DIFFICULTIES FOR SCHOOLS IN THIS AREA

A key phenomena present in many British secondary schools has been that of reactivity. By this I mean the way in which a school can allow its agenda and functioning to be defined by outside forces. Here I am not proposing that schools should be impervious, nor am I underestimating the very

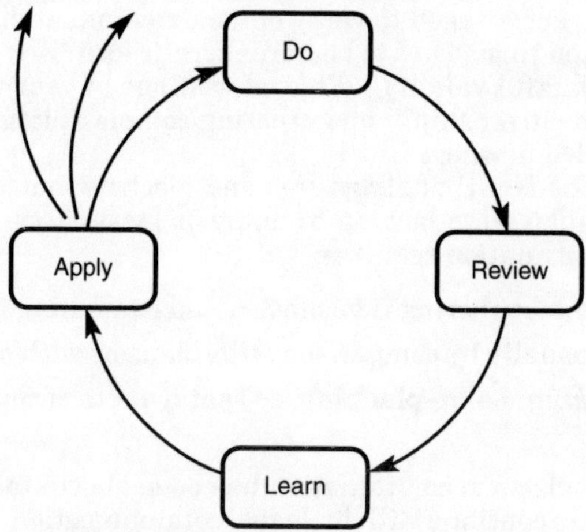

Figure 9.3 The process of action learning

major forces to which schools have had to respond. More I am remarking on the style of response. At one end of this spectrum is the school which seems to throw away its history and previous knowledge, saying 'We've got to do all this now', while at the other end is the school which evaluates the influences and proposals coming in its direction, and decides more critically which ones to develop. This dimension is similar to the one which David Hargreaves labels 'survivalist school versus empowered school' (Hargreaves, 1994).

In the area of PSE, reactivity has always been a particular problem, with the provision in a school being driven by the publication of resource packs, by particular staff predilections, by the anxieties of a range of adults and more recently perhaps by the rushed considerations of a government quango with an uncertain future.

A contemporary difficulty for PSE is to establish and to maintain its rationale, value and approach, and thereby reduce its vulnerability to whatever changes a school is facing. This vulnerability perhaps reflects the confusion which exists in some teachers' minds about the purposes and approaches which are appropriate for promoting young people's personal-social development. It is all too easy to polarize teachers on an issue, and PSE seems to attract more than its fair share of this.

In such a context, leadership is required, at school level and elsewhere. The need is for leadership which handles the polarizations, reaffirms the rationales and combats the fragmentation which has increased in recent years. At school level, this is in part the task of senior managers who play a key role in bringing status to a whole-school concern with personal-social development, and who continually articulate the link to other measures of achievement. Their contribution alone is not enough: it needs to be followed by a meaningful structure for whole-school co-ordination.

ISSUES OF CO-ORDINATION: WHAT MAY IT MEAN?

During the late 1980s the notion of co-ordination was at one and the same time raised and trivialized. For reasons of overlap or coherence, senior managers were encouraged to carry out 'curriculum audits' of a range of sorts. These often turned out to be bureaucratic exercises asking teachers questions of doubtful validity ('What percentage of your year 10 English teaching covers citizenship?') and creating complex pictures which more often than not led nowhere.

This raised the fact that structures and mechanisms for whole curriculum co-ordination were lacking in many or most cases. To be effective, curriculum co-ordination requires:

- *monitoring*, i.e. gathering information and examining for patterns;
- *evaluating*, usually by comparison with plans or with outcomes;
- *decision-making*, i.e. re-planning, so that aspects of the curriculum change.

In many schools such co-ordination has been shown to be lacking, and separate subjects continue with little real communication. In some schools the responsibility (but not the power) has been given to new role-holders, often young, enthusiastic, and receiving a minor incentive allowance. With these colleagues I sometimes find it important to raise the following points under the apparently dramatic title of 'How to kill off a PSE co-ordinator'.

1 Give them no structure to work in.
2 Give them no budget.
3 Give them no symbolic support from senior managers.
4 Subject them to negative 'role-sending':
   - *'You're the expert. Your job is to do it.'*
   - *'You're stealing time from me.'*
   - *'You're just a co-ordinator: I'm the real thing.'*
   - *'We need someone to do this – you'll do.'*
5 Make sure you never make a clear statement about their role and what it's meant to achieve.

The development of improved management structures in the secondary school is a key need identified in discussions of whole-curriculum management and the management of pastoral care (see Chapter 2 by Caroline Lodge, above), and some schools have made inspiring moves in this direction.

Looking toward the next period, in which there will doubtless be another pot-pourri of forces impacting on our increasingly different schools, there will doubtless be further experiments with the form, structure and balance of PSE in the context of a 'slimmed-down' National Curriculum. Whatever these may be there is no doubt that a whole-school picture and some fundamental entitlements are vital to schooling and achievement, and that the need to improve our whole-curriculum thinking will remain.

REFERENCES

Allen, I. (1987) *Education in Sex and Personal Relationships*. London: Policy Studies Institute.

BBC Education (1992) *Personal and Social Education*. London: BBC.

Brown, C. (1990) Personal and social education: a timetable ghetto or whole school practice? In Dufour, B. (ed.) *The New Social Curriculum: A Guide to Cross-curricular Issues*. Cambridge: Cambridge University Press.

Bulman, L. and Jenkins, D. (1989) *The Pastoral Curriculum*. Oxford: Blackwell.

CBI (1989) *Towards a Skills Revolution: Report of the Vocational Education and Training Task Force*. London: Confederation of British Industry.

Curriculum Council for Wales (1991) *The Whole Curriculum 5–16 in Wales*. Cardiff: Curriculum Council for Wales.

Curriculum Council for Wales (1992) *Community Understanding*. Cardiff: Curriculum Council for Wales.

Dearing, R. (1993) *The National Curriculum and Its Assessment: An Interim Report*. London: NCC and SEAC.

Department of Education and Science (1985) *Better Schools: A Summary*. London: DES.

Department of Education and Science (1987a) *Education Reform: The Government's Proposals for Schools*. London: DES.

Department of Education and Science (1987b) Letter from Kenneth Baker to Professor Blin Stoyle, Maths Working Group, 21 August.

Department of Education and Science (1987c) *The National Curriculum 5–16: A Consultation Document*. London: DES.

Department of Education and Science (1989) *National Curriculum: From Policy to Practice*. London: HMSO.

Donovan, J. (1989) Pastoral curriculum: examples from a London borough. *Pastoral Care in Education*, **7**(3), 39–43.

Goodson, I. F. (1990) Curriculum reform and curriculum theory: a case of historical amnesia. In Moon, B. (ed.) *New Curriculum – National Curriculum*. London: Hodder & Stoughton/Open University.

Graham, D. (1993) *A Lesson for Us All: The Making of the National Curriculum*. London: Routledge.

Hall, G. (1992) *Themes and Dimensions of the National Curriculum*. London: Kogan Page.

Hargreaves, D. H. (1994) The new professionalism: the synthesis of professional and institutional development. *Teaching and Teacher Education*, **10** (4), 423–38.

Hertfordshire County Council (1993) *Personal, Social and Health Education in the Primary Phase*. St Albans: Hertfordshire County Council.

HMI (1983) *Curriculum 11–16: Towards a Statement of Entitlement*. London: HMSO.

Lord, E. (1986) *The Whole Curriculum: A Contribution to the Debate*. London: School Curriculum Development Committee.

National Association of Careers and Guidance Teachers and ICG (1993) *Careers Education in British Schools*. Stourbridge: Institute of Careers Guidance, February 1993.

National Curriculum Council (1989a) *Interim Report on Cross-curricular Issues*. York: NCC.

National Curriculum Council (1989b) *The National Curriculum and Whole Curriculum Planning*, circular number 6. York: NCC.

National Curriculum Council (1990a) *Information Pack No. 2*. York: NCC.

National Curriculum Council (1990b) *The National Curriculum at Key Stage 4*, circular number 10. York: NCC.

National Curriculum Council (1990c) *The Whole Curriculum*, Curriculum Guidance 3. York: NCC.

Norfolk County Council Education Committee (1992) *Personal and Social Education: A Professional Paper Supporting a Statement for the Curriculum 5–16*. Norwich: Norfolk Educational Press.

Northern Ireland Curriculum Council (1989) *Cross-curricular Themes: Consultation Report*. Belfast: NICC.

Saywell, C. (1992) Personal-Social Education – one school's approach. *All-in Success*, **4**(4) 13–14.

Schools Council (1975) *The Whole Curriculum 13–16, Working Paper 53*. London: Evans/Methuen Educational for Schools Council.

Scottish Consultative Committee on the Curriculum (1989) *Curriculum Design for the Secondary Stages*. Dundee: Scottish Education Department.

Slavin, R. E. (1986) *Using Student Team Learning*. Baltimore: Johns Hopkins University Press.

Surrey County Council (1991) *Implementing the Cross-curricular Themes within the Whole Curriculum*. Kingston-upon-Thames: Surrey County Council.

Wall, W. D. (1947) *The Adolescent Child*. London: Methuen.

Wall, W. D. (1977) *Constructive Education for Adolescents*. London: Harrap/UNESCO.

Watkins, C. (1982) What's a turn-on? In Open University Continuing Education, Course Team, *Parents and Teenagers*. Harper & Row.

Watkins, C. (1985) Does pastoral care = personal and social education? *Pastoral Care in Education* **3**(3) 179–83.

Watkins, C. (1991) What can we expect of the pastoral curriculum? In McLaughlin, C., Lodge, C. and Watkins, C. (eds) *Gender and Pastoral Care: The Personal-social Aspects of the Whole School*. Oxford: Blackwell.

Watkins, C. (1992a) Whole school personal-social education. *All-in Success*, **4**(4) 12.

Watkins, C. (1992b) *Whole School Personal-social Education: Policy and Practice*. Coventry: NAPCE.

Watkins, C. and Thacker, J. (1993) *Tutoring: INSET Resources for a Whole School Approach*. Harlow: Longman.

Whitty, G. and Rowe, G. (1993) Five themes remain in the shadows. *Times Educational Supplement*, 9 April.

Whitty, G., Rowe, G. and Aggleton, P. (1993) *Cross-Curricular Work in Secondary Schools: Report to Participating Schools*. London: Institute of Education.

CHAPTER 10

Assessment and pastoral care: sense, sensitivity and standards

Stephen Munby

INTRODUCTION AND BACKGROUND

What is a chapter on assessment doing in a book on pastoral care and personal and social education? The supposedly mechanistic, narrow, bureaucratic, harsh and rigorous characteristics of assessment and record-keeping sit uneasily alongside the person-centred and sensitive aspects usually associated with pastoral care. Moreover, National Curriculum assessment arrangements have been roundly criticized of late. Those teachers concerned about the development of the whole child are fearful that assessment is becoming increasingly narrow and failure-orientated, leading to greater potential disillusionment amongst many students. Assessment, they say, is hindering rather than helping our aim of making schools more person-centred.

Many classroom teachers are also uneasy about the workload involved in National Curriculum assessment, complaining that they are so busy assessing that they no longer have any time to teach and that recent changes in assessment have made it increasingly difficult to avoid an assessment-driven curriculum. Moreover, teachers are, understandably, upset that as soon as they seem to have assimilated and implemented the latest set of regulations, the government introduces a different set. At the time of writing, these concerns and others are, at last, being taken seriously and are echoed in *The National Curriculum and Its Assessment – An Interim Report* (July 1993), known as *The Dearing Interim Report* (Dearing, 1993), and in the revised arrangements for marking SATs for 1995.

In addition, much concern has been expressed from a variety of quarters about the publication of assessment data in the form of league tables, especially since this is promoted by the government as a means of evaluating the quality of schools. League tables of raw assessment results are perceived by those who are concerned about the development of the whole child as evidence of an educational system which has lost its humanistic values – a system which has no clear rationale except the overriding importance of market forces. Meanwhile, government ministers, and those who have their ear, have wedded themselves to the notion of league tables and have criticized other assessment strategies, such as GCSE coursework, claiming that assessments need to be even more rigorous and should possess greater objectivity and reliability.

Against this background, it should be evident that assessment issues *must* be addressed in a book on pastoral care. Given recent legislation, perhaps the greatest challenge of any school which attempts to have a whole-school approach to pastoral care and personal and social development is how to tackle the assessment issue. A school's approach towards assessment and towards the use of assessment data is, I suggest, one of the acid tests of whether a school has a consistent whole-child and person-centred ethos.

As someone who for years has been excited about assessment and is an unashamed enthusiast for what it can do to promote learning and development, it is important for me to 'come clean' from the outset concerning my own views. Far from assessment getting in the way of teaching, I believe that on-going and effective teaching and learning cannot be achieved without assessment. Because we are rightly concerned about learning rather than just teaching, we need to know how much of what has been taught has been understood by the learners so that we can then help them to learn some more. Assessment provides the feedback loop to the teacher; it makes teaching a two-way process. Without assessment teaching is a sterile activity.

When the National Curriculum was first introduced, The National Curriculum Task Group on Assessment and Testing (TGAT) (DES/Welsh Office, 1987) was asked to develop an assessment system which would be formative, diagnostic, summative and evaluative. Although it is highly debatable as to whether a single assessment system can ever properly achieve all four assessment purposes satisfactorily, the TGAT *Report* tried to hold the four purposes in equal balance. The summative and evaluative assessment purposes were always going to be important, but the group sought to emphasize the formative and diagnostic purposes by recommending that end of key stage assessment should consist of a combination of the results of on-going teacher assessment and the results of Standard Assessment Tasks (SATs) and by suggesting that these SATs should be a combination of written and practical activities carried out by teachers as part of ordinary classroom work.

Successive Secretaries of State have, since then, attempted to move the emphasis away from formative and diagnostic assessment and further towards the summative and evaluative. As I wrote in 1990:

> The fact is that the concept of SATs is a very laudable one, since written testing tends to over-emphasise the importance of cognitive ability and memory recall whilst discriminating against those who have writing difficulties and those who tend to perform less well under pressure. Nevertheless, the problems of ensuring objectivity and lack of gender or race bias combined with the immense practical difficulties of implementing SATs makes their future by no means certain. Written tests are cheaper, more accurate, easier to compare and less complex to moderate. No doubt when the National Curriculum was first announced many traditionalists

were anticipating the return of brown envelopes with written tests inside them and were disappointed when the proposals of the TGAT report were accepted. However, if standard assessment tasks prove too difficult to implement they may yet get their wish.

(Munby, 1990, p. 120)

The Dearing Interim Report seemed to reinforce the view that the concept of SATs, though a great idea in principle, may have been overly ambitious and that the assessment tasks have, in reality, proved to be too costly and time-consuming.

The 1980s were an era of assessment-led curriculum reform but it was reform which had the potential to empower young people and to develop their self-esteem, typified by the emphasis on formative assessment in developments such as GCSE, CPVE (Certificate of Pre-Vocational Education) and, of course, records of achievement.

The 1990s appeared as if they were going to be a decade of assessment-led curriculum reform but along lines which, on the face of it, were less likely to be in the interests of many of the students in our schools. The emphasis from government ministers in the 1990s seemed to be away from on-going teacher assessment, which was dismissed as unreliable, and towards accountability, written testing and the publication of comparative results. They have since drawn back from committing everything to this emphasis, but where does the present situation leave those of us concerned about individual students and their learning and personal development? Have common sense and sensitivity towards individuals and their needs been squashed by the steamroller of National Curriculum assessment? Is the need to raise standards and to apply more focused assessment criteria in conflict with the notion of pastoral care for all students? Have we any room for manoeuvre or is our value system to be cast aside in the face of National curriculum testing and league tables?

SEVEN ASSUMPTIONS CONCERNING ASSESSMENT

It is important, in considering the assessment issues, to be clear concerning the principles and values which should underlie any assessment approach. These principles should be about ensuring that assessment is learning-centred. These are the key principles of learning-centred assessment which I propose:

The importance and uniqueness of the individual child

It is essential that we continue to remind ourselves that each young person in our schools is a unique individual and that it is therefore demeaning and dehumanizing to label students purely in terms of levels, numbers or grades.

One of the most important distinctions that we need to hold on to is the difference between attainment and achievement. I bought a table a few years ago that arrived in a box for self-assembly. It took me a day to put the table together but, by the time I had finished, it looked very good. It occurred to me that if it was in the National Curriculum it might be a level four for table-making. It also occurred to me that any of my colleagues could have made a similar table and, like me, have attained a level four. Our attainment, based on external agreed criteria, could have been identical but in my case the achievement was massive. I went around for days afterwards dragging people home to show them my table. It was a great achievement *for me*. Attainment is an external measurement irrespective of the individual's context. What turns an attainment into an achievement is the value that the person places upon their own attainment and whether their performance is good compared to their own previous performances.

We ignore this distinction between attainment and achievement at our peril. It means that a student can be on a high level in the National Curriculum but a low achiever because he or she is not working very hard and is not making very much progress, whilst another student can be on a much lower level in the National Curriculum and a high achiever because he or she is really making progress. Attainment-based approaches are liable to lead to complacency amongst some of the most able who feel that they are doing well and achieving high levels compared to other people but who may not be working to the best of their ability. Moreover, attainment-based approaches are liable to lead to unnecessary re-inforcement of feelings of failure amongst lower attainers, as students are compared with others who attained higher levels.

Assessment and recording strategies do not take place in a vacuum, they involve real students. To dismiss students as 'average' or to report to parents numbers or levels only without contextualizing them is to reject the notion of the uniqueness of the individual. One of the many positive things about records of achievement is that it provides something unique for each person. A student might have the same grades or levels as another student but he or she will not have identical records of achievement. We may need national standards and we may need nationally agreed attainment criteria but when we provide feedback to pupils and parents we must always take care to place attainment within the context of the individual learner. The regulations lay down the attainment criteria, but there is a great deal of freedom, and responsibility, as to how those criteria are used and concerning what is said or written about individual students.

Schools which are serious about whole-school approaches to pastoral care will ensure that sensitivity and respect for the individual pervade its approaches to assessment and that the assessment, recording and reporting of attainment is carried out using an achievement-based approach. They will ensure that students are given opportunities to be involved in their own assessment, that numbers and levels are never reported to parents in isolation. They will also ensure that proper, supportive reviewing procedures are built in to the school's tutorial system to help the individual student to make sense of her or his attainment and, through dialogue, to provide an individualized, person-centred context.

The need to recognize the whole child and a wide range of achievement, not just academic attainment

The danger of any assessment system is that it ends up assessing that which is easy to assess rather than that which is important. The recognition of personal achievement in addition to academic achievement and the value of recording progress in cross-curricular skills should not be neglected. Whilst we should be very careful indeed about issues such as confidentiality, intrusion and stereotyping, whilst we should be aware that reviewing personal achievement with students can be a subtle form of manipulation and control, and whilst we should be clear that the assessment of cross-curricular skills or competences only makes sense when it is assessed and reported within a context, it is nevertheless the case that schools are about more than academic attainment and we should do what we can to resist the pressures to reduce assessment to the ticking-off of statements of attainment in the National Curriculum. (For a further discussion of these issues, especially the issues involved in assessing cross-curricular skills, see Sutton, 1991, pp. 80–3; and Munby, 1989, pp. 54–83, 138–41, and 197–200.)

No approach to assessment in schools has much of a future if it flies in the face of established legislation and it won't succeed in enhancing learning if it is so unrealistic, burdensome and unmanageable that is endangers the health and sanity of those who are seeking to implement it. What is needed is a careful look at the legislation and a realization that the requirements are, perhaps, less demanding than some people realize (there is, for example, no legislative requirement to assess each individual statement of attainment). Many teachers seem to be weighed down and depressed by a sterile assessment system which is totally dominated by statements of attainment checklists, regular departmental tests and mounds of evidence for each student under the misapprehension that this is what they are legally required to do.

Having paired down to the bare minimum the legal requirements, it is possible to develop an *integrated* assessment and recording system which recognizes a wide range of achievement, including National Curriculum attainment, which meets the legal requirements, stresses the importance of professional judgement, and which holds on to the value systems of the school and the department. A whole-school policy which addresses these issues in a coherent way would seem to be the only sensible way forwards'.

The need to involve the learner in the assessment process

As part of my job, I must have interviewed hundreds of students concerning their views on self-assessment. The vast majority, perhaps 95 per cent, have stated that they think self-assessment is a good idea, although many are critical of the way particular teachers and schools have attempted to implement it. I did, incidentally, hear of one student who when asked what his favourite subject was, answered 'records of achievement'!

I would like to suggest that we need to involve students in the assessment process not only because it is more likely to motivate them as learners, not only because students should be entitled to such an involvement but also because, when done well, it can save the teacher time and make the process more manageable. Moreover, involving students in their own assessment is more likely to lead to accurate judgements about their attainments. It is, I suggest, the grossest form of egotism to think that nothing has happened in your classroom of which you, the classroom teacher, are not aware and that no additional evidence could possibly be brought to bear by the students that is not already known by you. Far from student self-assessment being a slur on the professionalism of teachers, it would be unprofessional to ignore the evidence of students' own perceptions of their learning. We should be involving students in their own assessment *because* we are professionals and because we want to ensure that our judgements about students' attainment are accurate.

Although the principle of the potential value of self-assessment may be agreed, the nature of it and the strategies for making it effective are less clear. If we are genuinely concerned about making self-assessment effective and useful we need to ensure that the following three aspects are present.

Clarity amongst students concerning the assessment criteria It may be the case that students perform poorly during assessment simply because the teacher failed to inform the students concerning the criteria for assessment. Students will not necessarily demonstrate what they know or can do unless they are clear as to what the teacher or assessor is looking for. As HMI have stated:

> Pupils produced work of better quality when their teachers explained the criteria used in its assessment. Relatively few teachers did this effectively, and pupils were generally unaware of any assessment criteria that the teacher might have been using. Pupils rarely understood the reason for grades and often felt, wrongly, that features such as length and presentation were most important.
>
> (OFSTED, 1992, p. 26)

Self-assessment as an integral part of the teaching, learning and assessment process Frankly, I see as many poor examples of self-assessment as useful ones. Many self-assessment strategies are paper-based only, take place inappropriately at the end of a topic or module and serve little purpose, whilst others actually interfere with effective learning. In almost every case where self-assessment seems to work it is implemented by teachers who believe in it and who have thought through the processes involved carefully from the student's perspective. As HMI say in their recent document:

> Many pupils were being encouraged to assess their own achievements but self-assessment was done with varying degrees of success. At best, pupils wrote perceptively about their achievements and were motivated by the process; and teachers reacted effectively to what the pupils wrote – for instance by doing something to remedy the weaknesses that the pupils had identified ... Pupils were frequently unsure about the purpose of self-assessment and unclear about the criteria they should use. In these circumstances, self-assessment became a chore and failed to support learning.
>
> (OFSTED, 1992, p. 26)

To be effective, self-assessment should:

- have a clear purpose understood by teachers and students;
- have clear criteria;
- be part of an integrated system so that the assessment criteria used by the teacher are essentially the same assessment criteria used by the students in self-assessment;
- have potential to save teachers' time;

- not be a 'play' activity or an activity tagged on to the end of modules of work but an integral part of the way in which the module or lessons are taught; and
- take a variety of forms, depending upon the context so that the approach remains fresh and relevant.

The development of focused learning targets, whenever possible Target-setting is particularly difficult to implement effectively. Nevertheless, it is disconcerting to observe that high attainers are rarely given challenging targets but, instead, are usually told to keep up the good work. Likewise, it is unusual to see low attainers given useful and graspable targets; instead they are asked to concentrate more in class or to work harder. Effective strategies for raising individual achievement often involve the setting or the negotiating of challenging, appropriate, specific and achievable targets – graspable challenges.

Far from militating against self-assessment, the National Curriculum with its clear criteria, can be a positive boost to meaningful self-assessment, provided we are asking students to do more than simply tick off statements of attainment on a grid. (For examples of how assessment strategies and target-setting can be built into teaching and learning see Richmond and Gilmour (1992).)

The importance of keeping the needs of the child central in the assessment process
If assessments are to have a positive impact they need to be communicated effectively and meaningfully to the students and, where appropriate, turned into targets and then monitored and reviewed closely. Students need to be told not just whether or not their work is good but what is particularly good about it. Likewise, students who perform less well or whose answers are incorrect need to be informed why their work is incorrect and how it could be improved. The attitude of many students towards unspecific and often banal feedback is to shrug their shoulders and carry on or, as one 9-year-old said when some of her work had been marked as incorrect: 'You win some, you lose some!'

The provision of feedback to students is a fundamental issue not only for the subject teacher but for the personal tutor too. It is too often the case that, in spite of the existence of tutorial groups and pastoral care systems, students do not receive coherent and integrated feedback concerning their learning and development at school. In many schools, information about students generated by the PSE teacher, the subject teacher, the tutor, the careers teacher or the careers officer is not passed on to the other people involved in providing guidance for the students, with the result that students are turned off learning because they are asked to complete similar and unnecessary self-assessment and personal interest sheets in a variety of different contexts.

Many schools are realizing that, in spite of the timetabling and human resourcing costs, one-to-one reviewing between a student and his or her tutor is fundamental. Without this kind of reviewing procedure, it is difficult to ensure effective support and guidance for students and their learning across the curriculum. Many schools are coming to the opinion that a structured reviewing process between individual students and a tutor is a very effective way to monitor the progress of individual learners and to help to make sure that pupils are reaching their full potential. In short, one-to-one reviewing can help schools to raise standards and to get good results in the league tables! This one-to-one reviewing process will rely for its effectiveness not only upon the skill of the tutor but also upon the communication systems and record-keeping systems used in the school. One question that I often ask when I visit a school is: 'If a student began to lose motivation or to struggle with work across a number of subject areas, how soon would it be before the student's tutor knew about it?' One of the keys to making assessment systems work for schools and students is to ensure that the school has effective communication systems to provide individual data about students so that each learner's work can be reviewed and monitored. It is encouraging to note that recently developed software is enabling this kind of information to be transferred effectively whilst keeping the student at the centre of the process.

Many schools see records of achievement and individual action planning as a way of valuing the individual student within the assessment and recording process but in some schools students are given no opportunity whilst at school to learn how to *use* their record and action plan. They are not given help, for example, in using their record of achievement to write a letter of application, or as an aid to talking about themselves at interview.

Schools which take the issue of raising individual achievement seriously are asking themselves hard questions about their assessment and guidance systems, what it is like to be a student experiencing these processes and whether the systems *really* operate to ensure that the child and his or her learning and development are as central as they might be.

The need to ensure that assessment approaches have potential to raise standards and enhance effective learning for all students, not just for a small minority

In a speech to the Council of Local Education Authorities in July 1992 in Liverpool, Eric Bolton, the former senior chief HMI, made this statement (*Times Educational Supplement*, 31 July 1992).

> English education's greatest success throughout its history has been to fail most children. Our system is better than any other in the developed world at failing people, and turning them out with a sense that they have achieved nothing of value. It is that issue above all others that we need to address if we are to raise the standards of education. (p. 10)

Any system of assessment in schools which ensures that the vast majority of people fail may raise standards for a small élite group but is very unlikely to raise achievement in the majority of students. There may be little that we can do to change the legislation or to effect the national culture but there is a great deal we can do at school and at classroom level to ensure learning-centred assessment for all students. If standards are to be raised for all, we need to look at the way in which assessment is implemented in classrooms and we need to ensure that it is carried out in a way which seeks to identify positive achievement. In this respect, it is important to guard against two extremes. The first extreme is to talk about achievements only – a mistake some of the early profiling and record of achievement schemes made. The effect of this is to produce complacency instead of challenged and motivated learners. The other extreme is to emphasize weaknesses and failure predominantly. Of course we learn from our failures, but we learn best from our failures when we largely succeed and achieve. If our main experience is one of failure, we soon stop learning from it and become disillusioned. The challenge to teachers is to try to ensure that students *mainly* experience positive feedback so that they can then talk to students meaningfully about their weaknesses and targets.

The need to maximize validity and maintain sufficient reliability in assessment

Validity John Major stated in July 1991 in a speech to the Centre for Policy Studies that short, regular, standardized written tests which the whole class can take at one time are the best and most objective method for measuring pupils' progress. The Prime Minister would seem to be correct in this respect, namely that written tests are the simplest way to ensure that assessment is as objective and reliable as possible. What seems to be overlooked, however, is the fact, known by all those who have any understanding of assessment issues, that though written tests may be more objective and reliable they are less likely to be valid. Even those who have given assessment issues no more than a cursory glance will be aware that written tests assess not what the candidate actually knows, understands or can do but rather the ability of the candidate during a single written performance on a given day at a given time.

One doesn't have to be a teacher to be aware that all kinds of factors can affect the ability of a person to perform well in a written examination – illness, problems at home, the weather, language difficulties, stress – and there are countless teachers who will testify to a significant number of students who have clear ability and understanding but who often fail to demonstrate it under examination conditions.

Much of the current thinking on assessment emanating from some politicians seems to rest on the assumption that education is largely about learning a body of knowledge, as if a teacher were pouring a full jug of knowledge into the pupil's empty mugs and then testing progress by sticking a measuring stick in the mugs to find out how much more still has to be poured in.

In reality, education is a far more complex and interesting process. It is about developing and practising skills, solving problems, widening understanding, clarifying confusions, making connections, and so on. It is precisely because learning is complex, and because it is about the development and use of skills as well as the increase of knowledge, that simple written tests are not always the best mechanism for assessing what has been learned. As Einstein is reputed to have said: 'Things should be made as simple as possible but not simpler.'

If learning is a complex process and if we want assessment to tell us about what has been learned, then assessment will need to be a complex process also. Those who argue for an assessment system based entirely upon written examinations are either intellectually bankrupt, lacking in plain common sense or have another agenda which is certainly not about fairness for all.

In order to ensure that assessment is as valid as possible, we need to do whatever we can to get inside each student's head and to find out what he or she actually knows, understands and can do. As one 7-year-old said: 'If you were me you would know that I can do that.' It is well documented that some people do better than others in multiple-choice tests, not because they understand the work more but simply because they are good at multiple-choice tests, and that other people will receive a better result if the assessment instrument used is questioning or observation of group-work. No single assessment instrument will always be the best way of finding out what everyone understands or can do. For the sake of validity, therefore, we need to use a variety of assessment instruments and techniques depending upon the context and upon the individuals involved. It is encouraging to note that the 1992–3 regulations for assessment in English, mathematics, science and technology stress the *requirement* to use a range of assessment techniques and types of evidence when making judgements for teacher assessment.

Reliability Although on-going teacher assessment, using clear, agreed criteria, is more likely to be valid than written tests, there is, rightly, a concern that assessment results should be reliable and comparable. Because of the need for greater reliability, there is a tendency to reduce the variables and to have assessment systems which involve as many students as possible doing the same written test at the same time under the same conditions. It is, however, important that we should nail the myth that written examinations lead to total accuracy and reliability. As Professor Desmond Nuttall has stated: 'Exam grades are the sum of fallible human judgements' (*Times Educational Supplement*, 11 September 1992).

In order to be fair and to avoid discrimination against students, consistency and standardization of assessment are needed. Some kind of balance between validity and reliability is, therefore, appropriate. I am not about to argue that there is no place at all for standardized written tests. I am, however, arguing very strongly that tests need to relate to the real curriculum, that they need to be thoughtfully constructed and well-trialled and that they should form only part of the information which we use to make judgements about students' learning and attainment. *The Dearing Interim Report* (Dearing, 1993) tries to solve this tension by emphasizing the different purposes of, on the one hand, end-of-key-stage testing and, on the other hand, teachers' own assessment. Teacher assessment, Dearing argues, is formative and diagnostic whereas the primary purpose of testing is summative. To try to develop tests which are formative, he maintains, is to miss the main point and to create potential additional work for teachers. He also argues that teacher assessment should be given greater status by being reported alongside test results (see Dearing, 1993, sections 5.9 to 5.20).

The Dearing Interim Report addresses many genuine concerns and is a courageous attempt to move forwards, but it will be interesting to see if these proposals for shorter tests can produce tests which relate sufficiently to the real curriculum to have the confidence of teachers and which do not lead teachers to 'teach to the test'.

Rather than simply waiting to see if teacher assessment and professional judgement are going to be given greater credibility and value as a result of the Dearing proposals, we need to be working hard to ensure consistency of teacher assessment standards within and across schools. Many departments and faculties have work to do in standardizing their assessments and in agreeing a common approach to the marking of work. Developing an agreed portfolio of levelled work across the department for reference purposes is a useful strategy. Standardization does not mean that we have to adopt the reductionist view of breaking up each statement of attainment into its component parts and making the criteria more and more detailed. To develop increasingly defined criteria is to disempower teachers and to make learning and its assessment sterile and uncreative. Our assessments need to be *consistent enough*. We have neither the time nor the capability to chase the holy grail of absolute consistency.

Once there is relative clarity concerning standards in the department which are monitored and checked out with local, regional and national standards, schools will need to be prepared to stand by their teacher assessments and not necessarily expect those assessments to be the same as national test results. Assessment based on a range of techniques over time may well produce outcomes different from assessment using one-off written tests. As the Dearing Report suggests, parents are entitled to know both sets of information about their child, and good schools will resist the pressure to make their teacher assessment results identical to the test results.

No assessment system can be entirely valid and totally reliable, but we need to work towards the best compromise between these two aspects in order to ensure that unfair discrimination against students is minimized.

The need to use assessment data within the context of a school-based quality assurance strategy

Clearly the publication of raw scores tells us very little about the quality of a school. Nor is the publication of results on their own likely to lead to more effective schools. Many states in the USA have been publishing SAT results school by school and district by district for more than a decade and there is no evidence that standards have noticeably risen as a result. It is, incidentally, interesting to note that there is a large reform movement in the USA which is moving schools away from standardized testing only towards much greater emphasis on what they call 'authentic assessment' and 'performance assessment' and what we would call formative assessment.

The value-added factor would be much more meaningful to publish than raw results, but at the time of writing we are a number of years away from being able to compare standardized assessment results for children at key stage 2 with the results of the same children at key stage 3 and 4. Even then, we would not necessarily be assessing children's real progress or the true value-added factor, since we would not necessarily be comparing like with like. There is no evidence whatsoever that a level five at key stage 3 has any clear connection with a level five at key stage 2 or at key stage 4. There is, incidentally, no evidence either that a level four in one subject has any clear relationship with a level four in another subject. If changes to the ten-level scale are introduced, as has been considered, such comparisons between performances at different key stages will be made even more difficult.

Even if we could be confident about the value-added factor, there are very grave concerns about publishing these scores and having value-added league tables since it may give the impression that improvement in academic results is the only criterion by which schools should be measured. Those of us who believe that schools are about developing the whole child and providing an environment in which they can reach their full potential will continue to find repugnant the notion that schools are to be judged on league tables of academic results, especially since those league tables for secondary schools currently give greatest emphasis to the percentage of pupils who attain grades A to C at GCSE, an indicator more appropriate to grammar schools than to comprehensive schools. Although the government has decided not to publish tables of results school by school for key stage 1 and key stage 3, it is currently determined, in spite of strong opposition, to publish key stage 2 results in tabular form and to continue to produce league tables for key stage 4 and beyond.

In view of the current political and social climate it would, therefore, be a foolish school which did not give the analysis and publication of results very serious consideration. To give this issue proper attention here would need a book in itself rather than a small part of one chapter but it is important to make two points.

Quantitative assessment data Quantitative assessment data is useful evidence for self-evaluation as long as it is contextualized, mixed with qualitative evidence and integrated into a whole-school approach towards quality assurance. 'A repudiation of quantitive indicators has prevented schools from devising robust systems of accountability, leaving a vacuum that has been filled by raw results' (Bill Chilton of the Audit Commission at the NAHT Conference, May 1992).

A school is not a caring school if it minimizes the importance of examination and assessment results. Schools which like to think of themselves as caring schools with well-developed pastoral systems have sometimes been schools which have been letting down their pupils by having low expectations concerning learning standards. Pastoral systems should help to provide an environment for learning which will maximize achievement and thus raise standards. A caring school will challenge its pupils, have high expectations of them and will take its assessment results very seriously indeed. Results, when carefully analysed and combined with other evidence, can help schools to identify areas of strength and weakness and to develop strategies for improvement. Rather than being frightened of the data, the enlightened school will take hold of the data, contextualize it, link it to other relevant evidence and use it as part of its quality assurance strategy. Assessment data need not be seen as a threat, provided the information is interpreted and used wisely as part of a larger evaluation strategy.

Records of achievement We need records of achievement for schools as well as records of achievement for students. The process involved in collecting, analysing and reporting data concerning National Curriculum results can be likened to the process of compiling records of achievement for students.

The formative process for students is designed to enhance learning, linked to self-evaluation and effective target setting. The formative process leads to the formulation of an educational record completed annually and the key points are then summarized on a written report. The report, combined with a portfolio of a student's work, is a record of achievement. The record of achievement recognizes attainment and achievement, putting the individual context and added value on to the attainment and emphasizing the importance of the individual's progress against previous performances ('ipsative' assessment). It also reports on other achievements which are non-academic.

In the same way, the formative collection and analysis of contextual data at whole-school level is designed to enhance the effectiveness of schools. It is linked to school self-evaluation and effective target setting. The key parts of the data are summarized in an annual prospectus or report for parents about the school. This report recognizes attainment and achievement, putting the school context and, where possible, added value on to the attainment and emphasizing the importance of 'ipsative' assessment. It also reports on the wide range of other achievements such as the school ethos, extra-curricular achievements, sporting achievements and personal and social aspects. Schools will need to be very clear about what is special and unique about their school and how it can both celebrate its own achievements and also set itself achievable targets.

CONCLUSION

It may be stating the obvious, but it is worth stressing that the processes involved in appraisal and staff development are very similar to those involved in learning-centred assessment. If the senior management team in the school implements strategies to recognize the achievement of the staff and to develop their self-esteem, it is more likely that students too will develop self-esteem and personal confidence. If staff are set challenging but achievable professional targets and have those targets reviewed, students are more likely to experience appropriate and effective target-setting. If staff experience what it is like to have some involvement in how the appraisal process is carried out and in the judgements or assessments that are made, they are more likely to implement similar self-assessment processes in classrooms. An appraisal and staff development process which addresses the individual needs of people on the staff may well lead to an assessment process for students that is more geared towards students' needs. An effective school is often one in which there is congruence between the management and evaluation strategies practised amongst the staff and the management and assessment strategies implemented with students.

This chapter has probably raised more questions than it has provided answers. But I hope, at least in part, to have demonstrated that, far from assessment being something of which those concerned about pastoral care and personal-social development should be fearful, there are approaches to assessment which sit comfortably within the value system of individual worth, whole-curriculum and whole-child. I hope to have shown that schools which give little value to assessment and to assessment data are unlikely to be entitled to call themselves caring schools. It is my belief that through common sense, sensitivity towards individuals and a determination to colonize existing legislation instead of being bullied by it, schools can ensure that assessment strategies enhance the personal development of students. In so doing, we can nail the myth that caring and standards are contradictory by demonstrating that learning-centred assessment is one of the keys to raising achievement in schools.

REFERENCES

Dearing, R. (1993) *The National Curriculum and Its Assessment – An Interim Report*, 1993.

Department of Education and Science/Welsh Office (1987) *The National Curriculum Task Group on Assessment and Testing* (TGAT), 1987. London: DES.

Department of Education and Science/Welsh Office (1992) *Regulations for Key Stage Three statutory assessment in English, Mathematics, Science and Technology*, Circular 13/92. London: DES.

Munby, S. (1989) *Assessing and Recording Achievement*. Oxford: Blackwell.

Munby, S. (1990) Assessing recording and reporting achievement in *Effective Learning – Into a New ERA*. London: Jessica Kingsley Publications.

OFSTED (1992) *Assessment, Recording and Reporting – A Report by HM Inspectorate on the Second Year, 1990–91*. London: HMSO.

Richmond, T. and Gilmour, J. (1992) *A Practical Guide to Developing Flexible Learning in Schools and Colleges*. Lancaster: Framework Press.

Sutton, R. (1991) *Assessment – A Framework for Teachers*. Windsor, Berks: NFER Nelson.

CHAPTER 11

Personal-social education for children with special educational needs

Phil Bayliss and John Thacker

It is the purpose of this chapter to examine the relationship between the personal-social curriculum, entitlement and children with special educational needs.

In order to address this relationship, it is necessary to determine what is meant by the term 'special educational needs'. The concept of 'needs' may be determined in various ways: all children and adults have 'needs', but whether these become 'special' is dependent upon several factors.

'SPECIAL NEEDS': A VIEW FROM THE BRIDGE

The term 'special educational needs' derives from the Warnock Report (1978), which became enshrined in law through the 1981 Education Act. Warnock states that, rather than thinking that there are two distinct groups of children, the handicapped and the non-handicapped, it must be accepted that 'the complexities of individual needs are far greater than this dichotomy implies'. Warnock adopted the concept of 'special educational need', 'seen not in terms of a particular disability which a child may be judged to have, but in relation to everything about him, his abilities as well as his disabilities – indeed all factors which have a bearing on his educational progress' (Warnock, 1978, section 3.5).

This view of special educational needs was further articulated (Fish, 1985) by taking into account not only the child's difficulties but also (and in Fish's view, more importantly) 'the curriculum, teaching materials, methods, and social and emotional climate with which the individual is faced in school' (Fish, 1985, p. 56). Here, children are seen as experiencing difficulty which is then exacerbated by the environment they find themselves in. The particular difficulties may be described, needs assessed and programmes of work detailed. This process is conducted within the framework of the 1981 Act, to produce a 'Statement of Need'. The 'statemented pupil' then receives extra help in some form (teaching resources, adapted materials) to support his progress, or the school may detail the need for special education within a new environment (the special school). The process of ascertaining the special educational needs in this way in order to underpin a full statement of need usually uses norm-referenced assessment (standardized) procedures which are carried out by local education authorities in a process which is controlled by educational psychologists. However, Warnock also described a wider range of pupils (the 'Warnock 18 per cent'), who are deemed to experience some form of special educational need at some point in their education but who have not received, or will not receive, a full statement of need. Caldwell (1989, p. 144) argues that because the definition within the Act is circular – 'a child is deemed to have a learning difficulty if he has a significantly greater difficulty in learning than the majority of children of his age' – it is possible for a school to argue that it has a significant number of pupils who need to be assessed for a 'statement' but who for a variety of reasons will not receive one. This process is reflected in the variability of statementing procedures nationally (Swann, 1987) which are governed more by resource considerations than by a clear view of what constitutes a special educational need.

Inherent in this discussion is the fact that children have difficulties which can be described, assessed and remediated. Although it is acknowledged that the educational environment (curriculum, teaching methods and materials) contributes to the special need, the 'difficulty', or the 'special educational need', still resides in the child, and the purpose of education is to meet the special educational need either by changing the educational environment (some form of special education) or by supporting the child (within mainstream settings) to achieve the common levels shared by his or her peers. Even a document ostensibly concerned with the curriculum (NCC, 1993) identifies groups of children. These groups are:

1 pupils with exceptionally severe learning difficulties, including those with profound and multiple learning difficulties (who may also have associated challenging behaviour) together with pupils who experience a severe learning difficulty arising from multi-sensory impairment;
2 pupils with other learning difficulties, including those with mild learning difficulties, moderate learning difficulties, specific learning difficulties, and emotional and behavioural difficulties;
3 pupils with physical or sensory impairment;
4 exceptionally able pupils.

A further group may also be described: those pupils with English as a second language.

Identifying groups in this way coincides with what Stuffelbeam (1977) describes as a *discrepancy* model for the definition of needs. An individual's needs will be defined by comparing that individual with his or her peers, using normative or criterion-referenced data (cf. Caldwell, above). Where a child differs in some characteristic this difference is seen as a lack and the purpose of education is to 'fix', to 'remediate' or to compensate for this discrepancy, this deficit. This process has led to what some authors have called the 'medical model of disability', which provides two intervention choices: 'either "cure" the individual condition ... or provide a system of care. Both forms of intervention assume that the problems of the individual disabled people originate in their deviation from essential and social standards of normality. Because the underlying assumption is that disabled people are dysfunctional, both approaches assume that helping interventions are introduced and administered to disabled people by able-bodied people' (Finkelstein, 1993, p. 37). Using the NCC groupings, there is a basic assumption that such classification of learning needs is required because such needs render children dysfunctional within an educational context and by meeting their needs we can render them 'functional'. It is possible, however, to define 'needs' in a different way.

TOWARDS A NEW DEFINITION OF SPECIAL EDUCATIONAL NEEDS

Needs, in a broad sense, may be determined *democratically*, that is they will be seen as a change which is desired by the majority of some reference group (society) (Stuffelbeam, 1977). Needs may also be described in *analytic* terms, in the sense that a starting point or baseline is described and a programme of study designed which will move the individual on to the next stage of development or progress. Where progression to this next stage is problematic, this lack of success will determine 'needs' for the individual. A *diagnostic* view sees a need as something whose absence or deficiency proves harmful for the individual, for example an adequate diet. Here, the identification of met and unmet needs for the individual may be seen within an entitlement framework in that some needs are seen as being absolute, and are described as rights for all. Within an educational context, a democratic definition of needs will determine the *goals* of the educational process ('equal opportunities for all'); an analytic view will determine the *processes* by which these goals may be achieved for any given individual, and a diagnostic view will describe, for the individual, the *starting point* of the process.

Special educational needs may also be described along continua which reflect the possibility of change for any given individual or group (Figure 11.1). A specific special need may be temporary and mild (a broken arm);

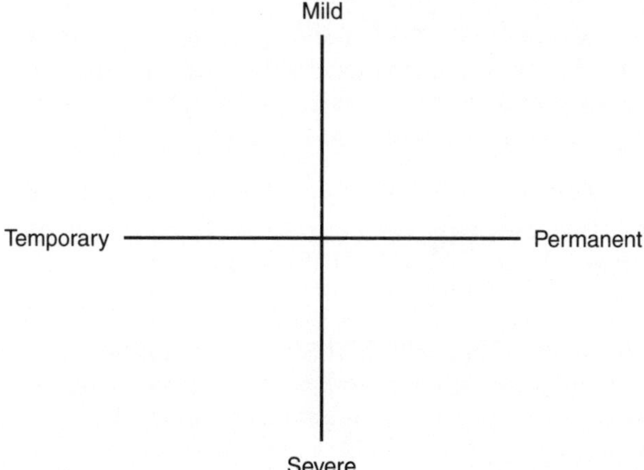

Figure 11.1 Continua in the description of 'special educational needs'

temporary and severe (bereavement), while for others their special needs are permanent and severe (for example, a child with Down's Syndrome). If a lifespan perspective (Sugarman, 1986) is adopted, the qualitative changes in 'needs' for an individual through childhood, adolescence and adulthood would require to be taken into account, whilst a developmental framework would describe the individual in terms of physical, emotional, intellectual, linguistic, social, moral and aesthetic development, where 'needs' are seen as arising through the interaction of the individual with his or her environment.

If all of these aspects of needs definitions are contained within what is termed an ecosystemic framework (Upton and Cooper, 1990), the definitions of needs (special or not) become complex, dynamic and relative. Within this perspective, special needs are not seen as residing in a particular, clearly identifiable group but are an inherent aspect which arises out of complex interactions between individuals and their environments, and which is a characteristic for *all* learners.

SCHOOLS AND SCHOOLING

Earlier in this volume it has been argued that PSE is an entitlement for all children, including, in our view, children with SEN. Let us take a starting definition of PSE as the intentional promotion of the personal and social development of pupils through the whole-curriculum and the whole-school experience.

A WHOLE-SCHOOL PERSPECTIVE

We will first of all look at PSE at the level of the whole school through a consideration of ethos.

This is the network of shared values which form the moral climate of the school, and which establish a democratic definition of the needs of its pupils. It is reflected in the climate of social expectations that influence relationships between pupils and between pupils and teachers and also, equally importantly, between members of staff inside and outside the classrooms.

The values portrayed will have both educational but also political implications. For example, one person's ideal school will stress attributes such as obedience, conformity and competition while another might stress pupil autonomy, co-operation and critical inquiry into the functioning of society.

The values expressed in a school are also in their turn affected by the wider society. For example, a comprehensive school committed to the concept of providing an integrated education for all the children in a neighbourhood will find itself in some conflict with an approach to education which espouses the values of the market-place.

Successive education acts since 1980 have extended parents' rights to information about their schools and have placed schools in the market-place, where their survival will depend on their ability to attract the parents of prospective pupils. Whether or not this is generally desirable is a matter of debate, but there is considerable concern over the well-being of pupils with special needs.

A pessimistic view is that this market approach will increase the tendency to locate explanations for problems in the individual pupil, following the discrepancy model. This would lead schools to seek to remove such children or at least to gain exemption for them from the National Curriculum requirements. Whether or not these moves are in the interests of any particular child, it is certainly in the interests of a school to ensure that its scores on the simple 'league table' results are as high as possible.

More optimistically the 1988 Act does at least require that all pupils should have access to the National Curriculum except in specified circumstances. This has counteracted the previous tendency for academically less able children in secondary schools to have alternative and usually low-status curricula. These changes may challenge headteachers and governors to take account of children with special needs more seriously and to work in partnership with parents. This positive effect would be amplified if it could be coupled to a view of the challenge being to the creativity of teachers and the appropriate group interaction rather than seeing an escape route through supposed deficits in individual children.

How these tensions are resolved in a school will have a material influence on PSE since it will affect how children with special needs are understood and treated. This in its turn will influence how the children see themselves. As Hargreaves (1983) points out, children's sense of personal identity develops in a social context. Outside the family, the principal influence is that of school. If the school has regard for the dignity and worth of each individual and for the development of the whole person, this will need to be reflected in all school policies and not just those with a PSE label.

CONTRIBUTION OF ALL CLASSROOMS: THE GROUP

In this section we will look at how learning in an ordinary class can help the learning of a child with special needs. Access to the mainstream curriculum is one of the major arguments for the integration of children with special needs into ordinary classrooms. However, an equally important reason for integration is the functional opportunities it offers to work collaboratively with their peers in the mainstream. As we shall see later, there are ways in which teachers can help in the social integration of children; but for the moment it is enough to note that to provide the opportunity to be in the same class is important.

However, integration into mainstream classes, while necessary, is not sufficient in itself to promote social development and the development of meaningful relationships. Conscious attention needs to be paid to creating a suitable climate. One of the main classroom strategies here is to encourage co-operative activities, especially in small groups where there is more opportunity for interaction. This can provide opportunities for pupils to learn how to co-operate; how to respect the views of others; how to question and challenge and how to listen. Again, simply putting the children into small groups and hoping that they will work together is not enough. Following the suggestion in the Plowden Report about the social benefits of groups, it became fashionable for teachers to group children around tables but often with work which was essentially individual. Classroom surveys since then (Bennett, 1987) have confirmed this picture. Also Guralnick

(1981) has argued that, when allowed a free choice, children tend to choose friends from among children who have similar cognitive ability to themselves.

To remedy this there have been at least two main approaches. One is to concentrate on the nature of the task and the outcomes of learning. This is represented in the work of Slavin, who has identified three key features of successful co-operative learning programmes (Slavin, 1990). Pupils must be operating under a regime which rewards team results, but where each individual remains accountable for their own contribution and where each individual has a chance of being equally successful. In order to ensure this, these approaches tend to be very highly structured. They have also been developed largely in the USA, and the results have been promising in helping the integration of children with special needs. For example, Slavin's own approach, Student Teams-Achievement Division (STAD), was used to attempt to integrate children performing two years or more below the level of their peers into the social structure of the classroom. It significantly reduced the degree to which the normal-progress children rejected their integrated classmates, and improved the academic achievement and self-esteem of all the children. This latter point is worth noting for those who are doubtful about integration of children with special needs on the basis of their possible effects on the learning of children who are making normal progress. As Slavin notes, 'Perhaps the most important fact about co-operative learning methods in the integrated classroom is that these techniques are not only good for the handicapped children, but they are among the very few methods for helping these children that also have a clear benefit for all pupils in terms of academic achievement', (1990, p. 238). However, Slavin's work has some limitations in that it can be strictly implemented only where pupils' work can be assessed in a relatively straightforward right or wrong manner.

The other broad approach to co-operative learning is represented by such writers as Thacker *et al.* (1992) at the primary level and Button (1981) at the secondary level. Here the approach is upon the use of a variety of groupings and activities to encourage a supportive social atmosphere in the classroom in which children can explore and value similarities and differences between themselves and find ways of resolving conflicts in a creative way. The stress here is upon raising the level of understanding of how groups can be helped to work well and to provide the opportunities for children to become more skilled in fostering good working relationships between themselves. Whilst these principles can be drawn on by children in any curriculum area, it has been commented that some of this work can be usefully done as part of personal and social education in tutorial groups at secondary schools and during reflective times for personal and social themes in the primary school.

Such group approaches also have the advantage of helping hard-pressed teachers see ways of working with classes of thirty children in realistic ways. Much of the legislation has concentrated on the identification and meeting of individual needs, and teachers can feel daunted by implementing individual programmes for each child. Group means can help in this as well as provide a realistic social context to foster children's social development.

Perhaps somewhat surprisingly, groupwork is also a way to foster autonomy or pupil self-direction. This cannot arise from purely individualized instruction, since this is most likely to lead to dependence on the teacher. It seems best thought of as a social product, developed through varied relationships with adults and peers. With effective peer interaction, the child has an alternative to counterbalance teacher dependence and control.

Overall, pupils working effectively with each other and thus developing better relationships with each other may simultaneously relieve the pressure from teacher dependence while at the same time providing a firm basis for autonomy from this co-operative working experience.

It should not be overlooked that teachers working collaboratively can provide an important model of co-operation for children. This is a bonus in addition to the other virtues of team teaching, which is becoming commonplace as a way of providing support for individual pupils with SEN. In the present context, the presence of a support teacher in a classroom may make it possible to cope with a wide variety of needs in a way which teachers might have found hard to achieve individually.

For children with particular needs, group-work is a skill which cannot be taken for granted, in that the individual's contribution is sensitive to the status of that individual within that group. At an interactive level, the concept of 'control' (Bayliss, 1992; Wells, 1981) reflects asymmetric relationships pertaining between children. Here, the power to initiate action or conversation resides in individuals or groups of individuals, with children of lower status assuming essentially passive (response) roles. Within true peer behaviour (symmetric relationships), co-participant status is spread throughout the group, which allows individuals to negotiate group outcomes.

For deaf children, Wood *et al.* (1986) showed that only by ceding control to individual children can teachers support language development, and in this respect a move towards equality of participation is actually necessary for development and learning. Further, where language is the main focus of development, 'the development of linguistic concepts per se is central to the children's overall intellectual and academic development' (Wiles, 1990, p. 83). For children with special needs who are seen as a low-status group, their participation in active learning situations may be inhibited if their generalized patterns of interaction are controlled by others – either within clearly didactic teacher–pupil relationships (Sinclair and Coulthard, 1975) or within didactic relationships assumed by their peers. There is evidence to support the view that pupils adopt teacher-like didactic styles of interaction with pupils with SEN and associated lower status (Bayliss, 1992). Such externally-directed social influences will exacerbate the learning difficulty experienced by the child. The child will see himself or herself as powerless, which may lead to a lack of confidence and low self-esteem, and may further lead to disaffection and final rejection.

If the purpose of PSE is to develop self-esteem and move the child towards internalized locus of control, to becoming an independent learner, it is crucial for the child with special educational needs to develop effective peer relationships to avoid being locked into a spiral of peer isolation, low self-esteem, failure and disaffection.

Given the increasingly prescriptive approaches developed under the direction of the National Curriculum, without an effective PSE curriculum for pupils with SEN (or for their peers) the prevalence of this spiral will grow – indeed for children with a wide range of learning needs, whose disaffection is shown through 'conduct disorder' which leads to exclusion, these spirals are already in place (Parffrey, 1993).

INDIVIDUAL

Our final level of analysis is that of the individual child. If we take our new definition of 'special educational needs' as being complex, interactive and relative, we need a new view of 'supportive education'. Traditionally the support role has been split in two aspects: the form tutor provides individual help for members of the tutorial group in situations of short-term, mild or severe, special needs, such as bereavement, while the longer-term (more permanent) special learning needs, both mild and severe, are seen as being the responsibility of the learning support staff.

In our view, the role of learning support is not restricted to these specific learning needs (although obviously this is central to the role). Rather, both the form tutors and learning support tutors mediate between the learner, the task and the classroom to enable the pupil not only to complete the range of tasks required across the whole curriculum but also to develop confidence and self-esteem. When these goals are clustered on personal development, as in the personal-social dimension of the whole curriculum, such goals will include: the empowerment of choice and the achievement of adult status. The general processes whereby these goals may be achieved will be the same for all individuals, that is giving responsibility, allowing choice and supporting the individual to accept responsibility and to make choices. However, it is necessary in the case of particular individuals to have a clear understanding of their capabilities as independent learners, where necessary support must be given to develop the specific skills which will allow them to act as independent learners, that is, providing the learner with the skills necessary to exercise choices together with offering them real opportunities for choices with *real* situations. How these strategies are executed in practice is the substance of our final section.

HOW DO WE ENSURE ACCESS TO THE ENTITLEMENT CURRICULUM FOR ALL PUPILS?

We have argued that for learners with special educational needs we require diagnostic definitions of the individuals' base-line needs, together with an analytic description of the processes necessary to achieve democratically defined goals.

Emerging from our discussion are ideas of structuring experiences; supporting independence in learning; extending choice; empowering all individuals to more autonomy within stable (symmetric) peer relationships. How can these aspects of the management of learning be supported in a system which is being seen as increasingly constrained by a narrow curriculum determined by didactic processes within the 'back to basics' movement?

It is possible to use the existing National Curriculum framework of dimensions, themes and skills to support the learning of the individual within a 'forward to fundamentals' approach (Phillips, 1990). Working within a cross-curricular framework allows us to develop structure (that is, planned frameworks within programmes of study), independence in learning (through project or course work), frameworks for choice (negotiation of learning outcomes for the individual or the group) and the empowerment of the individual by supporting pupils to take responsibility for their own learning. This may be undertaken within a PSE programme which uses structured group-work, involving the concept of co-operative goal structuring (Rynders *et al.*, 1980), STAD, etc. to allow the equality of participation for pupils with SEN.

If we take our notion of levels – whole-school, group and individual – our view is that particular needs, temporary and permanent, can be met only by coherent planning. Figure 11.2 offers a model for planning to meet special educational needs. Whole-school planning will establish the programmes of study (PoS) and the students' guide, and determine the allocation of resources. This process is informed by a partnership of tutor, subject tutors and learning support tutors. The PoS will determine a block of time (e.g. six weeks) during which a particular topic will be covered. The PoS will be described in National Curriculum terms to include attainment targets, levels, etc. and will use some form of task analysis or topic web to cover the range of subject and cross-curricular aspects of the task.

A student guide (see Figure 11.3) will be derived from the PoS. Here, the detail of the work to be undertaken will be described in language and content appropriate to the range of pupils taught. The student guide will prescribe content, but allow a range of responses which also offer choice of outcome to be negotiated with the pupil. Also, the pupil must contribute to an understanding of his or her own learning by using self-assessment procedures built into the student guide. (The completed student guide contributes to a final record of achievement, which also provides an extra benefit.)

For the specific aspect of meeting SEN, learning support will contribute at the level of whole-school planning (description of PoS and student guide, together with differentiated outcomes and responses) which will determine levels of support and resource allocation. Learning support will also contribute at the level of the group, by providing in-class support, and at the level of the individual pupil, by contributing diagnostic information and, where necessary, analytic information for the definition of specific support processes for given individuals (for example augmentative communication, or the use of targeted information technology to meet, for example, the needs of the pupil with specific learning difficulties, dyslexia, etc.).

This process is of benefit for all children, in ensuring a wide range of choice and self-determination in a whole-school personal and social curriculum offering. For pupils with special needs this process is not only desirable but is crucial, in our view, for promoting the self-worth of individuals. That this is necessary is supported by research: 'The most noticeable aspect of [this research] is how much students [with special needs] do not see themselves as "good" or "nice" or likeable. Nor are these views restricted to the adolescent group, which might be expected to have some

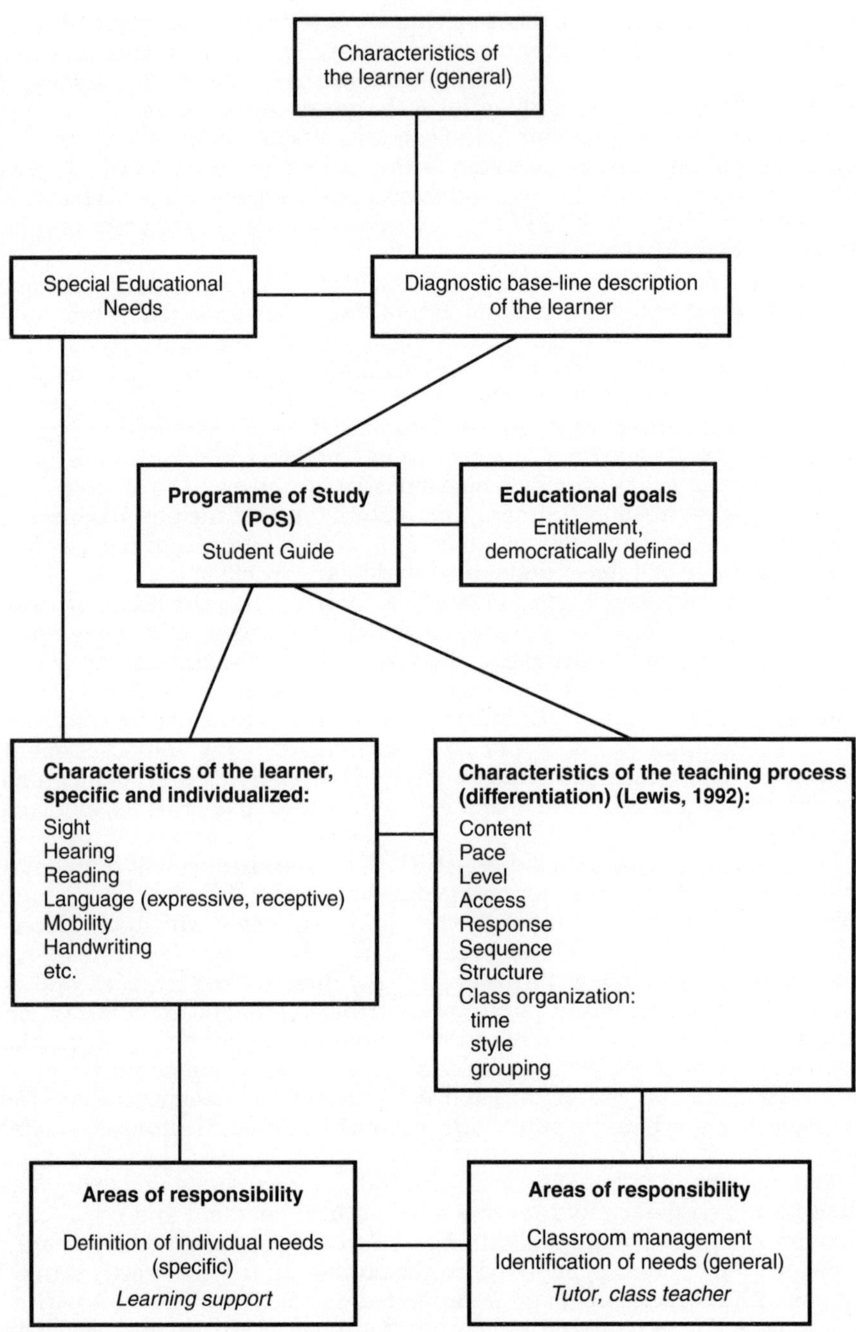

Figure 11.2 A planning model for special educational needs

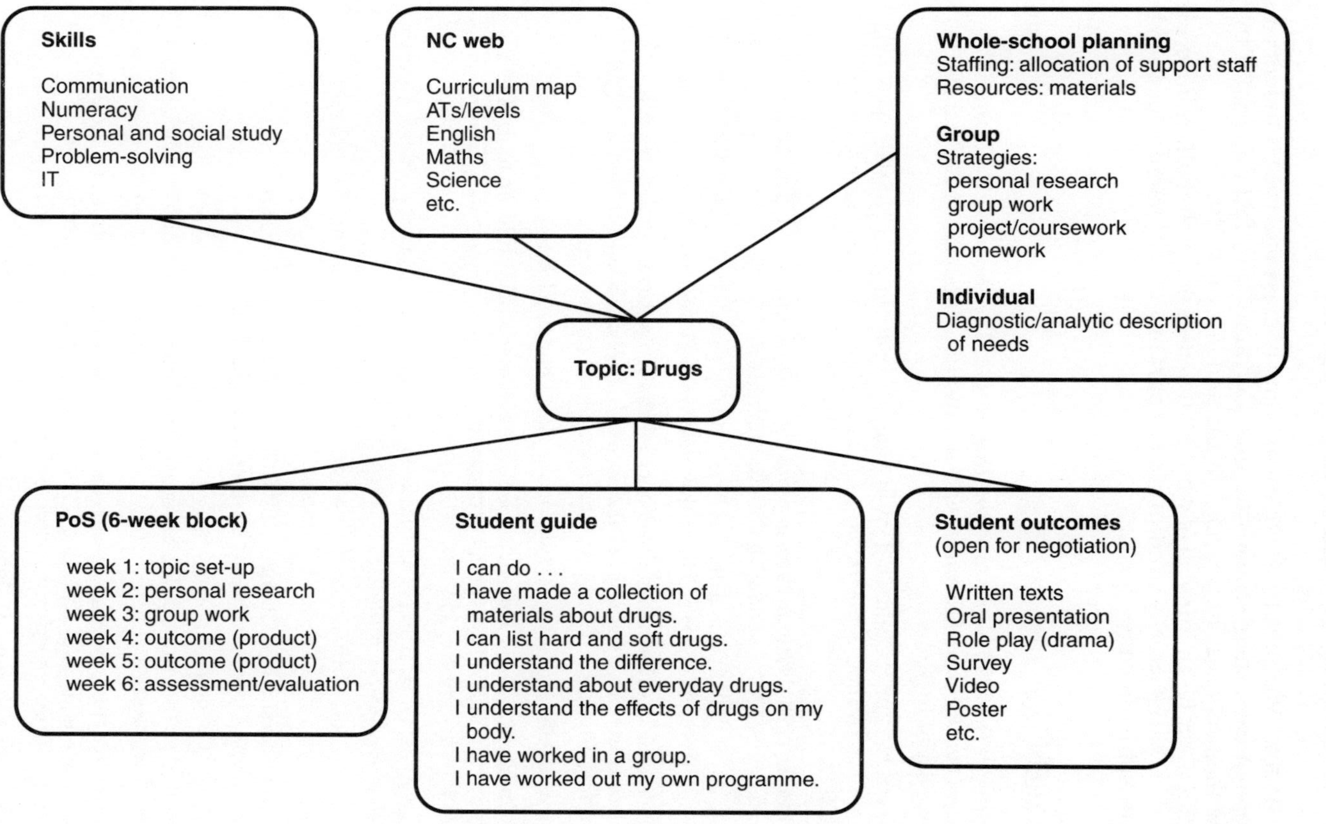

Figure 11.3 Levels of planning to meet special educational needs

self-doubts. We have to wonder what kind of messages these students are receiving from their school situation. Certainly they feel different if they view themselves so negatively' (Wade and Moore, 1993).

PSE must be an integral of what all teachers do, so that all children can progress satisfactorily to adulthood as part of an entitlement education by right, not by favour.

REFERENCES

Bayliss, P. D. (1992) *Language and Integration: The Discourse Processes of Students with Severe Learning Difficulties in FE*. Unpublished Ph.D. thesis, University of Bristol.

Bennett, N. (1987) Children do it in groups – or do they? In Thacker, V. J. (ed.) *Working in Groups. Educational and Child Psychology*, monograph edition **4**(3&4), 7–19.

Button, L. (1981) *Group Tutoring and the Form Tutor*, vol. 1, *The Lower Secondary School*. London: Hodder & Stoughton.

Caldwell, P. (1989) The Education Act 1981: a current view. In Bowers, T. (ed.) *Managing Special Needs*. Milton Keynes: Open University Press.

Finkelstein, V. (1993) Disability: a social challenge or an administrative responsibility? In Swain, J., Finkelstein, V., French, S. and Oliver, M. (eds) *Disabling Barriers – Enabling Environments*. London: Sage.

Fish, J. (1985) *Equal Opportunities for All?* London: ILEA.

Guralnick, M. (1981) The social behaviour of pre-school children at different developmental levels: the effects of group composition. *Journal of Experimental Child Psychology*, **31**, 115–30.

Hargreaves, D. H. (1983) *The Challenge for the Comprehensive School: Culture, Curriculum and Community*. London: Routledge.

Lewis, A. (1992) Differentiation: ways forward. From planning to practice. *British Journal of Special Education*, **19**(1), 24–7.

National Curriculum Council (1993) *Special Needs and the National Curriculum: Opportunity and Challenge*. York: NCC.

Parffrey, V. (1993) Exclusion: failed children or systems failure? Paper presented at the Annual Conference of Educational and Child Psychologists (BPS), Torquay.

Phillips, T. (1990) Beyond lip-service: discourse development after the age of nine. In Wells, G. and Nicholls, J. (eds) *Language and Learning: An Interactional Perspective*. London: Falmer.

Rynders, J., Johnson, J., Johnson, R. and Schmidt, B. (1980) Effects of goal structuring in producing positive interactions in Down's Syndrome and non-handicapped teenagers – implications for mainstreaming. *American Journal of Mental Retardation*, **85**, 268–73.

Sinclair, J. and Coulthard, R. M. (1975) *Towards an Analysis of Discourse*. London: Oxford University Press.

Slavin, R. (1990) Co-operative learning. In Rogers, C. and Kutnick, P. (eds) *The Social Psychology of the Primary School*. London: Routledge.

Stuffelbeam, D. (1977) Needs assessment in evaluation. Paper presented at the AERA Evaluation Conference, San Francisco, Calif.

Sugarman, L. (1986) *Life Span Development*. London: Methuen.

Swann, W. (1987) Trends in special school placement to 1986: measuring, assessing, and explaining segregation. *Oxford Review of Education*, **14**(2), 139–61.

Swann, W. (1992) Hardening of the hierarchies: the National Curriculum as a system of classification. In Booth, T., Swann, W., Masterton, M. and Potts, P. (eds) *Learning for All: Curricula for Diversity in Education*. London: Routledge.

Thacker, V. J., Stoate, P. and Feest, G. (1992) *Groupwork Skills*. Crediton: Southgate.

Upton, G. and Cooper, P. (1990). A new perspective on behaviour problems in schools: the ecosystemic approach. *Maladjustment and Therapeutic Education*. **8**(1), 3–18.

Wade, B. and Moore, M. (1993) *Experiencing Special Education*. Buckingham: Open University.

Warnock Report (1978) *Special Educational Needs*. London: HMSO.

Wells, G. (1981) *Learning Through Interaction: The Study of Language Development*. Cambridge: Cambridge University Press.

Wiles, S. (1990) Language and learning in multi-ethnic classrooms: strategies for supporting bilingual students. In Wells, G. and Nicholls, J. (eds) *Language and Learning: An Interactional Perspective*. London: Falmer.

Wood, D., Wood, J., Griffiths, A. and Howarth, I. (1986) *Teaching and Talking with Deaf Children*. Chichester: John Wiley.

Part 5

Trauma – Responding to the Unpredicted

CHAPTER 12

Child Protection

Steve Adams

THE SCHOOL PERSPECTIVE

In spite of the Butler-Sloss Report (Cleveland, 1988) and two editions of the multi-agency guidelines, *Working Together* (Department of Health, 1991), it is still a widespread public perception that child protection is the job of social services departments. Of course, it is true that social services carry the statutory responsibility for investigating concerns about abuse and other deficiencies in the care of children, and for ensuring the safety of the child, but neither of these are tasks which social workers could achieve alone.

Social workers work with a defined clientèle consisting of those children and families which they have identified as in need of support or other intervention. But they will begin to work with a family only if their attention is drawn to it, and they are therefore dependent upon those agencies which work with the generality of children for the raising of concerns about child abuse.

Only two groups work with all children: first, health visitors, who work with any family which has a child of between twelve days and five years of age; and second, staff in schools who work statutorily with all children from 5 to 16 years. The contact which staff in schools may have with those children is frequent, regular and often intensive, too, so that teachers, Education Care Officers, nursery nurses, midday supervisors and sometimes other staff may become trusted adults for some children. Even if a special relationship does not develop, staff have considerable opportunities for monitoring within school. As well as this, staff in schools may become specialists in what we might call 'the normal child' precisely because they meet so many children of the age range and locality concerned.

Unlike virtually all other professionals, staff in schools work with children in groups, and it is in their interactions with other children that changes in a child's behaviour are most evident, so that staff in schools have a particular opportunity to monitor such changes.

The result is that school staff are in a position second to none to notice behaviour which may indicate abuse or inadequate care, and to hear the child who is trying to draw attention to it. This places a responsibility on schools which cannot be set aside, and means that it is incumbent upon them to ensure that staff have a level of awareness of abuse and related care issues, and that they understand the importance of sharing any concern.

The responsibilities of the school staff, which schools need to recognise in a child protection policy, can be set out as follows:

Listening. Staff should endeavour in their interactions with pupils or students and with each other to be understanding, open and non-judgemental, the personal qualities defined by Truax and Carkhuff (1967) as those which facilitate helpful listening. Staff who are approachable in other situations, however trivial, will be more likely to be trusted about more sensitive issues. Staff need to be aware that children, especially younger ones, will find a range of ways in which to express what is happening to them at home, and that they may not be easily recognized.

Identification. Staff need to be observant, but they also need to be sufficiently well-informed to recognize those elements in a child's behaviour that may indicate that the child is being abused or otherwise suffering harm from parents or carers.

Referral. Staff need to be aware of the in-school child protection procedures, which in particular will mean that they need to know who the designated child protection liaison teacher is. That member of staff him/herself should be adequately trained for the role.

Support. Children who have been subject to abuse or lack of care need support if the effects of their experiences are to be minimised. The staff in school, because of their availability and frequently the closeness of their relationships with children, may have a significant role here.

The main task facing trainers intending to develop the capacity of a school to act appropriately within child protection procedures is to lower the levels of anxiety with regard to referral of concerns to social services. This is, more than any other, the main cause of a shortfall in referrals, and of delayed referrals. It also leads to unreasonable expectations of social workers: school staff sometimes expect to be able to control the outcome of a referral, particularly when their own perception is that they are phoning social services merely to discuss a case; and they may expect an immediate investigation in cases where that would be inappropriate.

The first and most common anxiety is that contacting social services will damage relationships with parents. It will, goes the argument, be seen by parents as a betrayal. If the school staff are wrong in their suspicions, the parents will never forgive them.

It is important first to stress that this anxiety conceals an ambivalence about who the client of the school is, an issue to which I shall return. We may work with parents, but it is in the interests of the child. When the interests of the parents are in conflict with those of the child, even if this is only so in principle, then the child's interests must be paramount – and of course this principle now has legal force in the 1989 Children Act.

Another issue embedded in this anxiety is that school staff – and indeed the parents and the public in general – have not recognized the school as a child protection agency. Hospitals for example are recognized as having the responsibility to interrogate parents of children presented with injuries with a view to checking whether parents may have caused the injuries. A confusing factor is the fact that the relationship between parents and the school is on-going in a way that with the hospital is not. Similar anxieties have been expressed by GPs and by health visitors. Part of the solution may be to publicize the child protection responsibilities in material to parents, so that parents do not expect the school to collude when staff are suspicious. Another element may be staff being more open with parents about the concerns they have – as long as this does not put the child at greater risk. The 1991 *Working Together* document appears to support this line.

Finally, there are issues here about the school losing control over what happens next. This probably arises out of the fact that many schools seem to have to sort out their own problems without outside help in most contexts, and staff expect to be able to do the same when a child protection issue arises. In the past, the sense that social workers would act without respect to the school's wishes was often well founded, and for schools which only infrequently contact social services such experiences may have conditioned staff attitudes. The media presentation of child abuse cases, too, dealing as it does exclusively with the sensational cases or with social workers perceived to have overreacted, confirms such preconceptions. Also, in some cases, notably concerns about actual physical injury, social workers may have little choice but to investigate, and the lack of room for manoeuvre may not be fully understood by schools.

A further anxiety which affects some schools arises from the sense of complicity which we all have for child abuse. Child abuse is possible only where children are seen as completely within the power of adults. Most adults expect children to obey them unquestioningly, and children grow up more or less accepting and expecting this to be the case. The work done in some schools aimed at making children less vulnerable to abuse, in which children are encouraged to believe that they have the right to say 'no' to adults is generally entirely at odds with the rest of the school's expectations of the behaviour of children, and indeed at odds with the expectations of most parents and of society in general.

The sense of complicity is even clearer in the case of sexual abuse, and many men are threatened by the implication that lying behind the abuse of children is the social context of male power. A defensive attitude arising from this may make it difficult for male staff to accept the possibility of abuse occurring.

What is needed is that staff in schools should make a move towards recognizing, first, that the school is a child protection agency and, second, that their responsibility towards their clients – the children – means that they cannot risk inaction where they have a concern or suspicion of abuse. Many staff say that they are cautious where child abuse is concerned. Unaware staff mean by this that they will not contact social services (they tend to use expressions like 'start the ball rolling', indicating the fear of losing control) unless they are certain that they are right, a demand which is rarely satisfied. For aware staff, on the other hand, when they say that they are cautious, they will mean that they will not risk allowing a child who they believe may be subject to abuse to continue to be abused: the risk for them is far more in not acting when there is any doubt. Clearly, to damage a positive relationship that a school has with a set of parents is to be avoided, but not at all costs, if the cost is the continued abuse of the child.

THE CHILD AND THE FAMILY

The Children Act, 1989 attempts to balance the safety and rights of the child with the rights of parents, and the tension involved here is a familiar one for schools. Staff need to work with parents in the interests of students. Indeed, as I have said elsewhere (Adams, 1989), the parents of a child are a crucial resource for the school. Nevertheless, it is important that staff should recognize that there are circumstances where to maintain the relationship with the parents may be to sacrifice the safety or well-being of the child, and the key field in which this situation arises is where the parents are either abusing the child or supporting an abuser or, at the least, being ambivalent in their attitude to an abuser.

However, the Children Act, as it must, does (just about) come down on the side of the child, in its insistence that the welfare of the child must be the paramount consideration, and the school must take the same line. And it is not only that the Children Act says so; it is also that in the end the school has to recognize that its client is the child, not the parents. Some ambiguity has been introduced in recent years by the notion of the 'citizens' charter', which encourages parents to believe that they can act towards schools in the same way as they act towards a company which produces a product – namely, that if they are dissatisfied with the product they can take their custom elsewhere. There is a limited extent to which this is in practice a reality anyway, but the principle ignores the fact that the school is there to educate the child, not its parents. Society has placed the child in the care of the school to act as a good parent might be expected to, not to act as the agent of the parents, and this is a very significant difference, since the effect is to require that, when the parents do not act in accordance with the welfare of the child, the school must have recourse to other means of ensuring it.

Another assumption which staff in schools sometimes make about families is that they are substantially the same as their own. The government has made a similar assumption in the Children Act with the principle that a child's family is the best place for him or her to be brought up. That social workers should have to justify to the courts the removal of a child in terms of the intended placement being an improvement is entirely right, but the fact is that some families provide the worst possible environment for a child, and it is important that this is recognized. It is as bad to cling to the idea that the child must be kept in the family at all costs as it is to remove it at the drop of a hat. Similarly, within a school context, school staff need to be able to face the possibility that a child may be ill-treated, discounted, neglected or sexually assaulted within the home, and should not assume that it will always be possible to work with parents in the interests of the child.

The range of families which do not provide a satisfactory environment is far wider than that which is generally understood to be covered by the term 'child abuse', and schools need to be aware that it is not just the systematic torture or sexual assault of children which needs to be reported. Staff often resist seeing other inappropriate parenting – such as that arising from incompetence or from pressure – as coming within child protection procedures. This is partly because of the implication that far more cases will have to be referred, or because they are sympathetic to the stresses that the family may be undergoing which lie behind the child's treatment. But a major part of their resistance comes from the expectation, encouraged by media reporting, that social workers will remove a child from its parents as soon as any concern is reported, and that, by referring, the school and by implication the member of staff will have been responsible for this.

In fact, of course, social workers themselves cannot remove a child, since it is only a decision of the court which can do so – even, since the Children Act, in an emergency. Generally, social workers see themselves as a helping profession and resist the image of them painted in the press of unfeeling and censorious investigators, and it is true that most of the work which follows child protection referrals is actually supportive rather than punitive, a point which needs to be stressed with school staff, since it affects the readiness of the school to work with social services, as we suggested earlier. That so much of the work of social workers is a low-key support and monitoring response is a reflection of the fact that most of the investigations within child protection procedures are not of what might be termed hard-core abuse.

Physical abuse has been recognized for longer than other forms of abuse, and it is no coincidence that it is the area where the threshold is most clearly defined. Since in our society at present it is legal for an adult to assault his or her own child – indeed, my own child is the only person I can legally assault – the threshold for an investigation is generally taken to be the point at which the assault causes an actual injury. The Children Act, 1989 puts the threshold at causing 'significant harm', which means that physical assault may precipitate an investigation if non-physical harm is resulting, such as if a child were subjected to repeated and unwarranted assault even where there is no actual injury. Most cases investigated do concern actual injury, however, and staff in schools need to be prepared to report injury if they believe that it has been caused by parents or carers, whether or not they would see the parents' action as actually constituting 'abuse'.

Often, because school staff understand and sympathize with the situation of the parent in these circumstances, they fail to share the concern, in spite of the fact that parents causing an injury to a child may well indicate a level of violence and stress in the family which endangers the child, and which may not cease without intervention of some kind. Another situation in which school staff may not report an injury is if they have no previous concerns about the care of the children – what they sometimes describe as a 'one-off'. Ignoring or minimizing such cases has resulted in the death of the child in a number of documented instances.

It is essential that in cases where concern focuses on actual injury staff do not delay in referring – and delay is unfortunately not uncommon in such circumstances, and sometimes results in a child remaining unprotected. This is because injury constitutes objective evidence which needs to be examined by a medical practitioner who is experienced in assessing the cause of an injury. Once this evidence is no longer available, it becomes a matter of the parent's word against the teacher's. More seriously still, delay in referring will mean that the time for the child to return home may arrive before the safety of the home has been assessed, and a home in which a child has already been injured by parents or carers is a potentially dangerous one to which the child should not return until workers are sure that it is safe for him or her to do so.

The boundary between physical abuse and neglect is not clear cut, since some physical injury results from parents not supervising children sufficiently or from their not being prepared to protect the child from household dangers. Neglect is essentially not providing for the needs of the child. This is also the clearest interface between children in need and children in need of protection. There is some evidence that gross physical neglect is decreasing, but it is still possible, particularly for staff at the younger end of the primary phase, to see children who exhibit the thin hair, the distended stomach and the shiny, chubby limbs associated with malnutrition. Less obvious examples, where children's weight and height increase at uneven rates, slower in the school holidays when the school dinner is not available, also cause concern and need to be reported. In young children, non-organic failure to thrive may be associated with emotional neglect or abuse.

Neglect at the softer end will cover low-level care, at the boundary of what social workers call 'good enough parenting', which will be difficult to define, and inadequate supervision. The law on supervision is not widely known, and most parents who habitually leave their children with a young person under 16 would be shocked to learn that if their children are injured while in the young person's care, they themselves could be prosecuted for neglect. If no harm is sustained, however, there is no legal age below which it is illegal to have the responsibility for the supervision of children. Even so, social services will intervene if parents are suspected to be taking risks by lack of appropriate supervisory arrangements.

Physical neglect, where there are again objective indicators, is easier to define than emotional neglect or abuse, though the latter can result in physical signs. A major problem is the fact that everybody might be said to abuse their children emotionally some of the time. For example, all parents shout at their children unreasonably when under stress, ignore them on occasions, send them away, laugh at them, are sarcastic, and so on. The 'hard' end of emotional abuse, even when no other apparent abuse is taking place, is not too difficult to identify: where a child is physically provided for but is prevented from having any contact with the rest of the family, and is kept alone in a (well-furnished) room, most school staff would have little difficulty in recognizing that such treatment was damaging. But where does the boundary lie?

All forms of abuse cause emotional damage, of course, so the term 'emotional abuse' is generally used when there are no signs of physical ill-treatment or neglect and sexual abuse is not suspected.

Sexual abuse or assault is frequently at the centre of press attention, particularly where the media deem that social workers have acted inappropriately or have trampled on the rights of parents. It is also the 'growth' area in terms of reportage, though there seems little reason to accept the myth that it is actually on the increase. Indeed, sexual abuse is hedged around with mythology, much of which is maintained to protect people from having to recognize what the fact that children are sexually abused and exploited says about our society and about human beings: myths which purport to explain why men who are otherwise of apparently unimpeachable character 'suddenly' (*sic*) engage in sexual relations with a child; myths which restrict sexual abuse to enclaves, or relate it to the underclass; myths which lead us to think that we shall be able to pick out a perpetrator at fifty paces. The truth is that sexual abuse can be found in any section of society, in all professions and among all economic groups. Research overwhelmingly suggests that perpetrators start at a young age and abuse repeatedly, often committing hundreds of offences and abusing scores of children. Perpetrators are often successful at their careers, may be charming and personable, and good with children – just like us, in fact. They engage in complex and systematic strategies to gain the trust and affection of the child and often the trust of involved adults before abusing that trust by abusing the child.

Sexual abuse is characterized by two main features. First, the child is unable to consent to sexual activity, whatever the abuser may say, because s/he does not understand the implications of whatever s/he is being asked to engage in. Second, there exists between children and adults a power imbalance which means that whatever the child may feel about the activity, s/he is unable to prevent it. The power of the adult is based first and foremost upon size and strength, but it is also related to the authority over children which society gives to adults in general and to some adults – parents and teachers spring to mind – in particular.

The abuser is most often a man. Recent British research (Kelly, Regan and Burton, 1991) supports 1984 American figures, suggesting that 95 per cent of perpetrators of sexual abuse are male. A majority of victims/survivors are female by between two and three to one. Most girl victims are abused by members of the family, while most boys are not, but very few abusers are totally unknown to their victims. The British research suggests that a quarter of perpetrators are of a similar age to the victims, a statistic which has huge implications for schools.

An aspect of sexual abuse which needs to be stressed is the systematic nature of this form of abuse. There is no possibility of a perpetrator claiming as with physical abuse that his normal behaviour went 'over the top'. Both Steven Wolf (1984) and Finkelhor (1984) have shown that sexual abusers plan, target and groom their victims, and that, far from being a deviation from their normal behaviour, the abuse is habitual and constantly repeated. This image, supported by the work at the Gracewell Clinic by Ray Wyre (Wyre, 1987), presents child sexual abusers as both more ordinary and more dangerous than is often thought to be the case. It is important that staff in schools do not believe that they will be able to recognize perpetrators by some obvious indicators, or that they are people who have been temporarily led astray. Both views have caused staff to fail to recognize, and therefore fail to prevent, the problem.

As well as being able to react when it is suspected that a child may have already been abused, staff in schools need to accept that there are times when intervention may be necessary to protect children who have never experienced abuse because there is reason to believe that they may be likely to be abused in the future. There are two common situations in which child protection procedures need to be invoked where abuse has not actually taken place. The first is where children who are not known to have been abused are members of a household where there are children who have. For instance, in a family of five children, if three are known to have been physically abused, it is necessary to ensure that all five are safe. It is sometimes the case that one child is selected by the family for particular abuse (often called scapegoating or child-specific abuse) but it is also common for all children in a family to be subject to the same abuse.

The second type of circumstance is where a known perpetrator moves into a family where there are children. Even though these children have never been subject to abuse, it will be necessary to assess the risk to them. This is particularly the case where sexual abuse is concerned because of the cyclic and systematic nature of sexual abuse referred to above.

CHILD PROTECTION AND PASTORAL CARE

It might be said that a school which can get it right for child protection has got it right for pastoral care generally. This is mainly because child protection, operated ideally, puts the child's welfare at the centre. At a time in the history of education when pastoral care is in danger of being marginalized, one way of ensuring that its objectives are still maintained is to focus attention on developing whole-school policies for child protection.

The most obvious aspect of child protection is that of multi-agency working. This challenges the practice still to be found in some schools of coping within the school with whatever problems may surface. The principle of multi-agency working is that staff in school have specific tasks to perform for which they have appropriate training and experience; and where there are tasks which are better done by other professionals, information is shared with them and their help enlisted. Secondary schools are, on the whole, more used to working in this way, but paradoxically it is often the schools which have the pastoral tradition which are least geared to it. This may be because the staff are used to going beyond the tasks which are most central to education in its narrower sense.

Child protection demands that teachers should accept the responsibility for the welfare of the child beyond the classroom; at the same time, it requires teachers to recognize that other professionals have the skills and experience to provide some parts of the actual intervention. As the demands of the curriculum increase, this approach is an appropriate one for a range of concerns. It requires staff in different agencies to trust one another, and to develop an understanding of each other's characteristic objectives, skills and perspectives.

Child protection also requires that staff in schools have some grasp of the legal context within which they work, and in particular of the legal rights of children. The Children Act, 1989 does introduce rights for children, and the school can play a part in informing students about them. The Gillick Principle, requiring that children of sufficient age and understanding should have their wishes and feelings ascertained and taken into account, may also present staff in schools with the opportunity to play a supportive role where children are involved in legal processes.

Because of the legal context of child protection and the fact that a member of the school staff may find him/herself required to appear as a witness for the prosecution against an alleged abuser, the very highest standards of reporting and recording are necessary. First, there needs to be a school record of the relevant concerns, the actions taken and the reasons for those actions, including reasons when no action was taken or when action did not involve contact with social services. Second, any member of staff who observed relevant behaviour, overheard relevant comments, or listened to allegations by a child, should write a witness statement, which can later be read in court if necessary. Both types of report need to be written *immediately*, which means within an hour or so of the events. Records need to limit themselves to the factual, or where interpretations are given it should be clearly indicated that this is what they are.

Such records need to be kept securely, but either they should be kept with the rest of the material on a child's file, or, if not, there should be a clear and well-understood signposting system on the files so that staff who need to know will be aware that such material exists and may need to be consulted.

Such approaches to the recording and filing of sensitive documentation about a child are essential for child protection, but are also good practice for all material. The school should also have a clear policy for what is to happen if a parent requests sight of filed material about his or her child. The Education (School Records) Regulations, 1989 (DES Circular 17/89) do not authorize or encourage the sharing of material relating to actual, suspected or alleged child abuse with parents, but *Working Together* (DH/DES/WO, 1991) suggests that schools should be as open about the records kept as is consistent with the safety of the child.

The principles of confidentiality required in child protection provide a model for confidentiality in school generally. This means that, first, there can be no blanket confidentiality. The welfare of the child being paramount, it is never possible to assure a student that what s/he tells a teacher will never be shared. At the same time, information is shared only in accordance with the principle of 'need to know'. This means that assurance can be given that anything the student says will not be used for 'gossip-fodder' among the staff, and that remarks will not be made in any public context which might be a source of embarrassment to the student. The position of parents in this kind of situation is also clarified by taking child protection as the model. There can be no assumption that whatever a student tells a member of staff will be automatically passed on to parents. The client of the school is the child, not its parents. Nevertheless, parents have the right to be involved in decisions affecting their child as long as this does not prejudice the welfare of the child. (The Sex Education guidelines document (Department for Education Circular 5/94) advises schools that they should always inform parents where a student gives a member of staff information which implies that s/he has engaged in sexual intercourse under the age of consent (that is, where the girl is under 16). This action must not be taken until the school has assured itself that there are no child protection implications, since, if there are, social services need to be informed rather than (or at least before) the parents. It should also be remembered that sex with a girl under 16 is a criminal offence (Unlawful

Sexual Intercourse) – though the reaction of the police if it is reported to them is sympathetic where the boy is of a similar age to the girl. In general, the question of whether this aspect of the Gillick principle – that the child has a right to confidential advice without her or his parents' knowledge or consent – applies to staff in schools or only to health staff has (as 5/94 says) 'yet to be tested in the Courts'!)

Child protection requires that staff are approachable to students or pupils, that staff will make time to listen to whatever they may want to share. This in turn requires an ethos in which both students or pupils and staff are valued and respected as individuals. Specifically, child protection insists that the student's perspective in what s/he says will be respected. This means that, prima facie, what s/he says will be assumed to be true in the first instance. In a child protection context, too many children who have tried to disclose sexual abuse have not been protected because it has been assumed that they were lying. Too many other kinds of interaction between teachers and students have in the past suffered too from staff taking a position of disbelief about the student's perspective. For instance, a common reaction to 'John's just hit me' is 'What did you do to him first?', automatically assuming some culpability in the child who is disclosing. This assumption is recognized to be destructive in the extreme in a child protection context, and is unhelpful in any situation.

Child protection demands that efficient referral systems should be in place in schools, so that information is transmitted to the appropriate place as quickly as possible, so that the appropriate staff can react. This is a useful principle for a school to adopt, though it needs to be recognized that child protection will require a faster and more direct channel than is needed to most situations. It is not appropriate that a member of staff in a large secondary school who has a child protection concern should first approach the student's form tutor, who then refers it to the head of year, who then passes it on to the head of upper/lower school, who at last approaches the child protection co-ordinator (designated teacher). Not only will this take up unnecessary time which may constitute danger, but there is an increased likelihood of the concern being inappropriately filtered out at one or other rung of the ladder.

As staff's awareness of the need to be alert for indicators of child abuse increases, so staff may also note needs of children which are not being met, where the shortfall does not actually constitute abuse. This means that the school will become a more effective monitor of the levels of home care which children are receiving, and now that the Children Act requires social services departments to provide services to children in need, the school can share these concerns too.

The curriculum is another aspect of the school where child protection can have an impact. In saying this, I wish to stress that no programme of study can enable children to protect themselves, nor indeed is it appropriate that it should. It is not the job of children to protect themselves from abuse by adults: it is our job as adults who care for children to do that. Nevertheless, it is possible to help children to be less vulnerable to people who systematically abuse children.

We should recognize the nature of abuse and how perpetrators work in forming this area of the curriculum. First, it makes no sense to concentrate on so-called 'stranger-danger' work, when we know that the bulk of abusers are known to and trusted by their victims. One implication of telling children to beware of adults whom they do not know is that they will believe that they are safe with adults who are known to them – and this in itself makes them more vulnerable to those people. Second, a simplistic message that a child can say 'no' to an adult is not helpful. For a child who is or has been subject to abuse, this message will ring false in their ears or will exacerbate the sense of guilt and responsibility for the abuse that virtually all abused children feel. As well as this, the message that a child can say 'no' to adults is entirely at odds with all the other messages which adults in general, and schools in particular, give to children – namely, that children have to do as adults say. Indeed, a frequent source of teacher–pupil conflict is disobedience.

It is also important to embed work designed to help children to be less vulnerable to abuse in the personal, social and health education curriculum. It should not be free-standing or overt, and most of the activities should focus on what are to most children (happily) more familiar areas of life. What teachers must not do, it seems to me, is to create a sense of unspecified danger which will simply frighten children, when what we want is to give children more confidence. In the end, the most effective way to reduce vulnerability is to increase self-esteem.

The following aspects of the PSHE curriculum will all help children to be less vulnerable in a range of contexts:

- *The family*. Discussion of the stereotype of the 'normal' family addressed and confronted. Family relationships. Rights of family members.
- *Relationships*. Expectations of friendships of different kinds. Appropriate behaviour for different relationships.
- *Gender issues*. Consideration of male power and its implications.
- *Personal identity and self-esteem*. Understanding myself: Who am I.? How am I changing? What influences are there on me? How did I get to be like I am now? What are my special qualities?
- *Human/children's rights*. Personal rights. What special rights do children have? What responsibilities are involved?
- *My body*. Physical development. Terminology. Touching: good and bad touches; private areas.
- *Safety*. In the home. On the roads. Personal safety: awareness of dangers posed by different situations.
- *Assertiveness*. Asking for what I want. Saying no. Receiving criticism and pressure from others.
- *Parenthood/childrearing*. Needs of young children. Stresses of living together. Discipline.
- *Secrets*. Good secrets. Recognizing bad secrets.
- *Feelings*. Pleasant and unpleasant sensations. Comparing feelings. Validating our own feelings. Uncomfortable feelings. Sexual feelings and awareness. What is 'normal'?

All in all, a school which provides a therapeutic environment for its most damaged children will care effectively for all its children. For the child who is being abused, the school needs to be organized to provide a setting in which he or she can, in whatever way, communicate that fact to staff. They in turn must be sufficiently aware to understand what is being communicated, and to be able to take the appropriate action so that protection is provided. Having identified pupils or students who are being or have been subject to abuse, the school should provide firm guidelines for behaviour, while at the same time having flexibility and a recognition of the needs of the individual. Recording should be scrupulous, efficient and professional. Staff need to be approachable and, when approached, able to listen effectively without imposing their own attitudes. Staff also need to be prepared to see the life of the child outside school as not beyond their concern. If a school provides all this, then it will not only be the children who are or have been abused who will benefit: the school will be able to care for all its pupils or students.

THE WIDER CONTEXT OF CHILD PROTECTION

The school's reaction to child abuse cannot be seen as a matter of individual school or even local LEA policy. Because child protection is a multi-agency response, how the school reacts must mesh with the responsibilities which other agencies take. Multi-agency child protection procedures are produced by the local Area Child Protection Committee (ACPC), in consultation with its member agencies. Most LEAs will be coterminous with the ACPC, and the LEA will have a senior officer who is a member of it. A representative of school staff, usually a headteacher, will often be a member too. ACPCs are responsible for administering and monitoring child protection within their areas, and meet regularly to review practice and policy issues. They also have some responsibility for training of staff in the member agencies.

Because procedures for child protection have quasi-statutory force (the latest expression of this is to be found in the post-Children-Act *Working Together* (DH/DES/WO 1991), LEAs are required to ensure that all maintained schools have a copy. The LEA is also required to ensure that all its schools designate a senior teacher to be responsible for child protection within the school and for liaising with social services and other agencies in child protection cases (see DES Circular 4/88). The core of in-school child protection procedures will be that a member of staff who is concerned that a child in his or her care may be subject to abuse must contact the designated teacher and share concerns. This teacher will normally be responsible for contacting social services if this is deemed to be appropriate. Details vary from area to area, but this will normally be followed by discussions as to the strategy of the investigation, following which social workers, and, where appropriate, police officers will investigate the suspicions or allegations. The social workers will focus upon ensuring the safety of the child, while the police will be primarily concerned with the apprehension of anyone who may have committed an offence.

The investigation may be brief, or it may be a more prolonged operation. It may involve interviews with and/or medical examination of the child. It may result in the rapid removal of the child from the dangerous home, or, more frequently, in discussions with parents as to how best to improve the welfare of their child.

Principles of good practice have developed over time, and the school needs to be aware of them. Central is the principle that the process through which the child is put should not be any more abusive itself than is necessary. Medical examinations should take place only where there is some purpose in them, and only one should be undertaken, so, if forensic evidence is required, a police surgeon should be present as well as a paediatrician. Interviews with the child should also be reduced to a minimum: the child should not have to tell his or her story more than once, if possible. This means not only that the interview will probably have to be undertaken by a social worker and a police officer jointly but also that it is important that staff in school have not encouraged the child to tell the whole story to them first.

The school needs to recognize that interviewing in abuse cases is a specialist skill which is fenced around with the complexities of the legal process. A teacher can effectively blow a prosecution of an alleged abuser, if he or she asks questions in a way which is seen as leading or coaching a child. Moreover, the 1991 Criminal Justice Act has now made it important that interviews with children in abuse cases are videoed, since the video is admissible as the chief evidence in such cases. The practice of such interviews is subject to the guidance to be found in the Memorandum of Good Practice which followed the Act. (The Memorandum of Good Practice has also impacted on the way in which the 'pre-investigation interview', that is, any occasion when a member of staff receives an initial disclosure from a pupil/student, must be handled. Staff must not question the student if possible, but must confine themselves to supportive responses; they should not stop a child who is in full flood but should not encourage her or him to say more than is necessary to be clear what s/he is saying. Recording carefully and immediately is also essential.)

Schools should be careful about contacting parents inappropriately in the early stages of a child abuse investigation. Part of the problem here is that some of the most pastorally-oriented schools are actually those which work most closely with parents, and to operate behind the backs of parents does not come easily to them. But it is essential that decisions about parental involvement are taken in co-operation with social services and other agencies. It is particularly important where there are allegations of sexual abuse. The problem is that it is not easy to predict whether non-abusing parents will support their child or the perpetrator, and in a surprising number of cases it is the latter. If those having the care of the child support the person about whom allegations are made, there is a clear danger that they may put pressure on the child to change his or her story – and the pressure may be physically and/or emotionally damaging to the child.

A member of staff who has been selected by a child to hear him or her speak about abusive experiences which s/he has had is an important person for the child protection process. Generally, and especially if the child specifically requests it, such a member of staff will be able to be present through the police or social services interview with the child, and may have a role in supporting the child through court appearances as well.

This should always be encouraged if the member of staff is willing and if s/he can be spared from other duties. It should, however, be recognized that such responsibilities are demanding and stressful, and a member of staff taking them on will need proper personal and professional support from colleagues and elsewhere.

After the investigation, the initial child protection conference takes place. This is a multi-agency meeting at which all involved professionals gather with an experienced and professional chair to share information and views, and to decide whether the child needs a systematic plan of protection. The key question at such a conference is whether the child's name should be added to the list of those children within the ACPC boundaries who are felt to be at risk of further abuse, ill-treatment or inadequate care – the Child Protection Register. At present, there is no national register and criteria for inclusion vary, but essentially the child will be registered if s/he is felt to need professionals to be involved to secure his or her safety.

The school will always be invited to this meeting, and must ensure that a member of staff attends. Thought needs to be given to the choice of staff who should attend. Generally, the school representative should be someone who has up-to-date, face-to-face contact with the child, so the class teacher or form tutor may be most appropriate. This has to be weighed against the fact that others – the head or designated child protection co-ordinator – may have more experience and understanding of the processes involved in the conference, or may have more authority to say what the school can offer to the child. But there is nothing so frustrating to a conference as to find that the school representative is not able to give first-hand information about the child. Of course, if more than one member of staff can attend, this is the best option, but against a background of stretched budgets this is likely to be impracticable.

The school should prepare a written report for the conference, which should give detailed but relevant information. It should be kept in mind that the conference will focus on the safety of the child, rather than on other issues, such as the problems which the child may present to staff in school, and extraneous comment should be avoided.

Since 1991 (*Working Together* II), parents are likely to be present for all or some of a child protection conference, and older children (13 is a common age boundary) may also be invited. Standards of oral and written reporting need to be high, therefore: rumour or gossip should be avoided, the report being limited to the factual, with any matters of opinion being clearly distinguished.

If the child is registered, further 'review' conferences automatically follow, usually at six-month intervals. The child will have a key social worker, who should keep in touch with the school and to whom any concerns about the child should be reported immediately. The school may be asked to monitor as part of the child protection plan, but this should be done as a matter of course anyway. The school may be asked to provide other support to the child and staff will need to consider whether what is asked for is possible.

A child can only be de-registered (that is, removed from the Child Protection Register) at a Child Protection Review Conference, so the school will have a part in that decision. Attendance at conferences should never be seen as optional.

TRAINING FOR CHILD PROTECTION

School staff – especially the designated teachers and headteachers – should take every opportunity to meet with staff from other ACPC agencies, particularly social workers, to build up an understanding of their roles, their perspectives and their tasks within child protection. They should also ensure that all staff have appropriate training. This is required by both *Working Together* and DES Circular 4/88, though it is difficult to see what pressure can be put on schools to comply now that the training budgets are devolved and schools have to decide their own priorities for staff development. The guidance for inspections (*Framework for the Inspection of Schools*, OFSTED, 1992) may provide a possible answer, though there is nothing explicit which will point inspectors towards child protection. Another route may be to train governors, but this too depends upon their identifying child protection as a priority. Indeed, a major problem is that schools will take up opportunities for child protection training only if they have some awareness of child protection issues, but schools which have not had training often lack that awareness. A central issue is therefore how to ensure that staff in all schools have such training.

At present, the training of staff is largely the province of individual school policy. Indeed, it should be a source of concern to the Department of Health that the local education authority's power to insist that schools should fulfil the requirements of *Working Together* or indeed Circular 4/88 has virtually evaporated. Local management of schools started the process; the movement towards grant-maintained status for many schools has exacerbated the situation; and the impending demise of the LEA looks likely to complete it. Somehow, the Department of Health needs to find a way to ensure that the prime monitoring and referral agency of child protection – the school – is equipped to provide this service to children. It is a gross anomaly that schools are able to decide whether or not training in child protection for the staff (even for the designated member of staff) is sufficiently high a priority to warrant the spending of a portion of the limited budget on it. It is bizarre that there appears to be no systematic mechanism to monitor the ability and indeed willingness of the school to follow ACPC child protection procedures, nor is it clear what sanctions might be imposed upon a school which fails to do so. Tragically, it may once again take the death of a child before action is taken to make the school's role within child protection mandatory. For 1995–6, GEST funding now includes Activity 17, which will enable LEAs to devolve funding to schools whose child protection liaison teachers remain untrained. This funding will be sufficient for half the schools in the LEA area to have up to two days' training for their designated member of staff. This is clearly an improvement – particularly if this is to be a permanent feature of GEST funding.

However, as things stand, it remains the school's responsibility to ensure that staff are adequately trained for their child protection role, and it need hardly be stressed that a school which has claims to providing effective pastoral care should ensure that it is a staff development priority. The designated teacher should have a comprehensive understanding of child protection issues, and a thorough knowledge of local child protection procedures. All staff – not just teaching staff – need to have some awareness training and to understand their individual responsibilities within local procedures. In a large secondary school, staff having special pastoral responsibility need more than the basic level of awareness. Some training for all staff in listening is also important, and schools should recognize that children do not necessarily follow official structures: it may be the midday supervisor who is approached, and the child cannot be drafted on to someone whom the child or young person may be less willing to talk to.

It needs to be remembered, too, that child protection is constantly changing in practices and philosophy, and staff training needs regular updating. Child protection training should also be part of the induction training for new staff. For these reasons, the temptation to feel that child protection training has been 'done' is one which should be resisted.

Care should be taken to ensure that trainers employed have an understanding of and sympathy with the attitudes and philosophy of the multi-agency child protection community. This is child- rather than parent-centred and has a sensitivity to equal opportunities issues. Trainers should also be selected who understand the particular perspective which school staff have, and are prepared to address the concerns which follow from it (I drew attention to these earlier).

Most local education authorities have staff (at present) who have responsibility for training school staff, and who work with social services to ensure that courses are in line with ACPC policy. In some areas, the education social worker or education welfare service take responsibility for training school staff, but in other areas this would be inappropriate. Some authorities have advisers or advisory teachers with a child protection training brief. Alternatively, social services departments themselves are often able to provide appropriately informed and experienced trainers. Each LEA at present has a designated senior officer with responsibility for child protection who will be able to advise schools on trainers.

Some independent training organizations can do the job, too, but schools should be cautious, since some training units have simply jumped on the 'child abuse' bandwagon. Those which have developed from LEA advisory services may be the most appropriate, but advice should be sought from senior child protection staff within social services if in doubt.

ABUSE BY STAFF

Before ending this chapter, it is important to emphasize that schools and colleges are part of a world in which child abuse occurs. The rigour which is applied to protecting children and young people from abuse beyond the school must also be employed when the suspicions or allegations concern school staff themselves.

A basic tenet of child protection philosophy is that the child must be listened to and, in general, believed. Many, many adults have unresolved abusive experiences in the past which still impact on their lives because they were unable to talk about them to a believing adult at the time. While it is a part of our professional stance that we should not undermine colleagues, this line must never be allowed to result in a child or young person who is being victimized by a colleague remaining unprotected.

What we know about perpetrators of sexual abuse (see above) must leave us in no doubt that there are people who enter careers such as ours at least partly in order to abuse the children for whom they are responsible. Staff in school who are trusted to the extent that a child confides abuse by another member of staff must act in a way which is worthy of that trust, first by believing the allegation and second by acting upon it to protect the child and other children who may be vulnerable to abuse by the same perpetrator.

There are in most LEAs procedures which have to be followed in such cases, and the school has a responsibility to ensure that all staff are aware of their stipulations. Essentially, however, the allegations should be reported to a senior colleague, and should be investigated along three distinct routes: first, the protection of the child and any other children who may be at risk from the same source; second, the possibility of criminal charges against the alleged perpetrator; and third, disciplinary proceedings against the alleged perpetrator. Other agencies, especially social services and the police, will need to be involved in the process. Covering up the allegations is probably collusion in abuse, and puts children at risk, immediately and in the future.

Much more contentious are allegations from a pupil or student or parent of physical assault by a member of staff. Again, LEAs will often have procedures to be followed. But it should be stressed that, where a child is injured, and alleges that the cause of the injury is an assault by a member of staff, a course of action must be followed which echoes the procedure which would be followed in the event of a child being similarly injured by a parent or other carer in the home. The three strands, of child protection, criminal investigation and disciplinary proceedings are equally appropriate here.

There would be a profound inequity if children were to be believed and action taken against an alleged perpetrator where the alleged perpetrator was a parent, but not where the alleged perpetrator was employed as a professional child-carer. The implications in the event of such allegations for the need for support for staff so accused are obvious, particularly since clearly the allegations may not be substantiated in the investigation. The fact that such support may require special arrangements indicates what may be a significant shortfall in pastoral provision: pastoral care for staff.

Understandably, concern is often expressed (by the teaching unions most particularly) about the possibility that allegations made against staff by students may be false. Staff who do not abuse or exploit the children in their care need to be secure in the knowledge that they are not vulnerable to accusations which may markedly affect their future even if they are unsubstantiated. Procedures in place must provide such security as far as is possible without making it more difficult to protect children. (One Area Child Protection Committee (Derbyshire) has procedures for allegations against staff in any day care context. (i.e. not just schools), which are approved by the local teacher professional associations as providing safety for innocent staff as well as for pupils and students.)

What the education service must avoid, however, is responding to such allegations in ways which allow schools to brush inconvenient situations under the carpet. There are many examples of proven sexual abuse by staff in schools where the perpetrator has been able to continue his teaching career (and his paedophile career too) because the school was unwilling to bring the issue to the surface. What schools must not do is assume that any allegation of abuse by a child about a member of staff must be false. A common (perhaps the most common) factor inhibiting a child who has been abused from telling someone about it is the fear that s/he will not be believed. Assuming that a student will be lying is not a pastoral approach for any situation.

I have endeavoured in this chapter to outline the major issues concerned with child protection, and to indicate the responsibilities of the educational institution within the wider child care network. The challenge for schools and colleges is to develop appropriate reactive and proactive strategies in co-operation with other professionals within the multi-agency child protection community and in accordance with statutory and quasi-statutory requirements. To an extent, such responses are a natural extension of existing pastoral and personal and social education provision. The growing public and media recognition of the scale of the problem, however, and the anxiety which this provokes, has led to a much more rigorous and systematic response on the part of child care agencies in general, and it is vital that we recognize the school's role as a – perhaps the – key referring agency, and similarly address child protection more systematically than has generally been the case. I hope that this chapter has served to highlight some of the complexities of child protection which schools and colleges should take into account in developing an effective and comprehensive policy.

Acknowledgement: Thanks are due to Francis Luckcock with whom I discussed in advance the structure of this chapter.

REFERENCES

Adams, S. (1989) *A Guide to Creative Tutoring*. London: Kogan Page.

Children Act (1989). London: HMSO.

Cleveland (1988) *Report of Inquiry into Child Abuse in Cleveland* (Butler-Sloss Report). London: HMSO.

Department for Education (1994) DES *Circular 5/94: Education Act 1993: Sex Education in Schools*. London: Department for Education.

Department of Education and Science (1988) *Working Together for the Protection of Children from Abuse: Procedures within the Education Service*, DES Circular 4/88. London: DES/WO.

Department of Education and Science (1989) *Education (School Records) Regulations 1989*, DES Circular 17/89. London: DES/WO.

Department of Health (etc.) (1991) *Working Together (under the Children Act 1989)*. London: HMSO.

Finkelhor, D. (1984) *Child Sexual Abuse: New Theory and Research*. Berkeley, Cal.: Sage Publications.

Home Office/Department of Health (1991) *Memorandum of Good Practice (under the Criminal Justice Act 1991)*. London: HMSO.

Kelly, L., Regan, L. and Burton, S. (1991) *An Exploratory Study of the Prevalence of Sexual Abuse in a Sample of 16–21-year-olds*. London: University of North London.

OFSTED (1992) *Framework for the Inspection of Schools*. London: HMSO.

Truax, C. and Carkhuff, R. (1967) *Toward Effective Counselling and Therapy*. Chicago: Aldine.

Wolf, S. (1984) A multi-factor model of deviant sexuality, Conference paper, Lisbon.

Wyre, R. (1987) *Working with Sex Abuse: Understanding Sex Offending*. Oxford: Perry Publications.

CHAPTER 13

Separation, divorce and the school

Martin Desforges

INTRODUCTION

Separation and divorce are becoming increasingly common throughout Britain, and there are few families which have not been closely affected. Between 1970 and 1980 the divorce rate increased from 58,000 per year to 145,000 per year, and stayed at this level through the 1980s. Three-quarters of all divorces involve children under 16, and, because most divorces occur in the first ten years of marriage, many involve very young children. About one child in five is likely to experience parental divorce before he or she reaches the age of 16. Each school year some fifteen out of every thousand children, that is between ten and twenty children in the average secondary school, have to cope with the divorce of their parents. These figures do not include those children involved in parental separation; to include these, the numbers above should be doubled. These statistics are averages for the United Kingdom as a whole, but in some inner city areas the incidence of separation and divorce may be much higher. Some London boroughs have reported that between 40 and 50 per cent of a school's annual intake of pupils have separated or divorced parents.

Divorce is now seen as an acceptable adult solution to an unhappy marriage. Attitudes, however, have not always kept pace with the new behaviour, and, despite the increased prevalence of divorce, those involved often feel guilty and ashamed. Each divorce brings with it a sense of personal failure and causes much unhappiness, at least in the short term. The way western society is organized, and the support it usually makes available to parents, means it is best when children are brought up in happy homes with both parents sharing the responsibilities of childrearing and family life. Where children are involved it would generally be preferable if their parents did not separate. It would be better if marital relationships could be helped to improve and grow rather than fall apart. However, staying together for the sake of the children and perpetuating a destructive household seldom helps, and can cause chronic stress for all members of the family. If a marriage breaks down, the home is no longer happy; separation and divorce may be the solution the adults choose for their problem. This solution may cause unhappiness and create new problems for the children, whose needs and opinions are necessarily different from those of their parents. In divorce the adults may want a clean break from the former partner, and sometimes a fresh start in a new relationship. The children will usually need continued contact with both parents and reassurances that marital breakdown is not accompanied by a break in the parent–child relationship. They usually want things to stay as they are, and are not excited at the thought of moving house or school.

Although divorce causes much unhappiness, it need not necessarily be a long-term disaster. The way the divorce is managed makes a significant difference to children's reactions and their ability to cope. There are many books and articles helping parents to support their children through this difficult period (see the bibliography at the end of the chapter), but little has been written on how the teacher and the school can offer vital support to pupils at this time of stress and uncertainty. It is legitimate and increasingly necessary for teachers and schools to be interested in separation and divorce as they affect the social and emotional development of children as well as their ability to benefit from learning experiences.

Many teachers already possess considerable expertise in helping children under stress. They know the range of behaviour to expect in each age group. The knowledge they have of children enables them to be aware of changes in an individual's behaviour. Many children experiencing difficulties can best be helped within an existing relationship, such as with a teacher, rather than by direct referral to an educational psychologist, psychiatrist or social worker. Teachers, in daily contact with the children, are more likely to be available when the pupil is willing to accept help. By observing pupils objectively and listening to their concerns, teachers can assess the reactions to stress, and eventually decide whether referral to a specialist agency is required (for example when the reaction to parental separation is more severe, lasts longer or differs greatly from what is expected for the age and sex of the pupil). Knowing that a significant number of children are experiencing their parents' separation, expecting a prolonged reaction, being familiar with the normal range of responses, teachers can go a long way in supporting those of their pupils in this position. This chapter provides some information on the stages of marital breakdown, considers the typical range of age-specific reactions shown by children when their parents separate, and explores the various ways schools can help children through this period of stress.

STAGES OF MARITAL BREAKDOWN

Marital separation is a lengthy and confusing process, with many couples going through a number of temporary separations before the final break. Some families may get caught up in a repetitive cycle of some of these stages before a final breakdown, the whole process taking months or years (Figure 13.1). The problem is made even more complex by the fact that the bonds of marriage can be considered in several different ways: emotional, legal and economic. In the process of separation and divorce each of these bonds is broken at a different time. Emotional bonds may break down either before or after legal and economic ones. Partners may progress at

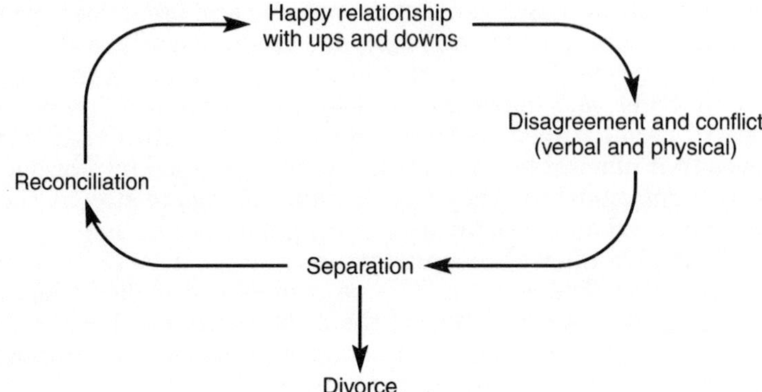

Figure 13.1

different rates, getting out of phase with each other, so adding to the conflict and confusion. As the parents grow apart they may talk less to each other, and spend less time together. The number of disagreements may grow with loss of temper and possibly physical violence. As each parent becomes preoccupied with his or her own problems they may spend less time sharing family activities and overlook the early signs of anxiety and upset in the children.

Having made a decision to separate, it is best if parents take time to explain what is going to happen before the break is made. Only a few children will want the household to break up, and most will want both parents to remain together, hoping desperately that things will improve. They will need to be told more than once, and reassured that both parents still love them. Practical details of where they will live and go to school and who will look after them is what will worry them. The reality, unpleasant as it is, is rarely as bad as the creative imagination of an upset child. It is important that parents are honest, and don't avoid telling their children for fear of the short-term upset. Reactions will vary: some children will cry, others remain silent or run to be alone. Reassurance at this stage is best given by physical comfort. It is likely that children will continue to ask questions for many weeks, and it is important that they are not embarrassed or ashamed by the situation. By creating the atmosphere that it's all right to talk about what is happening, they may get comfort from friends, be able to talk about their feelings and changes in their family life.

Schools can support this process in a variety of ways. A range of suitable books can be available within primary classrooms and school libraries which deal with parental separation and divorce in an appropriate way (see bibliography at the end of the chapter). Cox and Desforges (1987) deal at some length with curriculum issues in the area of family structure, family life and parenthood and discuss ways in which separation and divorce can usefully be raised within the framework of social education.

Immediately after separation parents are often depressed, anxious or physically ill. Preoccupation with their own feelings makes it difficult for them to provide their children with the attention, affection and support they need. Teachers can play a major role at this stage in listening to the children's concerns and offering reassurance. Knowing something of the stages that both parents and children go through also enables them to advise parents if their views are sought.

It is not the actual separation or divorce itself which affects children in the long term but the way it is managed, particularly by the parents. Children need both parents, even though after separation this can no longer be within the marriage. Although being married is ended by divorce, being a parent is not. When the children feel loved and cared for by both parents, even if apart, and both parents show this in what they say and do, the children are unlikely to suffer serious difficulties in the long term. This means working out a new relationship with the old partner, which is now for the benefit of the children, not for the adults. This is not easy, as strong, angry and bitter feelings between parents can get in the way. Each parent should try to respect the other's views, and not try to undermine them in the eyes of the children. It involves establishing a framework with clear expectations based on the children's needs, which avoids using the children as a focus for old quarrels. As soon as possible children should be encouraged to make their own contacts and arrangements with the absent parent. Even quite young children can be taught to use the telephone.

CHILDREN'S REACTIONS TO PARENTAL SEPARATION BY AGE

At each stage in the marital breakdown, the needs and perspectives of the children are different from those of their parents. In the middle of these emotionally charged events parents often have difficulty in meeting the needs of their children, and are unlikely to be aware of how best to help them. Teachers knowledgeable of the stages are able to respond to parental requests for advice, and to know when to suggest involving specialist agencies.

The majority of children are not told directly what is happening to the family during the period leading up to separation, and an atmosphere is created where children cannot ask questions, and remain anxious and uncertain. By being honest, remembering the age and understanding of the children, a great deal of confusion, uncertainty and anxiety can be avoided. Children should understand that they did not cause the divorce, that both parents still love them, and that they have no power to stop it. Most children feel angry and become preoccupied with their own thoughts, spending time day-dreaming and worrying about the future. They can become moody and bad-tempered, find it difficult to concentrate on school work and may over-eat. Within these generalizations there are important differences in how children of different ages and sexes react.

In our society boys and girls behave differently. Some people believe these differences are inborn and others believe they are caused by adults expecting them to behave in different ways, and therefore treating them differently. The differences are almost certainly due to a complex interaction of both these factors. However it is caused, it is true that boys and girls react differently in stressful situations, including reactions to parental divorce. Both boys and girls seek adult company and attention when parents divorce, but boys tend to prefer to be with men, whereas girls show dependency on men and women. Girls are not discouraged from crying and showing feelings of sadness, which evoke comfort and understanding from adults. Boys are usually expected to hide such feelings, leaving aggression as the only outlet. If boys do show distress adults are usually less supportive. All this causes boys more difficulties in dealing with problems involving personal relationships.

Adults should try to encourage an atmosphere where boys and girls feel comfortable in showing emotions – happiness, sadness, pain and grief. This is likely to lead to a reduction in the amount of aggression shown by boys, allowing a more satisfactory solution to emotional problems, and better personal relationships. Clearly adults have an important part to play in letting children see them display a range of emotions themselves, as well as offering support to boys in helping them demonstrate feelings of sadness, pain and grief.

Up to 5 years of age children have a limited understanding of events, but are usually capable of understanding much more than they are told. They can be helped by brief clear explanations. Routine security and being loved are the base from which they can explore an expanding world. Their sense of loss leaves them frightened and bewildered, often using fantasy in their play of united parents to ward off sadness. They may be so afraid of losing the remaining parent that routine separations they once coped with become difficult scenes. Bedtime may be accompanied by protest and crying, going to nursery or school can be traumatic. Regression is common, with the child behaving in more immature ways. Waking and crying in the night may increase, the use of soft toys or cloths as security objects reappear. The basic fear of the child is loss of the remaining parent, making separation very difficult. This can cause problems over visiting the absent parent unless both parents remember that the fear is separating from the parent the child is living with, not fear of being with the absent parent. Misunderstanding the nature of this fear can lead both parents to curtail visits to avoid immediate distress and worry. The situation is best dealt with by acknowledging the fear, offering reassurance, and giving the visits a predictable time and duration so that the children learn to cope with their anxieties, realize their fears are unfounded and begin to relearn the acceptance of separation and reunion.

Between the ages of 6 and 8 children are beginning to be independent in many ways, but still need a secure home base from which they can explore the world. They are badly shaken when they see that what they had taken for granted as permanent can be broken. They are not easily able to use the fantasy of younger children or the anger of older children. Their biggest fear is to be left with no family – if one parent can leave why not both? They are aware of their limited independence, and may worry that they may have to go to strangers, be adopted or taken into care. At these ages children are least able to put all their energy into alternative activities like play or school. They can be highly emotional, with aggression, crying and sobbing being very common. They long for the absent parent to return home, and may use their emerging literacy skills to write heart-rending notes. Rather than expressing anger towards the absent parent, it is shown to other important figures in the child's life: remaining parent, teacher and siblings.

Children in the 8 to 12 age range have strong feelings and are aware of themselves and the community of which they are part. They may feel deeply ashamed and embarrassed that the family is breaking up. To save face they are often extremely reluctant to discuss this at school or with their friends, and may cut themselves off from those who could help. Avoidance and denial of problems are common, often compounded by the adults in their life. This is the age at which children have aches and pains in their stomach for no medical reason. They tend to apply the major concerns of their age group – loyalty and fairness – to their present situation. They complain that it is not fair, and are often angry with the parent they believe is to blame for their unfair situation. They can easily be seduced into allying themselves with one parent, rejecting the other and refusing to see them. If parents encourage this behaviour it is unlikely to be in the best interests of the child in the long term.

The job of teenagers is to begin to put their childhood behind them and look to the time when they separate from the family unit. When parents leave their children instead of the other way round, this upsets the expected way of things, and may be a premature separation for the children. Although they may consider that they do not need their parents to provide day-to-day care, they still require support and look to the family for a sense of identity. Even though they are capable of understanding the reasons for the separation, they will tend to look at the situation from their own point of view. They will often feel angry and see the parents as selfish and spoiling their lives. Disliking their powerlessness in the face of unwanted parental separation, teenagers often seek to exercise power elsewhere. They may refuse to do school work, indulge in acts of delinquency or reject parental values and lifestyles. Within two years of parental divorce about 50 per cent of teenagers have lost contact with their natural father. Younger children in the family often develop a strong relationship with their older siblings following parental divorce, and may miss them intensely as they grow away from home. This places the whole family under further stress, and places a responsibility on to teenagers that they may find hard to handle.

DOES THE SCHOOL HAVE A ROLE?

The role of the school towards children whose parents separate is ill-defined. Teachers, pupils and parents are equally unsure about how school might be usefully involved. Some teachers regard themselves simply as educators. They feel they have been trained for this task and resent being called upon to act as social workers. They recognize that worries caused by parental separation may make pupils less receptive to teaching and influence their general attitude towards school, but feel they can do little about it.

Some parents think their separation is of no concern to the school and are reluctant to let teachers know of the home crisis. They may fear the teacher will be prejudiced against divorced parents and their children. They may decide to keep such a personal matter private, not realizing that family disruption can have profound effects upon behaviour and learning in school. Others, hoping for a reconciliation, do not wish to inform the school of what they hope will be temporary disruptions.

Some pupils prefer their home life to have nothing to do with school. This can be a useful strategy when difficulties arise, as wholeheartedly joining in school activities is an effective relief from domestic concerns. They actively resent what they see as prying by teachers who may appear over-anxious to help. It is important to respect this point of view, and respecting privacy can lead to a valuable trusting relationship. However, with 20 per cent of children experiencing the divorce of their parents before their sixteenth birthday, and an unknown number affected by parental separation, it is no longer possible for school to ignore events involving such a large proportion of their pupils.

Like children themselves, the schools are 'caught in the middle'. Whilst there is a general awareness that parental separation may interrupt a pupil's education, there is only limited knowledge of what to expect and do. The starting point is for the school to take active steps to define what can be expected of teachers, parents and pupils in these circumstances. Teachers need to know the particular difficulties children are likely to face, and the reactions common to each age group in order to help those of their pupils whose parents are separating.

About two-thirds of children will show marked changes in school behaviour following parental separation. Common changes are a deterioration in work, restlessness, an inability to concentrate on school work and a big increase in daydreaming. About one-fifth will exhibit sadness, some may become aggressive and disobedient, others depressed. The changes often disrupt friendship patterns, with friends understanding even less than the pupils themselves and avoiding contact. The deterioration in academic work can have profound effects at some stages in a pupil's educational career, for example a young child just starting to learn to read and write, adolescents taking public exams. The period of acute stress may last several months, and some children are not performing as well even two years after parental separation.

The problem for teachers is how they can help their pupils through this period of stress, minimize the effects it has and ask for further support if it is needed. They can do it best with the help of the parents and a supporting policy from the school. Schools are in a unique position to help, as all children are obliged to attend. They can offer practical and emotional help which may be needed when parents separate. The familiarity of school can itself provide comfort and security to a child, without any special efforts on the part of the staff. Predictable routines and activities can afford stability at a time when home and family are undergoing change. For the post-divorce family, schools can be one of the places where separated parents can cooperate and work together for the well-being of their children. School can be a neutral place to meet and discuss unemotively a topic of mutual concern, their children's education. Parental co-operation following separation can be a valuable way to help children recover from the trauma of the split.

Pupils and teachers develop relationships through routine daily contact. The same relationship between the teacher and the taught which is effective in the learning situation creates personal trust which can be used to help with personal problems. A sensitive teacher who enables children to express worries and fears in a calm atmosphere can help them to re-establish their own sense of place and purpose in a changing situation.

Active listening is one useful method of helping. Listening attentively is a powerful palliative to a person with a problem, and can itself help resolve difficulties. Allowing time and space for people to define their own problems in their own way and to search for their own solutions can avoid the two major temptations when confronted by the problems of others: imposing a hasty, inappropriate solution or taking on the problems oneself.

Some parents turn naturally to school to help them with their own problems. In times of stress adults, feeling childlike, look to figures like teachers who have been helpful in the past. This occurs frequently in young parents whose children attend the same school as their parents, perhaps even have the same teachers. At the outset of a parental interview it is essential to establish whether it is the parents' or the pupils' problems that are under discussion, and to draw a clear distinction between the two. Most teachers wisely feel unwilling to involve themselves in the parents' difficulties directly, but may usefully suggest alternative sources of help (see References). With regard to the parents' view of the child's difficulties, active listening rather than advice-giving is required from the teacher. Having listened, parents and teachers can then try to establish together what can be done to help the child who is their joint concern.

Pupils' emotional and social development may be impeded as well as their academic work. Some may regress to an earlier stage of development and become more immature, whilst others will simply cease to make progress emotionally. Friendship patterns may be disrupted as a consequence of changed lifestyles, old friends no longer enjoy the company of someone whose behaviour has changed, and valuable peer support is lost. Pupils' social development might benefit from more active help from school in order to overcome impediments which slow down normal social maturation. Teachers' objectivity in observing pupils can make a valuable contribution to an assessment of the severity of their reaction to stress. Being aware of the range of behaviours expected of children in a particular age group, and being sensitive to unusual behaviours, will allow them to assess the significance of any behavioural changes. They can then use this information to decide if outside agencies should be contacted and advise parents appropriately.

Children experiencing stress have greater difficulties with learning than previously. Their work usually deteriorates as they have difficulty in concentrating, are restless and spend more time daydreaming. This period of disturbance can last longer than many people expect, perhaps for two years or more. It may be necessary to ensure that the pupil is listening and be gently and sympathetically reminded to pay attention. Many teachers are uncertain whether to continue to expect the same progress as before, or whether they should make concessions, allowing pupils to stand still and recover from the emotional turmoil they are experiencing. As far as possible goals should be maintained, but extra help and support will be necessary if they are to be attained.

SCHOOL POLICIES AND PROCEDURES

Every school should define what can be expected of teachers, parents and pupils in the event of parental separation, even if it is only regarded as temporary. At the outset of contact with parents, schools should establish that they would like to be informed if the child experiences any major disturbance to home life, including parental separation. This can be written in the school booklet and stated at introductory meetings with parents, along with other statements of policy. Putting separation on the agenda also helps members of staff who are themselves separated parents to see their own position in a more positive light. Their personal experiences can be valuable in helping them relate to pupils and parents undergoing similar events, although it is seldom helpful to the parent if a teacher recounts personal experiences, as all situations are different.

School organization should ensure that the practices developed to support pupils and parents reflect the variety of family structures found in Britain, and do not simply assume that their pupils are brought up in a traditional nuclear family. Parents no longer living together may require separate copies of letters, reports, etc. Practice and procedures used in record keeping should ensure that the facts about a pupil's life are recorded and updated as necessary, and are available to those who need them. Suggested school record sheets for this information are provided by Cox and Desforges (1987). Sending two invitations to parents for school events shows that schools know that not all children are brought up in stereotypical families, and conveys acceptance of themselves and their lifestyles to pupils and their families.

At a practical level, it may become apparent that the school could complement existing parenting if the quality of parenting at home is temporarily diminished. Extra attention from a teacher prepared to listen to children's news when their parents are too preoccupied with emotional concerns can be very helpful. Parenting of a more tangible nature may be needed if providing the support materials required by the school curriculum (home economics or PE) becomes a low priority for a harassed parent. Somewhere to leave weekend bags packed ready for a weekend visit to the absent parent would be appreciated by many pupils. For pupils whose homes are being divided around them, homework can become an impossibility. Schools with a serious homework requirement should make facilities available in school where study can take place in a quiet atmosphere. When emotions are running high at home, to have a place of calm to work can mean that a pupil can continue to achieve and take satisfaction in those achievements, a valuable boost to self-esteem which might be badly needed at such a time.

THE CURRICULUM

The assumptions about family life are reflected not only in the practices of the school but also in the curriculum content of some subjects. The images presented by the media and many textbooks reinforce the view that the white, middle-class, Protestant family structure is the norm, if not ideal. They ignore the multiracial society in which we live and gloss over the different racial, religious and social backgrounds from which pupils come, thereby diminishing many children whose parents choose, or find themselves living in, different circumstances. Current stereotypes of family life regard the nuclear family as the basic unit in which happy, healthy children are brought up to maturity. In the minds of many, a normal family consists of a healthy man and woman in their mid-thirties, a boy aged 8 to 12, a girl aged 7 to 9, all sharing a joke and having a good time. Our image of the normal family does not allow much variation, and one consequence is that children may worry that there is something wrong with their family because it does not fit this ideal. One or both parents may be too old, there may be too many children, one member may be disabled or ill. There may be only one parent, or the children may not be living with their biological parents. If the family looks seriously different it is frequently felt by those inside, and judged by those outside, to be abnormal or inadequate. In fact only about 5 per cent of households consist of two-parent, two-child families. Living in a one-parent family, a step family, an adoptive family, a foster family are all common experiences, but rarely acknowledged in popular culture. All are perfectly capable of meeting the social and emotional needs of children.

The school curriculum may help to bolster this narrow view of a 'normal' family. In modern languages the vehicle for conversation is often the nuclear family in stereotyped form. Although intended to put pupils in a situation with which they are familiar, it probably no longer reflects the life circumstances of the majority, not only the 20 per cent whose parents have separated but also those with unemployed fathers and working mothers. Children may be encouraged to make things for homes and people that are not a central part of their everyday life, such as Mother's or Father's Day cards.

Education about family life in Britain in the 1990s is immediately relevant to all pupils. There is information that their limited experience has not yet provided, which may eventually have a direct bearing on their own lives. There are already many alternatives to the two-parent, two-child family: childless marriages, professional parenthood, as well as a variety of one-parent families by accident or design. A pluralist dimension should be included, providing knowledge and appreciation of the variety of family structures and childrearing practices that occur in different societies. In this way pupils can develop a heightened self-awareness and can interpret personal experiences of family living within a wider context.

As with sexism and racism, a close scrutiny of the practices, curriculum and teaching material of the school is necessary. It is likely that many practices no longer reflect the same situation as when they were put into operation. These changes will not only help the substantial minority of pupils whose parents are separated but also help prepare all pupils for situations that may affect themselves or their friends some time in the future. One example is the inclusion in the school library of books where separation and divorce occur. Many people find reading fiction a valuable aid to the resolution of their own emotional problems. Including such books in the library accepts the occurrence of separation, and enables pupils to select books in relative privacy that may help them to understand events in their own lives and those of their friends.

In recent years there has been growth in courses in health, personal and social education. All of these cover some aspects of family life, but deal with it separately, from the different perspective of each course. For example, the Northern Examining Association has at least six syllabuses containing some aspects of education for family life (sociology, community studies, integrated humanities and home economics, child care and development, welfare and society and law in society. This method of dealing with family life produces a fragmentation of knowledge, and contradictions in how the same topic is approached in different subject areas. Separation and divorce are dealt with only by the law in society course, and the causes and nature of family breakdown are raised in the welfare and society syllabus. Current thinking suggests that social education should be non-prescriptive and child-centred, placing more emphasis on attitudes and skills than on knowledge-based learning. It must be non-prescriptive and open-ended to take account of the rapidly changing, pluralist society in which we live, and because it is impossible for a teacher to know what form family life will take in thirty years' time. More fundamentally, its main focus should be on pupils taking responsibility for their own lifestyles. The starting point is the pupil's own experiences, which are used as the raw material from which they can learn. Formal knowledge is only one aspect of learning, and there is much evidence that on its own it does not significantly influence behaviour. Almost all the schoolgirls who unintentionally become pregnant know about contraception, but lack the skills to apply this knowledge within the context of their everyday lives.

The application of knowledge in personal and social situations is dependent on a variety of social and interpersonal skills. Communicating, self-expression, negotiating, clarifying expectations and decision-making are all skills relevant to family life. Deficiency in these skills can mean that people are unable to fulfil the marriage contract they have entered into. Social education should acknowledge the essential interdependence of knowledge, attitudes and skills, and acknowledge that the methods used in teaching about personal relationships and family life are more important than the curriculum content. Learning about families must be included at many stages in the curriculum, beginning with the child's own experience of home life, and widening out to include the varieties of family life and structure. This conveys the idea that there are many types of normality, preparing for the realization that marriages are relative to other aspects of the society in which they occur. The changing roles and shapes of families as people develop from being a couple primarily concerned with each other to being parents, grandparents, and then single widowed people can be observed, discussed and assimilated.

CONCLUSION

Schools can help pupils whose parents are separating in a variety of ways. They can help pupils by providing individual attention and counselling. They can ensure that their organization offers help and support to children and their families at the time of parental separation and when new families are created. They can examine their curriculum to ensure that a knowledge of family diversity leads children to understand that many of their peers will have undergone similar experiences. Through appropriate personal and social education they can ensure that pupils are developing attitudes and skills which will help them develop stable relationships in adult life.

REFERENCES

Burgoyne, J., Ormond, R. and Richards M. (1987) *Divorce Matters*. Harmondsworth: Penguin.

Cox, K. M. and Desforges, M. F. (1987) *Divorce and the School*. London: Methuen.

Cox, K. M. and Desforges, M. F. (1990) *Children and Divorce: A Guide for Adults*. Available from: 6 Whinfell Court, Sheffield S11 9QA.

Mitchell, A. (1985) *Children in the Middle*. London: Tavistock.

Wallerstein, J. and Blakeslee, S. (1989) *Second Chance*. London: Transworld.

Wallerstein, J. and Kelly, J. (1980) *Surviving the Break-up*. London: Grant McIntyre.

SUPPORT AND ADVICE AGENCIES

In addition to the usual range of support services currently available to schools such as School Psychological Services, Youth and Community Services, Child Guidance Services, there are many specialist services offering help to separating families. Note that many of these organizations may have local offices, and you should consult your local telephone directory or Citizens' Advice Bureau for information about your locality.

Association of Separated and Divorced Catholics, The Holy Name Presbytery, 8 Portsmouth Street, Manchester M13 9GB

Catholic Marriage Advisory Council, 15 Landsdowne Road, London W11 3AJ

Children Need Fathers, 97c Shakespeare Walk, London N16 8TB

Divorce Counciliation and Advisory Service, 38 Ebury Street, London SW1W 0LU

Families Need Fathers, 37 Garden Road, London SE15

Gingerbread, 35 Wellington Street, London WC2

National Council for the Divorced and Separated, 13 High Street, Little Shelford, Cambridge CB2 5ES

National Council for One Parent Families, 255 Kentish Town Road, London NW5 2LX

Relate – Local telephone directory or: Herbert Grey College, Little Church Street, Rugby CV21 3AP

BOOKS FOR CHILDREN FOR LIBRARIES, SCHOOL READERS AND HOME READING

The National Council for One Parent Families, 255 Kentish Town Road, London NW5 2LX provides a list of over a hundred suitable titles. Some popular ones are listed below.

Althea (1980) *I Have Two Homes*. Cambridge: Dinosaur Press.

Baurn, L. (1986) *Are We Nearly There?* London: Bodley Head.

Blume, J. (1979) *It's Not the End of the World*. London: Heinemann.

Butterworth, J. (1982) *Summer Island*. London: Kay & Ward.

Cleary, P. (1983) *Dear Mr Henshaw*. McRae.

Donnelly, E. (1983) *Tina into Two Won't Go*. London: Anderson.

Drescher, J. (1986) *My Mother's Getting Married*. London: Methuen.

Erup, B. (1979) *Susanna's Parents Get Divorced*. London: Black.

Gydal, S. and Danielson, D. (1985) *When Gemma's Parents Get Divorced*. London: Hodder & Stoughton.

Jong, E. (1984) *Megan's Book of Divorce*. London: Granada.

Krasny, L. and Brown, M. (1987) *Dinosaurs Divorce*. London: Collins.

Leach, C. (1980) *Decision for Katie*. London: Macmillan.

Leeson, R. (1981) *It's My Life*. London: Fontana.

Maddock, R. (1972) *Sellout*. London: Macmillan.

Mitchell, A. (1982) *When Parents Split Up – Divorce Explained to Young People*. Edinburgh: McDonal.

O'Connor, J. (1984) *Just Good Friends*. Harmondsworth: Puffin.

Sinberg, J. (1983) *Divorce Is a Grown-Up Problem*. New York: Avon.

Snell, N. (1983) *Sam's New Dad*. London: Hamish Hamilton.

Townsend, S. (1982) *The Growing Pains of Adrian Mole*. London: Methuen.

BOOKS FOR PARENTS

Ambrose, P., Harper, J. and Pemberton, R. (1983) *Surviving Divorce*. Brighton: Wheatsheaf.

Billing, J. (1985) *The Divorce Book*. Rugby: Marriage Guidance Council.

Brown, R. (1980) *Breaking Up: A Practical Guide to Separation and Divorce*. London: Arrow.

Burgoyne, J. (1984) *Breaking Even: Divorce, Your Children and You*. Harmondsworth: Penguin.

Fish, B. (1981) *Re-building When Your Relationship Ends*. San Luis Obsispo: Impact Publishers.

Hodder, E. (1985) *The Step-Parent Handbook*. London: Sphere.

Hooper, A. (1983) *Divorce and Your Children*. London: Unwin.

Maddox, B. (1980) *Step Parenting*. London: Unwin.

CURRICULUM SOURCE BOOKS

Clark, M. and Simmons, T. (1980) *The Family*. London: MacDonald Educational.

Study Commission on the Family. (1983) *Families in the Future*. From SCF, 3 Park Road, London NW1 6XN.

Cox, K. M. and Desforges, M. F. (1987) *Divorce and the School*. London: Methuen.

Fyson, N. and Greenhill, S. *Investigating Society: People Talking – Family Life*. London: Macmillan.

Hopkins, D., Ronder, J. and Cork, D. (1982) *Screen Scripts 3*. Harlow: Longman.

Levine, J. (1982) *Home Truths*. Harlow: Longman.

Lindsay, G. (1983) *Problems of Adolescence in Secondary Schools*. London: Croom Helm.

National Children's Bureau (1990) *Divorce and Children*. From NCB, 8 Walkley St, London EC1V 7QE.

Open University (1985) *Family Lifestyles*. Milton Keynes: Open University Press.

CHAPTER 14

Schools and pupils: developing their responses to bereavement

Patsy Wagner

THE AIM OF THIS CHAPTER

The aim of this chapter is to help teachers working in primary and secondary schools to explore and develop their ideas about death and loss. The view held by the writer of this chapter is that, by increasing our knowledge and understanding of death and loss, we can help children and young people to understand more about change and loss, death and bereavement. We can also support them through informed and practical school action when a death occurs.

In response to this, some may say, 'But isn't this going beyond the role of the teacher?', or, 'Haven't we got enough to deal with in schools already without this?' You, the reader of this chapter, may not need to be convinced of the usefulness and importance of addressing death and loss in school, but you may need to convince other teachers as well as students, parents and governors about its relevance and importance. The section, 'Why deal with death and bereavement?' explores the rationales.

This chapter addresses a rationale for dealing with the theme in school, before examining what we need to know in order to be able to help. It then considers what the school can do when a bereavement occurs, affecting a pupil at any of the various phases, or a member of staff. Finally it examines how we can address bereavement and loss through the taught curriculum and the resources available, and how we can adapt them.

SOME INITIAL THOUGHTS

We all have some views about death and bereavement. These views may have the force of convictions. They have all been acquired and developed through experience. Each reader will gain by reflecting on the views about death and bereavement which s/he has assimilated from her or his family of origin and other sources. This will help in working out, through further reading and reflection, how these views can be utilized, changed, adapted and augmented for the school context and the role of the teacher.

Questions that may help in the process of reflection are:

- How did you find out about death?

- How was death talked about in your family of origin (outside the occasion of a death in family) – comfortably, awkwardly, secretively, openly?
- Who talked about it? – parents, guardians, siblings, older generations, children?
- To whom?
- On what occasions?
- How was death, dying and mourning coped with in the family?
- Was death talked about with children in your family, by whom, how and on what occasions?
- How much were you kept informed about and involved in illness and death in your own family?
- How have your experiences affected your views about whether children can and cannot be told?

This process of examining experiences and perspectives is not a once and for all activity, but one we can return to.

WHY DEAL WITH DEATH AND BEREAVEMENT AT SCHOOL?

Most people would agree that death is a significant event. It is also a normal event – although the circumstances may be tragic. It is the one fact of life of which we can be certain. We will all die.

When a child is bereaved, teachers can help to ameliorate the devastating effects that death and loss can have on the child, in particular the effects it can have on a child's development, and on his or her progress or success in school. This links clearly to the main task of the school, which is to promote the success, achievement and personal and social development of each child.

Many teachers find that when a child is bereaved they feel at a loss to know what is best to do. Their school may have no agreed procedures for dealing with death, and they are often left feeling they have to work out for themselves what might be best. Many are not sure what is appropriate for a teacher to do, or how best to do it, or when they will find the time to do it. Most teachers err on the side of caution.

Most children are considerably at risk when a significant bereavement occurs in the family. They are at risk because of the normal effects of bereavement on concentration, feelings and behaviour. They are also at risk because of their dependence on the adults who look after them to understand and to meet their needs. When there is a death in the family, not all families are clear about, or fully able, at the time, to meet a child's needs. At these times, teachers are often the professionals best placed and best qualified, through their training in children's learning and development and their experience as teachers, to help a family understand more about the developmental needs of the child, and how they can be addressed.

This would include ideas about:

- how children understand death;
- how they can be helped to cope with it;

- their need (whatever their age) to have clear and comprehensible information when someone is dying or has died;
- their need (whatever their age) to be included in the sharing of grief and the processes of grieving.

The teachers who would be appropriate to this role would, ideally, be those who have a responsibility for the overview of the development of the child or young person. In primary schools this is the class teacher, and in secondary schools the form tutor. More experienced members of staff are also needed to provide guidance and to assist in this process.

The numbers of children affected by what we will call a 'significant bereavement' (of a parent figure or sibling) while they are at school is not insignificant. According to *Good Grief* (Ward *et al.*, 1988; 1989), approximately 3.3 per cent of the child population of 16-year-olds has experienced a significant bereavement. Added to this, one in three marriages results in divorce, and there are separations that do not result in divorce. The numbers of children involved, therefore, justifies our work in this area, and if we further consider the sometimes traumatic loss associated with migrations, illnesses and so on, the argument is even more compelling.

Finally, a reason put forward over the centuries, by a variety of sources, both secular and religious, can be summed up as: those who get the most out of life are those who are most at ease with the fact that they will die. That is to say, by knowing and accepting that our lives will end (whether or not we believe in any afterlife) we can commit ourselves each day, more fully, to living and growing, to becoming ourselves and to reaching out to other human beings. In this sense death is the key to living and learning.

Currently, in most schools, death is a crisis which is managed often reasonably well, sometimes not at all well, frequently at considerable emotional cost to some teachers. While we can never be totally prepared, we can set up frameworks and procedures in schools, known and understood by everyone in the school, which will help to guide us when a death occurs.

In a society which has 'swept death under the carpet', it is unsurprising that teachers feel uncertain, unconfident and sometimes reluctant about this aspect of their role. Clearly, in-service training and support is needed for all teachers, with a small core of more highly trained teachers who can act as a resource to other colleagues when a death occurs.

CHILDREN AND BEREAVEMENT: DEATH AND LOSS

What makes death difficult

Although death is such a significant and important event in our lives, it is one with which few of us in Britain are both familiar and at ease. This was not the case for previous generations. Before 1900 and in the earlier decades of the twentieth century death was all around. Children died through common childhood illnesses, such as whooping-cough, diphtheria and scarlet fever, for which there were no vaccinations or effective treatments; fatal, infectious and contagious diseases were easily passed around; fatal accidents were common; infections could lead to death. When people became ill they were more likely to be cared for and to die at home. When they died it was an event that the local community knew about and were involved in mourning and commemorating.

Nowadays, developments in medicine have dramatically reduced the chances of dying from childhood illnesses. Even severely-damaged accident victims can be kept alive. Hospitals care for the ill, and aim to offer treatment and cure.

Death and dying, when it occurs, is hidden from view. Dying mostly takes place in hospitals rather than in people's homes. The dying are screened from other patients and linked to machinery to prolong life. A major exception to this is, of course, the hospice movement, which provides a significantly different experience for the dying person and their family and friends, where living-while-dying is emphasized. Hospices make the environment welcoming and homely. The dying person's comfort and freedom from pain (whether physical, psychological or spiritual) is put first, and their family and friends also helped. In the main, however, dead bodies are hidden from view. Death in this context seems a failure.

When it comes to the arrangements following a death, we find a similar pattern of avoidance, compared to earlier times. In previous generations, in Britain, it was usual for the corpse to be kept in the house, for relations and friends to call, to visit the bereaved family and to pay their last respects to the dead person. Grief was shown more openly in the form that funerals took, in the involvement of the local community, by the wearing of mourning clothes. People in Britain now seem to consider these practices morbid and have brief funeral services and arrangements for mourning. The result is that the bereaved persons tend to be isolated in their grief. Notable exceptions to this are found in particular religions and cultures. For example, in Judaism there is clear recognition of the phases and stages in the grieving practices: the first three days of deep grief, seven days of mourning, thirty days of gradual readjustment and eleven months of remembrance and healing. This process involves both the bereaved and the local community, with everyone clear about their role and the bereaved helped, through the process, to grieve. The Irish wake recognizes the same important need to share grief and happy memories with friends and relations after the funeral. Sadly, many of these practices are, as time passes, being affected and watered down through their exposure to the predominant attitudes and practices in Britain.

It seems that over the last couple of generations we have lost something important in our approach to death. In the 1960s the anthropologist Geoffrey Gorer suggested that death had replaced sex as the ultimate pornography: a subject that was rarely if ever talked about and never in front of the children! Schools in Britain are now required to have sex education policies (Education (no 2) Act, 1986). Many schools, including primary schools, teach sex education within their curriculum for personal and social education, but very few schools address death and loss through the curriculum. Is it felt to be not as relevant – or is it just too difficult to deal with? The way that death is trivialized and distanced in the media – especially in films and television and computer games where characters 'die' several times – seems to confirm that we have lost touch with the realities and the meaning of death.

Identifying all these issues may help us to understand why death, dying and loss are an area in which many of us in a western society feel deskilled and unconfident. This leads us to the question of what will be helpful if we want to change things in school.

What we need to know in order to be able to help: understanding loss and its effects

In order to help it will be useful to know something about what to expect in terms of loss and the processes of grieving, and to know about how children grasp the notion of death.

We experience losses throughout our lives, and yet we tend not to acknowledge these losses except when they are 'significant', such as death or the breaking-up of an important relationship. By ignoring the effects of small losses we miss out on understanding the processes involved, so when the losses are much bigger we feel in unfamiliar territory. At a time of major loss the degree and intensity of the loss and the grieving which occurs can be psychologically overwhelming and emotionally devastating. Knowledge about loss and grieving will not protect us from these effects but it will help us to understand more about what is happening to us when it occurs.

Phases of grief

There are generally accepted phases of grief which are expected to arise when a loss occurs. These are:

Early grief

Initial effects:

- shock
- alarm
- denial and disbelief →

Acute grief

Medium to long-term effects:

- yearning and pining
- searching
- strong feelings of:
  - sadness
  - anger
  - guilt
  - shame
- disorganization
- despair
- reorganization → *Integration of loss and grief*

(Jewett, 1982)

With a significant loss these phases and elements take on a high degree of intensity and take a long period of time to work through. Of course, the phases of grief are not as clear cut as they appear on paper, nor do they follow a strict order when a person is grieving. There is more of a progression through them which includes some weaving back and forth between them. Sometimes a person may become 'stuck' in one phase. When grieving takes its course the whole process takes at least two years (when the bereavement is of a life partner or spouse). This does not mean that it is over after two years, but rather that the bereaved person will, when the grieving has progressed, have moved on to integrating the loss into their identity. Even so, the triggering of particular memories by people, objects, sounds, smells, music, or certain days or particular dates or anniversaries, which is especially powerful throughout the immediate period of grieving, can have powerful effects even after several years. The phases of grief help us to understand more of what a bereaved person may be going through and to remember the time it takes to 'recover' from the death of a loved one. Schools may need to be sensitive to this.

Features of children's grief

The grief of children is similar to that of adults, but certain features are particularly pronounced. Anxiety, for example, is very common in children. When someone very close (on whom the child is dependent) dies, the child's sense of security can be badly shaken. When a parent has died, a young child may become very anxious that the same thing might happen to the surviving parent. The child may show this anxiety by becoming very clinging or demanding and reluctant to go to school. The more grief-stricken and depressed the surviving parent, the more anxious the child will be. Children may also become frightened that they themselves will die. The grieving adolescent is very likely to focus on her or his own mortality, and for some this can become a major preoccupation. These anxieties and fears need to be addressed so the child can be helped to understand and overcome them. This is not something that the adult needs to wait to hear the child express openly before addressing.

All children are likely to feel anxious when a surviving parent shows any sign of illness, especially if the symptoms are anything like those of the person who died. These are the occasions which also lead children to want to stay off school. This can become a major problem if it is not understood and addressed promptly.

Physical complaints following a bereavement – such as headaches, stomach aches, or other minor ailments – can increase in some children. 'Illness' may be a way of getting attention from a bereaved parent, or staying physically close to that parent. Sometimes the child staying off school is a real comfort to the bereaved adult. These ingredients can sometimes lead to a diagnosis of 'school phobia', which in these circumstances is both inaccurate and unhelpful. Extremely careful and sensitive handling is needed on these occasions, and a routine of continued attendance at school is usually vital.

Sometimes children can become much more tense and jumpy, especially if the death was sudden. Difficulties in sleeping can be common, through fear of being alone at night, of leaving the surviving parent alone at night, or through vivid memories, especially when the child witnessed a violent death, or came unexpectedly upon the dead body. All of these affect the child's ability to concentrate in school and to apply himself or herself to work.

Anger and acting-out is another response to grief which is found in children. The child may become very angry with the person who died for deserting them, with the surviving parent, with the adults for excluding them from the grief, or for not telling them the truth about the illness or circumstances of the death. They can be angry with themselves or others for not doing more to prevent the death. Children may withdraw from members of their family, and/or switch off learning in school. Sometimes this anger can spill over into school. The less talking there has been in the family about the death and the less understanding there is of the likelihood of anger occurring as a normal part of grieving, the more likely there are to be more long-term difficulties with anger. Sometimes, children regress in their behaviour and their learning also regresses. All of these responses can be anticipated and largely averted or addressed by clear communication within the family, and between school and family.

Sometimes children become socially isolated following a bereavement. The form of illness or death can be significant, in terms of whether it was an illness or death which the family or others might feel is socially stigmatizing. Children may anticipate this and withdraw from others. Peers at school may trigger this response by teasing or name-calling. Sometimes the family may move from the area and the new school may be a 'fresh start'. But the effects of a bereavement are not, of course, avoided by geographical relocation.

When a child has not been told the full story about a death in the family, especially if that death was particularly horrifying, then the child may be troubled by fears and fantasies about what happened. The truth when shared is always much better than a story which is deduced in loneliness through guesswork.

By being aware of all of these possibilities, the school can play an important role: letting families know the ideas that will be useful to them; offering them support; understanding what children may be going through; helping them to cope, without making them feel different or strange; monitoring children and their progress in school and involving their families when they seem to be having difficulties which are affecting their development or learning.

Features of death which make it more difficult to deal with

It is understandable that, if an old person dies after a long and painful illness, death can be a release from suffering and, amidst the sadness, some degree of relief for the family. A death which was sudden, unexpected, painful, horrifying, mismanaged or violent, and/or the death of a child, partner or parent, will usually be harder to deal with. A death by suicide will trigger additional difficult feelings. Certain social circumstances also tend to increase the difficulty, such as: no family or social support; other losses; unemployment; dependent children; an ambivalent relationship with the person who died (for example, if the person was abusive).

It is usually the untimely death of a child or parent with which we try to help bereaved children or young people in school. If a death has been particularly tragic or horrifying, most people feel awkward, and family members are avoided because of 'not knowing what to say'. Contact between the school and the family and support of the child in school are especially important on these occasions.

How a child recovers from a bereavement is most affected by the coping skills and strategies of the adult carer(s) of the child. If the carer is able to care, then the child usually copes well. If the carer is both devastated and profoundly depressed then the child is more likely to become depressed too. In these cases the child is doubly bereaved and effectively loses both parents. The school can help the surviving parent to understand the needs of the child and help to locate sources of assistance, such as other family members, friends, community networks, or professional sources of help, such as child and family consultation services.

What children understand about death – it depends on what we tell them!

There is a tendency for many writers to place children's understanding of death within the framework of Piagetian notions of stages of development. In her excellent book about children's thinking, *Children's Minds*, Margaret Donaldson (1978) challenged those ideas about fixed stages of intellectual development and limited competences. Child development studies have also been helpful in illuminating what very young children are capable of. For example, it is now clear that even infants have some concept of loss.

If children have no experience of change and loss and/or no adequate explanations about it, then that will develop ideas that may be confused and frightening. When dying, death and grieving in a family are surrounded by secrecy as well as pain and fear, the child's vague and frightening feelings about illness and death increase. These children learn not to ask questions and are isolated in their grief. But even very young children are able to grasp ideas about the nature of change, the irreversibility of death, and the feelings and processes involved in loss, for example by examining phases and changes in plant and animal life.

WHAT THE SCHOOL CAN DO WHEN A BEREAVEMENT OCCURS

When a child in your school is bereaved (or about to be bereaved) there are some very practical things which can be done to help that child or young person and the family at certain key periods. This section considers action when someone is dying, and then action when a death has occurred.

When a person is dying

When a person is dying at home, or more likely in hospital, the child – no matter how young – will need to be told how seriously ill the person is by a close relative.

Parents and family often feel unprepared to tell a child about the severity of the illness. Often they feel that it is better to 'protect' the child or young person from this knowledge. Sometimes they feel they cannot face telling the child and ask someone outside the family to tell him or her. But the more a child is told by loving relations about these matters the more able s/he is to cope in the short, medium and long term. S/he is far less likely to be traumatized, far more able to recover and far less likely to suffer in later life.

When the school is aware that there is a life-threatening illness in the family it can offer practical help in relation to the child and school by addressing these areas with the family:

- How are the family coping with all of the demands and the practical arrangements for the child getting to school and home?
- Are there any particular difficulties which make it likely that the child or young person will be late for school? For example, taking a sibling to school – is there any way that this can be ameliorated so that s/he is not always late?
- Is there anything the school can do to help?

It is much better if the child is attending school than helping at home – there may be local networks or services which might be sources of help, for example, home helps.

The school can also help the family understand the child's need for information about what is happening; about what we know of the importance of including the child in family discussions about illness, dying and death; in the sharing of tears, grief and sorrow; in the talking and planning with the person who is dying. Schools also need to be clear about who else could support them and who else they can suggest to the parent as a possible support; the local education psychology service, child guidance, CRUSE could all be possible sources.

When a death occurs

When a death occurs the main things that the school might need to address are telling the child about the death, telling others about the death, making and keeping contact with the family and preparing for the child's return to school.

Telling the child about the death It is always best if the child can be told by a family member about a significant death in the family. If that is not possible then the school may be in the position of having to break the news to the child. In that case it should be done by someone who knows the child well and to whom the child feels some closeness. The place should be free of disturbance and there should be time allowed for it and given for the child to respond as s/he wishes. It is better, if the death is sudden, that a family member who is close to the child can come to the school to tell the child. In every case arrangements should be made to escort the child home – whatever his or her age – rather than having to wait for the school day to finish. When this is impossible a teacher will need to offer time to the child and be available to him or her until the family can take over.

Telling others in school about the death The class teachers or form tutor (and any others who work closely with the child) will need to know about the death as soon as possible. The teacher most likely to take on the role of supporting the child on her or his return will need time and support from the school to work out and check through the plan for the child's return. It is best if all the staff (including supply staff) of a school are aware and prepared when a child has been bereaved, so that absence from school and lessons, missed work, unfinished assignments or homework, etc. are all dealt with sensitively and supportively. Teachers who work with the pupil will be asked to think through possible issues in the forthcoming work, for example, particular content that might be sensitive, for which the child might need to be prepared. The friends and class or tutor group will be given time before the child returns to school to talk over how they will support the bereaved child on his or her return, including the possible insensitivity of other children.

Parents will need to know the school's arrangements for telling others in the school and this will be part of the school's guidelines on helping the school cope with a bereaved member. The child's closest friends need to be told as soon as possible, and then the class or tutor group. The details of the death do not need to be spelled out if there are any highly sensitive issues, such as death by violence. For example, 'a sudden and tragic death' can be sufficient. Generally, it is better to be as open as possible, given the wishes of the family on the matter. This can help to prevent the spread of rumours. In a school which has a policy on bereavement, which everyone knows about, this is less likely to happen.

Making and keeping contact with the family The school will need to be in contact with the family as soon as possible, in order to:

- express condolences;
- enquire if any practical help is needed, for example, over arrangements for children reaching school;
- find out about the funeral arrangements and to arrange representation of the school at the funeral;
- support the family in meeting the child's need for involvement in the events and arrangements for mourning, for example:
  - Seeing the dead person can help to actualize the loss. The family will often not appreciate the usefulness of this in the grieving process.
  - Attending the funeral also helps to actualize the loss and provides a sense of support and belonging, and helps the child to feel included in the sharing of the love and grief – as long as the child is familiarized beforehand with what is going to happen, and someone who is a close relative is able to look after him or her during the funeral service.
- prepare the family for the possibility of separation anxiety and to encourage them to return the child to school as soon as possible.
- find out how much they have told the child. This will help the school to assess how much help the family may need with this task.
- find out the family's religious beliefs. This will help the school be sensitive to the religious practices and requirements of the family.

Returning to school after the death When the child returns to school the following ideas and actions will be useful:

- Acknowledge the loss and encourage other adults close to the child to do the same.
- Provide a person for the child to talk to when s/he wants. It is usually best to offer time for this initially – if the child does not use it that is not problematic. The person should be someone that the child has chosen.
- Provide a suitable private place as a bolt-hole should the child need it (depending on the age of the child).
- Support and encourage the child's friends in being supportive.
- Consider whether it would be useful to involve an older child in providing support.
- Monitor the child and be aware of changes in behaviour.
- Help the child understand some of the normal effects of bereavement on concentration and behaviour and to cope with them.
- Keep up contact with the family. Talk to them about what has happened and how their child is coping.
- Consider what support the class teacher or form tutor might need.
- Consider whether the child may need extra help in school, in catching up with work or homework or if work or behaviour deteriorates.
- Consider whether the child or family might need specialized help from outside school.

If after three terms the effects of the bereavement on the child seem not to have ameliorated, remember that bereavement is a life event which lasts for ever. Ensure that significant bereavements are recorded so that this is not lost as the child moves up the school or transfers to another school.

When a child or staff member dies, how can the school mourn? When a child or staff member dies the whole of the school community will need to be involved in the process of mourning, and the contact with the family will need to be close to elicit their wishes over involvement in the funeral and in commemoration of the dead person.

Some key issues are to:

- Inform the members of the school community as soon as possible, providing sufficient information to reduce the incidence of rumour. Arrange this in groupings appropriate to the person or group's closeness to the dead person, to help the process of informing and grieving:
  - with all teachers and staff; with teachers in the team, year group or department; with teachers who taught the pupil;
  - with all pupils in the school; with pupils in the year group; with pupils in the class or tutor group.
- Acknowledge the need for teachers, as well as pupils, to express their feelings, and provide structured occasions for this to occur.

- Make arrangements for members of the school community to attend the funeral.
- Acknowledge the death in the school community – in class time, in assemblies, through memorials such as planting a tree, through commemoration, for example, making a book about the person, etc. taking into account the wishes and the involvement of the family.
- Keep contact with the family following the funeral.

PREPARING FOR LOSS, BEREAVEMENT AND DEATH: DEVELOPING A CHANGE AND LOSS CURRICULUM

What the school can do through the taught curriculum

This element in the school curriculum would be primarily about change. Children would have structured opportunities to learn about how change and loss affects people and how to help when it occurs. Through this the school would work in a preventative way with children so they were more prepared for changes at school, in their own lives outside the school, and to understand and help each other when a bereavement occurs. This would be part of an on-going programme in personal and social education which would be co-ordinated across the whole-school curriculum.

An aim for the primary school would be that by the end of the primary school phase a child could talk about death as part of life. By the end of the secondary school, in addition to the above, the young person would understand, in more breadth and depth, the processes involved in change; in coping with loss; the importance of acknowledging loss; the importance of grieving; the phases of grief; the issues and skills in helping a bereaved person; sensitive issues around death and dying.

This would be a spiral curriculum in which aspects would be developed and revisited as the child progressed through the school. Death would not, therefore, be something that was 'done' at a particular time in the child's school career. It would, rather, be something that was introduced at a very early stage and developed over time.

Other important aspects of this would be: times of transition – between classes and phases of education; and how to care for others when a loss or bereavement occurs. In this way, when a child or teacher left the group or was bereaved, or a major local or national tragedy occurred that affected the school as a community, preparatory work would have taken place and more in-depth work could then be carried out with individuals and groups (Yule and Gold, 1993).

How we can address bereavement and loss through the taught curriculum?

The guiding principle for us in working in this area is death as a part of life and loss as a part of life and death, and bereavement as part of a curriculum about change and loss.

The strategies that will be adopted will depend on how the taught curriculum is organized and delivered. The approach which makes the most sense is through topic work. Other more subject-bound approaches require more careful planning and co-ordination between teachers to make sure that the appropriate links are made between different subjects so that fragmentation is avoided.

The areas that would be relevant are:

- occasions of change and the feelings associated with change, both the gains and the losses in:
  - starting school
  - changing class
  - changing teachers
  - changing and losing friends
  - changing schools
  - developing, maintaining and changing friendships
  - preparing for life after school
  - changes in life outside school: in the family and in society;
- experiences of change in the life of others through:
  - stories
  - plays
  - poems
  - biographies
  - historical accounts
  - role-plays
  - pictures
  - music;
- physical changes in the life-cycle of plants and animals;
- feelings, beliefs and rituals which accompany major transitions and changes in human life from the perspective of different societies, cultures and religions in relation to:
  - infancy, childhood, adolescence, adulthood, old age
  - birth, marriage, dying, death and mourning;
- community involvement with the elderly and with the ill
  - as contributors in school to the topics planned
  - through community links and service.

These would need to be planned, co-ordinated and delivered in a way that was age-appropriate and developmental, so that children worked in progressively more depth.

In any planning, what is to be taught, when and how will need to be detailed. One way of starting this is by looking at what would be appropriate to include in the curriculum offering for each year group, using a simple device such as that in Table 14.1. The 'who' and a more detailed version of 'when' can subsequently be added to this.

Whole-school curriculum planning allows for the development of the overview on how themes connect across subjects and how they can be developed as a spiral curriculum. In using the planning device of a spiral curriculum, any overlap is deliberate: themes are not repeated in the same way but are developed in age-appropriate ways. For example, a plan for the topic of death within the overall change and loss curriculum might look like Figure 14.1. This plan is an amended version of one example from the very

Table 14.1

Year	What	How
1		
2		
3		
4		
5		
6		

helpful and highly recommended book *Loss and Change: Resources for Use in Personal and Social Education Programme* by Sue Plant and Pam Stoate (Plant and Stoate, 1989).

Bereavement is, of course, only one aspect of a change and loss curriculum. It is, however, the most sensitive and needs to be handled with care. This will involve preparing parents, as well as the pupils and other teachers, when it is addressed directly. Teachers who work on this should have some training and support. The team co-ordinators for personal and social education will have a significant contribution to make in this and the RE specialist will have an important role from the multi-faith perspective.

What resources are available and how can we adapt them?

It will be no surprise to the reader that there are few resources dealing with death and bereavement for the classroom. There follows a brief account of some of the materials available, representing a sample of different angles on the themes.

Good Grief (Ward *et al.*, 1988; 1989) was the first major publication in this area. It comes in two versions, one for under-11s and one for over-11s. It appears to aim to provide most of the materials, activities and references that might be needed for a course on death and loss. *Good Grief* draws on a range of professionals from health and educational backgrounds. It contains an enormous amount of very useful information and references. The writers have worked to make the activities user-friendly and useful for teachers, but many require considerable amendment and adaptation if they are to be successfully used.

Loss and Change (Plant and Stoate, 1989) is written by educationalists from the personal, social and health education field and is a resource pack for use in a personal and social education programme. Its activities are clearly presented and well structured. They focus on beginnings and endings as well as loss and change. The workshop activities which make up the main part of the book, which is on A4-sized paper, need no amendment to make them usable in a primary or secondary classroom. They also provide a very good example and model of workshop activities for personal and social education. In addition to the workshop activities, the authors have written very accessible and succinct introductory chapters on loss and change, and on issues in the content and process of developing a curriculum for loss and change. This book is an invaluable resource.

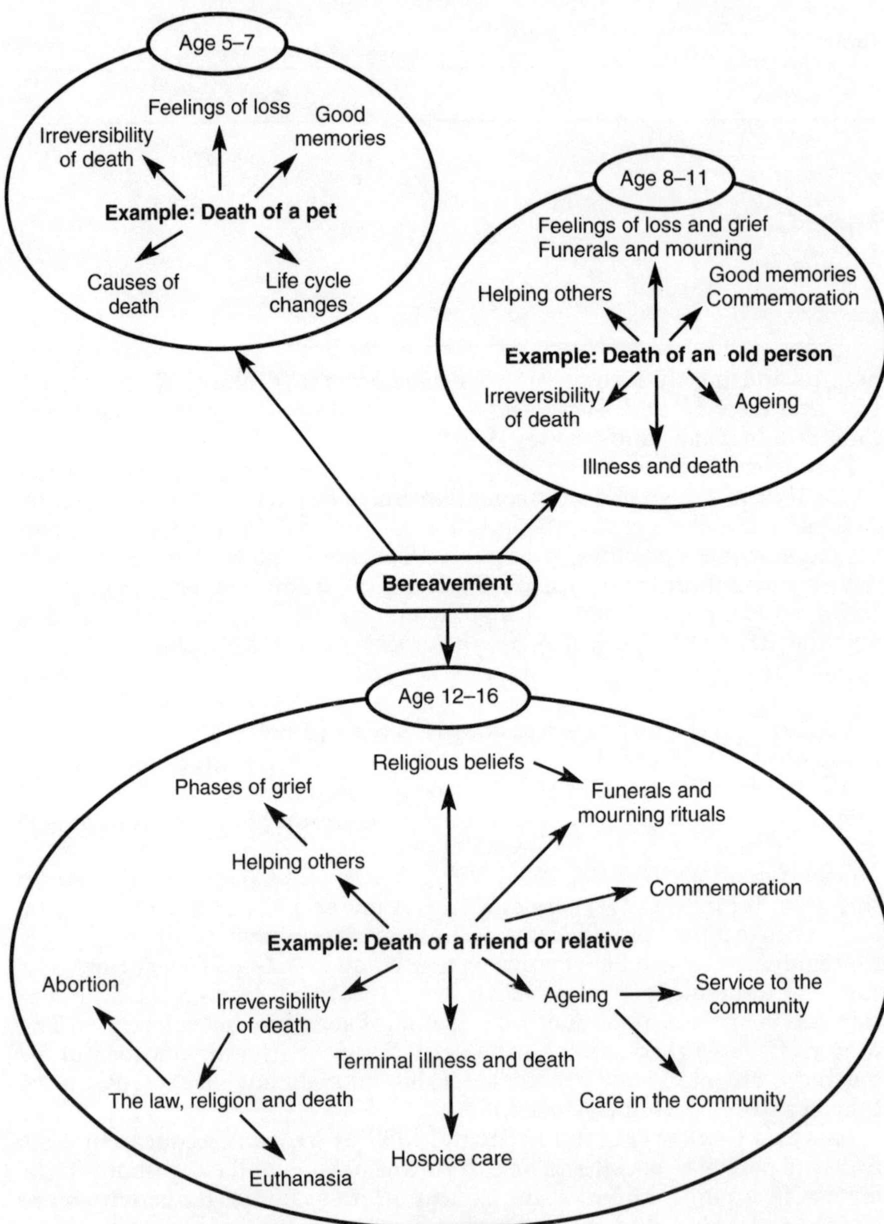

Figure 14.1 Planning for working on bereavement: a spiral curriculum approach

Death in the Classroom (Gatliffe, 1988) is a helpful book by Eleanor Gatliffe, an RE teacher. It is geared towards secondary-age children and aims to be a resource book for teachers specifically on death education. In this book Gatliffe examines the issues in working with children in this area, how the topic fits into religious studies or education and what the goals of death education might be. She also provides some examples of activities that might be used in the classroom and presents ideas on a range of religious and non-religious beliefs and practices.

A different style of resource is *Grief* (Neti-Neti Theatre Company, 1990), a video produced by an experienced theatre company. *Grief* covers a range of themes in a very condensed and powerful way. It is acted by older adolescents and young adults, using English, Bengali/Sylheti and sign language. The content is very much oriented to the upper part of the secondary school and could be a useful resource for an experienced drama and English teacher in an upper secondary school, sixth-form college, FE or youth and community setting. The company is also launching an audio tape in Sylheti synchronized to the video and a radio adaptation, and is planning to publish a resource pack.

In order to evaluate and adapt published activities for use with children and young people in school, teachers will need to consider their aims, methods, resources, planning and preparation. This checklist is intended to help with the process:

Analysing an activity

Aims

- Does the activity have clear aims?
- Are the aims relevant and appropriate to the needs of the intended students?

Method

- Are active methods used? For example varieties of activity-based group work including:
  - presentation of the aims of the topic;
  - structured opportunities for individuals, pairs or group work, reflection and discussion or simulation or role-play;
  - opportunities for feedback or presentations from groups;
  - processing of ideas through structured whole-group discussion;
  - structured opportunities for debriefing, transfer and application of what has been explored and how it can be applied;
- Is the suggested method appropriate to the content and the aims?
- Does it help in making the content more accessible?

Content

- Is the content relevant to the students?
- Is it sufficiently accessible so that all students can participate?
- Is there a link to other activities around on this theme?
  - If so, where would you locate this activity in the overall work?
  - If not, how would you justify its use?

Age

- What age is the activity appropriate for in its current form?
- If it is not appropriate for the age range or developmental stage of the students you deal with, would you adapt it, and if so how?

Timing

- Has the timing been worked out? – if not how would you work out how long to spend on the different elements?

Materials and resources

- What materials and resources would be required? Are they easily accessible?
- What might you need to prepare or preview?

Preparation and planning

- What would you need to do to prepare for this activity – materials and resources, students, other colleagues, parents, others?
- How could you ensure that it was part of a spiral curriculum?

Teachers will need in-service training and education (INSET) opportunities if they are to address these areas with some confidence, and the school will need to work out its guidelines for coping with bereavement. To address this need the National Association for Pastoral Care in Education has recently published a pack entitled *Children and Bereavement, Death and Loss: What Can the School Do?* (Wagner, 1993). This pack, produced by the writer of this chapter, was refined over time through INSET sessions with teachers, advisers and educational psychologists in the London Boroughs of Waltham Forest and Kensington and Chelsea, and with colleagues from a range of other LEAs. The course currently takes place at the University of London Institute of Education. Participants on the course have reported that the opportunity to work through the workshop material has the effect of increasing their feelings of confidence and competence in working in this area. The Inset Pack is available from the NAPCE base at a low cost (see Appendix 1 for contact details).

I hope to have shown in this chapter that there is a real need for schools to address this theme, that they have an appropriate role to play, and that practical action is within reach. In such a way we may make a vital contribution to learning about experiences which might otherwise disempower us.

REFERENCES AND FURTHER READING

Death, dying and bereavement

Krementz, J. (1991) *How It Feels When a Parent Dies*. London: Gollancz. 0 575 05183 3.

Kubler-Ross, E. (1974) *Questions and Answers on Death and Dying*. London: Collier Macmillan. 0 02 089150 4.

Kubler-Ross, E. (1975) *Death: The Final Stage of Growth*. New York: Simon & Schuster. 0 671 62238 2.

Kubler-Ross, E. (1983) *On Children and Death*. New York: Macmillan. 0 02 567110 3.

Pincus, L. (1976) *Death and the Family: The Importance of Mourning*. London: Faber & Faber. 0 571 11735 X.

Helping the bereaved

McCarthy,. S. (1988) *A Death in the Family: A Self-help Guide to Coping with Grief*. Vancouver: Self-Counsel Press. 0 2856 5069 6.

Owens, R. G. and Naylor, F. (1989) *Living While Dying: What to Do and What to Say When You Are, or Someone Close to You Is, Dying*. Wellingborough: Thorsons Publishing Group. 0 7225 1620 7.

Raphael, B. (1984) *The Anatomy of Bereavement: A Handbook for the Caring Professions*. London: Unwin Hyman. 0 04 445362 0.

Staudacher, C. (1988) *Beyond Grief: A Guide for Recovering from the Death of a Loved One*. London: Souvenir Press. 0 2856 5068 8.

Helping children

Dyregrov, A. (1990) *Grief in Children: A Handbook for Adults*. London: Jessica Kingsley. 1 85302 11 X.

Grollman, E. A. (1990) *Talking about Death*. Boston: Beacon Press. 0 8070 2363 9.

Jewett, C. (1982) *Helping Children Cope with Separation and Loss*. London: Batsford Academic. 0 7134 4707 9.

Rosen, H. (1986) *Unspoken Grief: Coping with Childhood Sibling Loss*. Lexington, Mass.: Lexington Books. 0 669 110221 1.

Wells, R. (1988) *Helping Children Cope with Grief*. London: Sheldon Press. 0 85969 559 X.

Resources and materials

Gatliffe, E. (1988) *Death in the Classroom: A Resource Book for Teachers and Others*. London: Epworth Press. 0 7162 0441 X.

Hopson, B., Scally, M. and Stafford, K. (1988) *Lifeskills Now – Transitions: The Challenge of Change*. Leeds: Lifeskills Associates/Mercury Business Books. 0 8525 2120 1.

Neti-Neti Theatre Company (1990) *Grief: The Video*. London: Neti-Neti.

Plant, S. and Stoate, P. (1989) *Loss and Change: Resources for Use in Personal and Social Education Programme*. Crediton: Southgate Publishers. 0 08 036355 5.

Rayner, C. (1978) *The Body Book*. London: Pan Books. 0 330 25807 9.

Wagner, P. (1993) *Children and Bereavement, Death and Loss: What Can the School Do?* Coventry: NAPCE.

Ward, B. and Associates (1988) *Good Grief: Talking and Learning about Loss and Death with Under 11s*. London: Jessica Kingsley Publishers. 0 85302 161 X.

Ward, B. and Associates (1989) *Good Grief: Talking and Learning about Loss and Death with Over 11s*. London: Jessica Kingsley Publishers. 0 85302 529 1.

Stories for children (and adults)

Donaldson, M. (1978) *Children's Minds*. Glasgow: Fontana. 0 00 635287 1.

Mathias, B. and Spiers, D. (1992) *A Handbook on Death and Bereavement – Helping Children Understand*. National Library for the Handicapped Child, Ash Court, Rose Street, Wokingham, Berks RG11 1XS (tel.: 01734 891101). 0 948664 10 X.

Yule, W. and Gold, A. (1993) *Wise Before the Event: Coping with Crises in Schools*. London: Calouste Gulbenkian Foundation. 0 903319 66 7.

Part 6

Making the Links

CHAPTER 15

The school in its community

Bernard Clarke

For years writers about sociology and education have failed to agree about what precisely they mean when they use the word 'community'. In his review of the literature in the United States, G. A. Hillery found ninety-four different definitions! He was left to reflect that 'beyond the recognition that people are involved in community, there is little agreement on the use of the term' (Hillery, 1955, p. 23). The number of definitions has probably increased since 1955!

Rather than enter that particular minefield and attempt a definition, this chapter will describe the efforts of one school to develop relationships with groups of people in different contexts with the aim of enhancing the personal and social education of its students. In doing so, it will make a number of assumptions about what characterizes a community.

For our purposes, a community is a social group which is more than the sum of its parts. It involves unity, belonging and shared purposes and interests. It embodies a sense of mutual responsibility and provides opportunities for participation in corporate activity.

PEERS

Peers is a comprehensive upper school on the southern fringe of the city of Oxford. Many of its five hundred 13- to 18-year-old students live in the three housing estates which surround it.

The LEA in Oxfordshire has never had a formal policy of community schools, but has been supportive of those which choose to move in that direction. Successive governing bodies, heads and teachers at Peers have drawn on that encouragement and the school thinks of itself as a community school without ever having been formally designated as such.

The campus is home to the Peers Community Library which serves the local neighbourhood as well as the school, a joint-use sports and arts centre, a community education centre, a self-managed workplace day nursery and the local rugby football club. Oxfordshire County Council moved the central offices of four major departments into a spare building on the premises in January 1992. Several thousand people use the facilities every week.

Pastoral care and PSE have been and remain vital parts of the curriculum at Peers. There is a well-established tutorial structure in which all staff and students participate, and the tutorial programme is under regular review as, increasingly, it provides the means of ensuring that students have access to the cross-curricular themes of the National Curriculum.

There is, however, a strong feeling amongst the staff that much of the most important and effective learning that any of us does occurs as a result of what we experience first-hand rather than as a result of what we are taught. So the relationship between what we say and what we do – 'the hidden curriculum' – is critical to the development of our students as people and has been a constant subtext to recent developments at Peers. We occasionally remind ourselves of the words of the high school principal to his teachers on the first day of school, quoted by Pring:

> Dear Teacher
>
> I am a survivor of a concentration camp. My eyes saw what no man should witness:
>
> Gas chambers built by learned engineers.
>
> Children poisoned by educated physicians.
>
> Infants killed by trained nurses.
>
> Women and babies shot and burned by high school and college graduates.
>
> So, I am suspicious of education.
>
> My request is: Help your students become human. Your efforts must never produce learned monsters, skilled psychopaths, educated Eichmans.
>
> Reading, writing, arithmetic are important only if they serve to make our children more human.
>
> (Pring, 1984)

Such thoughts seem neither irrelevant nor far-fetched the morning after the mass suicide of religious fanatics at Waco, Texas; the funeral of Chris Hani and subsequent racial violence in Johannesburg; and the attempts to prevent a massacre of Bosnian Moslems at Srebrenice.

For many years, at Peers, we have tried to create an atmosphere in which individuals are helped to develop through their working relationships with other people. We have chosen to see this as everybody's responsibility and not the special province of a particular group of teachers or section of the timetabled curriculum. This theme of individual development through working relationships will recur in the examples which follow.

WHICH COMMUNITIES?

As it stands, the chapter title gives the impression that 'the community' is something which surrounds a school, rather as the sea surrounds an island.

The image prompts others. Tides of people moving in and out; sea defences erected to prevent flooding; periods of calm interrupted by occasional storms. Best to stop, perhaps, before we get to LMS-inspired thoughts of 'treasure' or 'desert'!

In other ways the island image is not particularly helpful. It implies that 'the community' is a single, identifiable thing and, moreover, that it is different and separate from the school. For the purposes of this chapter it is more helpful to think of the *school* and its *communities*.

The list of groups of people with which a school has relationships is extensive. There is the community of local schools; those schools which have common philosophies (LMS, open enrolment and opting-out have produced a few changes there!); the teaching profession; former students; the LEA (how important that remains for some of us!); the community of those involved in the training of new teachers. And so on.

The importance of strong relationships with people in the local neighbourhood ('the community') has been written about on numerous occasions by others and is emphasized in the work of such organizations as the Community Education Association and the Community Education Development Centre. The key role for schools of working with parents is dealt with by Sally Tomlinson in Chapter 16, below.

The perspective I have chosen of the school lying at the centre of a number of communities, each making a contribution to the personal and social development of the students, will be illustrated by three examples. Each represents a set of relationships which are particularly important to the school for reasons which, I hope, will become clear as they are described. They are:

- our dealings with the local business community;
- the Peers/Katumba II Link ('the global community');
- the school as a community.

THE LOCAL BUSINESS COMMUNITY

It is as well to remind ourselves that 'industry links' were not invented when the 1986 Education Act obliged governing bodies to ensure that their membership included representatives of the local business community. They have been an outstanding feature of the life of many schools for a long time. Indeed, the richness and relevance of the educational experience for many young people has come, at least in part, from the influence, both direct and indirect, of local employers.

Countless teenagers have had their attitude to education changed by visiting speakers, work experience, careers conventions, work shadowing, etc. In only a few cases, though, has the full potential of these relationships been realized. There are a number of reasons for this, one of which is the pressure on time at both ends of the partnership. Some schools and businesses may see getting involved with each other as incidental to, or even a distraction from, their primary function and, consequently, not make it a high priority. Certainly, the climate of recession during the late 1980s and early 1990s did not encourage employers to offer work experience opportunities to youngsters from school at a time when they were having to reduce their own staffing levels.

Two other possible reasons come to mind. One is the view of school as 'preparation for working life'. It is embarrassing to think of the number of times one has said to students, 'When you leave school and go to work' or something similar and, in so doing, made it more difficult for young people and business partners to see that we are involved in the same enterprise.

School is working life. Furthermore, learning does not stop when you leave school. Increasingly, people 'at work' need to see themselves as lifelong learners. The separation in people's minds of school and work has led to the unspoken view that they are two different worlds. And yet the skills, knowledge and attitudes essential for success in one are equally vital in the other.

The second possible reason is the idea that all the benefits of partnership between schools and industry flow in one direction, that is to the school: that, in offering our students work experience opportunities, local employers are being selflessly generous and not seeking or getting anything in return.

At a celebratory party for stakeholders, the chief executive of a large local industrial concern with an international reputation explained just how important local schools are to its prosperity. They provide not only its future workforce but also its future customers. Its relationships with local schools have a direct effect on its well-being. Furthermore, he said, businesses do not exist in vacuums. They are situated in local communities and have a vested interest in making a contribution to the life of those communities.

For these reasons, teachers at Peers have attempted to integrate our work with business and industry as fully as possible into the life of the school and make the most of the benefits for everybody concerned. All staff visit students on their work experience placements and, in so doing, identify themselves with the companies concerned. Most staff have already spent time on placements with local businesses, usually with curriculum development in mind but also in order to acquire a greater understanding of the local business community.

Three further examples will illustrate the point. They will also show how additional benefits, unforeseen at the outset, can result.

The Oxfordshire two-way compact

In 1992, the Heart of England Training and Enterprise Council and Oxfordshire LEA, through the Education Business Partnership, applied to the Department of Employment to establish a two-way version of the well-known Compact idea. As well as seeking to raise students' levels of attainment through the involvement of people from local firms, it was intended to address the problem of low take-up of training opportunities by local employees.

Peers was selected as one of the two first-phase schools. Within six months over sixty 'mentors' from local firms had offered to devote at least one hour per month to working alongside individual students in year ten. Their meetings with students focus on progress towards agreed targets in relation to academic work, attendance, punctuality, extra-curricular activities etc. and plans for the future. The intention is that students will be helped to make progress through the personal interest of adults who know about life after school but, unlike parents or teachers, have no axe to grind.

People from all sectors of industry have volunteered to become mentors. The list grows almost daily and includes factory workers, nurses, managing directors, police officers, retail workers, accountants, academics, research workers and teachers. Once established, mentors tend to become involved in other aspects of school life like curriculum development and providing technical assistance to individual students with their work.

As a result of this contact, an increasing number of employees are taking up opportunities for further training and education on the school's premises through day or evening classes. More and more are using the sports facilities during the lunch hour and after school. There is an incidental, but significant, benefit for all students' personal and social development through these routine encounters with adults from local businesses in a variety of different contexts at school.

Commercial services

Having successfully tendered for the contract, Oxfordshire County Council Commercial Services (i.e. the school meals, cleaning and caretaking, highways and grounds maintenance department) needed a base for their central offices. A surplus building in the middle of the Peers campus was offered and accepted.

The benefits to the school of having a thriving business concern in the heart of our premises are enormous, apart from the obvious one of work experience opportunities. Students have daily contact with people at work; they have to be sure not to disturb the work-place, particularly on their way to and from school, at morning break and at lunchtime; visitors to Commercial Services quite often find themselves in the wrong place and need to ask students for directions. When we say to visitors that Peers is a place of work, the presence of a business in the heart of the school is evidence that we mean it.

Recently, the school council became concerned that some Commercial Services employees were leaving their offices to smoke in the car park right in the centre of the school grounds. On a basis that sauce for the goose is sauce for the gander, the headteacher was despatched to ensure that the strict no smoking policy for all members of the school was not breached!

There have been material gains from the arrangement like enhanced car and cycle parking and campus signposts. Whenever the school meals service needs to try out a new idea, it tends to do it in our school kitchen. And, of course, if there is ever a problem over meals or caretaking or the grounds, we don't have to go far to sort it out!

Education/industry seminars

A number of people, including some members of the local Education Business Partnership, identified the need for a series of seminars on education/industry matters, the purpose being to bring together policy-makers from both worlds. In partnership with the Oxford University Department of Educational Studies, a format was agreed upon. We would invite forty senior people for a buffet supper, prepared and served by students in the school's training restaurant, followed by an introductory talk from an eminent person in the field, and discussion.

Sir John Cassels, secretary of the National Commission on Education, spoke at the first seminar, and such was its success that the chief executive of a local business made a substantial donation to the school to help it 'keep up the good work'. The money has enabled us to establish Education Plus, a programme of twilight enrichment classes for students in year 9. In consultation with their families, students are invited to choose two from a list of courses which are related to but different from the mainstream curriculum. In the first year of the scheme the list consisted of effective English, electronics and robotics, statistics, beginners' Spanish, advanced chemistry, information technology and art appreciation. The courses run for one hour after school, so, by selecting two, students commit themselves to two hours' additional study per week.

The fundamental purpose of Education Plus is to foster positive attitudes to academic work in our students and an appreciation that the more you put into your education the more you get out of it in the long run. The fact that the scheme is sponsored by a local employer is not lost on the students or their families, particularly as the chief executive presents certificates to them at the end of the course (Neumark, 1993).

THE PEERS/KATUMBA II LINK

The link between Peers School and Katumba II School in the remote rural highlands of southern Tanzania was established in 1984 through contact with the Ministry of Education in Dar es Salaam. Its aim was to create a bond between the two schools based on partnership and exchange. As a result it was hoped to make a significant impact on the life of both schools and to bring about a wider awareness of and interest in our respective local communities and beyond.

These aims were based on the belief that a proper understanding of the issues of world development – including the increasing interdependence of different parts of the world – is of fundamental importance and relevance to us all. Further, our belief is that such an understanding needs to be promoted actively through direct exchanges of experience, especially among young people.

The first visit was by a group of students and teachers from Peers who spent four weeks in Tanzania in the summer of 1985. Twelve months later a group from Katumba came to Peers and the pattern was established. Reciprocal visits have taken place each year since then. The link is based on the twin principles of work and reciprocity. So, in Tanzania the students and teachers from Peers divide their time between helping in the school 'shamba' (plantations of coffee, bananas and vegetables) and classrooms. At Peers, students from Katumba spend a great deal of their time in classrooms. Sightseeing is kept to a minimum.

What has this to do with the school and its communities? A great deal. Visits involve everybody at the host school. At Katumba the Peers groups are invariably honoured on their arrival and at intervals during their stay with wonderful displays of singing, dancing and drama which involve the entire school and many members of the local community. In Britain, because we are more inhibited in such matters, the involvement of the whole school, whilst just as real, is less obvious. Relationships quietly evolve during the month as a result of contact in the classroom and during social time. It is interesting to watch 'sophisticated' Oxford teenagers, unable to conceal their interest, hovering around the Tanzanian students until their confidence grows sufficiently for them to join in the conversation. By the end of the visit many lasting friendships have been formed and very few of our students are untouched by the presence of the students from Katumba in their midst.

Friendships are important, but if the link is to achieve its aims and develop the understanding of all students, it must influence the whole curriculum. At various times, every area of the curriculum has drawn on the link to enrich the learning of students: design projects based on finding 'low-tech' solutions to everyday difficulties for the disabled; creative writing in English; the mathematics of a game involving dried beans which is played throughout Tanzania; a creative arts project based on Tanzanian sculpture. Each year brings new ideas and additions to the curriculum.

The most recent is Project Gemini, a scheme, sponsored by British Telecom, for computer linking between schools in different parts of the world to promote development and environmental education. The original plan envisages one class of 14-year-olds in Katumba and one class in Peers using the link directly as part of their work on environmental issues across the curriculum and them disseminating their findings throughout their respective schools.

This comparatively simple idea raises extraordinarily difficult technical issues which have to be discussed thoroughly with our students. For instance, how do you transport computer equipment to a remote area of Tanzania? How do you ensure it works, given the erratic nature of the local electricity supply? What about maintenance?

Even more important are the moral questions. What are the implications of introducing computers to a school in a society where, at present, they are almost non-existent? How do we avoid the charge of 'cultural imperialism'? How does it square with the link's founding principle of reciprocity? Raising and working through these knotty problems with our students is an essential part of the educational process which flows from the link. By reaching answers or not, as the case may be, they arrive at a deeper understanding of the relationship between ourselves and the wider world.

As with our contacts with the local business community, unexpected benefits have a habit of emerging from the link. When, in 1990, Archbishop Desmond Tutu came to Oxford to receive an honorary degree, he accepted our invitation to pay a visit to Peers. The experience for us all of meeting a great world leader and worker for peace was something we will never forget. It also gave us a sense of communion with South Africa that no amount of lessons or television programmes could provide.

When the BBC decided to make a schools television programme about international exchanges, they decided to focus on the Peers/Katumba II Link. All of us – students, staff, parents, governors, the Parish Council – derived immense pleasure from seeing the 1991 visit to Tanzania sensitively portrayed for a wider audience (BBC, 1992). The second programme following the progress of the Katumba II group's visit to Peers in 1992 was in some ways even more moving because it showed how affected the Tanzanians were by so much that we regard as humdrum (BBC, 1993).

The involvement of other communities in the life of a school is only effective if it alters the way young people see the world. The evidence we have gleaned from eight years of the Link is that it really does change young people's attitudes. As one student summed it up: 'This trip has changed my life. When I go back I'm going to be a different person ... definitely ... hopefully, anyway.'

THE SCHOOL AS A COMMUNITY

The essential prerequisite for any school to develop relationships successfully with its communities is that it should aim to be a coherent community itself. That is much easier said than done. Most schools struggle, with varying degrees of success, to create a sense of unity amongst the range and diversity of people that inhabit them. It is one of those tasks that is never done. As soon as everybody appears to be pulling together, something always seems to happen to remind us how fragile the cohesion is.

But that is to miss the point. In any community the members are never identical and the differences are often greater than the similarities. Even in the most close-knit group the members have varied interests, attitudes and roles. The strength of the community lies in its ability to recognize, contain and nurture differences at the same time as achieving an overall sense of unity.

Our attempt to achieve this impossible task is embodied in the Code of Conduct – a statement of the principles which must guide the action of every member of the school. The Code of Conduct ('Rights and responsibilities of peers') rests on two basic assumptions:

- Peers is a place of work where we all have a job to do. It is the *right* of everybody to get on with their job without being hindered by anybody else.
- Adults should not expect young people to do what they are not prepared to do themselves.

The strength of the Code of Conduct lies in the fact that all those groups of people with a stake in the school – students, staff, parents and governors – were involved in drawing it up. The process of drafting and redrafting took several months and only when all the groups were happy with the result was it published in its final form.

The Code of Conduct summarizes what we have agreed we have a right to expect of each other and serves as a reminder to us all. It does not assume that everybody will get everything right every time. After all, as somebody else once said, 'schools should be full of second chances'.

Of course, there is a bottom line. But, here again, the list of unacceptable behaviour was produced as a result of discussion. If any of us had written down a list it would have been a lot quicker and, almost certainly, very similar. But the process of discussion is what gives it strength. We have *agreed* that these things are unacceptable.

So, for instance, we all understand why we cannot accept bullying. If somebody is afraid of what another person might do to them, their right to get on with their work is being interfered with. In affirming this, we are bound to accept that bullying by teachers is just as unacceptable as by students. So teachers have agreed that shouting, threatening and punishing arbitrarily will not be used.

Peers is not a rose garden, but neither is it a bear garden. When, as not infrequently happens, one of us falls short of the expectations, we can remind each other of what we have agreed and consider ways in which the mistake can be avoided again.

Producing a Code of Conduct does not, of itself, create a community. The *process* by which it is produced can be a very significant step on the road, but *only* if it is rooted in the young people's experience of the school. If it were simply a form of words, we would be better off without it, because the students would see through it as a sham straight away.

At the start of each year the Code of Conduct is discussed by the students (those in their first year with us have already been introduced to it with their parents as part of the induction process for new families) and there is the opportunity to revise it, although, so far, it has not been changed. The significance of the Code of Conduct is that we want our students to learn from the experience of living and working in a community where we have agreed to treat each other as we expect to be treated ourselves. It is our intention that they will take that learning with them into the other communities in which they live, now and in the future.

This chapter has attempted to describe the efforts of one school to promote the personal and social development of its students through its work with various communities. Without ever taking a conscious decision about it, the school has developed an attitude of mind, based on practical experience over many years, that our communities represent a huge learning resource.

It is our belief and experience that, in essence, effective community education is about the working relationships between people. Young people learn and develop more as a result of their dealings with others than from what they are taught in classrooms, important as that obviously is. As a result, visitors are always welcomed, not for reasons of altruism or politeness, but through enlightened self-interest!

That attitude of mind is probably the best safeguard we have against the obvious danger of complacency or staleness. The three illustrations I have used in the chapter were intended to show how, so far, one thing has always seemed to lead to another. The challenge is to ensure that that continues to be the case.

REFERENCES

BBC (1992) *Tanzania, O Yea*. BBC Television, Life School.

BBC (1993) *Welcome, Dear Friends*. BBC Television, Life School.

Hillery, G. A. Jnr (1955) Definitions of community: areas of agreement. *Rural Sociology*, **20**, 110–21.

Neumark, V. Peers pressure. *Times Educational Supplement*, 9 April 1993.

Pring, R. (1984) *Personal and Social Education in the Curriculum*. London: Hodder & Stoughton.

CHAPTER 16

Home–school links

Sally Tomlinson

The case for involving parents in their children's development and education has been established by innumerable studies and many schools are now committed to pursuing home-school links.

(Wolfendale, 1989, p. ix)

This chapter is largely about the development of links between homes and schools which create a partnership. For most of the twentieth century education has been equated with schooling, teachers have defended their professional territory and there has been a separation of home and school. Now, there are increasingly moves to reverse this situation and to recognize that children's school performance and their personal and social development are most successful when a partnership is established between home and school. Home–school relations figure prominently on the agendas of politicians, professionals and parents, although from different perspectives, but there is a widespread acceptance that 'good' relations include effective communication and information-giving, accountability of schools to parents, encouraging parents to support children's learning and development and creating a sense of shared purpose and identity between parents, pupils and teachers. However, there is currently a political divide as to the form parental involvement should take. The Conservative government, via the 1986, 1988 and 1993 Education Acts, has encouraged parents to regard themselves as consumers in an educational market and as managers via representation on governing bodies. Parental choices of schools are intended to promote competition between schools and to help close ineffective ones. Whether the role of parent as consumer and agent of competition will actually improve children's educational performance and enhance their personal and social development is debatable.

This chapter briefly reviews home–school contacts in Britain up to the present, noting that much of the literature on home–school relations has used a simplistic social class model in which 'working-class' homes have been regarded as deficient and less likely to care about children's achievements or pastoral needs. The chapter also covers problems inherent in creating partnerships, especially with ethnic-minority parents and parents of children with special educational needs, the experiences of other

European countries, and policies for closer home, school and community co-operation.

HOME–SCHOOL CONTACTS

Home–school contacts have never figured large as a priority in English education, and up to the 1970s talk of partnership in education usually referred to that between central and local education authorities. Within the Department for Education the responsibility for overseeing home–school relationships is still relatively a minor chore. The social history of parent–school contacts indicates that – in the State system – relations have often been marked by tension and sometimes overt conflict. Willard Waller, an American sociologist, wrote in the 1930s that 'parents and teachers usually live in conditions of mutual mistrust and enmity' (Waller, 1932). In the Victorian era, and particularly from 1870 when mass elementary education was introduced, it was easy to see why this should be the case. Apart from removing potential wage-earning children into school, the type of education offered was rigid, inflexible and authoritarian – teachers were enjoined to 'civilise and control' their pupils (Grace, 1978), a task which involved not only harsh discipline for pupils but also the denigration of homes and parental values. Many teachers came to see themselves as compensating for the deficiencies of homes – a view that lives on in the 1990s – and teachers felt free to criticize parents, especially mothers, for perceived inadequacies. Staffrooms have always been familiar with the theme of 'what can we do with Johnny, have you *seen* his mother?' (Tomlinson, 1988).

Literature discussing the relationship between school attainments, personal and social behaviour and homes has always worked to the disadvantage of working-class homes and parents. On measures of achievement, children from manual workers' homes and those with unemployed parents have tended on average to do less well, and it has usually been children from the lower socio-economic groups who have acquired the labels and reputation for being 'troublesome'. Explanations for this have, over the past hundred years, run a gamut from Victorian beliefs in the genetic inferiority of the 'lower classes' (Tredgold, 1908) through material and social disadvantage, cultural and linguistic deprivation, apathetic parenting and ineffective homes (Rutter and Madge, 1976). The misuse of Basil Bernstein's 1960s work on language codes (Bernstein 1973) reinforced teachers' views that working-class speech was 'deficient'. Many teachers came to believe that school influence was marginal when set against a 'poor' home background, and held low expectations of large groups of children. This included, from the 1960s, pupils from ethnic minorities who were also subject to stereotyped beliefs about their culture, language and potentialities.

The middle–working class divide appearing in much of the literature undoubtedly led some teachers to underestimate the ambitions and capabilities of working-class and minority parents and their children, and many of the perceived problems in home–school contacts do have a class and a racial dimension. Research during the 1980s demonstrated that working-class and minority parents actually have very positive attitudes to education but lack the knowledge and information about the education system, and how to 'manage' it, that middle-class parents usually have (Roberts, 1984; Tomlinson, 1984, 1991; Gewirtz, Ball and Bowe, 1992). It has become a truism that it has always been the more informed and articulate parents who can obtain most from the education system.

Over the past twenty years major efforts have been made to improve home–school contacts and more information has become available on parental views. As the authors of the Royal Society of Arts Home–School project recently wrote:

> Among parents there has been a slow but definite shift in attitudes away from deference, puzzlement and helplessness, clearly documented in the 1960's and 1970's, towards a general recognition that parents do have a formal right to information and access concerning their children's schooling, and to a share in the decisions regarding this.
>
> (Jones *et al.*, 1992, p. 13)

HOME–SCHOOL LINKS

The Plowden Report (Plowden, 1967) proved to be a watershed in helping schools to understand why closer home–school links were desirable, although Edwards and Redfern (1988) have pointed out that, ironically, the underlying message from the Plowden Committee was similar to traditional views that poor educational performance and unacceptable social behaviour were likely to emanate from 'deficient' homes. Whilst it is undoubtedly true that there are some children whose home backgrounds are such that they need special pastoral care and attention, this is not necessarily linked to socio-economic status.

The Plowden Committee did, however, set out a minimum programme by which schools could inform parents and encourage home–school links. This included welcome to school, open days, regular reports and written information, and meetings with teachers. By the 1980s the extent of home–school links in a majority of schools had gone beyond this minimum programme. Visits of teachers to homes, and parents to school, letters, circulars, pupil reports and records of achievement, governors' reports, school prospectuses and education–employer–parent compacts all constituted very direct forms of communication and linkage. Parental involvement in day-to-day activities as classroom helpers, translators, materials-makers, assistants on outings, and in home–school reading, maths and homework schemes, and involvement via parent–teacher and other associations had also become more commonplace.

Parental partnerships and home–school links have been furthered, to some extent, by the existence of parents' voluntary organizations. The Home–School Council, founded in 1930, and the National Confederation of Parent–Teacher Associations, founded in 1956, have acted as pressure groups on government to improve home–school links, as have more radical groups such as the Campaign for State Education (1962), The National Association for Governors and Managers (1970) and local groups such as the All London Parents Action Group, and the Haringey and Brent Black Parents Associations. The only national parental advisory service, ACE

(Advisory Centre for Education, 1962) is currently encouraging the creation of local advisory services, to help give parents a local power base from which to influence schools and government policies.

Legislation in the 1980s gave parents far more rights to information about schools, access to curriculum documents, governors and HMI reports, and equal representation on governing bodies. From 1988 parents were, however, encouraged to 'choose' between schools rather than opt for a local neighbourhood school, and to vote in ballots for their children's school to opt out of local authority control and become grant-maintained by central government. A Parents' Charter published in 1991 set out existing parental rights and promised a variety of new rights but devoted only a short section to the notion of parents as partners. While this legislation and approach placed a premium on home–school links best described as customer–provider, and actively *discouraged* parents from supporting local schools in their local community, there has also been, over the past ten years particularly, a countervailing movement. There has in practice been an expansion of many different kinds of home–school links which indicate an increasing desire on the part of teachers and parents to work together. The most up-to-date (to 1992) record of such links is contained in a *Directory of Home–School Initiatives in the UK* compiled by John Bastiani at Nottingham University (Bastiani and Bailey, 1992). Some of the initiatives described are Lewisham's development of a code of practice on home–school links, an advice service to parents with independent advocacy, a project to improve school–community practices in seven primary schools and funding for a project on 'Raising pupil standards in the inner city'. In rural Devon the LEA has a policy of developing family education through schools and works with the Devon Federation of Home and School to produce materials. There is also an advisory teacher on family initiatives, home–school files and workshops for parent–governors. Cleveland has a team of home–school liaison teachers, City-Challenge-funded home–school link projects and a focus on parents of special educational needs pupils.

The most comprehensive project in England to date, exploring expanded partnerships in education, was set up in 1989 by the Royal Society of Arts and the National Association of Headteachers. This project was initially based in twenty schools around Britain, the schools being selected on the basis of an interest in developing home–school relations. The essence of the project was that it set out to:

- consider changing legal and contractual requirements to develop effective partnerships between schools and homes. This means that partnership will be not an optional extra but an essential requirement, and will include all parents, not just the 'active and unrepresentative' ones.
- develop whole-school approaches to policy and practice – reviewing existing home–school relations, developing home–school contracts or signed understandings, and planning, organizing and evaluating home–school activities.

This project, which included a strong European dimension, is described in Tomlinson (1991) and Jones *et al*. (1992).

PARENTS AS PARTNERS

Whatever the political context and desires of government, home–school links cannot be forced. Contacts take different forms and are at different levels, most parents initially becoming involved in school activities to improve the progress and well-being of their own child. From this point parents may become involved at whole-class and whole-school level, but only a few go on to influence school policies via governance and management. There are, as a wide variety of studies testify, different dimensions and kinds of parental involvement and there are also parents who chose not to be involved with schools (see Cunningham and Davis, 1985; Pugh and De'Ath, 1989; Wolfendale 1989). A major obstacle to the creation of partnerships has been that many teachers have embraced a notion of professionalism that excluded parents, and needed to be persuaded that professional teaching does recognise the integral role of parents in education. Macbeth (1989) suggested that there were four stages of progression in the growth of home–school partnerships which depended on a developing teacher and school acceptance of a new professionalism:

- *The self-contained school* is characterized by teacher autonomy, limited and formalized contacts with parents, little parental choice or consultation, a denial of access to school records, and with curriculum and teaching methods regarded as the teacher's domain.
- *Professional uncertainty* is characterized by tentative experiment with home–school liaison and participation but teachers still restricting consultation and blaming homes for low pupil attainment.
- *Growing commitment* is the stage at which the school leadership encourages liaison and consultation with parents, recognizes the value of home teaching, encourages parents onto governing bodies, and generally begins to adapt the school system to include parents.
- *The school and family concordat* represents the ultimate stage in the attempt to involve all families in formal schooling, recognizing that home learning is part of education and the role of parents is crucial in this, and emphasizing the obligation of parents to be involved and to co-operate with schools.

Schools in Britain could certainly be rated along this continuum with many being at stages one or two. On the parental side, many parents are still reluctant to become involved in their children's formal education, lacking confidence and knowledge, or regarding classroom affairs as the teacher's domain.

Asking teachers to incorporate a 'practice' of home–school contacts into their professional activity, to accept criticism of their practice and to accept parents as equal partners requires justification. Teachers must be convinced that it is in their interests, as well as the interests of parents and children, to regard parents as integral to the whole process of education and training from pre-school to post-16. They will also have to work out the different kinds of partnership required as children progress through school.

New requirements for teacher-training, however, do not encourage student-teachers to think of parents as partners, but as consumers to be informed of their children's comparative achievements *vis-à-vis* other children's. The Council for the Accreditation of Teacher Education published new guidelines for teacher-trainers in November 1992 which noted that, as the Parents' Charter requires teachers to 'report comparative information about pupils in relation to others in schools ... it is expected that students will be given some opportunity to demonstrate ability in reporting and discussing pupil progress with parents' (CATE, 1992, p. 11).

It would be unfortunate if teacher–parent relationships were to be confined to such a narrow professional–client role, as there are compelling reasons why a partnership model is to be preferred. One reason is *legality*. Parents are the primary educators of their children and are responsible in law for their education up to 16. The United Nations Declaration of the Rights of the Child also places the final responsibility for the education and guidance of their children on parents. A legal framework is in place to enhance the teacher–parent link. Another compelling reason is adherence to democracy. In a democracy parents have a right to be involved in decisions which affect the education, development and future of their children beyond merely receiving reports and 'discussing' them.

There are other problems inherent in the notion of partnership – particularly from the parents' side. Parents, for example, have no distinctive power-base. There is a plethora of local and national groups but no single group that the government could negotiate with or fund. Parents' organizations may influence policy on single issues but are not regarded at national, local or school level as integral to decision-making. Parent governors still have limited influence, especially given the historically dominant position of headteachers in England.

Parents often find the language of education difficult, particularly as the educational reforms have introduced a whole new curriculum and assessment language, and initials and acronyms abound. In addition, many aspects of school are beyond actual parental influence. Inadequate resourcing and poor teachers are two issues which worry parents but which are difficult to address, particularly if parents are regarded simply as clients and consumers.

ETHNIC MINORITY PARENTS

A group of parents who have particular problems with the notion of partnership are ethnic minority parents. The involvement of ethnic minority parents as partners in the education process is more difficult to achieve than with white parents, given that the majority of teachers are from the white, majority culture. Over the past thirty years, minority home–school encounters have perforce taken place in a society marked by racial antagonisms and intercultural tensions. Teachers, having not been equipped during their training to deal with minority parents, have often clung to negative, stereotyping and patronizing views. The research literature into the 1990s still indicated that minority parents were perceived as a problem for schools rather than as equal partners (Brar, 1991; Tomlinson, 1993).

There has long been a mismatch of expectations between what minority parents expected of education and what teachers felt they could offer. Minority parents – Afro-Caribbean, Indian, Pakistani, Bangladeshi,

Chinese and others – have all indicated that they not only want their children equipped with the credentials and skills on a par with white pupils, they also want their backgrounds and cultures taken seriously in schools, and they want racism and racial harassment eradicated. While some schools and local authorities have always taken these issues seriously, others have found it more difficult. The insensitive treatment of the parents of Ahmed Ullah, the boy murdered at Burnage School, Manchester in 1986, received wide publicity (MacDonald, 1989), and research by Brar in Birmingham has demonstrated that stereotyped ideas of minority families and communities continue to be held. He found that teachers' knowledge of the 'black community' in Handsworth was based on 'common sense, or racist media distortion' (Brar, 1991, p. 33). The Handsworth community was presumed to be all-black, all-working-class and often all-male. Teachers continued to stereotype parents as uninterested in their children's education and perpetuated a blame-the-parents syndrome which 'has often been the excuse for schools to sit back and avoid developing school-community consultation' (p. 34).

During the 1980s, ethnic minority parents, in common with other parents, did benefit from improved home–school contacts and from legal requirements to pass over more information to homes. Some urban schools in areas of high minority settlement have been in the forefront of pioneering imaginative contacts and developing LEA and school policies on multicultural and anti-racist education, although it does remain the case that minority parents are less likely than white parents to be involved in day-to-day school activities or represented on governing bodies (National Consumer Council, 1990).

White parental antagonism to the education of their children alongside minorities, a feature of our multi-racial society since the 1960s, has become more vocal and open since the 1988 Education Act. During the passage of the Bill through Parliament in 1987, opposition Peers in the House of Lords moved an amendment to remove the duty on LEAs to comply with parental preference for choice of school if it was believed to be on racial grounds. The amendment was withdrawn after a government Minister gave assurances that it was unlikely that white parents would openly use racial reasons for choice of school. This had in fact, already happened in Cleveland, where a white parent had requested her child be transferred to a majority white school on what were deemed to be racial grounds (Commission for Racial Equality, 1989). There are now legal dilemmas over the precedence given to educational and to race relations legislation, and white parents have also been using the clauses in the 1988 Act requiring religious education to be 'predominantly Christian' as a way of moving their children away from multiracial schools (CRE, 1989).

SPECIAL EDUCATIONAL NEEDS

A second, and often overlapping, group of parents who have particular problems in creating partnerships with schools are the parents of those children designated as having special educational needs. Over the past twenty years there has been an increasing emphasis on involving the parents of these children in assessment discussions, but evidence continues to suggest that many parents, particularly minority parents, feel uninvolved or inadequately consulted in decisions about the assessment of their children, and uninformed, misinformed or overwhelmed by professional expertise once the children are actually in a special education programme (Tomlinson, 1982; Chaudhury, 1990). This is perhaps unsurprising, as the fact that their children are regarded in a negative light, as '*dis*-abled', '*in*capable' and so on makes it less likely that parental views will be taken seriously, or the notion of partnership be considered. The parents of children with special educational needs have, historically, been subject to more strategies of persuasion and coercion than any other parents, and it still remains the case that there are legal sanctions against parents who refuse to accept final placement decisions.

There has been rhetoric about parental partnership in the special education area which has never quite coincided with reality. The Warnock Committee, reporting in 1978 on *Special Educational Needs*, wrote that 'we have insisted throughout our report that the successful education of children with special needs is dependent on the full involvement of their parents. Indeed, unless parents are seen as equal partners in the educative process the purpose of our report will be frustrated' (Warnock Report, 1978, p. 150).

However, research during the 1980s has continued to demonstrate that, while ostensibly committed to parental involvement, teachers and other professionals still expect parents to be passive partners, accepting professional decisions without questions. In a study following the assessment of thirty children as 'emotionally and behaviourally disturbed' (Galloway *et al.*, 1993), The professionals claimed that their overriding concern was to act in the interests of the children and involve parents at the centre of decision-making, but parents felt they were listened to only when they were confirming professional views, and that ultimately the professionals knew that, in any conflict of interest, they had the sanction of coercion against uncooperative parents.

One way in which parents are becoming more involved in special education is through litigation, which does not encourage the formation of partnerships. There is a growing consciousness amongst some parents, particularly articulate and knowledgeable ones, that their rights under the 1981 Special Education Act are not being respected, as during the 1980s local education authorities, with budgets reduced by central government, have sought to minimize spending on special educational needs. The production of inadequate statements and the failure to specify resources has resulted in more legal challenges from parents (Audit Commission, 1991; Pyke, 1993).

EUROPEAN POLICIES

It is useful to consider some other European home–school policies and learn from positive developments. An EEC-funded project in the early 1980s, 'The school and family in the European Community', suggested that politicians, educators and parents themselves often assumed that home–school partnerships could be achieved by simple strategies (Macbeth, 1989). An EEC conference held in Luxembourg in 1983 noted that 'there is widespread recognition that parents and teachers should be partners in educating children but there are difficulties in putting this ideal into practice'. However, it is possible that Europe-wide parental initiatives are now in advance of governmental or educationalists' thinking. The European Parents Association – and a more recent French initiative the Centre Européan des Parents l'Ecole Publique (CEPEP) – aim to work out joint goals for the future of publicly-funded education in Europe which will include parental partnership. CEPEP has representation from parents' organizations in France, England (via Parents Initiative), Eire, Italy, Germany, Spain, Portugal and Belgium, and interest expressed by groups in Holland, Denmark, Greece, Austria and Luxembourg. This group has set in train discussion of a common educational philosophy for EEC countries and has suggested that national education systems should all include a home–school association in every school, government-funded parent associations, home–school links to be compulsory study in teacher training, and parents to be represented at all local and national levels where educational policies are formulated.

In *France* the schooling is secular and centralized, teachers are civil servants and there is a national curriculum. However, dialogue with parents has been a feature of the education system for some time. The Ministry of Education publishes material explaining the education system and a bulletin, 'A letter to parents'. All French primary schools are required by law to have a joint committee of teachers and parents and parents are consulted over the choice of books and materials for schools.

In *Italy* co-operation with parents has been included in Ministerial decrees since 1955, and a *decreti delagati* in 1974 introduced an elaborate system of councils which were intended to involve parents and local communities in all aspects and levels of education. The complexity of the pyramid of councils – school class, school, district, provincial, and a national council – and the elaborate system of representation has not notably included parents in actual decision-making but the councils have reduced mutual mistrust between parents and teachers, given parents better information and encouraged parents to regard education as a joint home–school process.

In *Germany* the postwar Federal Basic Law laid down broad guidelines for the control and administration of education in (West) Germany, which is undertaken by the eleven provinces (Länder). The Basic Law incorporated principles of parental rights and responsibilities for their children's education and all the provincial constitutions require co-operation between schools and families, although each province varies in the details of its written requirements. The Bavarian constitution, for example, notes that 'The common educational task which confronts school and parents requires co-operation carried out in mutual trust'. In Rhineland-Palatinate, 'parents have the right and duty to co-operate with school in the education of their children'.

All provinces have legal requirements for parents' councils at different levels of education. In Baden-Württemberg, for example, there are school class councils chaired by a parent, school, district and provincial councils. The provincial parents' council offers advice to the Minister of Education and must be kept informed by the Ministry.

The *Danish* school system is rooted in the notion of community education and gives more legal recognition and informed support to partnership between the family and the school than any other country. The Danish Basic School Law of 1975 reads:

> The task of the Basic School is, in co-operation with parents, to offer possibilities for pupils to acquire knowledge, skills, working methods and forms of expression which will contribute to each individual's development.
>
> (Macbeth, 1989, p. 174)

The Danish approach recognizes that schools can do no more than make facilities available; they cannot, unaided, educate the 'whole child' and make no claims to this. Pupils attend the basic school (Folkeskole) for a minimum of nine years, and the class teacher moves with the pupils accentuating the possibilities of partnership with families. Municipal committees oversee the folkeskoles and there is parental representation on these committees. Each school board comprises parents with voting rights, teachers and pupils in its participants. Within schools, class associations of parents, teachers and pupils have developed, and the Education Ministry publishes a guide to co-operation between homes and schools. The national parents' organization Skole og Samfund incorporates all school boards and voluntary parental associations. Danish parents are recognized in law and in practice as sharing partnership rights and responsibilities at all levels of schooling.

In *Spain* one approach to parental involvement has been to recognize that parental involvement means educating parents in school and educational matters in ways not hitherto envisaged. At the University of Navarro 'schools for parents' have been devised, working on a modular basis with university staff and parent co-ordinators. Sexton, who learned about this development at a European Parents Association Conference in Italy, was so impressed by the way such courses improved parental participation in education that he has introduced pilot 'schools for parents' in the UK (Sexton, 1992).

NEW POLICIES

In considering new policies which will improve home–school links and create genuine partnerships, it has to be recognized that it will not be easy to work out a practice of education based on the reversal of a 150-year-old process. Educational policies have until the 1980s sought to *reduce* the impact of parents on their children's education, since mass schooling had been created partly because *parents* in the nineteenth century could not communicate the knowledge and skills required for an industrial society. Policies were geared to *replace* parental influence. Now it has become apparent that *schools* on their own cannot communicate the knowledge and skills required for an advanced technological society or the moral, social and political skills for living in such a society. Schools must now *reorient their work to collaborate with parents as an educational force*.

New legislation which requires schools to pass over much more information to parents is to be welcomed, although presenting information in the form of league tables (of exam results, attendance figures, post-16 destinations, etc.) without close parental involvement in the life of the school may be more a recipe for conflict and alienation than closer co-operation.

Offering a wide range of information to parents, in conjunction with 'schools for parents', perhaps as suggested by Stuart Sexton (1992) constitutes one policy for improving home–school links. It has already been noted that particular groups – ethnic minority parents and the parents of those with special educational needs – will require particular attention.

A second and crucial policy which could easily be implemented and which would go a long way towards including *all* parents in home–school co-operation would be a new legal requirement that all schools should set up a home–school association, open to *all* parents, teachers and representative pupils. Given the history of parent associations in England, such associations, if voluntary, might be dominated by white middle-class parents. If associations have a statutory base, all parents being automatic members when their child joins a school, this objection would be overcome.

The associations would:

- not principally be concerned with fund-raising or social activities. They would be a forum for passing over knowledge and information about formal schooling to parents, and the passing of information on home learning to teachers.
- discuss matters relating to children's learning, progress and achievement, debate matters related to curriculum, assessment, recording teaching methods, behaviour in schools and school organization.
- include class associations as the main way to bring teachers and parents together. Parents would work with teachers to involve those parents who, for practical or other reasons, find it difficult to involve themselves with school. (This would help remove the teacher complaint that 'the parents we really want to see never come'.)
- inform themselves of the professional services teachers offer, their rights, their conditions of service and their needs as a professional body.
- be statutorily consulted at local level when important decisions were being made on education, and representatives would be similarly consulted at national level. The associations would liaise with, but not replace, governing bodies.

The associations would organize home–school communications, make arrangements for obligatory consultation about individual children, co-ordinate home–school learning schemes and homework arrangements and arrange parental involvement in day-to-day school activities.

Given the interest in written home–school educational agreements (contracts) pioneered in the RSA home–school project, the development of such agreements within the framework of a home–school association could be explored.

CONCLUSION

This chapter started from the premise that improving children's educational performance, enhancing their personal and social development and creating genuine home–school links could happen only if the current stress on parents as consumers of education and agents of competition gave way to a belief that parents must be partners in the educative process.

If we are really concerned to raise educational standards and improve the quality of education, a *convergence* of home and school and a partnership between parents and teachers is a necessity. Policies must be geared to the understanding that schools and homes are *joint producers of education* and that in future parents will need to be more centrally involved in the process of schooling.

Any government which is seriously concerned about raising standards and offering an improved education to all pupils will concentrate on enhancing parental support, involvement and obligation to participate in formal education. It will also recognize that a more equal relationship between parents and teachers will require a different legislative framework to the present one. The legal framework will need to include more rights to information, for parent education, for parents to be involved in their children's day-to-day schooling, to be automatically members of a home–school association and to make an educational agreement with the school.

Home–school partnerships can remain empty rhetoric, be a cover for enhancing professional powers or become another mechanism for 'policing' pupils. We need open and equal relationships between schools and homes to contribute to better understandings, higher standards and an improved quality of education.

REFERENCES

Audit Commission (1991) *Getting in on the Act: Provision for Pupils with Special Educational Needs*. London: HMSO.

Bastiani, J. and Bailey, G. (1992) *Directory of Home–School Initiatives in the UK*. London: Royal Society of Arts and National Association of Head Teachers.

Bernstein, B. (1973) *Class Codes and Control*, Vol. 1. London: Routledge.

Brar, H. S. (1991) Teaching, professionalism and home–school links. *Multicultural Teaching*, **9**(1), 32–5.

Chaudhury, A. (1990) Problems for parents: experiences in Tower Hamlets. In Orton, C. (ed.) *Asian Children and Special Educational Needs*. London: Advisory Centre for Education.

Commission for Racial Equality (1989) *Racial Segregation in Education: Report of a Formal Investigation into Cleveland LEA*. London: CRE.

Council for the Accreditation of Teacher Education (1992) *The Accreditation of Initial Teacher Training Index, Circulars 9/92 and 35/92. A Note of Guidance*. London: CATE.

Cunningham, C. and Davis, H. (1985) *Working with Parents: Frameworks for Collaboration*. Milton Keynes: Open University Press.

Edwards, V. and Redfern, A. (1988) *At Home in School*. London: Routledge.

Galloway, D., Armstrong, D. and Tomlinson, S. (1993) *Whose Special Educational Needs?* London: Longman.

Gewirtz, S., Ball, S. and Bowe, R. (1992) Parents, privilege and the education market place. Paper to the British Educational Research Association, Stirling, Scotland, August.

Grace, G. (1978) *Education Ideology and Social Control*. London: Routledge.

Jones, G., Bastiani, J., Bell, G. and Chapman, C. (1992) *A Willing Partnership: Project Study of the Home–School Contract of Partnership*. London: Royal Society of Arts.

Macbeth, A. (1989) *Involving Parents*. Oxford: Heinemann.

MacDonald, I. (1989) *Murder in the Playground*. Manchester: Longsight Press.

National Consumer Council (1990) *Minority Ethnic Communities and School Governing Bodies*. London: NCC.

Parent's Charter (1991) *You and Your Child's Education*. London: DES.

Plowden Report (1967) *Children and Their Primary Schools*. London: HMSO (2 vols).

Pugh, G. and De'Ath, E. (1989) *Parents, Professionals and Partnership: Rhetoric or Reality*. London: National Children's Bureau.

Pyke, N. (1993) Parents take to High Court, *Times Educational Supplement*, 15 January.

Roberts, K. (1984) *School Leavers and Their Prospects*, Milton Keynes: Open University Press.

Rutter, M. and Madge, N. (1976) *Cycles of Disadvantage*. London: Heinemann.

Sexton, S. (1992) Parents can be teachers too. *The Times*, 3 November.

Tomlinson, S. (1982) *A Sociology of Special Education*. London: Routledge.

Tomlinson, S. (1984) *Home and School in Multicultural Britain*. London: Batsford.

Tomlinson, S. (1988) Why Johnny can't read: critical theory and special education. *European Journal of Special Needs Education*, **3**(1), 45–58.

Tomlinson, S. (1991) Home–school partnerships. In *Teachers and Parents*, Education and Training paper no. 7. Institute for Public Policy Research. London: pp. 1–18.

Tomlinson, S. (1993) Ethnic minorities: involved partners or problem parents? In Munn, P. (ed.) *Parents and Schools: Customers, Managers or Partners*. London: Routledge.

Tredgold, A. E. (1908) *Mental Deficiency*. London: Balliere, Tindal and Cox.

Waller, W. (1932) *The Sociology of Teaching*. New York: Wiley.

Warnock Report (1978) *Special Educational Needs*. London: HMSO.

Wolfendale, S. (1989) *Parental Involvement: Developing Networks between Home, School and Community*. London: Cassell.

Part 7

Developments

CHAPTER 17

Evaluating PSE and pastoral care: how shall we know success?

Mary James

Any kind of development that is important enough to promote is important enough to be assessed in some broad sense of that term. If one knows what personal development means, then one must have some rough idea of what counts as having achieved it in some respect. One must be able to state what counts as appropriate evidence of success. It is therefore important to attend to the ways in which both the school and the individual are succeeding – the school in helping the individual to develop as a person, the individual in his or her own personal development. If it is argued that personal development is much too subjective or private an affair for any form of assessment, then one should retort that it is much too subjective or private an affair for the school to get involved in. But that is not to say that personal development should be assessed through tests or examinations. It does mean that one has to make judgements, and that to make judgements one needs to think by what criteria and on what evidence one is to make them.

(Pring, 1985, pp. 139–40)

Before I begin I should say that this is not a 'How to do it' chapter. My intention is not to offer a framework or recipe for evaluation but to explore some issues about how the quality of PSE and pastoral care might be judged. The emphasis is on the *process* of delineating criteria and deciding what kind of evidence it would be appropriate to collect. I have no interest in making dogmatic statements about what I think should count as good practice because I prefer, for the purposes of this chapter, to explore the value pluralism that characterizes this area, as it does all areas of education. By remaining agnostic, as it were, I hope to show just how important are the decisions that need to be made by stakeholders about what constitutes quality in PSE and pastoral care and how debate about, and development of, success criteria are a vital part of any evaluation – perhaps the most vital. It is in this process that the questions of what is of value, what is worthwhile and what is good practice are addressed. After all, it is this act of valuing that distinguishes evaluation from research which sometimes aspires to be value-neutral.

Unfortunately, and perhaps surprisingly, questions about judgement are not well dealt with in the evaluation literature. Most texts, including the book that I co-authored (McCormick and James, 1983, 1988) and the only book on the theme of evaluation in pastoral care (Clemett and Pearce, 1986), give more space and attention to the important technical and ethical issues associated with evaluation roles, data-collection methods, analysis and reporting than to the difficult conceptual questions associated with developing criteria for judgement. This can contribute to an impression that evaluation is essentially a technical and strategic enterprise. It is all this, but it is also about engaging in principled debate at the most fundamental level – about the aims and purposes of PSE and pastoral care and the extent to which educational provision promotes their fulfilment.

With this in mind I propose to begin my discussion by outlining the *kind of criteria* that might define success in PSE and pastoral care. I identify three broad categories of success criteria:

1 success defined by the quality of student outcomes (outcome criteria);
2 success defined by the quality of student experience (process criteria);
3 success defined by the quality of the environment for learning and change (context criteria).

In relation to each of these categories, I will describe some approaches to evaluation that have the capacity to provide the *kind of evidence* to which these criteria might be applied. In doing this, I will also try to identify the particular opportunities or difficulties that arise when applying these approaches in the field of PSE and pastoral care.

APPROACHES DEFINED BY STUDENT OUTCOMES

Outcome criteria

If the purpose of certain forms of educational provision, whether through specific courses or more generalized whole curriculum approaches, is to develop in youngsters certain behaviours, skills, attitudes or understandings, then it would seem logical to delineate what these outcomes should be. The success of provision would then be judged according to the extent that youngsters demonstrate what they know, understand and can do. The attitudes they display may also be considered important outcomes. *Evaluation* of educational provision is therefore achieved through *assessment* of student achievement. This is the classical approach to evaluation in many western societies and is currently embodied in National Curriculum assessment in England and Wales; league tables of aggregated results of assessments are regarded by government as the most important measures of the effectiveness of teachers and schools. (Interestingly, this link between students performance and school effectiveness is not taken for granted in all societies. In Japan, for instance, despite an inordinate amount of testing, there is no assumption that student outcomes are a reflection of the quality of the curriculum or teaching (see Abiko, 1993). Students are held to be more accountable for their results than either their teachers or their schools.)

The argument for giving priority to outcome criteria are usually considered to be very strong in our society. In the context of PSE and pastoral care, therefore, it is often claimed that there is little value in educational provision that does not result in recognizable improvements in students' understanding, attitudes, skills and behaviours. For example, if teenage pregnancy, racial harassment and bullying show no signs of improvement after extensive programmes to address these issues, then there would be justifiable cause for concern. If the purpose of PSE and pastoral care is to promote student development, learning or change, it seems reasonable to expect that provision should be judged according to whether it achieves this aim. The implication for evaluation is that judgement of effectiveness is based on the analysis of student outcome data. The mode is outcome evaluation.

Outcome evaluation

Traditionally, outcome evaluation has been associated with a particular model of curriculum and teaching which assumes that planning begins with the specification of objectives for student learning. Sometimes these can be quite broad but often they are defined in terms of precise student behaviours, such as demonstrating through writing that they know certain facts, or displaying particular skills. The objectives are often set by 'experts' (in the case of the English National Curriculum by subject working parties) and the task for the school is to plan schemes of work and to provide teaching to give students the best opportunity to achieve these objectives. Student outcomes are then measured, by assessment techniques, to determine changes in knowledge, attitudes and behaviour. The success of the educational programme (the intervention) is therefore judged according to the extent to which student outcomes reflect the pre-specified objectives. The objectives therefore become the criteria for success.

This objectives model of curriculum planning and evaluation has always been popular both at the level of theory and in teachers' common practice. It has been challenged, particularly in the 1970s (more of which later) but it is currently experiencing a resurgence in the shape of the National Curriculum for England and Wales. To date, the model is strictly applied only to the core and foundation subjects but it will be interesting to see whether the cross-curricular themes, dimensions and skills (some of which overlap with PSE and pastoral care) will eventually be viewed in this way. There is considerable precedent for this, particularly in relation to health education which was one of the five cross-curricular themes to be identified by the National Curriculum Council (NCC, 1990). I shall use health education as an illustration here, and elsewhere in this chapter, partly because I have had some involvement in evaluating it but also because health education is often incorporated into programmes of PSE (or vice versa). I recognize that the relationship between the PSE and health education is problematic, so I should make clear that what follows is not an attempt to equate them, although some writers have sought to do so, or to argue for priority to be given to one rather than the other.

On the whole I take the view that PSE is the broader area although this depends on a particular view of what health education is. Definitions of health education have varied from the broad to the comparatively narrow. Some are so broad as to encompass PSE, if not the whole of education. Katherine Mansfield's definition of health is often quoted: 'By health I mean the power to live a full, adult, living breathing life in close contact with what I love . . . I want, by understanding myself, to understand others.

I want to be all that I am capable of becoming.' The definition given by the World Health Organization in 1946 was almost equally broad: 'Health is a positive state of mental, physical and social well-being and not merely the absence of disease or infirmity.' In both cases the aim is so broad, and deep, that the extrapolation of measurable outcomes becomes exceedingly difficult and threatens the feasibility of evaluation within the classical objectives model. To delineate operational objectives for measurement purposes would undoubtedly trivialize the aim.

It is clear that educators often work with a much narrower definition of health than that given above. Beattie (1984) has identified four approaches which may be identified in health education:

- education for bodily regulation
- education for personal growth
- education for awareness of the environment and political limits to health
- education for community action on health

These can be handled alongside one another, with schools giving greater or lesser emphasis to each dimension according to their circumstances. In this way the four approaches can be related, rather than polarized, as in some of the literature.

However, when confronted with the problems associated with drug abuse, teenage pregnancy and the exponential spread of HIV, definitions become narrowed again. Faced with these immediate threats to the well-being of both individuals and society, the pressure for educators is to intervene to bring down morbidity and mortality rates. A social consensus in support of this is assumed and liberal arguments for the individual's right to choose are not always considered relevant in these circumstances. Nevertheless, the 'intervention' often targets *individuals*, and particularly their cognitive or affective faculties, in order to persuade them of the need to change or modify their behaviour in a direction that accords with current 'expert' knowledge. Many health promotion campaigns are of this nature and some, it has to be said, are highly successful. For example, on the day that I wrote the first draft of this chapter (9 October 1992), the newspapers reported that the Foundation for the Study of Infant Deaths claimed that a 35 per cent decrease in sudden infant deaths (cot deaths) between 1988 and 1991 was likely to be attributable to a Reduce the Risk campaign, which was launched in 1991 to disseminate new advice through television, doctors and health visitors. The evidence on which this claim was based was essentially epidemiological: mortality rates were monitored and, on the basis of statistical probability, changes had been associated with the intervention. The procedure was little different from the evaluation of the efficacy of a new drug, except that a control group was lacking which reduced the certainty with which cause and effect could be established. Not surprisingly, this approach to intervention and its evaluation is sometimes referred to as 'the medical model'.

In some circumstances, the effectiveness of educational programmes in terms of changes in knowledge, attitudes, behaviours and disease rates can be established with even greater apparent certainty through what is known in the jargon as a 'quasi-experimental non-equivalent control group design' (Campbell and Stanley, 1963; Bynner, 1980). In simple terms, this means that two groups of students, with roughly similar characteristics such as age, sex, social background, educational attainment and school experience, are chosen but only one group is exposed to the programme that is to be evaluated. The performance of students who have followed the programme can then be compared with the performance, on the same measures, of the control group. Inferences about the effectiveness of the programme are then made according to whether statistically significant gains are registered for the 'treatment' group over the control group.

This was the main approach to evaluation adopted in two dental health programmes with which I was associated in the early 1980s (see Dental Health Study, 1986; James, 1987). The programmes were curricular programmes available for use by teachers in schools but they were sponsored by the then Health Education Council whose Dental Health Advisory Panel was the steering group for the project. This panel was largely made up of dental and medical professionals who were predominantly concerned with the reduction of disease through encouraging preventative behaviours. Their medico-scientific training also led them to expect rigorous evaluation along the lines of the medical model with which they were familiar. Therefore, continuation of funding became dependent on the provision of reliable information about improvements in children's knowledge and attitudes (as assessed through structured interview and questionnaire) and behavioural outcomes (as assessed through clinical examination to give measures of plaque deposits and gingival bleeding). The extent to which any improvements were attributable to the programme was determined by the use of 'control groups' in schools which had not, at this point, been offered the programme.

In both the cot deaths campaign and the dental health programmes *some* of the messages were relatively simple (sleep your baby on its back; brush your teeth and gums regularly) and *some* of the effects of behavioural change were observable in a relatively short time. For example, brushing quickly reduces gingival bleeding – an indication of gum disease. However, in many areas of health education, and in PSE and pastoral care more generally, it is not easy to measure outcomes or even define, in precise operational terms, what they might be. What, for instance, would be a reasonable expectation of measurable student outcomes from teaching or counselling about personal relationships, HIV/AIDS, citizenship or environmental stewardship? The scope of PSE is much broader than that which can easily be measured. Furthermore, many behavioural outcomes will truly be demonstrated only in the real-life choice situations that children encounter in late adolescence and adulthood.

Attempts have been made to predict outcomes reliably from what people say that they intend to do in certain future situations (Becker, 1975; Fishbein and Ajzen, 1975). Thus measures of knowledge, understanding, intention and attitude, rather than explicit behaviours, become the focus of outcome evaluation of educational programmes. However, there is always some doubt about whether the intention to act in a certain way will, when circumstances arise, lead to the desired action itself. One of the main difficulties with the outcomes approach framed in this way is that it often assumes that individuals will make rational choices on the information available when the time comes. It therefore ignores or minimizes powerful social constraints on an individual's freedom to act.

There are other problems too. First, there is the question of whether social consensus on what outcomes are worthwhile can be assumed. In some circumstances the right of an 'expert' group to impose its definition of the situation on others poses both political and ethical questions. For example, programmes promoting birth control raise such questions if they fail to address underlying issues associated with poverty. As Williams (1992) has pointed out, 'sexual activity and parenthood are two of the few aspects of life in which the poor can achieve some form of parity with the rich' (p. 281); children are still 'poor men's riches' in many late-twentieth-century communities.

Second, if outcome data are taken to be the sole indicators of the success of PSE and pastoral care, it is unlikely that satisfactory *explanation* will be found for failure if the objectives are not achieved. This has a crucial bearing on the usefulness of evaluations. In its pure form the objectives–outcomes model treats the intervention (programme and processes) as a kind of 'black box' since what goes on inside it is not scrutinized. Attention falls only on the objectives for the programme and what it appears to achieve. How objectives are achieved is of little interest. The assumption is that what needs to be done if the programme fails to do what it was intended to do will be self-evident. It is worth noting that this seems to be the assumption underlying National Curriculum assessment. Given the specification of objectives in the form of statements of attainment, it is assumed that knowledge of whether children have achieved them or not will be the key to future curricular planning. However, as Simpson (1990) has argued, if we wish to find out why children have failed to learn certain things we need to know *how* they have learned what they have actually learned. In other words, if we want *explanations* for particular outcomes we need data about processes (of both teaching and learning) and criteria with which to judge their worth.

Third, there is the question of whether it is ever possible to attribute outcomes unequivocally to a particular intervention. Since students are not rats enclosed in mazes but human beings who are exposed to rich and varied material and social environments, there is always the possibility that the outcome might have been brought about by something else entirely. In this is a strong argument for making sure that the intervention or teaching programme is worthwhile as an experience in its own right.

If, as argued above, there are a number of objections to an exclusive focus on outcomes as indicators of quality in PSE and pastoral care, are there alternatives? The next section examines the possibility of developing and using process criteria as a conceptual basis for evaluation.

APPROACHES DEFINED BY STUDENT EXPERIENCE

Process criteria

Like outcome criteria, process criteria, which have reference to the quality of educational experiences, are derived from underlying models of curriculum and learning. For this reason their formulation can be equally problematic. For example, if educators believe that the only thing that stands in the way of an outcomes approach is the fact that students are not likely to encounter the relevant 'real-life' choice situation for some years (for example, preparation for parenthood) then the curricular programme, and the way it is taught, might be very similar to the objectives approach outlined above. In other words, facts and information might be presented to students in line with current expert knowledge. Understanding would be encouraged through illustrations of hypothetical or real-life situations, and students might be encouraged to develop decision-making competence in line with the instruction they have received. Again the appeal would be to the individuals' cognitive faculties on the assumption that when the time comes they will make rational choices. In this case, process criteria relating to the educational experience might look something like this:

Students should have an opportunity to:

1 listen and pay attention to the teacher;
2 work in an orderly and quiet atmosphere;
3 be given correct information and explanations;
4 be given or shown evidence of ideas in practice (perhaps through examples of what is likely to happen if certain courses of action are, or are not, followed);
5 receive clear guidance on how they can avoid problems encountered in 'real life';
6 demonstrate that they have absorbed and understood the instruction they have received (orally or in writing).

This, of course, will be instantly recognizable as the traditional 'transmission model' of teaching and learning. An alternative model, with which teachers involved with PSE and pastoral care will be familiar, is the 'self-empowerment model'. This is less 'content-centred' and more 'learner-centred' and aims to encourage the development of personal competence, self-esteem and life-skills (including decision-making), through experiential learning strategies. In so far as the aims are about personal growth, the precise long-term outcomes for any individual are difficult to define and predict. Again the most realistic approach, for the purposes of evaluation, may be to focus upon the educational experiences that students are given access to, and to judge the quality of these. The process criteria within a self-empowerment model of curriculum and learning might therefore look something like the following:

Students should have an opportunity to:

1 encounter a problem (perhaps through the use of stimulus material, such as a trigger film, an extract from a television programme, a dramatic presentation, a newspaper article or fictional narrative);
2 gather information on the problem for themselves (by investigating what constitutes the problem, who is affected, and how it develops, perhaps by using libraries, making inquiries of specialist agencies, conducting mini-surveys);

3 discover and disclose their own values and feelings in discussion with one another (probably requiring group work in which certain ground rules are clearly articulated and understood – concerning the importance of listening, being supportive and respecting others, not interpreting others' experiences for them and not being judgemental);
4 propose a number of alternatives for action that take account of people's different values, different personalities and abilities, different cultures and different social and material circumstances;
5 consider the likely consequences of each course of action, especially the reactions of others (which requires empathy and imagination);
6 decide on a course of action and try it out with someone who will give feedback (perhaps through role play);
7 evaluate whether the decision was wise or appropriate (perhaps in whole class discussion, small group work or through written work).

(adapted from James, 1987)

What I hope will be clear from this discussion is that the precise formulation of process criteria depends on a fundamental analysis of what counts as worthwhile curriculum experience for students. This is a form of curriculum deliberation (intrinsic evaluation) which needs to go hand in hand with empirical data collection and analysis (empirical evaluation).

Process evaluation

Whatever process criteria are arrived at, and whether their identification precedes or follows the collection of evidence, the fact that they have reference to the *educational experiences* of students demands the collection of data that are very different from the data appropriate to outcome evaluation. What is needed are data about curriculum materials and classroom processes and techniques for analysing it.

During the 1970s, as the shortcomings of outcome evaluation became known, there was a tremendous growth of interest in process evaluation in Britain, in North America and in Australia. A reader entitled *Beyond the Numbers Game* (Hamilton *et al.*, 1977) was pivotal in the international debate among professional programme evaluators. At the same time Lawrence Stenhouse in Britain was looking at similar issues in the development of his concept of 'teachers as researchers' in their own classrooms (Stenhouse, 1975; Rudduck and Hopkins, 1985). At both levels, the move was away from developing ever more sophisticated techniques for the measurement and testing of student outcomes, and towards greater use of the data-gathering methods previously associated with ethnography and social anthropology – observation, questionnaires and interviews, journal keeping, photography and document analysis. As Parlett and Hamilton (1972) argued in their manifesto for 'evaluation as illumination', the need was for greater understanding of the 'instructional system' and the 'learning milieu', that is, the processes and contexts for learning.

As a result of this new orientation, the 1980s saw a growth in publications, projects and in-service courses which aimed to give the necessary research skills to those who wanted to engage in enquiry into classroom experience (for example, see Burgess, 1985; Hook, 1985; Hopkins, 1985; Nixon, 1981; Walker, 1985; Walker and Adelman, 1975). In essence these all advocated the adoption of a research perspective on classroom and curricular processes so that the 'black box' might be opened up to scrutiny. The intention was to enable teachers to make judgements about the effectiveness of curricula and teaching on the basis of evidence that did not depend solely on data about student outcomes.

In terms of the techniques available for data-gathering, the emphasis shifted from the use of assessment instruments, often dependent on quantitative analysis of students' written responses to prescribed tasks, towards collecting qualitative data through direct observation of classroom processes or talking with teachers and students about their classroom experiences. If one takes the process criteria set out above, the appropriate evidence for determining whether these had been achieved would probably take the form of observational data of what actually happened in the classroom, or participants' perceptions of the impact of what happened. This more qualitative approach to the evaluation of PSE and pastoral care has characterized a number of fairly recent substantive studies. For example, the national evaluation of active tutorial work located itself within the 'illuminative paradigm' (Bolam and Medlock, 1985, p. 4); the data collected were qualitative rather than quantitative and drawn from observation, interviews, questionnaires and document analysis.

Of particular note has been an increasing recognition of the importance and value of eliciting students' views of their experience (Ellenby, 1985; Lang, 1983, 1985; Thorp, 1982). In my own early evaluation efforts, as a secondary school teacher of social studies and PSE, I discovered that talking with students about their experiences of the curriculum provided the kind of insights that enabled us to rethink provision (James, 1980). It might seem rather obvious to ask students about their views but until recently this source of evidence was neglected. Lang (1985) attributes this neglect to the dominance of the teachers' perspective although, for a long time, *all* kinds of data involving people's perceptions or personal judgements were suspect because the dominant positivist paradigm of research claimed that the validity and reliability of findings depended on so-called 'objective' measures. Yet common sense tells us that perceptions count; 'If people perceive things as real, they are real in their consequences' (Thomas, 1928).

The assumption behind all approaches to evaluation is, of course, that if evidence (of whatever kind) and judgements indicate that something needs to be done – to improve students' educational experiences or to bring about the desired outcomes – then action will be taken to improve the existing situation. In both outcome evaluation and process evaluation the focus of attention is generally at the micro level, on individuals and classrooms. This assumes that any action for change will take place at this level, most obviously by adapting teaching programmes so that they might become more effective in process or outcome terms. But process evaluation, like outcome evaluation, can fall into the trap of ignoring social constraints on the development of personal autonomy and decision-making competence. A moment's reflection is usually sufficient for us to realize that, in order to bring about desired change in individuals, or to empower them to take control over their lives, action may need to be taken to remove barriers to the exercise of individual freedom. And these barriers are often located in social structures, at the macro level. For example, however successful teachers appear to be in motivating individuals to eat a healthy well-balanced diet, to stop smoking or to disclose bullying, little is likely to be achieved if the diet proposed is beyond a family's economic means, if children are being (insidiously) bombarded with contradictory messages on smoking from a powerful industrial lobby (and government is perceived to take a passive stance towards this) and if social codes and values are not taken into account over issues involving disclosure. There is an argument therefore for turning the evaluation spotlight on structural and environmental barriers to change. According to this argument the success of programmes of PSE and pastoral care might reasonably be evaluated according to the extent to which such barriers have been removed or overcome.

APPROACHES DEFINED BY THE ENVIRONMENT FOR LEARNING

Context criteria

The case for shifting the focus of attention from the individual and the classroom to the social structure of nations and communities is a radical one. In the field of health education it has been debated extensively (see Tones, 1987) and contributed in the mid-1980s to some shift of interest away from health *education* per se towards more emphasis on health *promotion* (although there were more conservative interests operating in this direction as well). This also influenced some reconceptualization of success criteria towards consideration of the extent to which the following promote or hinder the achievement of health goals:

1 mass media and marketing strategies by industry;
2 the provision of public services and incentive systems;
3 organizational and community development and change;
4 economic and regulatory activities;
5 local and national legislation.

Here attention is focused at the macro level, so one might reasonably ask what the implications might be for school-level health education, PSE and pastoral care. After all, teachers and schools can hardly be expected (for political and practical reasons) to take on governments and multinational corporations and be judged by the results. It would contravene the principles of natural justice to hold them accountable for change which is beyond their power to effect, except in minimal ways. Yet surely schools are still expected to have a role in promoting personal and social development in a context of structural constraints. And there is some expectation that these efforts will be evaluated. It seems to me that the response to the evaluation problem is, as in the previous two approaches outlined above, rooted in a view about what constitutes an appropriate curriculum in this context.

In relation to school health education, Tones (1987) outlines what he calls a 'radical' approach. This is an *approach*, not a *curriculum* as such, but the elements of a planned curriculum might be extrapolated from it:

the main function of education is considered to be that of 'critical consciousness raising' (a process which has an excellent educational pedigree – originally in the adult literacy field [Freire, 1972]). People should first be made aware of the existence of the social origins of ill health and then should be persuaded to take action. According to Freudenberg (1981) health educators should 'involve people in collective action to create health promoting environments' and should help people organise 'to change health-damaging institutions, policies and environments' (Freudenberg, 1984). This might, at first sight, seem far removed from the concerns of health education in school, but . . . a combination of social education and lifeskills training as a precursor to 'mainstream' health education may lay the foundations for such radical activities. However, before any such action is feasible, people must believe that they are capable of acting. In other words, they must come to accept that they have the capacity to influence their destiny and acquire the social skills to do so.

(Tones, 1987, pp. 11–12)

Tones's view of social education and life skills as a foundation for 'mainstream' health education is highly problematic. So is his advocacy of a 'self-empowerment approach' to school health education as the appropriate model for curriculum in this context. If this alone were adequate then effectiveness might be judged in terms of the criteria set out in the previous section, which would allow no distinction from the process approach previously discussed. The focus would remain at the level of the individual and interpersonal interactions and would not pay sufficient attention to environment change, which is claimed to be the major rationale for the approach. It seems to me that the so-called 'radical approach' demands that both curriculum and evaluation should focus deliberately on 'critical consciousness raising' and 'collective action to change environments'. Therefore the criteria by which this approach might best be evaluated would probably be a combination of process criteria and outcome criteria: concerning the development of individuals and groups in terms of self-esteem, life skills, critical awareness of social constraints on action, and their capacity to work collaboratively towards action with some attention to the results of such action. This last criterion might reasonably be assessed in school settings in limited ways since, as sociologists of education have shown, there is much in the structure of schools and the 'hidden curriculum' that obstructs the achievement of educational goals. Students might be encouraged to address these issues, and the results could be monitored. To take one small example, again from health education, the recent demise of the tuck shop can in many schools be attributed to students realizing and taking action to reduce the mismatch between what they learn in lessons and what the school promotes in other ways. The key evaluation question implied here is: 'Is this a health-promoting school?'. This can be widened to 'Is this a healthy school?', at which point it resonates with 'Is this an empowering school?' which is a central evaluative question for those who promote whole-school approaches to pastoral care and PSE. In relation to all three questions, answers probably require an analysis of process, outcome and contextual data and the relationships among them.

Although, in the radical approach, outcome, process and context criteria are all considered to be important, the key concepts are 'critique' and 'action'. For this reason the mode of evaluation with which this approach is often associated is known as critical action research.

Critical action research

Critical action research is not a new approach but has a history stretching back almost fifty years. Its origins are usually associated with Kurt Lewin (1948) who worked with minority groups to help them overcome barriers of caste and prejudice. His ideas have probably been taken up and extended most effectively in the field of development studies (that is Third World development). However, they have also had an impact in the field of education, although, in their most radical form, more at the theoretical level than the practical level (Carr and Kemmis, 1986; Oja and Smulyan, 1989; Elliott, 1993; McKernan, 1991).

In essence, the central idea is that action and research should proceed together hand in hand. (This contrasts with conceptualizations of evaluation as a 'bolt-on' to the main activity.) There have been a number of attempts to represent the action research process in diagrammatic form (see Ebbutt, 1985, for a review). Most have been successful only in confusing would-be participants and convincing them that the process is esoteric; instead of empowering them it threatens to make them even more authority-dependent. Cognisant of this danger, I am hesitant to offer a further such representation. I therefore offer Figure 17.1 merely as a means of showing how the two key elements are integrated. The assumption is that participants (students and teachers in the school situation) begin with some idea about what is wrong and what they might do about it (a general idea). They then go about finding out more including whether their assumptions are justified (fact-finding). On this basis they devise an overall plan which they break down into action steps. They try the first step out and evaluate the results. This may lead them to revise their overall plan or it may give them the confidence to go on to the next action step. The action they next take will also be evaluated as it is implemented. This pattern would be repeated until the ultimate goal is felt to have been achieved. In this way, evaluation is not a 'bolt-on' but becomes an integral part of the development process. If evaluation is a fundamental part of the process, it also follows that it should not be delegated to a specialist 'evaluator' but should be taken on by the collaborative group of participants. The logical implication for schools that choose to adopt this approach would be that both teachers and students should be involved, as well as any consultant whose specialist skills might also be enlisted. The emphasis here is not so much on specific *methods* (qualitative and quantitative techniques of assessment, observation, interviewing might all be useful) but on the evaluation *strategy*. In order to maintain coherence, the evaluative element of action research has to involve all participants, including students, in an active way, not merely as research 'subjects'. I have to admit that I can find few references to examples of this approach in practice in British educational contexts although the work of Jean Rudduck (1990) provides a notable exception. There have been numerous educational projects which describe themselves as action research (such as the Ford Teaching Project and the Teacher Pupil Interaction and the Quality of Learning Project,

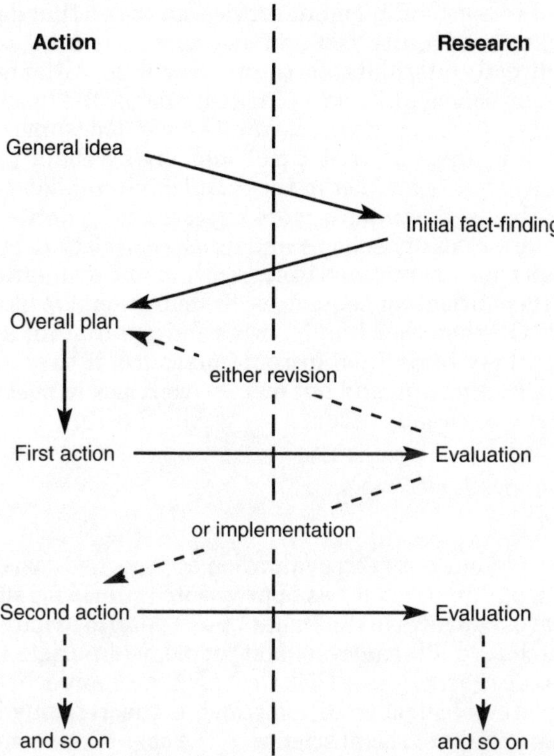

Figure 17.1

directed by John Elliott, and the more recent Pupil Autonomy in Learning with Microcomputers Project, directed by Bridget Somekh) but these have mainly defined the participant group as teachers and educational consultants. Students have provided data but have not been centrally involved in conducting the research. In the examples given, this may be legitimate because, despite their titles, the focus was actually on *teachers* and the constraints on their action. However, if interest shifts to the learning and empowerment of *students*, and structural constraints on their freedom of action, then it follows that the participant group should be redefined to include students who would need to be involved in all the decisions about, and processes of, evaluation. In many ways this would represent a fundamental shift in our view of what constitutes evaluation and who does it. If worked out in practice it could be very exciting and thoroughly educational. But this radical approach is, by definition, also highly political, which is probably why examples cannot easily be found.

As I mentioned earlier, there was once a time (in the mid-1970s) when I was a head of social studies in a secondary comprehensive school. One of my abiding memories is of being hauled over the coals by the headteacher who viewed my practice of getting students to do little social investigations of their own as a threat to the status quo in the school. One cold day when the boiler had broken down the girls decided on collective action (to sit down in the school playground) to try to persuade the head to allow them to wear trousers. I was attending an in-service course on that day but when I returned it was made quite clear to me that this kind of action was perceived as directly attributable to my teaching. Although I was not accused of making school uniform a particular focus, the head implied that making students aware of social constraints on action (some of the content of social studies courses at that time) and giving them the skills and confidence to investigate and act in the social environment was politically unacceptable. Above all, students were expected to be docile – to obey the rules – as they are in many schools and much of society today.

If one adopts a radical approach to curriculum and evaluation, one needs to be aware of its political consequences; by definition it is likely to disturb the status quo. On the other hand, one can argue that all approaches to evaluation are likely to do this, in some measure, if they are genuinely concerned with 'finding out' and not merely exercises in post hoc rationalization for decisions already made.

CONCLUSION

In drawing distinctions between evaluation approaches based on different conceptions of what might count as appropriate criteria for success in PSE and pastoral care, I am aware that what I have described may be perceived as mutually exclusive alternatives. Methodological purists might indeed say that this is the case, arguing that each of these approaches is grounded in a distinct epistemological tradition which is theoretically incompatible with the others: positivist social science in the case of outcome evaluation; interpretative social theory in the case of process evaluation; and critical theory in the case of emancipatory action research (see Carr and Kemmis, 1986, for the clearest account). However, evaluation, whilst having a theoretical dimension, is essentially a practical activity, and the long-established criterion of 'fitness for purpose' may yet be the best guide to choosing the most appropriate strategy and methods for evaluation in a specific context.

For example, in areas where there is acknowledged social consensus, where objectives for learning and change can be clearly defined and where outcomes can be accurately measured and attributed to a specific educational programme with some certainty, then outcome evaluation might be very appropriate. Where these criteria cannot be met then another approach might be called for. Best of all might be an approach to evaluation that attempts to tap all the relevant dimensions – outcome, process and context. As long ago as 1967, Bob Stake wrote a paper called 'The countenance of educational evaluation' which still provides perhaps the most comprehensive answer to questions about what we should attend to in evaluation. He said that any educational programme should be fully described and fully judged and that this description and judgement should relate to antecedents (including environmental influences on teaching and learning), transactions (processes) and outcomes in the widest sense (immediate and long-range, cognitive and conative, personal and community-wide) – and the relationships that can be found to exist among these dimensions. This still stands as an ideal for a comprehensive evaluation.

However, alongside this ideal one has to bear in mind the practical and resource implications of trying to investigate all these things.

Although many evaluations aspire to be multi-dimensional and comprehensive, practical constraints usually mean that priorities have to be decided. The outcome of these decisions usually endows evaluations with a particular (and inevitably skewed) character. For example, the national evaluation of pilot records of achievement schemes (see Broadfoot *et al.*, 1988), on which I worked from 1985 to 1990, set out to investigate all aspects of the phenomena called records of achievement, including their effects on students' self-concepts and self-esteem and attainment. However, methodological and resource limitations led us to decide to concentrate our efforts on investigating content, process and context. Our case studies provided rich information for helping to frame policy (which was our brief) but they were unable to provide unequivocal evidence about student outcomes. We would argue that techniques for doing this were simply not available. However, a residual feeling remains that, had we been able to provide 'hard' evidence on this dimension, government might have made a more committed response.

Evaluation, then, is an inexact science and is likely to remain so. In the area of PSE and pastoral care, as in general education, its value rests on the quality of the judgements that are made about the appropriateness of approaches to particular contexts. This calls for basic thinking skills as much as for the specialist skills of the social investigator or test expert. Indeed, since no educational programme is like quite any other, the idea of ever producing a foolproof technical manual is likely to remain elusive. These insights should convince people that evaluation is not an 'experts only' activity but one that teachers, students and others can participate in at all levels. But they need to see the point of it; their views need to be taken seriously; and they need help to develop skills of deliberation on the basis of evidence.

REFERENCES

Abiko, T. (1993) Accountability and control in the Japanese national curriculum. *Curriculum Journal*, 137–46.

Beattie, A. (1984) Health education and the science teacher: invitation to debate. *Education and Health*, **2**(1) 9–16.

Becker, M. (1975) Socio-behavioural determinants of compliance with health and medical care recommendations. *Medical Care*, **13**, 10–24.

Bolam, R. and Medlock, P. (1985) *Active Tutorial Work: Training and Dissemination: An Evaluation*. Oxford: Blackwell.

Broadfoot, P., James, M., McMeeking, S., Nuttall, D. and Stierer, B. (1988) *Records of Achievement: Report of the National Evaluation of Pilot Schemes*. London: HMSO.

Burgess, R. (ed.) (1985) *Field Methods in the Study of Education*. Lewes: Falmer.

Bynner, J. (1980) Experimental research strategy and evaluation research designs. *British Educational Research Journal*, **6**(1), 7–19.

Campbell, D. and Stanley, J. (1963) Experimental and quasi-experimental designs for research on teaching. In Gage, N. (ed.) *Handbook of Research on Teaching*. Chicago: Rand McNally.

Carr, W. and Kemmis, S. (1986) *Becoming Critical: Education, Knowledge and Action Research*. Lewes: Falmer.

Clemett, A. J. and Pearce, J. S. (1986) *The Evaluation of Pastoral Care*. Oxford: Blackwell.

Dental Health Study (1986) *Natural Nashers: Evaluation Report, Dental Health Study*. Cambridge: University of Cambridge Department of Education (mimeo).

Ebbutt, D. (1985) Educational action research: some general concerns and specific quibbles. In Burgess, R. (ed.) *Issues in Educational Research: Qualitative Methods*. Lewes: Falmer.

Ellenby, S. (1985) Ask the clients! *Pastoral Care in Education*, **3**(2), 144–9.

Elliott, J. (1993) What have we learned from action research in school-based evaluation? *Educational Action Research*, **1**(1), 175–86.

Fishbein, M. and Ajzen, I. (1975) *Belief, Intention and Behaviour: An Introduction to Theory and Research*. Reading, Mass.: Addison-Wesley Publishing Co.

Freire, P. (1972) *Pedagogy of the Oppressed*. Harmondsworth: Penguin.

Freudenberg, N. (1981) Health education for social change: a strategy for public health in the US. *International Journal of Health Education*, **24**(3), 1–8.

Freudenberg, N. (1984) Training health educators for social change. *International Quarterly of Community Health Education*, **5**, 37–51.

Hamilton, D., Jenkins, D., King, C., MacDonald, B. and Parlett, M. (eds) (1977) *Beyond the Numbers Game: A Reader in Educational Evaluation*. London: Macmillan.

Hook, C. (1985) *Studying Classrooms*. Waurn Ponds, Victoria: Deakin University.

Hopkins, D. (1985) *A Teacher's Guide to Classroom Research*. Milton Keynes: Open University Press.

James, M. (1980) On the receiving end: pupils' perceptions of learning sociology and social studies at 16. *The Social Studies Teacher*, **10**(2), 61–8.

James, M. (1987) Outcome evaluation, process evaluation and the experience of the dental health study. In Campbell, G. (ed.) *Health Education, Youth and Community: A Review of Research and Developments*. Lewes: Falmer.

Lang, P. (1983) How pupils see it. *Pastoral Care in Education*, **1**(3), 164–75.

Lang, P. (1985) Taking the customer into account. In Lang, P. and Marland, M. (eds) *New Directions in Pastoral Care*. Oxford: Blackwell.

Lewin, K. (1948) *Resolving Social Conflicts*. New York: Harper.

McCormick, R. and James, M. (1983; 2nd edn 1988) *Curriculum Evaluation in Schools*. London: Croom Helm and Routledge.

McKernan, J. (1991) *Curriculum Action Research: A Handbook of Methods and Resources for the Reflective Practitioner*. London: Kogan Page.

National Curriculum Council (1990) *Curriculum Guidance 5: Health Education*. York: NCC.

Nixon, J. (ed.) (1981) *A Teacher's Guide to Action Research: Evaluation Enquiry and Development in the Classroom*. London: Grant McIntyre.

Oja, S. and Smulyan, L. (1989) *Collaborative Action Research: A Developmental Approach*. Lewes: Falmer.

Parlett, M. and Hamilton, D. (1972) Evaluation as illumination: a new approach to the study of innovatory programmes, Occasional Paper 9. Edinburgh: Centre for Research in the Educational Sciences, University of Edinburgh. Reprinted in Hamilton *et al.* (1977).

Pring, R. (1985) Personal development. In Lang, P. and Marland, M. (eds) *New Directions in Pastoral Care*. Oxford: Blackwell, in association with NAPCE and ESRC.

Rudduck, J. (1990) *Innovation and Change: Developing Understanding and Involvement*. Milton Keynes: Open University Press.

Rudduck, J. and Hopkins, D. (eds) (1985) *Research as a Basis for Teaching*. London: Heinemann.

Simpson, M. (1990) Why criterion referenced assessment will not improve children's learning. *Curriculum Journal*, **1**(2), 171–83.

Stake, R. E. (1967) The countenance of educational evaluation. *Teachers College Record*. **68**(7), 523–40.

Stenhouse, L. (1975) *An Introduction to Curriculum Research and Development*. London: Heinemann.

TGAT (1988) *Task Group on Assessment and Testing: A Report*. London: DES.

Thomas, W. (1928) *The Child in America*. New York: Knopf.

Thorp, J. (1982) Evaluating practice: pupils' views of transfer from the primary to the secondary school. *Pastoral Care in Education*, **1**(1), 45–52.

Tones, K. (1987) Health promotion, affective education and the personal-social development of young people. In David, K. and Williams, R. (eds) *Health Education in Schools*, 2nd edn. London: Harper & Row.

Walker, R. (1985) *Doing Research: A Handbook for Teachers*. London: Methuen.

Walker, R. and Adelman, C. (1975) *A Guide to Classroom Observation*. London: Methuen.

Williams, C. (1992) Curriculum relevance for street children. *Curriculum Journal*, **3**(3), 277–90.

CHAPTER 18

International perspectives on pastoral care (affective education)

Peter Lang

INTRODUCTION

Some years ago I was due to deliver a paper 'Pastoral care: an English Perspective' at a conference of the Canadian Guidance and Counselling Association in Vancouver. This was a large conference, and my session was one of some twenty simultaneous ones from which participants could choose. At breakfast on the day of my presentation I chatted to the Canadian counsellors who were sitting at my table. Gradually it emerged that the title of my paper suggested to them that I would be discussing a religious theme, and the likelihood was that those who attended my session would do so expecting a theological discourse. Eventually the conference organizer felt it appropriate to announce that I would be talking about aspects of care in English schools, rather than priests ministering to their flocks. This, of course, worked to my advantage as my session was very well attended, the curiosity factor playing an important part. I include this story not just to entertain but to draw attention to the fact that educational terminology, like wine, does not always travel well.

But this was not the end of the story, for though the term 'pastoral care' meant nothing so far as education in Canada went, I found that this did not mean that its concerns were ignored. Further experience, and an increasing understanding of what was actually done, suggested that in fact most if not all the concerns that pastoral care and personal and social education express in England also exist in Canada. But they were found under the names of counselling and guidance, and operated through different organizational structures and approaches. For example Young (1994, p. 42), writing of the Canadian situation generally, confirms this view: 'In Canada guidance, and more particularly, guidance and counselling, subsume much of what elsewhere is referred to as pastoral care.' He goes on to spell out the goals of guidance and counselling:

> Traditionally, the primary goal of school guidance and counselling programs has been to facilitate development in three areas of the student's life: educational, vocational, and personal social. Specifically, these programs were intended to help students adapt to school and the educational process, assist them in determining

and implementing vocational goals and plans after secondary school, and ameliorate the personal-social concerns as they arise.

(Young, 1994,14 p. 43)

It hardly needs remarking that 'the amelioration of personal-social concerns' is very close to one of the major aims of pastoral care in England. I found evidence of further commonality when I examined a number of guidance programmes produced by some of the different Canadian States.

For example a programme for secondary schools from Ontario listed the aims of guidance as follows.

Students acquire the skills, knowledge, and attitudes necessary to:

- know and appreciate themselves
- relate effectively to others
- develop appropriate educational plans
- explore career alternatives

(Ministry of Education Ontario, 1984, p. 3)

A similar programme from Alberta included:

Career, personal finance, and life management skills, including personal development, interpersonal relationships, effective learning skills, career planning, skills and attitudes required in the workplace, preventative alcohol and drug education, and other relevant societal issues.

(Ministry of Education Alberta, 1988, p. 7)

Finally a programme from Ontario entitled 'Personal life management' included the following modules for study:

- Aesthetics
- Aging
- Career Planning
- Decision Making
- Entrepreneurship
- Home Maintenance and Care
- Human Relations
- Law
- Nutrition
- Parenting
- Resource Management
- Well-Being

(Ministry of Education Ontario, 1985, p. 2)

Clearly many of the concerns and topics that appear in these programmes can be found in a typical PSE or pastoral programme in England.

I became interested in the extent to which the situation I had identified in the case of England and Canada was shared elsewhere. Visits to or correspondence with those working in a number of other countries has shown that there are potential parallels to be drawn in a significant number of cases.

Having established this common ground, how might we move from simply noting the underlying parallels to a more systematic comparison? What is the relationship of the different examples, to what degree has their origin been unique to their particular country, and to what extent has what happened in one country influenced another? The next part of this chapter will seek to begin to answer these questions. After I have raised a number of problems that need to be taken into account, an example of shared views on outcomes will be given. A model will then be presented which it will be argued can be used to consider examples from different countries. It will also be suggested that there are ways that the nature of provision can be categorized. The value of this model will be considered in relation to a number of examples, starting with what appear to be the two most significant traditions in terms of both development and influence, though it will be noted that not in every case can developments be accounted for in relation to these traditions. The final section of the chapter will suggest that the significance of these comparisons goes beyond a simple contribution to the body of comparative knowledge and has considerable pragmatic relevance both in terms of advancing practice and possibly in raising the status of an undervalued area. Before we consider how one might begin to make sense of this area, there are some initial issues which have some implications for this process.

SOME INITIAL PROBLEMS OF MEANING AND PROFILE

The problem of different terminology for approaches which often appear to have very similar aims has already been highlighted, using England and Canada as illustrations. However, perhaps an even greater difficulty is the situation where a particular term is used, but given different meanings according to the context. This is not surprisingly the case in relation to the same term used in different countries or areas. For example the term 'guidance' in Scotland means something significantly different from 'guidance' in Canada, and something different again in New Zealand.

> In New Zealand the term 'guidance' is used to encompass a wide range of services, including 'pastoral care', (as understood in England), classroom programmes of personal and social education, educational and vocational guidance and specialist individual counselling.
>
> (Arnott, 1994, p. 67)

Research for an entry into an international encyclopaedia of education (Lang and Ribbins, 1985) found that in every State in Australia the term 'pastoral care' was used at a policy level, but the policies it represented varied considerably, from the welfare-orientated to the purely disciplinary. A current example of the disciplinary can be found in Western Australia where the Ministry of Education operates a unit named 'Behaviour management and pastoral care'. But it is not only when the same term is used in different places that the issue of different meanings may arise; in some cases, it seems that a term used may be given different meanings depending on the level at which it is operating. This can be seen to be one of the implications of the following quotation relating to pastoral care in a particular English secondary school.

There are grounds for arguing that there is a serious mismatch between theory and reality at a number of levels: at the level of what the 'conventional wisdom' says pastoral care is/ought to be and what is actually happening in schools: at the level of the school's official pronouncements about pupil welfare and what the school actually does about it; and at the level of what teachers claim to mean by 'pastoral care'; and the day-to-day practices in which they actually engage.

(Best, *et al.*, 1983, p. 29)

I would suggest that it is possible to relate these different usages of the same term to at least three levels of operation (there may be more).

The first is a broad administrative policy level; second a level of individual institutions; finally a third level which relates to the different groups within an institution.

In the case of the broad administrative policy level, the context is national or more local – that is, province, state, school board or local education authority. Here definitions or meanings may be found in such things as official reports, policy pronouncements and sets of guidelines. Here, in part unavoidably, things tend to be expressed at a very general level, and can often be categorized as rhetorical.

The second level is generally at the level of individual institutions, expressed through such means as staff handbooks, school prospectuses and pronouncements at parents' evenings. Partly because this is a public view it tends to be unproblematic and idealized.

The third level is that of the different groups and individuals within the institution. Here things may be fairly complex in so far as meanings are concerned. First, the actual practice may be very different from what is claimed in the official rhetoric. Again, at institutional level the assumption is often that all concerned share the same meanings whilst in reality the meanings that different groups and individuals give to the affective area can be very different: often this will be along a continuum from a perception of great value to one of total pointlessness.

Richard Young in the paper quoted earlier suggests that some elements of this situation exist in Canada in relation to the term 'counselling'.

More recently, counsellors have used the terms developmental, preventative and remedial to further differentiate the goals of school guidance and counselling programs. In practice, the emphasis of the counsellor's work has been in the remedial domain. However the rationale that underlies these programs is based on a developmental perspective.

(Young, 1994, p. 43)

A further level of complexity may be added by the fact that different commentators may interpret a situation differently. For example, both of the following authors are talking about the current position of counselling in the USA.

Selection, placement, and adjustment remain, but are included in the concept of development. Organisationally the framework of a comprehensive program has incorporated the vocational guidance, counselor-clinical-services models, and, in the 1990s, has become the major way of organizing and managing counseling and guidance in schools. The position orientations of the past have been transformed into developmental, comprehensive counseling and guidance programs.

(Gysbers, 1994, p. 57)

We are now a beleaguered profession on the verge of extinction. The irony, whether tragic or not, is that in many ways we are much stronger theoretically, with a more robust research base, and with an increasing variety of program applications. Why then the pessimism? What has happened in the past few years to cause such a dire diagnosis? In a word the problem we now face has its roots in our continued shift from a developmental conception of counselling psychology to a therapeutic framework. What was once the exception for our field has now become the rule.

(Sprinthall, 1991, p. 27)

It seems likely that if asked Gysbers and Sprinthall would offer different versions of what was currently meant by counselling in the USA, and what counsellors themselves meant by it must depend on which of the interpretations is the most accurate.

In seeking information about ideas and practices in other countries which correspond to pastoral care I have frequently found that preliminary enquiries have been met with claims that no equivalent activity existed. For example, although enquiries made to the education sections of the Portuguese and Italian embassies received assurances that nothing comparable existed, later investigations revealed that personal and social education is a mandatory part of the Portuguese curriculum and that in Italy a major health education project has many pastoral aims (these developments will be discussed later). Similarly the director of a highly prestigious German comparative educational research institute assured me that no equivalent existed in his country. Later I found that in a number of Gesamtschule (comprehensive schools), particularly in the Saarland, not only was the term 'pastoral care' understood but it was felt that a number of the practices which were common to these schools could be described as pastoral. In fact this is an issue that was partly identified by Dockrell some years ago.

Of the 32 countries represented at the 8th World Congress of the World Association for Educational Research ranging alphabetically from Argentina to Zimbabwe at least 30 assumed that education had a role in the development of personality. Yet there is a marked Anglo-Saxon reluctance to be concerned with research in this area. At the last meeting of the American Educational Research Association I looked for sessions which were concerned with affective or social development. There were some in the index but none of those sessions saw affective development as anything other than a peripheral issue as it related to some more important concern...

Now this is strange. If affective education is important and indeed inevitable because schools intentionally or unintentionally contribute to the social and personal development of their pupils, then it should be a major item on the agenda of researchers in Britain and America as well as in 30 odd other countries in the world. Yet it does not seem to be.

(Dockrell, 1987, p. 5)

Thus what Dockrell has described as affective education (so far described in this paper as an area of common concern) can be seen as a low-profile phenomenon. The implications for those involved in comparative work are that relevant data may exist, but it may require a very thorough investigation to unearth it. The information we receive about good practice in other systems is always limited; in the case of affective education its low profile means there is a very small chance we will hear anything about what goes on elsewhere.

Dockrell uses the term 'affective education', and there is some value in using this as an umbrella term to cover the number of different usages found internationally. Though not familiar everywhere, it is a term which appears to have wider currency than any other comparable one. Used in this overarching way, I suggest that the phrase 'affective education' can encompass all current educational approaches to this aspect of student development, in whatever country they are found. A working definition might be as follows: 'affective education' includes all work (individual, group and programme) that is concerned with the student's feelings, emotions and personal and social development, the positive encouragement offered by schools and the support they provide when difficulties are encountered in these areas.

So far the discussion has focused on potential similarities in approaches to affective education. What of the outcomes of these approaches? Are there similarities in the actual qualities it is hoped to develop in students? Some small-scale research undertaken by the writer suggested that this could be the case.

PARENT AND PUPIL VIEWS

In a small-scale study by the writer, using the European schools (run by the European Community) fifty-five parents of English, French, German, Dutch, Danish, Belgian and Italian nationality responded to the question:

> What personal qualities would you hope that you and the school can encourage in your child during their secondary education?

There was a very considerable amount of overlap in their responses, including frequent mention of such qualities as empathy, responsibility, tolerance, self-awareness, self-esteem, ability to take decisions, ability to listen, compassion, honesty, self-confidence, consideration for others, independence. A similar question was asked of a group of 30 teachers from the nine European schools, who had come together in Belgium for an in-service training course. This group included the same nationalities plus Spanish and Portuguese, and very similar responses and overlap were recorded.

Though they were not derived from a large or particularly representative sample, these results are important, because they suggest that in Europe, in so far as the feelings of parents and teachers about outcomes are concerned, the correspondence may be greater than in terms of approaches to affective education.

A MODEL OF AFFECTIVE EDUCATION

This model was initially developed on the basis of my Canadian experience, but has since been related to situations in other countries. Earlier Young was quoted as saying that Canadian counsellors used the terms *developmental, preventative* and *remedial*, and this corresponded to my own experience there. I felt this threefold categorisation could also be applied to pastoral care and personal and social education in England, and it is on the basis of this that the model was first produced.

This model seeks to provide a basis for identifying and analysing relevant areas of educational policy and practice in different countries. It is concerned with purpose, aims and type of response. The three categories, are potentially of equal importance but likely to be given different emphasis in differing systems and situations. Though it was not designed as such, the model is in part a historical one. There appears to be a tendency for development to start with a strong emphasis on the first category, but for a greater concern in the second and finally third categories to develop over time.

Responsive (cure)
Support and individual guidance for students who have already encountered difficulties and problems of an educational, personal or social nature, that is, crisis counselling, individual support from teachers or form teacher/tutor, educational psychologist welfare officer, or referral to outside agencies.

Proactive (prevention)
Individual guidance and programmes or activities designed to equip students to deal effectively with common personal, social and educational difficulties such as drug abuse, solvent abuse. AIDS programmes, group-work on handling bullying, conflict, gender issues, aspects of health, moral and values education could contribute here.

Developmental (enhancement)
Individual guidance, programmes and curricula-based inputs designed to enhance the student's social development and personal effectiveness, namely assertiveness training, interpersonal skills development, self-esteem building. There are aspects of health, moral, values and human rights education that could contribute.

This model, like most, is intended to provide a working tool of analysis, and should not be seen as possessing definitive theoretical qualities. Other models and approaches could be equally valuable. For example this model has some resemblance to Maslow's hierarchy of needs (Maslow, 1975), and his conception of a hierarchy starting with safety needs, moving to belongingness and love needs, on to esteem needs, and ending with the ultimate goal of self-actualization could have been used as a model in its own right.

There is another dimension to affective education where different approaches may be found to be in direct contrast to each other. This relates to the nature of the provision of affective education. The contrast is particularly significant in terms of the personnel involved in the provision. Thus in England the key emphasis is normally on the involvement of all staff in the provision of pastoral care, whilst in Canada it is on the part played by the counsellors, who are only a small fraction of those working in or with schools. Of course in England there are special roles associated with pastoral care, and equally Canadian counsellors cannot operate without the co-operation of teachers. The point is that provision in England is seen as operating through the work of 'generalists' and in Canada through that of 'specialists'. I would suggest that most approaches to the provision of affective education can be seen to fall somewhere along a continuum from total reliance on the work of 'specialists' to total reliance on that of 'generalists'. Usually associated with this is the degree of training that is seen as necessary for those involved, specialists normally receiving more than generalists.

TRADITIONS OF AFFECTIVE EDUCATION

Investigation and examination of the literature suggest that there are cases of approaches or traditions that have developed in one country influencing developments in others. Two major and contrasting traditions will now be considered. Though they are contrasted in terms of the degree to which they involve specialists or generalists, they are both firmly within the affective tradition in relation to the threefold model.

Pastoral care in England

> The problem of numbers has been partly solved by putting each boy under a tutor whose connection with him remains unbroken during his whole stay in the school and whose duty it is to bestow that attention on him and undertake that responsibility for him that cannot be expected of the class teacher.
>
> (an Eton tutor giving evidence to the Clarendon Commission in the 1860s quoted in Lang, 1984, p. 140)

Here we see an element of the early development of pastoral care in England: a public school master talking in the early 1860s of aspects of his school which could be seen as simple pastoral care. In fact the evidence given to the Clarendon Commission contained several examples from a number of different public schools. In the same article I went on to argue:

> What I would suggest however, is that by providing a vocabulary and new ideology of wider concerns for pupils than had existed before the nineteenth century, public school laid the foundation for what was ultimately to follow in terms of pastoral care in the comprehensive school.
>
> (Lang, 1984, p. 140)

In this paper I sought to trace the origins of pastoral care as it exists in England. I suggested that in terms of structure (house systems and later year systems), approaches (the role of the tutor) and ideology (care and welfare and responsibilities for all-round development of pupils), the origin of pastoral care could be traced from the early nineteenth century to the present. A distinctive terminology came relatively late. 'In 1954 (Education Year-book) the term pastoral care was first used in print though it was over a decade before it began to be used in schools and probably the early seventies before its use became universal' (Lang, 1984, p. 145). Coventry had already established house systems in its new comprehensive schools in the early 1950s.

The development of pastoral care from these early house systems to the 1980s was charted in a booklet produced by the National Association of Pastoral Care in Education (NAPCE, 1986). Four phases of development were suggested. Phase 1, from the middle 1950s to late 1960s was one where

> The key skills of those with pastoral responsibilities were perceived as essentially organisational insofar as they were concerned with the management of large numbers of young people, the collection, recording and dissemination of a great deal of information and with control, discipline and punishment of difficult and disruptive students.
>
> (NAPCE, 1986, p. 11)

Phase 2 began to emerge towards the end of the 1960s. It was characterized by an increasing awareness that a significant number of students faced severe learning and personal problems. Increased support was provided in school for vocational and educational counselling. Emphases were placed upon the development of interpersonal relationships and co-ordination of welfare provisions for students with the school at the centre of the network.

Phase 3, from the late 1970s to the early 1980s, saw the emergence of 'pastoral curricular' that focused on personal, social and moral development and the acquisition of personal and interpersonal skills. Emphases in schools shifted from individual to group-work in the area of pastoral care. The fourth phase was predictive in nature and need not concern us here.

Thus there appears to be a strong historical tradition so far as pastoral care in England is concerned: a tradition which could be characterized as a progression through the categories of the model of affective education, from the 'responsive' to the 'developmental'. The strength of this tradition is indicated by the fact that in spite of the emergence, during the 1970s and 1980s, of the parallel affective strand of personal and social education, and a limited amount of attention in terms of national policy and legislation, pastoral care continues to be seen as an important part of the work of the vast majority of secondary schools. It should be noted, though, that personal and social education is the affective approach preferred by most primary schools, where explicit notions of pastoral care never developed.

Guidance and counselling in the USA

The second major tradition is that of the United States, where the main area in which the affective appears to have developed was initially that of vocational guidance, and its origin and current manifestations seem to be intimately tied up with this. These origins were very different from those in the traditional English public school. This development is well summarised by Norman Gysbers:

> Thus, what began at the turn of the century in the schools of the United States under the term vocational guidance with a selection and placement focus, and then shifted in the 1920s, 1930s, 1940s, and 1950s to a focus on personal adjustment, organised around a counselor-clinical-services model, has now assumed a developmental focus, organised around the framework of a comprehensive program. Selection, placement, and adjustment remain, but are included in the concept of development. Organisationally the framework of a comprehensive program has incorporated the vocational guidance, counselor-clinical-services models, and, in the 1990s, has become a major way of organising and managing counseling and guidance in schools. The position orientations of the past have been transformed into developmental, comprehensive counseling and guidance programs.
>
> (Gysbers, 1994, p. 57)

Thus in both England and the United States the development of an affective dimension to education has progressed through a number of stages, which in both cases can be seen, in relation to the model and its historical dimension, as moving from an exclusive focus on the first two categories, 'responsive' and 'proactive', to an incorporation of the third, 'developmental'. It should be recognized that the stages are to some extent ideals, and the degree to which individual schools or services have moved through them varies considerably. For example, in a paper assessing the degree to which pastoral care had progressed through stages of positive development, I referred back to the concept of pastoral incantation or fantasy, a concept I had developed in an earlier study. I had described them as dialogues which were heavily interspersed with words or concepts which had strong favourable and warm connotative meanings for the speaker, and usually for at least some of those with whom they are engaged in discussion. I went on to comment:

> The point about pastoral incantation is that it lets you off the hook, talking in itself becomes sufficient. I would suggest that statements about the positive development of pastoral care are in danger of becoming pastoral fantasy on a grand scale.
>
> (Lang, 1994, p. 38)

In the same way the quotation from Sprinthall earlier, where he suggests a shift from a developmental conception of counselling psychology to therapeutic framework, indicates that in the USA affective education's development in terms of the inclusion of the developmental may be uneven.

The influence of the English and American traditions

There is considerable evidence that both these traditions have influenced affective education in other countries, though this is most likely to be in terms of one aspect or phase of their development.

> The early New Zealand secondary schools were private institutions, based on the model of the British public school with 'house' systems, where 'house parents' offered advice and guidance to their young charges. As in Britain, the expanding state education sector adopted this model which developed into a variety of pastoral care systems.
>
> (Arnott, 1994, p. 66)

> The Canadian experience in school guidance and counselling is long and varied, beginning with recognizable efforts immediately after World War II (Herman 1981). In its inception, it was almost entirely influenced by practices in the United States.
>
> (Young, 1994, p. 42)

Equally it appears common that both traditions may influence the way things develop in a particular situation.

> Experience in both Britain and U.S.A. has influenced the approach taken in Australia. The historical pattern in schools in U.S.A. has involved the use of specialist personnel whilst that in Britain has tended to place more emphasis upon the use of the resources of the teachers themselves. Whilst specialist services have tended to serve those students with special and obvious needs, pastoral care, which

utilizes a larger proportion of the personnel of the school, attempts to reach all pupils.

(Martin, 1994, p. 141)

In the case of affective education in New Zealand, which was initially strongly influenced by aspects of pastoral care, Arnott goes on to describe how in the 1960s and 1970s:

the New Zealand system broadened its perspective, incorporating ideas and influences from the United States of America (Webb 1981) along with those of the increasingly influential Maori community. Guidance counsellors were introduced to complement the system of tutorial care, and guidance networks developed from there.

(Arnott, 1994, p. 66)

There is much to suggest that the influence of the American model of affective education has been significant in many parts of the world. This is particularly the case in terms of its counselling dimension. Educational counselling which has developed from the American model is found in a wide variety of countries. Some examples are Nigeria, the Philippines, Thailand, Japan, Hong Kong, Taiwan, Brazil (Oliveira, 1993), Israel (Katz, 1992) and the Netherlands (Stern, 1985). The influence of English pastoral care appears to have been less widespread, and has tended to be particularly associated with countries with strong connections with Britain, in particular Australia and New Zealand.

There is, however, one country where English pastoral care has had a direct and unusual influence, and this is Singapore. Salim and Chua (1994) suggested that up to 1987:

Most schools ... tended to relegate pupil welfare to a low priority level or continued to hold on to a very narrow perception of it ... A reactive approach continued until 1987, when a group of 12 secondary school principals visited successful schools in the United Kingdom and the United States of America, and made several recommendations in their report 'Towards Excellence in Schools', including one for the introduction of a proactive approach through pastoral care and career guidance, to enhance the quality of education in Singapore.

(Salim and Chua, 1994, p. 77)

Thus, pastoral care was introduced in Singapore using the English approach as an explicit model. The process involved can be seen as corresponding to the model's historical dimension, in representing a move from reactive through preventative to developmental approaches. Since 1987 pastoral care has been gradually and systematically introduced into an increasing number of secondary schools, the long-term aim being for all schools, both secondary and primary, to be involved.

By 1990 pastoral care was being defined in Singapore in a way that embraced all categories of the model.

A simple definition will serve to focus attention on the principal reasons for introducing pastoral care to schools, which is to improve the education of our children even further.

At its simplest, pastoral care may be described as the practice of identifying the particular needs (including vocational needs) of each child in a school and of trying to meet them through a carefully thought-out developmental programme.

This programme would be concerned with the personal, social and moral growth of the child and would rank in importance with the academic programme. It would complement the existing Moral Education programme in our schools.

(Ministry of Education Singapore, 1990, p. 1)

AFFECTIVE EDUCATION IN EUROPE

In the case of Europe, although a considerable number of education systems include affective aspects, these are generally harder to relate to a particular tradition. For example, the class teacher system in Denmark has its own tradition going back some hundred years:

Concurrently with the social advantages of non-streaming, children in Danish Folkeskole can look forward to the additional support of the class teacher system, whereby each class can have the same teacher throughout the whole or greater part of its 10 years. Each pupil group can thus develop its own profile under the guidance of its own class teacher, who comes to know and not infrequently also to cherish every aspect of each individual pupil's abilities, skills, character and aspirations. The class teacher will also be well acquainted with the pupil's parents and home background, functioning as counsellor and encouraging maximum contact between the family and the school.

(Ministry of Education Denmark, 1988, p. 8)

Reinsholm *et al.*, who have researched the work of the Danish class form teacher, offer an elaboration of the picture presented in the official rhetoric above:

in some cases, the tasks undertaken by class form teachers have closely resembled therapy, which naturally raises the question whether class form teachers should take on problems which in general they do not have training to solve. Be that as it may, there is a clear tendency for class form teachers to tackle such problems on the promptings of their own conscience, simply because no one else is prepared to support the children – or the families – who are in difficulties.

... Some class form teachers are aware that this type of help is extrinsic to what goes on in the classroom, and they attempt to maintain in principle the position that the caring work of the school should take place not primarily on a one-to-one basis, but in the classroom, between the teacher and the pupils as a group. A very special aspect of the work of the Danish class form teacher is perhaps this search for an intrinsic connection between the functions of caring and teaching.

(Reinsholm *et al.*, 1994, p. 179)

The development of this Danish manifestation of affective education appears to be unique to that country. However, it is interesting to note that the process described by Reinsholm *et al.* has close similarities to the way pastoral care has been described as developing in England. The process can also be seen as an attempt to move away from the first 'responsive' category of the model to the second two categories, 'proactive' and 'developmental'.

There are undoubtedly further examples of approaches to affective education in other northern European countries. For example, in the Netherlands it appears to depend on the school.

Dutch schools have a large measure of autonomy in how they deal with guidance, counselling and other non-teaching activities. It is the principal and teaching staff of each school who decide how to allocate hours they receive for all non-teaching duties, and these may or may not include counselling.

(Stern, 1985, p. 239)

Work akin to pastoral care in some German Gesamtschulen has already been mentioned and some form of personal and social education exists in Belgium. The following quotation might be seen to imply affective work in the Swedish system, but more would need to be known about how these ideals are put into practice.

Schools must provide upbringing. This means that they must actively and deliberately condition and encourage children and young persons to embrace the fundamental values of our democracy and to express those values in practical and everyday actions.

(National Swedish Board of Education, 1980, p. 9)

In some countries in Europe affective education has not developed over a long period of time but been introduced from scratch for political or social reasons. The following extract from a set of guidelines for the work of the tutor in Spanish schools relates to an example of this.

Two facets of education are equally important and complementary, an instructive action through which it is possible to transmit knowledge, and on the other hand education to help students in development and personal evolution. Education well understood must have two aspects, instructive and formative. Through the first the student progressively acquires culture and mastery of knowledge and science, with the second he develops as a person, integrating values, attitudes and aspirations until he reaches a personal maturity which enables him to integrate into society as an individual person free and responsible...

... if it is important that students should know and learn it is also important he should acquire attitudes, criteria and values which will enable him to assimilate to society and life in an adequate form. This second aspect is what tutorial work is about.

(CEVE, 1990, p. 4)

In the case of this model the major emphasis appears to be on the 'developmental'. Significantly, tutorial work of this kind was introduced in Spain only after the Franco era with the clear intention of acting as an antidote to aspects of its legacy.

The situation in Portugal is similar. The Education Act of 1986 included the field of personal and social education, and in 1989 legislation set out how this should be implemented. Currently work is in its early stages, but training has been given to a number of teachers and more will be trained. The ultimate aim is for personal and social education to be explicitly taught at all phases of education. As in Spain, affective education has been consciously initiated as an antidote to the legacy of years of dictatorship.

Though the idea of including PSE in the curriculum was Portuguese, the original model on which the programme was based came from Quebec where the Université Laval has developed a personal and social education course. This course, which appears to be the only one of its kind in Canada, comprises a detailed programme for the secondary phase, 'Formation personnelle et social' (Pelletier, 1988).

In the case of Malta, Sultana suggests that personal and social education was introduced in the late 1980s as the result of a form of 'moral panic'.

> It was this scenario of stress and anxiety in the junior lyceum and the primary school sector on the one hand, and absenteeism in trade schools on the other, which facilitated the acceptance of personal and social education as a panacea for various ills.
>
> (Sultana, 1992, p. 239)

In Italy for a number of years legislation has sought to involve both parents and pupils actively in the education process. Recently a major health education project has been set up where schools or groups of schools design appropriate projects and bid to a central agency for funding. Though at least in part motivated by anxieties about drug abuse and other youth-related problems, it is envisaged as something that goes well beyond negative proaction. The Ministry information states:

> The problem of health education, intended as an educational process committed to the formation of individuals conscious of health risk, free from conditioning, and capable of making choices founded on rediscovered and responsible assumed values, has been, and is still, one of the Ministry of Education's prime undertakings.
>
> In fact, the initiatives carried out are based on the principle that every educational activity has a preventive value if it aims to strengthen the resources of the individual so as to make him or her capable of facing the challenges of school and life. The initiatives, therefore, aim to become part of normal school life, as a contribution towards the rethinking and replanning of the everyday school situation according to models through which the plans for learning and relationships, the cognitive dimension and the socio-emotional dimension of the scholastic experience, can interact effectively.
>
> (Italian Ministry of Education, 1992, p. 1)

Details of the programme undertaken by a group of schools in Salerno illustrate the project in practice. Here the emphasis is mainly on the model's first two categories. The programme involved:

- lectures, debates, small group work concerned with the themes of 'Progetto Giovani' (the title of the secondary level health education initiative): health education, drug abuse prevention, multi-cultural and peace education, moral issues (at classroom level);
- conferences of experts working in the area (psychologists, health service personnel, etc.) about AIDS, sexuality and adolescent problems, career education (addressed to several classes together);
- service (in school, during lesson time) of psychological counselling, carried out by a clinical psychologist;
- extra-curricular activities: sports, cinema, theatre, school newspaper.

A PHENOMENON OF INDUSTRIALIZED SOCIETY?

It is far easier to find examples of affective education in relation to traditional industrialized countries, but other societies also furnish them. The following example, taken from information provided by a lecturer at the University of Malaysia, suggests that in at least one newly industrialized country some aspects of affective education exist.

As far as affective education/pastoral care/counselling goes in the secondary school, we have a subject called moral education. This is a subject which is compulsory for all non-Muslims (the Muslims take religious education). Through moral education students are taught values such as honesty, loyalty, open-mindedness, etc. etc. Beside moral education these values are also incorporated in all other subject areas taught at the secondary schools. For English language and the national language syllabuses, these values are incorporated through topics selected from the textbooks. To quote from the secondary education syllabus:

> The teacher should use materials that emphasize the principles of good citizenship, moral values and the Malaysian way of life. The moral values should be introduced and taught through situations so that students will internalise these values and put them into practice.

In the Third World affective education might be expected to be a low priority, other more pressing concerns taking precedence, but there are some examples here as well. Nigeria, where a nationwide counselling service exists, has already been mentioned, and a course in pastoral care is currently being developed at the University of Ibadan. Pastoral care is also given a place in the new education system being developed in Namibia (Turner, 1990).

SHARED PROBLEMS

The issues identified at the beginning of this chapter suggested that there were aspects of affective education that were problematic, in particular in terms of the way it was understood and its status. It seems probable that just as affective education itself is an international phenomenon, so are its problems. Quotations from Young have indicated that in Canada what counsellors talk about and what they actually do differs. Best *et al.* (1983) suggest that the same thing happens in England in so far as teachers are concerned. This problem is elaborated by Lang and Hyde in a comparison between England and Western Australia.

During the early 1980s, accumulating evidence indicated that the rhetoric of pastoral care was somewhat different from the reality to be found in schools. This evidence which was mainly subjective, resulted from academic contacts between teachers and academics involved with pastoral care. Best et al. (1983) reported that this experience in England led them to the view that

> . . . there exists among teachers and others an 'unofficial' version of pastoral care which stands in stark contrast to the 'official' version of the conventional wisdom.

Some three years earlier Dynan (1980) had reported similar dysfunctions in Western Australian secondary schools. She stated:

> The responses of students in this survey indicate that the formal structures and

organisation are not fulfilling their intended purpose of providing pastoral care for students ... teachers indicated some frustration with the school system.

(Lang and Hyde, 1987, pp. 10, 93)

The issue of status, long significant in relation to pastoral care in England, is reflected in this quotation from Spain:

We can verify that there is a lot of emphasis on the first role, the instructive aspect. Present society puts a lot of emphasis on all things related to evaluation, marking and assessment, and it demands that students know a lot, that they should have lots of culture and good qualifications.

However, the formative aspect frequently receives secondary value and it is assumed that by emphasising the first you achieve the second, this is not always true.

Teachers usually give less emphasis to the formative and guidance aspect of the school, which is a mistake.

(CEVE, 1990, p. 2)

There appear to be a significant number of shared problems when affective education is viewed from a comparative perspective. Often there is a considerable gap between rhetoric and reality, and in many countries it is a low-profile phenomenon. Coupled with this low profile is a problem of lack of status. This is not usually found at the level of official pronouncements, but is expressed through the attitudes and priorities of some schools and teachers. In close relationship to this is a tendency for affective work to be under-resourced.

CONCLUSION

In this chapter I have sought to demonstrate that what we in England describe as pastoral care and personal and social education is part of a broader concern, affective education, found in many parts of the world. I have attempted to start making sense of this situation through the use of a model in relation to which a number of different examples have been considered. I believe that the development of a clearer understanding of affective education from an international perspective would be valuable to teachers as well as academics and researchers. This chapter is intended as a small contribution to this. However, there are problems! All involved in a particular education system tend to suffer from a kind of occupational myopia when it comes to the way things are done elsewhere, or at best can handle things only in terms of educational 'sound-bites'. For example, in 1991 four HM Inspectors visited twelve French primary schools for one week. Their report (HMI, 1991) was taken up by the media as demonstrating that French primary education was more effective than English and in particular that the superiority of more formal teaching methods had been proved. An earlier and much more thorough study had been ignored by all but academics. Here four hundred primary schools in England and four hundred in France were compared and a much more balanced view, presented as a question, put forward.

For pupils, what is the respective impact of coping, as in France, with an impersonal, often harsh, pedagogy and an often arid curriculum as compared to a typically more liberal, but highly varying, set of teacher expectations as in England?

(Broadfoot *et al.*, 1987, p. 300)

Thus, part of the task of understanding affective education will be to change this myopic media-orientated culture. We should seek to create a situation where our education system was not, as John Patten sought to suggest in a recent party political broadcast (31 March 1993), 'the envy of the world' but a system which sought to learn from other systems and equally had much to teach them. In the case of affective education the potential is there. A greater understanding from an international perspective could bring at least two major benefits. First, it could bring together those committed to it in different countries and this could lead to stronger support and more persuasive arguments, which through mutual support and encouragement could turn the international tide in a positive direction, and in particular raise the status of affective education and its various manifestations in different countries. Equally it could enhance what we do. I have already argued for certain valuable and unique qualities of pastoral care as it is practised in England (Lang, 1989), but there is no monopoly: it is likely that many of the particular manifestations of affective education found throughout the world have something unique and valuable about them, something which we could all learn from, and as a result do a little better in the future.

REFERENCES

Arnott, R. (1994) A whole-school approach to pastoral care: a New Zealand perspective. In Lang, P., Best, R. and Lichtenberg, A. (eds) *Caring for Children: International Perspectives on Pastoral Care and PSE*. London: Cassell.

Best, R. and Ribbins, R. (1985) Pastoral care: theory and the growth of research. In Lang, P. and Marland, M. (eds) *New Directions in Pastoral Care*. Oxford: Blackwell.

Best, R. Jarvis, C. and Ribbins, P. (eds) (1980) *Perspectives on Pastoral Care*, London: Heinemann.

Best, R. Ribbins, P. Jarvis, C. and Oddy, D. (1983) *Education and Care*. London: Heinemann.

Broadfoot, P., Osborne, M. with Gilly, M. and Paillet, A. (1987) Teachers' conceptions of their professional responsibility: some international comparisons. *Comparative Education*, **23**(3), 300 295–303.

CEVE (1990) *Orientacion y Tutoria*. Madrid: CEVE Estudios a Distancia.

Dockrell, D. (1987) The assessment of children's affective characteristics. *British Journal of Educational Research*, **13**(1), 3–13.

Dynan, M. (1980) *Do Schools Care?* Co-operative research project, no. 29. Perth, Western Australia: Education Department of Western Australia.

Gysbers, N. C. (1994) Developmental counselling and guidance programmes in the schools: developments in the USA. In Lang, P., Best, R. and Lichtenberg, A. (eds) *Caring for Children: International Perspectives on Pastoral Care and PSE*. London: Cassell.

Herman, A. (1981) *Guidance in Canadian Schools*. Calgary: Detselig Enterprises.

HMI (1991) *Aspects of Primary Education in France*, HMI Report 295/91NF/91. OFSTED.

Italian Ministry of Education (1992) *A Special Programme for Youth*. Rome: Ministry of Education Italy.

Katz, J. (1992) Integrational policies for the ethnically heterogenous school. *Pastoral Care in Education*, **10**(1), pp. 32–5.

Lang, P. (1984) Pastoral care: some reflections on possible influences, *Pastoral Care in Education*, **2**(2), 136–46.

Lang, P. (1989) What's so special about pastoral care? *Pastoral Care in Education*, **7**(4), pp. 21–7.

Lang, P. (1994) Trying, but could do better: a review of pastoral care in England and elsewhere. In Lang, P., Best, R. and Lichtenberg, A. (eds) *Caring for Children: International Perspectives on Pastoral Care and PSE*. London: Cassell.

Lang, P. and Hyde, N. (1987) Pastoral care: not making the same mistake twice. *Curriculum Perspectives*, **7**(2), 91–9. Australian Curriculum Studies Association.

Lang, P. and Ribbins, P. (1985) Pastoral care in education. In *Pergamon Encyclopaedia of Education*. London: Pergamon.

Martin, D. C. (1994) The organization of pastoral care in independent secondary schools in Australia. In Lang, P., Best, R. and Lichtenberg, A. (eds) *Caring for Children: International Perspectives on Pastoral Care and PSE*. London: Cassell.

Maslow, A. (1975) *The Farther Reaches of Human Nature*. New York: Wiley.

Ministry of Education Alberta (1988) *Career and Life Management*. Calgary: Ministry of Education.

Ministry of Education, Denmark (1988) *The Folkeskole: Primary and Lower Secondary Education in Denmark*. Copenhagen: Ministry of Education.

Ministry of Education Ontario (1984) *Guidance 1984*. Toronto: Ministry of Education.

Ministry of Education Ontario (1985) *Personal Life Management*. Toronto: Ministry of Education.

Ministry of Education Singapore (1990) *Pastoral Care: A New Focus*. Singapore: Ministry of Education.

National Association of Pastoral Care in Education (1986) *Preparing for Pastoral Care: In-service Training for the Pastoral Aspect of the Teacher's Role*. Oxford: NAPCE.

National Swedish Board of Education (1980) *The 1980 Compulsory School Curriculum*. Stockholm: Skolverstyrelsen.

Oliveira, L. (1993) A counselling experiment in Brazil: difficulties and opportunities. *Pastoral Care in Education*, **11**(1), pp. 26–9.

Pelletier, D. (1988) *La Collection, formation personnelle et sociale*. Quebec: Les Editions Septembre.

Reinsholm, N., Kryger, N., Moos, L. and Reisby, K. (1994) Caring, upbringing and teaching: the Danish class form teacher system. In Lang, P., Best, R. and

Lichtenberg, A. (eds) *Caring for Children: International Perspectives on Pastoral Care and PSE*. London: Cassell.

Salim, J. and Chua, E. (1994) The development of pastoral care and career guidance in Singapore schools. In Lang, P., Best. R. and Lichtenberg, A. (eds) *Caring for Children: International Perspectives on Pastoral Care and PSE*. London: Cassell.

Sprinthall, N. (1991) Towards a generic definition of counseling psychology: development versus therapy. In Campos, B. (ed.) *Psychological Intervention and Human Development*. Porto: Instituto de Consulta Psicologica Formacao e Desenvolvimento.

Stern, E. (1985) A Dutch contribution to counsellor education: an in-service model. *International Journal for the Advancement of Counselling*, **8**, 240–5.

Sultana, R. (1992) Personal and social education: curriculum innovation and school bureaucracies in Malta. *British Journal of Guidance and Counselling*, **20**(2), 164–85.

Turner, J. (1990) *Education in Namibia*. London: Overseas Development Administration.

Webb, S. (1981) *The Development of Guidance Counselling in New Zealand Secondary Schools*. Unpublished B.Phil. thesis, Exeter University.

Young, R. A. (1994) A systems perspective on whole-school guidance/pastoral care programmes. In Lang, P., Best, R. and Lichtenberg, A. (eds) *Caring for Children: International Perspectives on Pastoral Care and PSE*. London: Cassell.

Conclusion

CHAPTER 19

Pastoral care and PSE: principles and possibilities

Ron Best, Peter Lang, Caroline Lodge and Chris Watkins

INTRODUCTION

There are good reasons for bringing together in one volume the thoughts and experiences of a number of teachers and educationalists who, from their different professional roles, share a concern for pastoral care and for personal-social education.

First, the different emphases to be found amongst the contributions are an important reminder of the breadth and diversity of activity which is represented by the concept of pastoral care.

Second, it is possible to see in such a collection of accounts the ways in which pastoral care and personal-social education have developed and continue to develop. Like twigs on a tree, our pastoral activities bifurcate and differentiate as growth takes place and new foci for pastoral work are identified. A comparison between the topics of the chapters in this volume and those of an earlier generation of writers (e.g. Best *et al.*, 1980) reveals both change and growth in our understanding of what these concepts entail by way of both theory and application.

Third, to attempt to define the area today – as Marland and Haigh could do in the mid-1970s (Marland, 1974; Haigh, 1975) – would seem a vain endeavour. The attempt of HM Inspectors to summarize what pastoral care comprises (see Chapter 1) becomes a long, and by no means exhaustive, list of where pastoral care might be manifest in the work of the school. A tight and definitive statement remains elusive.

What the literature of the last twenty years reveals is the growth in interest in – and, it seems, in the practice of – pastoral care and PSE. It is not easy to say with any confidence that there is 'more' or 'better' pastoral care in schools now than when some of the contributors to this present volume undertook the first empirical studies of this phenomenon (e.g. Lang, 1982; Best *et al.*, 1983). The surveys of research undertaken by NAPCE and reported in *New Directions in Pastoral Care* (Lang and Marland, 1986) revealed a patchwork of individual studies, many reported in theses and dissertations at master's degree level (Ribbins and Best, 1986). Together, these gave an impression of the situation in schools across the UK, but, as the editors of that volume made clear, this was no substitute for a comprehensive research programme which would provide data which are reliable and representative. This need remains unmet. The HMI inspections of 1986–7 and 1987–8 (DES, 1988, 1989) provide some kind of overview, yet (as is often the case with such reports) the methodology is insufficiently clear and the samples (21 and 27 schools respectively) too small to satisfy the canon of rigorous educational research.

None the less, there are grounds for arguing that this is an aspect of schools' work where there have been significant developments in thought and practice. The HMI inspection reports are themselves evidence of a growing awareness of the importance of pastoral care and personal-social education, and are indicative of a general raising of awareness in schools. The evidence – certainly impressionistic and probably unrepresentative – of the experiences of the contributors to this book, in attendance at conferences and workshops, and in providing INSET courses and training days up and down the country, is that teachers are much more conscious of the contribution schools may make to the personal, social and moral development of their pupils than they were twenty years ago. Moreover, this awareness is institutionalized in schools' mission statements and prospectuses, and in their staff development priorities, in ways which are quite new.

Overall, it is our impression that the last decade has been a period of growth and consolidation for pastoral work in schools. It has witnessed the growth of personal-social education in and across the curriculum, the elaboration and increasing complexity of the role of the form tutor, a greater awareness of the relationship between pastoral work and the curriculum, and (in response to the Warnock Report and the 1981 Education Act) more integrated approaches to meeting children's personal, social, emotional and learning needs. Not least, it has witnessed the establishment and success of a significant professional association (NAPCE) concerned precisely with the promotion of such developments.

As we noted in the Introduction, this book was conceived at a time of rapid and on-going change in education, epitomized by the 1988 Education Act and all that follows from it. The attainment of a kind of dynamic equilibrium (to borrow the economists' term) of stability and steady growth in pastoral work may be disrupted by developments elsewhere. In particular, the creation of a National Curriculum and the assessment systems associated with it, and the promotion of greater legal and financial independence for schools through LMS and opportunities for grant-maintained status, are highly significant. They pose some fundamental questions about what education has come to mean in our society, and thus for the place of personal-social education in our schools and in the roles teachers perform. In this context, it is necessary to remind ourselves of some of the fundamental principles which underpin the work schools do, and to reflect upon the implications of recent developments in the context of schooling.

FIRST PRINCIPLES

It is our contention – and, it seems, a logical prerequisite for a legitimate pastoral role for teachers – that *education must begin from a commitment to meeting the developmental needs of the individual*. In one sense this is a truism, for a reasonable definition of education is precisely that it *is* the intentional promotion of individual development. What schools set out to do must be guided by an accurate assessment of where the child is, and by what the child needs in order to develop. To begin from any other point (it may be argued) is not to be engaged in education at all.

Yet it is clear that there are conceptions of education which have other starting points, and that some of these are, to say the least, influential. Media and parliamentary debates, for example, often begin with a commitment to the needs of the economy rather than those of the child. Orthodox curricula, teaching methods and so on are castigated by some representatives of commerce and industry because they are inappropriate for the creation of the technologically-skilled and economically-efficient workforce necessary to secure competitive advantage in international markets.

Other lobbies emphasize the intrinsic worth of cultural pearls enshrined in the literature, art and history of our society. They argue that it is by acquaintance with and appreciation of these that a society remains civilized and grows in its civilization. By exposure to such experiences are the tastes and sensitivities of the cultivated person to be acquired. Others may press for the curriculum to reflect the particular sets of religious or moral beliefs which they hold (Welford, 1994).

Yet others are concerned primarily for the social order and lawfulness which schools, especially in their socializing and disciplinary procedures, are supposed to promote. Recent emphasis on the place of spiritual and moral development within the curriculum is an example of this. The Secretary of State, John Patten, suggested in 1993 that a more potent religious education, with a greater emphasis on learning right from wrong, would help to stem the perceived rise in juvenile crime.

It is not our intention to challenge the importance of these functions for schooling. Sociologically, schooling has long been recognized as performing a range of functions which include selection for the occupation structure, the enculturation and socialization of each generation, the production in appropriate proportions of skilled labour for the economy and the achievement of social integration, cohesion and political stability by the promotion of a national identity (Musgrave, 1965). Nor are the expectations of the various lobbies particularly new. Raymond Williams identified pretty much the same perspectives amongst participants in the debate about State provision of education in the nineteenth century (Williams, 1961).

Such concerns may not necessarily be incompatible with the developmental needs of the individual. The point is that in such conceptions of education, individual developmental needs are recognized, if at all, as inferences from the kind of 'educated person' society requires, rather than as setting the parameters within which learning experiences must be conceived and structured.

It is important to recognize the dangers of such approaches. For one thing, they seem to carry the seeds of their own destruction. It is frequently assumed that those bodies of knowledge which have been respected in the past are necessarily of value in the future. As representatives of industry frequently point out, such a view is more likely to contribute to stagnation than to progress. Moreover, the evaluation of such knowledge is a subjective matter; witness the debates of the early 1990s about which literary gems should be included in the National Curriculum programme of study for English.

The foundations for such curriculum planning are indeed shaky. As Lawton and others (Lawton, 1973; Lawton *et al.*, 1978) long ago pointed out, the curriculum is a *selection* from the culture, and such a selection must needs be guided by principle rather than taste or fiat. A fundamental principle which underpins every chapter in this book is that of *the primacy of individual needs.* The selection from the culture which schools make must be directed towards meeting these needs, and that is a matter ultimately of how individuals develop into persons, not of whether Shakespeare is a better writer than Bacon, or of how many metallurgists the country will need by the turn of the century.

THE WHOLE PERSON

Some articulation of the nature of developmental needs is necessary. In order to begin such an articulation, we require a conception of *what* it is that is to be developed.

A simplistic answer is that schools are instrumental in converting children into adults: the beginning of schooling may be said to correspond to the end of 'babyhood'; the end of schooling to the beginning of adult life. However, this is to identify only rough stages which are, after all, socially defined rather than biologically determined – puberty, by contrast, is a biological watershed which does not now (if it ever did) correspond to the end of schooling. In any case, such a response tells us nothing about the *needs* of any individual at any stage of this development. In order to establish needs, we must recognize that, throughout its development, the child is already, and is constantly in the process of becoming, a *person*. The needs which education must meet are thus the needs of the person-in-the-process-of-becoming.

One way of exploring these needs is to recognize the many different 'selves' which make up the person. Within the context of schooling, these may be said to include the physical, social or moral, sexual, intellectual, spiritual, vocational and emotional selves, together with the self within the school organization and the self as a learner (Watkins, 1985). To fail to meet the needs of the individual in any of these 'selves' is by implication to fail to contribute to the development of the whole person. A second principle, therefore, is that *education properly conceived must be oriented towards the development of the whole person in a balanced and measured way*. In this context it is important to remember that the emphasis which those involved in pastoral care and personal-social education place on the affective domain must not distract attention from cognitive needs. Nor should it be allowed to obscure the vital relationship between experience in the affective domain and the quality of pupil learning.

What any specific individual needs at any precise moment in time is, of course, unique. There are dangers in assuming that teachers and other educational decision-makers simply know what they are. Indeed, there is a strong argument for saying that the child has a better idea of what she or he needs than anyone else, but in our conventional practice we are not very good at asking our clients for *their* perception of their needs (Lang, 1985). A further principle follows: that *the identification of the educational needs of the individual requires the willing participation of the learner in the needs-identification process.*

To write of 'developing the whole person in a balanced and measured way' is resonant of the 1988 Act's statement of the entitlement of each child to a 'broad and balanced curriculum'. Yet it is arguable that the experiences of most of our children in schools have been balanced in the past, and that the advent of a National Curriculum has not significantly increased this balance.

Personal, social and moral education have never enjoyed a prominent position in the curricula of most schools. In the context of the National Curriculum, the concerns of citizenship, health education and other aspects of personal-social development may receive attention, but with the questionable status of cross-curricular elements rather than discrete programmes of study. It can be argued that to restrict such issues to a particular subject would be to reflect an inadequate recognition of the nature of personal-social education, and might suggest that other parts of the curriculum were not concerned with such development.

None the less, in a scheme which discriminates 'core' and 'foundation' subjects from the rest of the curriculum – let alone from the 'hidden' curriculum of the values, attitudes and sentiments which the school environment promotes – the low status of cross-curricular themes and skills may subordinate the social or moral self to the intellectual self to which the core and other foundation subjects are directed. In practice this may mean that PSE is abandoned or neglected. Nor does the physical self receive much attention in such a scheme, while the entitlement of the individual to sex education is now a matter of parental choice.

As the chapters by Marland and Watkins in this volume make clear (see Chapters 8 and 9 above), there are serious tensions between statutory requirements, the historical facts of the evolution of the National Curriculum and the entitlement of individuals to be educated as whole persons.

EQUALITY AND RESPECT

Two further principles which we take to be central to the concept of education are the *principle of respect for persons* and the *principle of equality* (Peters, 1964).

The first of these reminds us that the means by which we go about making possible the development of the person must be in harmony with the concept of personhood itself. We have seen already that there are many selves which, together, make up the person, and that an essential feature of personhood is that one is constantly in the state of becoming. One does not achieve personhood as a destination; rather, personhood resides in the endless journey of becoming.

A further feature of personhood is that we can recognize it only by virtue of our own experience. As the symbolic interactionists and phenomenologists of another age (e.g. Mead, 1934; Husserl, 1960; Schutz, 1967) were concerned to establish, we apprehend others as persons like ourselves only by the recognition of features of ourselves in them: features of gesture, motive, predictable response, communication through shared symbols and so on.

By recognizing others as like ourselves, we are logically obliged to respect them (Peters, 1964) and to universalize our prescriptions for moral action to all others in similar circumstances (Kant's categorical imperative). Our rights are their rights in-as-much-as they, like us, are persons in comparable situations to ourselves.

This is both the root and the outcome of empathy. In the practical context of social interaction, we cannot recognize the personhood of another without valuing its development, and without treating it with that respect to which we, as persons, feel entitled. One does not need a humanistic account of the worth of each individual – though it helps – to recognize the importance of the way we treat others. Certainly, to treat children without respect is neither logically nor heuristically defensible if we are genuinely committed to their personal development. Unless teaching methods and the relationships which teachers form and promote with and amongst their pupils are based on respect for one another as whole persons – as rational, morally autonomous and feeling individuals – their efforts will come to nought. In developing whole persons, the medium really *is* the message.

Again, there must be doubts about the impact of the National Curriculum upon such a conception of appropriate social relations in schools. A preoccupation with a pre-packaged curriculum which is somehow to be 'delivered' to the learner is likely to reduce social relations to ones of subordination and receptiveness to what the teacher presents. It is unlikely to promote an awareness of the prior need for persons to have orderly and equitable social relationships within which to develop themselves, rather than merely to take delivery of packages of knowledge. In our experience (and this is supported by an increasing body of research: see Appendix 2), it is precisely this awareness which characterizes schools which are most successful in meeting the needs of all their pupils.

The connection between *respect* and *equality* is significant, and (we think) logical as well as empirical. For respecting persons in the school context is not a question of respecting 'able' children, or 'nice' children, or 'children from good homes'. Nor is pastoral care to be reserved only for 'those children who need it', as though only children from certain kinds of background, or 'problem children' have a right to be cared for. All children need understanding, support, warmth, acceptance and so on. All children need to be respected and valued for themselves. All children have an entitlement to a learning environment which will promote their development and provide enriching and fulfilling learning experiences.

The principle of equality is presumed in such statements, for it asserts that individuals are entitled to similar treatment under similar conditions; that *there should be no discrimination in the provision made for individuals unless there are good grounds for it, unless there are relevant differences between them; in short, unless their needs are different*.

It is clear throughout the chapters of this book that the principle of equality is fundamental to pastoral care and personal-social education. All pupils have a right to develop personally, socially, morally and so on, but in the planning which schools do for this part of the curriculum, and in the reactive casework which tutors (and others) regularly undertake, schools should be properly discriminating. Otherwise, the individual provision which unique needs require cannot be made.

We may wonder if all this is not so self-evidently true as to need no further comment. But this is not the case. Our respect for individuals is too often determined by our perception of their visible achievements, rather than a necessary respect born of a recognition of our common humanity. In the context of schooling, this can reduce a concept of intrinsic equality to a rather instrumental concept of *equality of opportunity*. Thus (it may be argued) although the creation of secondary grammar, technical and modern schools after the 1944 Education Act may have been justified in terms of access for all, regardless of ability and aptitude, to secondary education as a right, it soon became a matter of providing an equal opportunity merely to compete for a place at a superior school. While the rhetoric of the 11-plus examination was that it identified relevant differences in aptitude and ability, and thus in developmental needs, the reality was of a contest in which the life-chances of those who won and those who lost were determined. The concern to refine the tests themselves was founded not on the idea of the equal worth of the education of every child but more narrowly upon how to ensure that this contest was fair: that those who won, won fairly, and those who lost had at least had their chance.

The comprehensive movement of the 1960s and 1970s sought to redress the balance, but in recent years the creation of an 'opted-out' sector of grant-maintained schools, the growth of the independent sector and the advent of city technology colleges has undone much of what was achieved. It is arguable that the competition entailed in this process is fundamentally opposed to the idea of equal access to that education which is the entitlement of every person, however humble or auspicious their origins. We believe that proper provision for the development of every child based upon the principle of respect for persons *and* of the ultimate equality of persons requires that personal-social education is a major, well-planned and properly resourced dimension of the whole curriculum. But it also requires a recognition of the corollary of equality of individual worth: that permitting the distribution of resources according to the fluctuations of parental preference, influenced by raw data included in 'performance' and 'truancy' tables, is profoundly wrong. For the principle of equality entails that one receives according to one's need, not according to 'performance' or 'success', however that may be measured. As Brighouse and Tomlinson (1991, p. 1) put it, 'it ought to be the entitlement of every child to attend a 'successful school"'.

ENTITLEMENT

What is at issue is the conception of entitlement. There are direct parallels to be drawn between attitudes to pastoral care in education and attitudes to State provision of welfare benefits in society at large. In the latter, it is possible to distinguish between a case for the entitlement of every citizen to certain benefits (for example child benefits, free medical services) regardless of the affluence of the recipient, and a case for provision only according to individuals' need – the kind of arrangement usually associated with some kind of means test. Much of the debate down the years (and on-going at present) about the need for and shape of the Welfare State is precisely about these two perceptions of entitlement.

Best and Decker (1985) have argued that pastoral work in schools is analogous to welfare services at large, standing in a similar relationship to the mainstream curriculum as the welfare services stand to the commercial and industrial sector of wealth-creation. Their intriguing prediction was that, if the Welfare State were to be dismantled or seriously diminished, the same fate might be expected to befall pastoral systems in schools. There is some evidence to suggest that both these things are happening.

The present government is certainly diminishing the role of the State-provided welfare services, and radically re-shaping (if not dismantling) some of its structures (regional health authorities, local education authorities, etc.). It is also true that curriculum-led developments in schools may be diminishing institutionalized pastoral work, although in some schools this is enhanced in the metamorphosis of the head of year to the year curriculum co-ordinator. Where the new role is creatively interpreted, pastoral work may be strengthened by bringing it into a more organic relationship with planning, monitoring and promoting the individual child's academic development. As Caroline Lodge argues in Chapter 2 above, the need to integrate these concerns has become especially urgent as a response to the fragmenting effect of the National Curriculum on the experiences of individual children.

The parallel between pastoral care in education and the caring provisions of the Welfare State invites further research. What is more important in the present context is to recognize that to prioritize reactive (rather than proactive) policies in meeting individual needs is tacitly to acknowledge failure: failure successfully to take those developmental steps which enhance the quality of life of the citizen. While it is important to repair the damage when the quality of life (for whatever reason: illness, unemployment, disability) is reduced, a system which is limited to remedial help is clearly unsatisfactory.

An important principle, therefore, for schools to follow is that *the learning experiences which promote personal-social and moral development are an entitlement, and any reduction of pastoral care to reactive casework is an unacceptable dilution of the mission of the school.*

TEACHING AS A PROFESSION

The considerable government intervention of the 1980s – through legislation on the curriculum, changes in the legal status of schools and their governing bodies, the disempowerment of local education authorities and so on – has also affected the nature of teaching as a profession.

Perhaps we need to remind ourselves that teaching is an *intentional* activity. It is true that people can learn unintentionally – children do it all the time – but the role of the teacher cannot be performed by accident (Oakshott, 1967; Dearden, 1967). It is part and parcel of the concept of teaching that there is an intention that learning should occur and that steps are taken to bring such learning about. It is by the systematic, planful and structured provision of relevant and effective learning experiences that the role of the teacher is defined and recognized.

The performance of such a role presumes a certain freedom on the part of the teacher to choose what to teach and how to teach it. The teacher who accepts the role of promoting the development of all those 'selves' which comprise the whole person must be so placed as to be able to respond to the associated developmental needs as and when they arise. In other words, there is a presumption to be made of a measure of professional judgement and discretion for the teacher without which teaching is not really possible. We may style this the *principle of the professional judgement of the teacher*. This is not to claim that 'the teacher is always right', but that informed and reflective judgement is as essential a part of the role of the teacher as it is of any other profession.

It is arguable that the developments of the late 1980s and early 1990s have been profoundly antagonistic towards the exercise of such a principle. Teachers' judgements are not, it seems, to be trusted as compared with those of others (including parents – hence the Parent's Charter), and those who have until recently trained, supported, advised and inspected teachers in their work have been subject to a 'discourse of derision' (Ball, 1990) as an accompaniment to their systematic disempowerment.

The issue of 'parent power' is particularly interesting. Parents generally value teachers' judgements, and in the main teachers value parental interest and support. However, it is important to maintain a sense of balance, as Adler has argued:

> Liberal economic theory assumes that individuals are the best judges of what is in their own best interests. Whether or not this is true, it is fairly clear that parents are not necessarily the best judges of what is in their children's best interests.
>
> (Adler, 1993, p. 62)

TRAINING AND SUPPORT

When, some years ago, NAPCE undertook its small survey of training and support for pastoral care (Maher and Best, 1985), the intention was to provide some valid data for evaluating the quality of provision in order to press for improvements. It was relatively easy to establish the inadequacy of initial training, and to make a case for greater attention to be given to preparation for the role of the form tutor. The progressive tightening of the requirements of initial teacher training courses under the Council for the Accreditation of Teacher Education (CATE), with emphasis on increased work in schools and on core curriculum subjects, seems unlikely to have improved the situation.

The NAPCE survey showed the quality of In-service Training and Education to be rather better. Provision was patchy and uncoordinated but there were significant courses and training opportunities on offer. In the years that followed, these opportunities were at first expanded, not least by NAPCE's own programme of conferences and workshops.

Before the end of the decade, the tide had turned. Changes first in the funding of INSET, then in the power and roles of LEAs and their inspectors, advisers and advisory teachers, and finally in the radical restructuring of HM Inspectors, have effectively taken many successful courses and their providers out of the system. Whilst it is true that some schools are providing their own staff development activities aimed at improving their work in pastoral care and PSE, there is little check to ensure that these events are more than what one commentator has termed the mutual recycling of schools' own inadequacies.

Whether faith in teachers' professional judgement can be restored remains to be seen. In the short and medium terms, the damage done to teacher morale by the pace of change and the deprofessionalization of teaching must be recognized, and the need of teachers themselves for counselling, guidance and support acknowledged with action. The principle here is that *it is not only the pupils who need pastoral care: teachers are human too!*

WHOLE SCHOOLS

If teachers should be in teaching with the intention of bringing about learning, then schools ought to be institutions set up by society to facilitate teachers' work. We say 'ought', because, in respect of personal-social education and the pastoral casework which complements it, teachers often feel that this has been neglected in the planning and resourcing of schools.

This is significant, for a theme which runs throughout this book is that the well-being and development of the pupils should be the concern of the whole school, and not just of those teachers who hold designated pastoral roles, or of the staff of the PSE department. The authors of the National Curriculum got it right when they recognized that the development of social skills and qualities of character, such as respect for the truth, could not be confined within one subject but needed to be an aspect of the whole curriculum. More importantly, such values are promoted by the climate or ethos of the school as a whole – the 'hidden' (or not-so-hidden!) curriculum of school rules, traditions, customs, celebrations and so on.

Nor can pastoral casework be confined to the more or less specialist activities of school counsellors and pastoral middle-managers when they counsel, guide, support (and discipline) individual pupils, nor to those of the more generalist supportive work of the form tutor. Others cannot merely turn their backs, or pass the buck through a convenient system of referral, whenever they encounter a child in need. Nor ought they to pass lightly over issues of moral principle and personal crisis when they arise in (say) a maths or geography lesson, simply because such issues are not on the syllabus.

There is an important principle here, and it is that *pastoral care and personal-social education are whole-school responsibilities and require whole-school policies*. This suggests a further principle: that *schools should be properly organized and appropriately resourced to this end*. Here too, there are concerns about recent developments.

The growing official endorsement – nay, *fostering* – of competition between schools, through the publication of 'league tables' of examination results, truancy rates and the like, encourages parents to exercise what the economists are pleased to call 'consumer sovereignty'. This has serious consequences for the proper resourcing of schools. If resources 'follow' pupils on register (which they do), and are more or less supplemented by fund-raising PTAs (which they are), it is difficult to see how the creation of an 'underclass' of 'sink schools' in impoverished neighbourhoods with impoverished resources can be avoided.

Moreover, where resources are limited, schools are forced to prioritize and economize, and, in the present climate, pastoral work and PSE are unlikely to be high on the list of priorities. The reason is simple: the structure of the National Curriculum and its assessment requirements, together with the publication of league tables, is creating a climate in which things are valued not foremost because they contribute to human development but because they are capable of assessment, required to be assessed and the outcomes of their assessment matter. They matter, most significantly, in terms of their effect on market demand and, in turn, on the capitation a school attracts. Since personal-social education and pastoral care are assessed at the most by some mysterious and invisible means as cross-curricular elements in the assessment of National Curriculum programmes of study, and at the least not assessed at all, they cannot be expected to be taken very seriously when resourcing priorities are being determined in a reactive and sometimes paranoid climate.

IN CONCLUSION

In this concluding chapter we have chosen to focus upon the principles which underlie a commitment to the education of children as whole persons rather than merely 'empty buckets to be filled with knowledge' (Haigh, 1975). In such a conception of education, personal-social education and pastoral care are central.

Other principles follow, some to do with the morality of schooling, others to do with more practical concerns such as training and resourcing. Inevitably, such issues must be addressed with reference to the social and political context within which teachers have to operate.

We are aware that we have been highly critical of some of the recent trends in education policy, and of the values which underpin them. We make no apology for this. Education is, after all, a moral matter. To engage in education is to take a stand on the nature of humanity, and thus on what is required to realize that humanity more fully through the curriculum and through the social and institutional arrangements we make for its delivery. A discussion of education which ignored the possibilities and the constraints posed by this context would be shallow indeed. It would be especially shallow where personal-social education is concerned precisely because the exploration of morality, the consideration of values and the development of moral sensibilities are at its very heart.

The pastoral work which teachers do is also an intensely moral matter. Children are likely to achieve more in the conventional curriculum if they are valued and cared for, and if the impediments to learning posed by social, emotional and personal problems are cleared out of the way. But this is not its primary justification. Pastoral care is justified as an expression and an application in practice of a commitment to the value of the individual as a person. As such it requires no further justification.

If we have said more of the constraints than of the possibilities, this is because the constraints of recent developments seem far to outweigh their potential. We have been critical of changes which have taken place in the structures and policies for education in recent years because they seem to us inimical to the effective development of pastoral care and PSE. If this suggests that they have, at their roots, values which are incompatible with those which underpin the professional commitment of teachers to the total well-being of their pupils, then this is to underline the paucity of principles underlying government 'reforms' in education in the 1980s, and directly to challenge their educational value.

Education *is* an intensely moral matter: what could matter more than a nation's young people? The tasks and the challenges facing those in education whose primary concern is to defend and promote the all-round development of our children have never been greater.

REFERENCES

Adler, M. (1993) Parental choice and children's interests. In Munn, P. (ed.) *Parents and Schools: Customers, Managers or Partners?* London: Routledge.

Ball, S. (1990) *Politics and Policy Making in Education*. London: Routledge.

Best, R. and Decker, S. (1985) Pastoral care and welfare: some underlying issues. In Ribbins, P. (ed.) *Schooling and Welfare*. Lewes: Falmer.

Best, R., Jarvis, C. and Ribbins, P. (eds) (1980) *Perspectives on Pastoral Care*. London: Heinemann.

Best, R., Ribbins, P., Jarvis, C. and Oddy, D. (1983) *Education and Care*. London: Heinemann.

Brighouse, T. and Tomlinson, J. (1991) *Successful Schools*, Education and training paper no. 4. London: Institute for Public Policy Research.

Dearden, R. F. (1967) Instruction and learning by discovery. In Peters, R. S. (ed.) *The Concept of Education*. London: Routledge & Kegan Paul.

Department of Education and Science 1988 *Report by HM Inspectors on a Survey of Personal and Social Education Courses in Some Secondary Schools*. Stanmore: DES.

Department of Education and Science 1989 *Report by HM Inspectors on Pastoral Care in Secondary Schools; an Inspection of Some Aspects of Pastoral Care in 1987–88*. Stanmore: DES.

Haigh, G. (1975) *Pastoral Care*. London: Pitman Publishing.

Husserl, E. (1960) *Cartesian Meditations*. The Hague: Martinus Nijhoff.

Lang, P. (1982) *Pastoral Care: Concern or Contradiction?* Unpublished M.A. thesis, University of Warwick.

Lang, P. (1985) Taking account of the views and feelings of pupils. In Ribbins, P. (ed.) *Schooling and Welfare*. Lewes: Falmer.

Lang, P. and Marland, M. (1986) *New Directions in Pastoral Care*. Oxford: Blackwell.

Lawton, D. (1973) *Social Change, Educational Theory and Curriculum Planning*. London: Hodder & Stoughton.

Lawton, D., Gordon, P., Ing, M., Gibby, B., Pring, R. and Moore, T. (1978) *Theory and Practice of Curriculum Studies*. London: Routledge & Kegan Paul.

Maher, P. and Best, R. (1985) Preparation and support for pastoral care: a survey of current provision. In Lang, P. and Marland, M. (eds) *New Directions in Pastoral Care*. Oxford: Blackwell.

Marland, M. (1974) *Pastoral Care*. London: Heinemann.

Mead, G. H. (1934) *Mind, Self and Society*, edited by Charles W. Morris. Chicago: University of Chicago Press.

Musgrave, P. W. (1965) *The Sociology of Education*. London: Methuen.

Oakshott, M. (1967) Learning and teaching. In Peters, R. S. (ed.) *The Concept of Education*. London: Routledge & Kegan Paul.

Peters, R. S. (1964) *Ethics and Education*. London: Unwin.

Ribbins, P. and Best, R. (1986) Pastoral care: theory, practice and the growth of research. In Lang, P. and Marland, M. (eds) *New Directions in Pastoral Care*. Oxford: Blackwell.

Schutz, A. (1967) Husserl's importance for the social sciences. In *Collected Papers*, vol. 1. The Hague: Martinus Nijhoff.

Watkins, C. (1985) Does pastoral care = PSE? *Pastoral Care in Education* **3**(3).

Welford, G. (1994) The new religious grant-maintained schools. *Educational Management and Administration*, forthcoming.

Williams, R. (1961) *The Long Revolution*. Harmondsworth: Penguin.

Appendices

APPENDIX 1

The National Association for Pastoral Care in Education

NAPCE was founded in 1982 and is an established and thriving professional association.

As an educational charity NAPCE's goals are:

to support all those who have a professional concern for pastoral care, whether general or specific;

to promote the theoretical study of pastoral care in education;

to disseminate good practice in pastoral care in education;

to promote the education, training and development of those engaged in pastoral care in education;

to liaise with other organizations having similar objects.

The Association represents over two thousand members drawn mainly from secondary schools but including primary, special and further education, advisers, inspectors, lecturers, consultants, students, etc. NAPCE has thirteen regions, and a national base with paid staff: it is run through a National Executive Committee with elected officers and an Annual General Meeting.

In addition to sponsoring books such as this, NAPCE publishes the journal *Pastoral Care in Education*, staff development resource packs, broadsheets and response documents on a range of national issues.

Activities include conferences, workshops and training at national, regional and local level. Active links with other complementary associations are maintained.

Further details of membership, publications and activities is available from: NAPCE Base, c/o Education Department, University of Warwick, Coventry, CV4 7AL (tel.: 01203 523810; fax: 01203 524110).

APPENDIX 2

The value of pastoral care and PSE: a compilation of research

Chris Watkins

This appendix aims to bring together evidence and arguments to show the impact and value of pastoral care and personal-social education in schools.

When resources for education are scarce, the aspects of school which are not obviously direct teaching can sometimes come under threat. This is a wrong-headed approach if we are to maintain a central focus on learning and achievement, and are to develop the features of the effective school: 'Effective schools are *demanding* places, where teachers expect and ensure high standards of work and behaviour; at the same time they are *responsive* to pupils, for the teachers are approachable and, since they value pupils, seek to *involve* them in the life and work of the school' (Hargreaves, 1990).

Pastoral care and PSE are at their most effective when they are demanding, responsive and involving. 'We recommend that headteachers and teachers should ensure that pastoral care in schools is characterised by a healthy balance between challenge and support for pupils' (Department of Education and Science, 1989).

In talking about the value and impact of pastoral care and PSE, the question of how to identify them and their effects arises. Both have a general and a specific aspect to them, which might include:

Pastoral care		Personal-social education	
specific aspects	*general aspects*	*general aspects*	*specific aspects*
tutor groups individual pupils guidance links to parents other professionals	school climate care of staff whole curriculum all contexts teaching and learning	personal-social in all classrooms whole curriculum ethos school environment	specialist PSE: careers, health, tutorials other guidance

The effects of the specific are influenced by the general: the effects of the general are long-term, linked to other factors, difficult to measure. It is certainly not possible to create simple outcome measures of personal and social development (Assessment of Performance Unit, 1981).

This appendix brings together evidence under headings which identify the value for major stakeholders. In the final analysis it is not advisable to force a strong separation between these: they are interconnected, and what benefits one has positive spin-off for others.

In this book, extra arguments, commentary and analysis have deliberately been withheld. The overall message is that there is available evidence to construct professional arguments for provision in this area. The evidence speaks for itself.

Pastoral care and PSE bring attention to achievement and social development. The two are linked, and promoting both is important. 'In years gone by, educationalists have debated whether *either* a task-oriented, nose-to-the-grindstone approach *or* an emotionally supportive approach designed to make children want to be at school and enjoy their learning was better. The choice is artificial and misleading. *Both* aspects are necessary for optimal learning' (Rutter, 1991).

Approachability of and access to teachers or tutors is important for achievement. 'Pupil outcomes tended to be better in schools where ordinary teachers were available to see children about problems at any time (not just at fixed periods) and where pupils reported that, if they needed to, they would talk to a member of staff about a personal problem' (Rutter, 1983).

Learning is a personal-social process and is enhanced by personal-social attention. 'The successful learner is knowledgeable, self-determined, strategic, and empathetic' (Jones and Fennimore, 1990).

A focus on the personal-social aspects of learning, and on co-operative approaches to learning, enhances achievement. 'The theoretical support for co-operative endeavours appears to be borne out by the research evidence' (Bennett and Dunne, 1992). 'In our studies we have found considerable evidence that co-operative learning experiences promote higher achievement than do competitive and individualistic learning experiences' (Slavin, 1990).

Studies of approaches to learning demonstrate that study skills which focus on surface matters such as reading, note-taking and time management are largely ineffective, whereas a focus on purpose, strategy and review is more effective. Learners need occasions to reflect on their strategies to learning (Gibbs, 1992; Ramsden, 1988; Selmes, 1987).

Tutoring across ages of pupils has been shown to be more effective and more cost-effective than reducing class size, increasing instructional time, or computer-assisted instruction (Fitz-Gibbon, 1988).

Programmes which help students to analyse real life situations, set goals and take responsibility for their actions result in increased motivation for learning and in improved academic achievement (deCharms, 1972).

Adolescents experience and express personal-social difficulties which limit their performance, and which form one strand of personal-social education.

From this date, it is quite clear that these young people had considerable difficulties in relating to parents and teachers, in asserting themselves to achieve their goals, and in relating to the opposite sex and to people in authority. They had inaccurate and damaging ideas on the degree to which they could change themselves or their life situation.

(Hopson and Hough, 1976, considering 235 15- to 16-year-olds)

Adolescent concerns may be adequately described along the dimensions of: Myself, At Home, Assertiveness, Opposite Sex, Communication, Powerlessness, School Work, Coping with Change, Choosing a Job, Job Finding, Job Information Seeking, Starting Work, Money Matters (Millar *et al.*, 1993, considering 378 15- to 16-year-olds; Gallagher *et al.*, 1992, considering 446 15- to 18-year-olds).

'Planning, decision-making and taking responsibility may be central to young people's perspectives of life skills' (Poole and Evans, 1988, a study of fifteen facets of life skills with 1,084 15- to 18-year-olds).

Pupils' personal problems can be increased or decreased by school atmosphere.

First it appeared that pupils in over-controlling schools expressed more problems with authority. In such cases it seemed that the school engendered problems by being over-controlling in its climate. Secondly, where low levels of concern for pupils were perceived, it seemed that pupils experienced more problems in peer group areas. In other words, schools with concerned atmospheres had pupils who were more likely to get on well with each other.

(Porteous and Kelleher, 1987, considering 349 pupils in fifteen secondary schools)

Helping students tutor each other has positive benefits for all.

These programs have positive effects on the academic performance and attitudes of those who receive tutoring. Tutored students out-performed control students on examinations and they also developed positive attitudes toward the subject matter covered in the tutorial programs. The analysis also showed that tutoring programs have positive effects on the children who serve as tutors.

(Cohen *et al.*, 1982, an analysis of sixty-five evaluations of peer tutoring)

Students who are deemed at risk can continue to succeed in supportive schools: 'The key finding from our research is that effective schools provide at-risk students with a community of support . . . in which school membership and educational engagement are central' (Wehlage *et al.*, 1989).

Nearly a quarter of the teenagers who could talk to a member of staff about personal relationships said they would turn to their form tutor. The importance of pastoral care was underlined by the fact that nearly a fifth of the teenagers who felt they could ask a member of staff about sex or contraception cited a form tutor, head of year, head or deputy head of school, with the older teenagers more likely to cite the latter, mainly, it appeared, because they had more contact with them or because they taught the personal and social education programme.

(Allen, 1987).

The young people we talked to felt that their learning about preparation for parenthood in schools was patchy and inadequate . . . They identified that things like communication, relationship and personal development skills are sometimes included in tutorial time at school – but only if the teacher is interested. (Braun and Schonveld, 1992, considering 83 young people)

THE VALUE FOR PARENTS

Parents gave substantial support to these two statements:

Children's personal and social development at school is at least as important as their academic development.

The most important thing about a school is whether the children are happy and enjoy their lessons.
(Elliott, 1981, on fourth-year parents choosing from over forty statements: cited in Johnson, 1990)

Also:

Parental choice of school is most strongly influenced by pragmatic and pastoral considerations, 'factors which direct little attention, if any, to the actual structure of what the child will receive by way of educational content or method' ... 'the majority of parents who are exercising choice on behalf of their child are doing so from a humanistic rather than technological perspective, being less concerned with measurable criteria than with the creation of an atmosphere supportive to the child's well-being'.

(Johnson, 1990, quoting Petch, 1986, a survey of one thousand parents)

Of parent-teacher associations, 64 per cent consider that staff do not have adequate time to develop pastoral contact with pupils, and that this is one of the most important problems facing schools; 55 per cent consider that staff do not have adequate time to talk to parents (National Confederation of Parent–Teachers Associations, 1991, a survey of 2,051 parent–teachers associations).

Of parents, 96 per cent think that schools should provide sex education to children and young people (Allen, 1987).

THE VALUE FOR THE SCHOOL

Pastoral care is concerned with the 'health' and functioning of the organisation as well as with individual pupils.

(Hamblin, 1981)

One could argue that the pastoral organisation was an intuitive response to regarding the child as the customer, an internal agency to make sure that each child got the best mix available out of the product range on offer ... that part of the organisation (which connects products and customers) ought to be the driving force of the organisation, the one that sets the priorities and the tone and calls the tune. My conversations suggest that in most schools it is the production system, not the internal marketing system, which is dominant. Excellent companies maintain a regular survey and feedback programme from customer to organisation. In schools the feedback system runs the other way round – from organisation to customer (child or parent). Accountability in the education system often means the school explaining what it is doing to its customers, rather than asking its customers whether and when they are satisfied.

(Handy, 1984)

Concepts of school and teacher effectiveness imply the sort of constructive and co-operative pupil–teacher relationships which are one of the characteristics of effective pastoral care.

(Galloway, 1985)

The evidence suggests that schools with high exclusion rates may be less successful than schools with low exclusion rates in persuading the majority of pupils that teachers are interested in them (apart from a natural interest in the quality of their schoolwork).

(Galloway *et al.*, 1982, on ten secondary schools)

Six characteristics of pastoral care in four secondary schools each selected for its low level of disruptive behaviour:

- The principal aim of pastoral care is to enhance educational progress.
- Distinguishing 'pastoral' and 'discipline' problems is seen as spurious.
- Class teachers are not encouraged to pass problems to senior staff.
- Pastoral care is based on tutors, from whom advice about pupils is sought.
- Pastoral care for teachers is in evidence.
- The climate promotes discussion of disruptive behaviour without recrimination.

(Galloway, 1983)

A school which fails to care for its staff is not likely to be caring effectively for its students.

(Murgatroyd, 1986)

Training research and research on teaching and learning have reached the stage where a system that increases student aptitude, achievement, and personal and social development can be designed with confidence ... The individual, school, and systemic components need to be oriented towards changes in practice that offer promise for student growth in the personal, social and academic domains.

(Joyce and Showers, 1988)

Schools in which form tutors carry out mainly administrative functions, such as taking registers and reading notices, tend to suffer from more disruptive behaviour than schools in which they are actively involved in disciplinary, counselling and guidance activities, monitoring academic progress and other pastoral work.

(Department of Education and Science, 1989)

THE VALUE FOR THE WORLD OF WORK

Sound careers guidance and advice in schools, further education and employment is central to providing each individual with a high quality personal guidance base throughout their career ... Broader occupational competence should be concerned with adaptability, management of roles, responsibility for standards, creativity and flexibility to changing demand. Task competence is not enough to meet this need although some employers, concentrating on their short term needs, may believe it is.

(CBI, 1989)

There still remains the need for a timetabled slot of careers education in the curriculum. Despite improvements with the introduction of careers education as a cross-curricular theme, this is not enough.

(Nicholson, 1993)

Following on the heels of basic skills and relevant knowledge, business expects from the education system 'motivated pupils and social/team skills' (CBI, 1988).

Students leaving school see employers as valuing most highly personal skills, and they value them themselves, but do not consider they are gaining them at school. On teamwork skills, they see employers as valuing these, and do not rate highly their advancement at school (CBI, 1992).

It is argued that Careers Guidance fosters efficiency and social equity. It supports individual decisions, reduced drop-out and mismatch, and contributes to improvements in the world of work (Killeen *et al.*, 1992).

> There is compelling evidence from our research that many young people and their parents are at sea with respect to what needs to be done to ensure their futures. The essential antidote is to give career and personal counselling a much higher status, not only through the specialists involved in it, but also in the jobs of teaching and training themselves.
>
> (Banks *et al.*, 1992, considering 4,830 16 to 19-year-olds in five areas of Britain)

A major study of the guidance needs of young people revealed that they viewed the development of social skills for work as a major requirement for their future (Eaton and Daws, 1987) and that they are influenced most in guidance by persons with whom they have a well-established relationship.

> Those having regular careers lessons had a greater knowledge of the world of work than their peers who had no such lessons, ... were less reliant on their family for careers advice, and used a wider range of sources for career knowledge, ... and were more aware of the preparations necessary for job interviews.
>
> (Chamberlain, 1982, considering 274 fifth-form students from six schools)

> Schools providing formal careers education in the fourth or fifth years had pupils whose scores suggested a gain of six months' vocational awareness.
>
> (Cherry and Gear, 1987, considering 1,366 pupils in twenty English secondary schools)

Where there is a careers education programme in the school, fifth-year pupils made much more progress in vocational awareness in interviews with careers officers (Bedford, 1982, on 680 interviews in two hundred schools)

THE VALUE FOR SOCIETY AT LARGE

> The benefits of learning are economic, personal and social ... Those nations that invest in learning gain economic, social and personal benefits for their citizens: those that fail to do so suffer decline. [We recommend] embedding careers education and guidance within the mainstream of the curriculum and education process, rather than positioning them as external and marginal adjuncts to formal learning.
>
> (Ball, 1992)

> We have unearthed a number of results which seem to indicate that
>
> - drinking rates are lower in schools where alcohol education is delivered through PSE
> - drinking rates are higher if the programme is delivered through Science'
>
> (Balding and Bish, 1992, considering thirty schools)

Preventive education on matters such as smoking is more effective when the personal-social dimension is addressed.

The implications of the school effects appear to show that smoking rates were significantly lower where the school gave a relatively high profile to social/health education as a firm, separate and important curriculum area ... The differences in smoking rate are such as to indicate that lessons embedded in social/health education curriculum seem more successful.

(Clift *et al.*, 1989; Eiser *et al.*, 1988; Jamison and MacNeil, 1992)

THE AGENDA FOR DEVELOPMENT

The evidence demonstrates the value of effective pastoral care and PSE as one dimension of the effective school. A continuing focus on these areas is necessary.

Development is the responsibility of the individual school, and requires a co-ordinated and collective approach to evaluation, review and planning.

Professional evaluations such as HMI reports and surveys have continued to present evidence and analyses which highlight the characteristics of effective work in pastoral care and PSE (HMI, 1988; HMI, 1989; HMI, 1992). These provide useful frameworks for a school to review its practice.

An additional stimulus to maintain the focus will be the regular inspection of schools. This will be developed according to OFSTED's Framework and Handbook (Office for Standards in Education, 1993) which currently include main sections on:

pupils' support and guidance;

pupils' social and cultural development;

pupils' spiritual and moral development;

links with parents and liaison with other schools;

attendance;

behaviour and discipline.

Schools will be expected to provide documentation on such areas, and inspection teams will seek evidence through indicators of performance in them. The management of the school will also be under scrutiny: pastoral care and PSE, however organized, will be expected to show evidence of systematic review, monitoring and evaluation of its performance in relation to pupils' achievement.

REFERENCES

Allen, I. (1987) *Education in Sex and Personal Relationships*. London: Policy Studies Institute.

Assessment of Performance Unit (1981) *Personal and Social Development*. London: DES.

Balding, J. and Bish, D. (1992) *Alcohol Education in Schools*. Exeter: Schools Health Education Unit, University of Exeter.

Ball, C. (1992) *Profitable Learning*. London: Royal Society for the Arts.

Banks, M., Bates, I., Breakwell, G., Bynner, J., Emler, N., Jamieson, L. and Roberts, K. (1992) *Careers and Identities*. Milton Keynes: Open University Press.

Bedford, T. (1982) *Vocational Guidance Interviews: A Survey by the Careers Service Inspectorate*. London: Department of Employment.

Bennett, N. and Dunne, E. (1992) *Managing Classroom Groups*. Hemel Hempstead: Simon & Schuster.

Braun, D. and Schonveld, A. (1992) *Preparation for Parenthood: Myth or Reality?* Coventry: Community Education Development Centre.

CBI (1988) *Building a Stronger Partnership between Business and Secondary Education*. London: CBI.

CBI (1989) *Towards a Skills Revolution: Report of the Vocational Education and Training Task Force*. London: CBI.

CBI (1992) *Survey of Students' Attitudes: 17- and 18-year olds going to Higher Education*. London: CBI.

Chamberlain, P. (1982) Careers lessons and career awareness of fifth form students. *British Journal of Guidance and Counselling*, **10**, 74–82.

Cherry, N. and Gear, R. (1987) Young people's perceptions of their vocational guidance needs: II. Influences and interventions. *British Journal of Guidance and Counselling*, **15**, 169–81.

Clift, S., Stears, D., Legg, S., Memon, A. and Ryan, L. (1989) *The HIV/AIDS Education and Young People Project: Report on Phase 1*. Canterbury: Christ Church College, HIV/AIDS Education Research Unit.

Cohen, P. A., Kulik, J. A. and Kulik, C.-L. C. (1982) Educational outcomes of tutoring: a meta-analysis of findings. *American Educational Research Journal*, **19**, 237–48.

deCharms, R. (1972) Personal causation training in the schools. *Journal of Applied Social Psychology*, **2**, 95–113.

Department of Education and Science (1989) *Discipline in Schools: Report of the Committee of Enquiry Chaired by Lord Elton*. London: DES/HMSO.

Eaton, M. and Daws, P. P. (1987) *A TRAWL Perspective on Guidance Provision*. Belfast: NICED.

Eiser, J. R., Morgan, M. and Gammage, P. (1988) Social education is good for health. *Educational Research*, **30**, 20–5.

Elliott, J. (1981) How do parents choose schools? In Elliott, J. (ed.) *School Accountability*. London: Grant McIntyre.

Fitz-Gibbon, C. (1988) Peer tutoring as a teaching strategy. *Educational Management and Administration*, **16**, 217–29.

Gallagher, M., Millar, R., Hargie, O. and Ellis, R. (1992) The personal and social worries of adolescents in Northern Ireland: results of a survey. *British Journal of Guidance and Counselling*, **20**, 274–90.

Galloway, D. (1983) Disruptive pupils and effective pastoral care. *School Organisation*, **3**, 245–54.

Galloway, D. (1985) Pastoral care and school effectiveness. In Reynolds, D. (ed.) *Studying School Effectiveness*. Lewes: Falmer Press.

Galloway, D., Ball, T., Blomfield, D. and Seyed, R. (1982) *Schools and Disruptive Pupils*. Harlow: Longman.

Gibbs, G. (1992) *Improving the Quality of Student Learning*. Bristol: Technical and Educational Services.

Hamblin, D. H. (1981) Pastoral care and pupil performance. In Hamblin, D. H. (ed.) *Problems and Practice of Pastoral Care*. Oxford: Blackwell.

Handy, C. (1984) *Taken for Granted? Understanding Schools as Organisations*. York: Longmans for Schools Council.

Hargreaves, D. H. (1990) Making schools more effective: the challenge to policy, practice and research. *Scottish Educational Review*, **22**, 5–14.

HMI (1988) *A Survey of Personal and Social Education Courses in Some Secondary Schools: Report 235/88*. Stanimore: DES.

HMI (1989) *Pastoral Care in Secondary Schools: An Inspection of Some Aspects of Pastoral Care in 1987–8*. Stanimore: DES.

HMI (1992) *Survey of Guidance 13–19 in Schools and Sixth Form Colleges*. Stanimore: DES.

Hopson, B. and Hough, P. (1976) The need for personal and social education in secondary schools and further education. *British Journal of Guidance and Counselling*, **4**, 17–27.

Jamison, J. and MacNeil, M. (1992) Can health education change school practices and young people's attitudes and behaviour? Paper given at NFER Annual Conference, Slough, 1992.

Johnson, D. (1990) *Parental Choice in Education*. London: Unwin Hyman.

Jones, B. F. and Fennimore, T. F. (1990) *The New Definition of Learning*. Elmhurst, Ill.: North Central Regional Educational Laboratory.

Joyce, B. and Showers, B. (1988) *Student Achievement through Staff Development*. Harlow: Longman.

Killeen, J., White, M. and Watts, A. G. (1992) *The Economic Value of Careers Guidance*. London: Policy Studies Institute.

Millar, R., Gallagher, M. and Ellis, R. (1993) Surveying adolescent worries: development of the 'Things I Worry About' scale. *Pastoral Care in Education*, **11**, 43–51.

Murgatroyd, S. (1986) Management teams and the promotion of staff well-being. *School Organisation*, **6**, 115–21.

National Confederation of Parent–Teachers Associations (1991) *The State of Schools in England and Wales*. Gravesend: NCPTA.

Nicholson, S. B. (1993) What are the needs? In Ball, S. C. (ed.) *Guidance Matters*. London: RSA.

Office for Standards in Education (1993) *Handbook for the Inspection of Schools*. London: OFSTED/DFE.

Petch, A. J. (1986) Parents' reasons for choosing secondary schools. In Stillman, A. (ed.) *The Balancing Act of 1980: Parents, Politics and Education*. Slough: NFER.

Poole, M. E. and Evans, G. T. (1988) Life skills: adolescents' perceptions of importance and competence. *British Journal of Guidance and Counselling*, **16**, 129–44.

Porteous, M. A. and Kelleher, E. (1987) School climate differences and problem admission in secondary schools. *British Journal of Guidance and Counselling*, **15**, 72–81.

Ramsden, P. (1988) *Improving Learning: New Perspectives*. London: Kogan Page.

Rutter, M. (1983) School effects on pupil progress: research findings and policy implications. *Child Development*, **54**, 1–29.

Rutter, M. (1991) Pathways from childhood to adult life: the role of schooling. *Pastoral Care in Education*, **9**, 3–10.

Selmes, I. (1987) *Improving Study Skills*. London: Hodder & Stoughton.

Slavin, R. E. (1990) *Cooperative Learning: Theory, Research, and Practice*. Englewood Cliffs, NJ.: Prentice-Hall.

Wehlage, G. G., Rutter, R. A., Smith, G. A., Lesko, N. and Fernandez, R. R. (1989) *Reducing the Risk: Schools as Communities of Support*. London: Falmer.

Name index

Subject index